The EMERGENCE *of* ONE AMERICAN NATION

The EMERGENCE *of* ONE AMERICAN NATION

The Revolution, the Founders, and the Constitution

DONALD J. FRASER

FRASER & ASSOCIATES
ROSEVILLE, CA

For information contact:
Fraser & Associates
Roseville, California
www.perspectiveshistory.com

978-0-9970805-0-6 (paperback)
978-0-9970805-1-3 (ebook)

Library of Congress Control Number: 2015920429

Book Design by Dotti Albertine

Printed in the United States of America

To Patty

for always believing in me

CONTENTS

Acknowledgments

In a letter to John Adams in 1813, Thomas Jefferson stated his goal in preparing the Declaration of Independence. "Neither aiming at originality of principle or sentiment, nor yet copied from any particular and previous writing, it was intended to be an expression of the American mind."[1] This book in some way follows the Jefferson model, in that it is not a work of history primarily grounded in original source documents. While I have relied on letters, reports, and the writings of the founders, I stand on the shoulders of the giants in the field of history and of historical scholarship that have developed over the past thirty years. The research and writings of the following historians have been of particular assistance in the writing of this book: Joseph J. Ellis, Gordon S. Wood, Jack N. Rakove, John Ferling, Richard Beeman, and Pauline Maier.

Writing a book seems like a solitary pursuit, but in fact that is far from the truth. Penny Hoffman read an early version of the first chapters and made a variety of comments and suggestions that are reflected through out the book. Vicki Gibbs, my copy editor, has been of immeasurable help in the production of this book. She saved me from numerous errors of syntax, questioned some of my arguments that were incomplete, and found all of those nagging typographical errors. Any remaining errors in fact or judgment are mine alone. I would also like to thank Hazel Abbuhl for her keen eye in completing the final proofreading and for her expertise in preparing the index. And to Dotti Albertine for her work in compiling the book and creating the cover art work, which has made this a professional looking endeavor.

To my family and friends, thank you for your encouragement and listening to me as I went on and on about what makes us one Nation.

Endnotes

1 Quoted in David McCullogh, *John Adams*, (New York, 2001), p. 121

Introduction

"We are a country bound
not by ethnicity or bloodlines
but by fidelity to a set of ideas."
– President Barack Obama, July 4, 2012 –

"We the people"...the most important words in the Constitution. They do not carry the force of law; nor do they establish a government of limited and enumerated powers; nor do they protect basic rights; all of which are addressed with other words in the Constitution. The value of these words lies in their recognition of America as one nation, a nation established by the Constitution.

But America did not start as one nation, and even in the aftermath of the ratification of the Constitution in 1788, the concept of nationhood was still in an embryonic stage. The term "American" was in fact an epithet, as historian Joseph Ellis writes: "English writers... used the term negatively, as a way of referring to a marginal or peripheral population unworthy of equal status with full-blooded Englishmen back at the metropolitan center of the British Empire." Perhaps that was why, at the close of the French and Indian War in 1763, Benjamin Franklin wrote, "I am a Briton." Or that a few years later, when George Washington attended the Continental Congress, he came as a Virginian.[1] It would take not only a break with Great Britain through the Revolutionary War, but also the space of time in the aftermath of that war for a "national" perspective to develop in the United States.

Proprietors and private companies established the original thirteen colonies, with the British government providing very little supervision.[2] The colonies had different natural resources, which affected the development of each region's culture and society. Land in the New England colonies proved poor for farming, but fishing, shipbuilding, logging and fur trading flourished. The middle colonies had good land for farming and natural harbors that led to the growth of major cities in New York and Philadelphia. The southern colonies had land that was suitable for growing tobacco, rice, and indigo—labor intensive crops—which led to the development of large plantations and the use of slave labor. The colonies were largely isolated from each other and had different interests. Colonists viewed themselves first as loyal British subjects, and second as owing allegiance to their individual colony. The idea that they owed any loyalty to America did not exist, since America did not yet exist as an independent nation. The colonies did share some common characteristics; for one, they spoke the same language. In the 1700s, most of the population was of British descent, with the exception of the slaves brought from Africa and pockets of population that came from other European countries. Plus, they were largely Christian Protestants, except in Maryland, where Catholics had settled. Yet these commonalities alone could not produce a new nation.

How did these separate and distinct colonies end up as one American nation? And just what does it mean to be a nation? What were the forces that led to unity among the colonies? How did resistance to British rule contribute to that unity but also create a countervailing ideology opposed to centralized power? Why did the first American Constitution fail, and what brought about the Constitution of 1787, which created the foundation for America as one mighty and sovereign nation? This book explores these exact questions.

Students who have taken an introductory college course in political science may remember that one of the first lectures typically includes a set of definitions for nation, state, nation-state, government, and sovereignty. The professor may have indicated, as mine did, that political science doesn't use the term *country*, since that is more of a geographical term. But in everyday use, people tend to use *country* and *nation* interchangeably; so when this book uses *country*, the reader should think *nation*.

Since *nation* is at the core of this book, we need a working definition of the word. Though dictionaries and the Internet offer numerous definitions, none seems to precisely fit the concept as used in this book. Gordon Bowen, in his class syllabus *Foundations of Political Science: Defining Concepts*, offers one that comes close. He defines *nation* as "a collective identity of a people as a result of common history, expectations of a shared future, and, usually, a common language."[3] To that, I would add that individuals must be aware of or conscious of their own unity and have a common vision of the future.[4] As we will see, the United States did not meet any of the elements of this definition at the time of the revolution.

Some would argue that a nation can only be defined in terms of some combination of common origin, language, ethnicity, religion, or culture. Colin Woodward, in his book *American Nations: A History of the Eleven Rival Regional Cultures of North America*, argues that America is made up of multiple nations, due to the substantial differences that different sections of the United States display.[5] But Woodward tends to conflate culture and region with nation. "Without the nation there could be no regions; without the whole there could be no parts," two historians have written.[6] Ask any person traveling outside of the

United States what his or her nationality is and they will tell you they are Americans. While culture and the other characteristics listed above can be important components of nationhood, no single one is determinative. France is certainly a nation due to its language and culture, yet at the time of its revolution in 1789, only half of its people spoke French. Israel is a nation based on ethnic and religious identification, but it is populated with Jews from all over the world, and the Hebrew language was revived as a way to bind all Israelis together. Switzerland is a confederation whose people speak four separate languages (German, French, Italian, and Romansh), with some regions linked culturally to France, while other parts are more Italian or German. But they have a common identity as "Swiss." Ultimately, nationhood is about self-identification: you are what you think you are. And a people must accept the sense of nationhood voluntarily, it cannot be coerced.[7]

Today, the United States is religiously, culturally, and ethnically diverse. Yet we see ourselves as Americans. Why? President Obama's quote that opened this introduction, from a speech he made to a group of newly naturalized American citizens, encapsulates much about what makes America a nation. At our core, America is a nation because of a shared set of ideas about what it means to be American—ideas developed during the founding generation, and that have evolved over time. Among these ideas are liberty, equality, and self-government. But even these ideas were not sufficient to knit us together into one coherent nation. The seminal act in that process was the creation of the Constitution, which placed the union of the states on a stronger basis; allowed the new federal government to act directly on the people; and made that government responsible to the will of the people. The historian John H. Murrin has equated the Constitution to a roof over an emerging nation, one that would require time before the walls of common experience could be erected.

Ultimately, the ratification of the Constitution provided a governmental framework within which citizens can debate issues of national importance and create solutions tailored to meet the needs of each successive generation. Given this, constitutional questions are at the heart of our political dialogue. They were of core importance in weaving together the disparate regions and sections that made up the United States in 1787, and remain so with those that make it up today as well. As the writer and columnist E.J. Dionne observed, "Constitutional questions enter the political conversation in the United States more than in most countries because our diverse nation is bound by our founding principles, not by blood, race or ethnicity."[8]

Why write a book about the founding of the United States of America, a subject that others have covered so extensively? In part, because I want to provide a historical account for the general reader, one that answers a basic question: why are we one nation, and not two, or four, or fifty? Other books on this subject, most of them not recent, typically were not designed for the general reader.[9]

As with all students of history, I carry forward my own biases, which are embedded in this work. In the interest of full disclosure, I believe that both government and the private marketplace are essential for the well-being and happiness of the nation. In this book, I strove to find why some members of the founding generation concluded that a strong central government was needed to make the United States into one nation. Works of history are influenced not only by a writer's own biases, but are also a reflection of the times in which the writer lives. "All of my books have been, in a certain sense, topical in their inspiration," historian Richard Hofstadter once wrote. "That is to say, I have always begun with a concern with some present reality." This work is no different, and one of the current debates that most interests me is the disputes that have arisen over the meaning of the Constitution. One side in this debate has attempted to hijack the meaning of the Constitution, and this book attempts to bring some balance to that debate.

As such, the book is an appeal to all Americans that we are one people, despite the divisions that exist in modern society. Disagreement is a part of what makes us Americans, and it is as old as the republic itself. In today's world, some put forward the notion that our Founding Fathers agreed with each other on the major issues they confronted. Nothing could be further from the truth. Some conservatives, including members of the Tea Party, believe that limited government and individualism were the sole values at the founding of our nation. While those were important components, so were the need to create a stronger central government, which culminated in the framing and ratification of the Constitution; the need to pursue policies that were in the broader public interest; and the need to balance liberty, equality, and self-government. Perhaps it will help all of us to be reminded that the founders of our nation also had great differences of opinion, and yet they found a way to reach principled compromise and knit us into one coherent nation.

Endnotes

1 Joseph J. Ellis, *Founding Brothers: The Revolutionary Generation*, (New York, 2000), p. 10; The Franklin quote is from H.W. Brands, *The First American The Life and Times of Benjamin Franklin*, (New York, 2000), p. 306; On Washington see James Thomas Flexner, *George Washington and the New Nation: (1783-1793)* (Boston, 1969), p. 85.

2 See History.com, retrieved July 20, 2012 from http://www.history.com/topics/colonial-government-and-politics.com

3 Bowen, Gordon. *Foundations of Political Science: Defining Concepts*. Retrieved June 17, 2012 from http://www.mbc.edu/faculty/gbowen/concepts.htm

4 The inclusion of unity in the definition of nation can be found at Dictionary.com. Retrieved June 17, 2012 from http://dictionary.reference.com/browse/nation

5 Colin Woodward, *American Nations: A History of the Eleven Rival Regional Cultures of North America*, (New York, 2011) is a useful study of the social, economic, and political differences that separated the colonies and some of its findings have been used in this work.

6 Edward L. Ayers, Patricia Nelson Limerick wrote those words in *All over the Map: Rethinking American Regions*, (Baltimore, 1996), p. vii.

7 The information on the French language is attributed to historian Eric Hobsbawm, as quoted from Answers.com. Retrieved June 17, 2012 http://www.answers.com/topic/nation-state; I attribute this idea to my first political science professor, John Buckley, at Orange Coast College in Costa Mesa, California. I am grateful to Professor Buckley for this insight.

8 *Keep in mind Founders' spirit, broader objectives,* Sacramento Bee, July 5, 2012; I have been heavily influenced by the work of Joseph Ellis in term of the ongoing nature of the American debate. I recently told someone that instead of a nation conceived in liberty, we are a nation conceived in argument. See for example his latest book, *The Quartet: Orchestrating the Second American Revolution, 1783-1789*, (New York, 2015), p. 175. That work was released after this book was largely completed and so his insights were not available to this author other than as after the fact reflections.

9 These include Hans Kohn, *American Nationalism: An Interpretive Essay*, (New York, 1957), which deals less with the founding period than the entire span of the American nation through the 1950's; Paul C. Nagel, *One Nation Indivisible: The Union in American Thought*, 1776-1861, (New York, 1964); A more recent contribution to the field that is referred to in the Introduction and Epilogue is John M. Murrin, "A Roof Without Walls: The Dilemma of American National Identity," in Richard Beeman, Stephen Botein and Edward C. Carter II (Ed.), *Beyond Confederation: Origins of the Constitution and American National Identity*, (Williamsburg, 1987).

Chapter 1

The Colonial Era / 1607 to 1750

"We shall be as a city upon a hill,
the eyes of all people are upon us."
– John Winthrop –

Certain elements rooted in the colonial past—the time between the establishment of the colonies, the distance between them, their geographic diversity, and the resulting cultural and societal differences that these engendered—would, in the future, make it difficult for the original thirteen colonies to form one new nation. To understand why, we need some understanding of the colonial period leading up to the Revolution.

Great Britain was a latecomer to colonial expansion. By the time England established its first colony in Virginia in 1607, the Spanish had been colonizing for over 100 years, and the French had found success in settling parts of Canada. Both of these countries had left the mid-Atlantic open to the English, deeming the area "too cool for tropical crops but too warm for the best furs."[1] The English version of colonization provided a great deal of independence to those who settled in the New World, which would provide fertile ground for their future separation from Great Britain.

In the early part of the seventeenth century, the English Crown lacked the capability to finance colonization, and so they instead established a proprietary colony in 1606 under a private venture called the Virginia Company. The initial attempt at establishing a presence at Jamestown was an abject failure. The Virginia Company had originally tried to follow the Spanish colonization model in which the local Indian tribes were subdued and forced to provide food and labor for the conquerors. The Indians of North America were not that pliable, and they also lacked surplus food and mineral resources (gold and silver) that had allowed Spain to become rich. Despite massive investments by the Virginia Company, by 1616, the colony contained only 350 mostly poor and sick colonists, and the company was on the verge of bankruptcy.[2]

Two major changes occurred in 1618 that forever reshaped the face of Virginia and would have impacts for the future United States. First, the "headright system" was introduced into the New World. Under that system, settlers received fifty acres of land, plus an additional fifty acres for each family member or servant they brought with them. Through this system, the ownership of private property was introduced into North America, which created the incentive for emigrants to work hard and prosper. The second major change was the growing of tobacco, which became a major crop for export to Great Britain and led to the development of large plantations and a colonial elite in Virginia. The population surged, growing to 13,000 colonists by 1650.[3]

Tobacco, a labor-intensive crop, demanded that workers toil under very harsh conditions, including exposure to malaria, dysentery, and typhoid fever. The larger plantation owners initially used indentured servants from England to work their fields. The indentured servants were released from their contracts after five years, and given fifty acres of land of their own to farm. Landowners used indentured servants because the life expectancy for those that worked the fields was so short that it was cheaper to purchase them for a limited time than it was to acquire a lifelong slave from Africa. "At mid-century, the Chesapeake became a bit healthier and many more servants lived long enough to claim their freedom and farms," according to historian Alan Taylor. The former indentured servants formed a new and middle level group of planters.[4]

Maryland, the second colony formed in 1632 in the Chesapeake Bay area, was named for Queen Mary, the wife of King Charles I. The King gave twelve million acres of land to Lord Baltimore, who was Catholic, to govern the new colony. Baltimore attempted to make Maryland a refuge for Catholics, but very few actually immigrated to the colony. Instead, the new colony was largely settled by Virginians of modest means, who took advantage of a very lucrative headright system in which they could receive 100 acres of land for every adult that emigrated, and fifty acres for each child. Over time, Maryland too developed into a tobacco colony.[5]

In the latter part of the seventeenth century, prosperity in England reduced the number of people that immigrated to Virginia. Life expectancy in the colony was also increasing as "many of the new plantations expanded upstream into locales with fresh running streams and away from the stagnant lowlands."

These factors, combined with longer life expectancies, meant that the large planters turned to African slaves to provide labor for their plantations. The slave population grew from about 300 in 1650, to 13,000 in 1700, to over 150,000 in 1750. In order to control such a large population of black slaves, the large plantation owners used harsh and demeaning methods. One slave owner commented that the "unhappy effect of owning many Negroes is the necessity of being severe. Numbers make them insolent, and then foul means must do, what fair will not." The slave owners also elicited the support of non-slave-owning white men of the colony as a means to control the slave population. In order to justify their harsh treatment, the slave owners treated the African slaves as less than human, "no better than dogs or horses." A sense of racial superiority emerged in Virginia, as every white man found himself superior to black slaves. The slave system helped to foster ever more concentration of wealth in the hands of fewer and fewer men who owned large plantations. As historian Daniel J. Boorstin writes, "Virginia had become an aristocracy…not more than a hundred families controlled the wealth and government of the colony," by the middle of the seventeenth century.[6]

The New England colonies developed in a very different way, as a refuge for the Puritans who wanted to escape what they perceived as religious persecution by the Anglican Church in England. The first settlement began in 1620, when a group of Puritans, known as the Pilgrims, established the Plymouth colony. Ten years later, John Winthrop led the "Great Migration." He wanted to make the New World a "Shining City on a Hill." For him, the phrase that meant a religious refuge would come to represent to the world America's destiny as an example of a free society.[7]

Unlike Virginia, which was largely populated by poor indentured servants and unwilling slaves, the Massachusetts colony attracted middle-class people from England. They generally came as families who had sufficient resources to pay their own way. Winthrop managed to secure a royal charter from the Massachusetts Bay Company. "Once in Massachusetts, the company leaders established the most radical government in the European world: a republic, where the Puritan men elected their governor, deputy governor, and legislature," according to historian Alan Taylor. The Puritans tended to settle in small towns in order to provide greater protection from the local Indian tribes, and also as a way to sustain the church. Out of this system emerged the New England town hall form of government, in which the public directly made the laws.[8] By 1691, four colonies existed in New England: Massachusetts, Connecticut, Rhode Island, and New Hampshire.

Initially, the economy centered around farming. Most families owned small farms of between 100 and 200 acres, not like the great plantations that developed in the South. The work was difficult since the soil was not rich, and the growing season was much shorter. The farms produced enough food to sustain the family, with small surpluses that they could trade for consumer goods. Fishing, shipbuilding, and the carrying trade (shipping products to overseas markets) led to the diversification of the New England economy. Boston emerged as a major city by the early 1700s, a center for commerce and trade. A wealthy, commercial elite also began to develop in Boston, along with a variety of artisan tradesmen that supported shipbuilding. But the wealthy elite "enjoyed less collective power than did the great planters" of the South "because the New England system of many nearly autonomous towns dispersed political power in the countryside," according to one historian. The Puritans also believed that a more equal distribution of wealth was more in line with a "godly life."[9]

The British initially ignored the middle colonies, the area between New England to the north and Virginia to the south. In the late 1660s, the Netherlands was an expanding maritime power, and to help sustain their massive trading operation, the Dutch established New Amsterdam in 1625. It served the Dutch interest in defending the mouth of the Hudson River and its lucrative fur trading operation in upstate New York. Farming settlements arose in the surrounding areas of New

Jersey and Long Island, and eventually extended south to the Delaware River.[10]

The Netherlands was a religiously tolerant country, and the middle colonies attracted a diverse mix of ethnic and religious groups. This included not only the Dutch, but also emigrants from Belgium, France, Scandinavia, and Germany. The newcomers were mostly family groups of farmers and artisans. New Amsterdam developed into a cosmopolitan trading center. The Dutch were also pioneers in banking and global business enterprises, two areas that the future New York City would inherit. Because life in the Netherlands was generally good, the Dutch had difficulty establishing a large settlement in the New World, with a population of only 9,000 in 1664. In that year, the English conquered the Dutch colonies in the New World and established control over most of the eastern seaboard. It would take almost 100 years before assimilation to the English language and customs would fully take hold in New York and the surrounding middle colonies of New Jersey and Delaware.

Pennsylvania, also considered a part of the middle colonies, experienced a different evolution.[11] It was founded in 1680 when the King granted William Penn a colonial charter to repay a debt owed to Penn's father. Penn, a very affluent man, was an odd convert to Quakerism, a religion that opposed great concentrations of wealth and most social hierarchy. The Quakers did espouse hard work and thrift, which helped them achieve success in the New World.

The Quakers settled along the western shore of the Delaware River in a city they called Philadelphia, the "City of Brotherly Love." The colony grew rapidly, with farms springing up in the area surrounding Philadelphia. Penn recruited a broad mix of people with different religious and national backgrounds to settle his colony, essentially anyone who had money and could purchase land from him and pay the annual quitrent. Pennsylvania attracted middle-class people, much like New England did, but the location provided a better climate and soil, allowing for more prosperity for the farming community. A group of merchants and artisans also developed in Philadelphia, which over time became a thriving metropolis.

The colonies established in the deep south of the Carolinas and Georgia had a very different experience than any of those that came before them, even Virginia. In 1670, a group of English aristocrats known as the Lords Proprietor, allies of the King, were granted a proprietorship over the area. But rather than immigrating to the Carolinas themselves, they recruited planters from the island of Barbados to lead the establishment of the colony. Barbados was an English outpost in the Caribbean notorious for a "slave system whose brutality shocked contemporaries," according to the author Colin Woodard. They would ultimately build a similar society in the Carolinas.[12]

The Carolinas, which served as an outpost for the English, were bordered by hostile Spanish territory in Florida. To expedite emigration in the 1670s, the Lords Proprietor offered numerous incentives, including "religious toleration, political representation in an assembly with power over public taxation and expenditures, a long exemption from quitrents, and large grants of land." Through these means, they were able to foster a rapid increase in population, with middle class farmers and artisans making up the bulk of the emigrants. Indentured servants were also welcome, and once they completed their contract, they received a grant of 100 acres of land. The Lords Proprietor attracted wealthy plantation owners from Barbados by offering each of them 150 acres for each slave they brought with them. The Lords told each great planter that he would have "absolute Power and Authority over his Negro Slaves," just as they had in Barbados. The large plantation owners very quickly came to dominate South Carolina.[13]

In 1650, Virginians had settled the northern portion of the Carolinas. They resented rule by the Lords Proprietor, and in 1691, they were allowed to establish their own colony of North Carolina. The Carolina elite and the Lords Proprietor fought for control of the two colonies in the early 1700s. In 1729, the King bought out the Lords Proprietor and both North and South Carolina became royal colonies. Except for the appointment of royal governors, who tended to be weak, the great planter elite controlled the governance of both North and South Carolina, including issues regarding taxation. With the introduction of rice as the main staple crop in the colony in 1690, the slave population exploded. Like tobacco, rice was a labor-intensive crop, and the work was grueling, especially in the lowland areas where heat and tropical diseases were rampant. "By 1730, enslaved Africans outnumbered free colonists in Carolina two to one," according to Taylor. In the lowland area where rice was grown, the number was as high as nine to one. The great fear of the planter class was that the slaves would revolt and kill their masters. They maintained order through a system of terror against the slaves and by recruiting the common farmers in a system of institutionalized racism. In putting down a slave revolt that occurred in 1739, the white masters "cut off the rebels' heads and placed them on posts, one every mile, between the battlefield and Charles Town," as a means to discourage other slaves from attempting any revolt.[14]

The planter elite of the Carolinas became the most affluent people in all of the colonies. Since slaves did all of the work for them, the planters spent their time "eating, drinking, lolling, smoking, and sleeping, which five modes constitute the essence of their life and existence," according to one observer of the period. Per capita wealth was quadruple that of Virginia and six times higher than that found in the major cities of the middle colonies, and that wealth was concentrated in the hands of very few families in North and South Carolina.[15]

In the 1720s, Georgia was split off from South Carolina to form a colony that the poor from England could immigrate to and begin life anew. By 1742, 1,800 poor Englishmen had been transplanted to Georgia and were given small farms. While the trustees that governed Georgia initially banned slavery, this policy changed under pressure from the more successful colonists. In 1751, Georgia, too, became a crown colony, and soon began to recreate life in South Carolina, with large plantations dominated by the use of slave labor.[16]

The Europeans did not come to a virgin land, far from it. The native peoples of the Americas may have started their migration across the land bridge of the Bering Strait as far back as 10,000 years ago. The native peoples represented a diverse and linguistically distinct people that gradually spread over much of North and South America. Beginning in 1492, with the journey of Christopher Columbus, the Spanish became the first colonizers of the New World. They came in search of gold, silver, and other raw materials, and they conquered all those who stood in their way. By the mid-1550s the Spanish controlled much of South America through superior guile, weaponry, and diseases that substantially reduced the native population.[17]

The English initially attempted to follow the Spanish model in Virginia, but the Indian tribes in the area were neither wealthy nor compliant. Waiting for the local Powhatan's to feed them while they explored for gold, the first colonists nearly starved. "The colonists did not understand that the local Indians had scant surplus to spare, raising little more than they needed every year," Taylor argues. The proprietors of Virginia then changed direction, deciding instead to develop a planation system that rewarded hard work among the settlers, a system that ultimately thrived with the production of tobacco. As the growth of the settlers exploded in the 1600s, the native tribes in the area began a slow decline. A combination of disease and war reduced their numbers from 24,000 in 1607 to 2,000 by 1669.[18]

The Indian experience in New England was no better. Despite the myth that evolved around the first Thanksgiving holiday, where natives and Englishmen shared a meal together, the Pilgrims considered the Indians as "savage people, who are cruel, barbarous and most treacherous." In the aftermath of the Great Migration, the New Englanders "openly bullied the various Indian bands, demanding their formal submission and the payment of tribute in wampum," according to Taylor.[19]

The English settlers could not comprehend the nomadic lifestyle of the natives and their indifference to exploiting the land and accumulating wealth. Indian men were the hunters who had intense periods of work in the fall and winter, but then did little work in the summer months. Women were responsible for the villages and hunting camps and also tended the crops. The New Englanders could not understand why the Indians did not extract more from the surrounding land. The Puritans also attempted to force the Indians to settle into fixed communities and to convert to Christianity.[20]

The two sides fought numerous wars. In 1637, the Puritans attacked a Pequot village, set it on fire, and killed all 400 people that lived there. In 1675, one of the local Indian tribes, the Wampanoag, fought back under the leadership of a chief named Metacom. Initially, the Indians had the upper hand, attacking and destroying twelve Puritan towns. The colonists eventually turned to other Indian tribes as allies, who taught them the fine art of bushfighting. While the New English lost about 1,000 settlers, the Wampanoag were nearly destroyed, losing over 3,000 people, almost a quarter of their population. In the aftermath of the war, the Puritan settlers expanded rapidly. Within one hundred years, "every native people along the Atlantic seaboard [would live] on a changed land among invaders," a common outcome in the future for Indians in the rest of North America.[21]

A dress rehearsal for the American Revolution occurred in 1685, when James II assumed the throne in England. He exerted greater control over the New England colonies, and merged them with New York and New Jersey into the Dominion of New England. "The Dominion dispensed with assemblies, entrusting administration to a governor-general assisted by a lieutenant governor and an appointed council," according to one historian. The New Englanders, accustomed to a strong local self-government, specifically over internal affairs and taxation, were outraged. Sir Edmund Andros became the governor-general, and immediately began to levy new taxes and charge landowners quitrents.[22]

Events in England soon opened a path of resistance for the colonists. James II, a Catholic, had raised the ire of several powerful Anglican Bishops. They encouraged the Dutch Prince William of Orange to invade England, which he did with the support of dissident factions in the British Army and Navy. He was then crowned the King, with his wife Mary as Queen. Given the support of the Bishops and the armed forces, William promised to cooperate with Parliament and uphold the Anglican faith. Because of his support of Parliament, the English Whigs (those who believed in power sharing between the King and Parliament) called his ascension to the throne the "Glorious Revolution."[23]

With William now on the throne, resistance to rule by the

Dominion broke out in New England and New York. Local officials in New England dissolved the Dominion and threw Andros and his supporters into prison, pledging support for William and Mary. But King William refused to return to a loose system whereby the colonials ruled themselves. Instead, the two sides agreed to a compromise; they shared power between royal governors appointed by the King and assemblies elected by the elite colonial property owners. The local assemblies generally controlled taxation and the spending of money, including the governors' salaries. Through this system, the colonies became more closely entwined with Great Britain, and a dual identity began to emerge in which the colonials saw themselves as part of a larger empire, with loyalty owed both to Great Britain and to their own colony. This was the system in place when the British and the French engaged in a war in the new world known as the French and Indian War.[24]

Historian Forest McDonald writes that "widely different and deeply rooted local traditions separated the thirteen British colonies in North America, and space and the available means of communication separated them further." These components, especially the time between the establishment of the different colonies and their distance from one another in an era without mass communication, would make it an uphill struggle to establish one nation. The colonies' varied climates and environmental conditions led to different economic circumstances and the development of distinct cultures. The economy of the South, dominated by large planters dependent on slaves to produce staples crops, led to a society where an aristocratic elite ruled. The middle colonies were more diversified, with small farms and fertile soils with reasonably long growing seasons, and a better distribution of wealth.

The growth of cities like New York and Philadelphia led to the creation of a merchant class that became the elite in the middle colonies. New England had the most equal distribution of wealth, an offshoot of the Puritan belief in simple living, but also a byproduct of the limited natural resources and colder climate of the area.[25]

McDonald argues that "logic dictated that if the colonies were to be independent of Britain they should also be independent of one another." Yet, certain elements would lend themselves toward consolidation of the colonies. With the exception of parts of Pennsylvania and New York, the colonists all spoke the same language. Daniel Boorstin maintains that the colonials spoke a more uniform English than did the British. John Winthrop, who emigrated from Scotland in 1781 to become President of the College of New Jersey, said, "there is a greater difference in dialect between one county and another in Britain, than there is between one state and another in America." Both New England and the South spoke with "what we now call a southern accent," according to Boorstin. And even those emigrants that came to the New World speaking different languages knew that in order to thrive, they needed to learn English.[26]

A second element that brought the colonies together was their common experience with local self-government. By the time of the French and Indian War, most of the colonies were governed under a structure in which local assemblies made decisions about taxation and spending. Tensions between the local assemblies and the royal governors existed, tensions that would mount during the 1760s and 1770s. This common experience was also a double-edged sword. While the colonies had a common experience of self-rule, it was grounded in their individual colony, and the conflicts they had with royal governors made them suspicious of a distant and centralized government.

The colonists were also largely from Great Britain. In 1700, the population was mainly drawn from England, but over the next fifty years, greater numbers of people came from Germany and other parts of Europe. But by far the largest non-English ethnic group was the Scotch-Irish that emigrated from Northern Ireland, a part of Great Britain.[27] By the mid-1750s, most of the colonists had a dual identity, believing they were both loyal British subjects, as well as members of their individual colony. As Englishmen, they believed they were "entitled to all of the inherent rights and liberties" as those that lived in Great Britain. "Despite their internal diversity, therefore, it is reasonable to speak on an American outlook, for a rough consensus would be achieved in the course of decade long controversy," that was about to unfold between the colonists and the mother country.[28] By the end of that controversy, when the colonists had achieved independence and were considering a new Constitution in 1787, John Jay wrote the following:

> *With equal pleasure I have often taken notice that Providence has been pleased to give this one connected country to one united people—a people descended from the same language, professing the same religion, attached to the same principles of government, very similar in their manners and customs, and who by their joint counsels, arms, and efforts, fighting side by side throughout a long and bloody war, have nobly established their general liberty and independence.*

Jay wrote these words as part of the Federalists Papers, and they were less a statement of fact than an aspiration for what the nationalists in 1787 hoped to achieve through ratification of the Constitution. John Adams expressed the difficulties of creating a sense of American nationalism more realistically in 1775, when he wrote that the differences between New England and the other colonies made them almost like "several distinct Nations." Looking back in 1818 at what the founders had achieved, Adams expressed a sense of amazement that a people with such a "great variety of religions…customs, manners, and habits," whose relations "had been so rare, and their knowledge of each other so imperfect, that to unite them…was a very difficult enterprise," could achieve a bit of a miracle: the eventual emergence of a common national identity.[29] But the miracle that Adams wrote of, the unity of the Americans, would emerge only gradually, and not without great debate, between the 1750s and 1787, and would continue to evolve and develop during the early years of the republic.

Endnotes

1 Alan Taylor, *American Colonies: The Settling of North America*, (New York, 2001), p. 118

2 Daron Acemoglu and James A. Robinson, *Why Nations Fail: The Origins of Power, Prosperity, and Poverty*, (New York, 2012), I Book edition, p. 45-57; Taylor, p. 33

3 Taylor, p. 133-134

4 Taylor, p. 142-144

5 Taylor, p. 136-137

6 Taylor, p. 142-144 and p. 153-157; Daniel Boorstin, *The Americans: The Colonial Experience*, (New York, 1958), p 103

7 Taylor, p. 165; Boorstin, p. 3-4

8 Taylor, p. 16.

9 Taylor, p. 172

10 Taylor, p. 252

11 This section is drawn largely from Taylor, p. 264-271

12 Woodward, p. 83; Taylor, p. 223

13 Taylor, p. 224-225

14 Taylor, p. 226-240

15 Taylor, p. 238; Woodward, p. 84

16 Taylor, p. 241-243

17 Taylor, p. 4-5

18 Taylor, p. 131-137

19 Taylor, p. 194

20 Taylor, p. 188-189.

21 Woodward, p. 62; Taylor, p. 188-189

22 Taylor, p. 276-277.

23 Taylor, p. 278; Woodard, p 74

24 Taylor, p. 282-288

25 Forrest McDonald, *E Pluribus Unum: The Formation of the American Republic 1776-1790*, (Indianapolis, 1965), p. 1.

26 McDonald, p. 18; See Boorstin, p. 271-277, for a complete discussion of the importance of a common language in the colonies.

27 Richard Hofstadter, *America at 1750: A Social Portrait*, (New York, 1971), p. 16-24

28 David C. Hendrickson, *Peace Pact: The Lost World of the American Founding*
(Lawrence, 2003), p. 74

29 The Adams quotes are from Hendrickson, p. 26-27

Chapter 2

The Roots of a Nation / 1753 to 1774

"It is proposed that humble application be made for an act of Parliament of Great Britain, by virtue of which one general government may be formed in America."

— from the Albany Plan —

The twenty-year period from 1753 to 1774 saw the unity of the colonists emerge. It began first as a reaction to the threat posed by the French and the resulting French and Indian War. In the aftermath of the defeat of the French, the British attempted to exert greater control over their colonial empire, which, historically, they had ruled lightly. They also implemented various taxation measures to pay for the war, which resulted in vociferous colonial protests, since the colonists had become accustomed to establishing their own policies for taxation.

The French and Indian War and the Albany Plan

The competition between two of the great European powers at that time, Great Britain and France, had a major impact on the future course of events. Both countries were vying for control of the hinterlands of the new North American continent. The British had established a string of thirteen colonies along the eastern seaboard, whereas "trappers and traders who operated along the Mississippi and Saint Lawrence

Rivers,"[1] represented the French presence. The French and the British had clashed over control of the continent multiple times since 1690.[2]

In 1753, the French attempted to hem in the colonies and reduce the influence of the British by building a series of forts along the Ohio River. If successful, the French would have controlled the heartland and confined the British to the Atlantic coast only. This would have foreclosed the ability of the British and the colonists to expand into the interior of the continent, perhaps forever.[3] Part of the British response, through its Board of Trade, was to call for an inter-colonial conference as a means to achieve greater cooperation between the colonies so they could support their own defense. They invited eight colonies, but Virginia and New Jersey both declined to attend. New York, the New England colonies, Maryland, and Pennsylvania all sent delegates to the conference in Albany, New York. At that time, little unity existed among the colonies, and the assemblies for seven of the colonies in attendance directed their delegates to "avoid any plan for colonial confederation."[4]

Though many colonists opposed the idea of a union, some delegates looked forward to the opportunity to discuss just such a plan.[5] Pennsylvania delegate Benjamin Franklin began developing his own plan of unification. Walter Isaacson, in his brilliant biography *Benjamin Franklin: An American Life* argues that "Franklin was among the first to view the British settlements in America not only as separate colonies but as part of a potentially united nation."[6] Franklin's nationalistic perspective is a product of his life's experiences as man who rose from humble beginnings to achieve incredible accomplishments.

Benjamin Franklin[7]

In the words of biographer H.W. Brands, Ben Franklin was the first American. A self-made man, Franklin excelled in many areas: he was a successful businessman, an inventor and scientist, a philosopher and diplomat, and a writer and politician. He was perhaps the first of the founding generation to develop a nationalist perspective. His experiences in business, in government, and even in his pursuit of scientific knowledge all gave him opportunities to travel widely and to interact with people of differing backgrounds, both in America and in Europe, giving him a wider perspective than many of his peers. Franklin also combined two core American principles: individual achievement through hard work and persistence, and a concern for helping others. He also had an uncanny ability to show up at key moments, from the signing of the Declaration of Independence in 1776, to negotiations in Paris over the treaty that ended the Revolutionary War in 1783, to the Constitutional Convention in Philadelphia in 1787.

Franklin was born on January 17, 1706, in Boston, the thirteenth child of his father Josiah and the eighth child of his mother Abiah. Benjamin was the youngest son of his parents with his next older sibling seven years his senior. He also had two younger sisters. According to Walter Isaacson, "Being the last of the litter often meant having to strike out on your own."[8] That would be the case for young Benjamin.

His father originally intended for Benjamin to train to become a minister, but the expense proved too much for Josiah. At the age of ten, after only two years of formal schooling, Ben went to work in his father's candle shop. Later, his father would arrange for him to work in his brother James' print shop, as an indentured apprentice, where he learned the business and became quite proficient at it. He also developed his skills as a writer. James, who was nine years Ben's senior, treated him quite poorly. Young Ben wrote that his brother treated him in a way that "demeaned me too much," with occasional beatings.[9] At the age of seventeen, he broke his indenture and fled to New York, where he stayed only a short while. He ultimately landed in Philadelphia, where he made his fame and fortune.

Young Ben was able to use his charismatic personality to achieve success. Isaacson writes, "At 17, Franklin was physically striking: muscular, barrel-chested, open-faced, and almost six feet tall. He had the happy talent of being at ease in almost any company, from scrappy tradesman to wealthy merchants, scholars to rogues. His most notable trait was personal magnetism; he attracted people who wanted to help him."[10] By the age of twenty, he owned his own print shop, which he managed to acquire through financial assistance from several friends. At a young age, Franklin impressed some very powerful men, whose patronage he was able to use in his rise to success. His patrons included the governors of Pennsylvania and New York, along with the powerful merchant Thomas Denham, and Andrew Hamilton, the speaker of the Pennsylvania Assembly, who in 1733 helped steer government printing jobs to Franklin. All "these friends were…of great Use to me as I occasionally was to them," Franklin would recall.[11]

Over the course of the next twenty years, he would purchase a newspaper, publish *Poor Richard's Almanack*, and franchise his print operation in other colonies. His experience in the print business, in which he had developed relationships with printers from as far away as Rhode Island, New York, and South Carolina, gave him a cosmopolitan point of view. He also read publications from throughout the colonies. By 1748, "Franklin's print shop had grown into a successful, vertically integrated media conglomerate." At the age of just forty-two, he had reached the point where he could retire from business, and pursue other interests. For Franklin, money was always a means to an end, and not an end to itself. His interests now lay elsewhere, including politics and the world of science. He would have the "leisure to read, study, make experiments, and converse at large with such ingenious and worthy men as are pleased to honor me with their friendship," he would write to a friend at the time of his retirement.[12]

Franklin launched his political career in retirement, first as a member of the Philadelphia City Council in 1748, and then as a member of the Pennsylvania Assembly in 1751. In 1737, the British government had appointed Franklin the postmaster of Philadelphia, and by 1753, he shared the role of Postmaster General for all of the colonies, which broadened his perspective even further. As Postmaster General, he traveled throughout the continent on postal inspection trips. His longest trip was a seven-month, 1,789-mile journey that occurred in 1763, with stops in Virginia, New Jersey, Boston, and New Hampshire. During travels such as this, he began to see the possibility of America as one nation. As his biographer Isaacson notes, "To [Franklin], the colonies were not merely disparate entities. They were a New World with common interests and ideals."[13]

From the distance of history, we might be tempted to view the founding generation as men with no weaknesses. But of course, they were all too human, and Franklin was no exception. In his business pursuits, Franklin was quite cunning and would do whatever was necessary to succeed, including driving his competitors out of business in order to secure his media empire. As with many of the founders, he owned slaves, and early in his life, he exhibited great prejudice against non-whites, although he ultimately changed his mind and became an abolitionist. He also made some major political mistakes. During a stay in London, he totally misread the colonists' reaction to the Stamp Act when he told the British government that he was "not much alarm'd about your Schemes of raising Money on us." In fact, the Stamp Act would trigger the beginnings of resistance to British rule. Though happily married, he continued to be attracted to younger women, with whom he entered into flirtatious relationships. And he fathered an illegitimate son, whom he loved, but whom he would break with over the issue of American independence.[14]

In many ways, Franklin represents the essential and idealized American story of the person pulling themselves up by their own bootstraps, one component in the overarching American dream: Through hard work, one can rise up the social and economic ladder, unlike the European aristocratic world, where individuals were restricted by their birth or social class. As historian John Ferling writes: "Opportunities were better in America for young men from humble backgrounds who were ambitious and industrious. They too could rise to be part of the middling sort of society."[15] Franklin rose even higher than "middling," but he was the exception and not the rule. And while one can apply such a rags-to-riches story, later made famous in dime store novels by Horatio Alger, to Franklin, his story is certainly more complicated than that. While his success can be in major part attributed to his own skills and abilities, he had help along the way. And such a path was not open to slaves, or to women of that era, but only to white males.

Franklin recognized that he did not make it on his own without the help of others. He received financial assistance when he was starting his own print shop and he saw firsthand the value "in encouraging and providing opportunities for all people to succeed based on their diligence, hard work, virtue and ambition." He also saw a role for government in fostering individual and community initiatives. Isaacson thought the essence of Franklin was that he was a civic-minded man. He writes, "A fundamental aspect of Franklin's life, and of the American society he helped create, was that individualism and communitarianism, so seemingly contradictory, were interwoven." Franklin started a subscription library, a volunteer fire department, a night watchmen patrol, a militia, and a college. In 1751, Franklin raised money for a hospital and was able to convince the colonial legislature to provide public matching funds equal to the private dollars that had been generated, thus creating the concept of the matching grant. "He believed in volunteerism and limited government, but also that there was a legitimate role for government in fostering the common good."[16] At the core of his being was a concern for his fellow man and a need to do charitable works. He saw a connection between civic virtue and religious virtue. In a letter to his wife, he expressed these convictions: "God is very good to us. Let us ... show our sense of His goodness to us by continuing to do good to our fellow creatures."[17]

Benjamin Franklin was also one of the earliest advocates of the Albany Plan, a proposal for creating an American union of the thirteen colonies under British control.

The Albany Plan

By 1751, Franklin had been considering some form of union for the colonies under British rule. One of the primary goals was to provide for the common defense. But he faced stiff opposition in establishing such a plan. The colonies were accustomed to acting independently; they each had their own governments, and they had separate and sometimes conflicting interests. In addition, the small colonies feared that the larger ones would dominate any union.[18]

But war, or the threat of war, had a way of creating unity. Delegates to the Albany Conference engaged in a serious discussion about a plan of union as first proposed by Franklin, expanded on by Thomas Hutchinson, and amended by the Conference. Hutchinson, who had graduated from Harvard at sixteen, was a man of great wealth who came to the conference as a representative from Massachusetts. His goal was to remove French influence from the New World to increase security for his own colony. Achieving this would require the assistance of Great Britain and the other colonies.[19]

The plan called for a union of eleven colonies. It excluded Georgia, because it had been founded only twenty years before, and Delaware, which was considered a part of Pennsylvania at that time. Under the Albany Plan, the King would appoint a President-General who would serve as the executive. A Grand Council would serve as the legislative body, with representation based proportionally on population and directly elected by the people in each colony. (Interestingly, this body would resemble the House of Representatives later formed under the Constitution.) The new government would have powers over war and peace, treaties, trade and land transactions, and would have the power to levy taxes. Its task would be to focus on issues common to each colony, such as national defense. Each colony would also maintain its own government under a federal scheme and maintain control over local matters. The delegates endorsed the plan unanimously.[20]

But the plan did not find acceptance, either in England or among the colonies. The English feared it could lead to demands for independence from the colonies. And for the colonies, old fears of a general union resurfaced with each colony afraid of losing power. Franklin, in looking back, argued that had the colonies adopted the Albany Plan, they could have avoided the American Revolution. "The colonies so united would have been sufficiently strong to defend themselves. There would have been no need for troops from England; of course the subsequent pretence for taxing America, and the bloody contest it occasioned, would have been avoided."[21] As with all roads not taken, we will never know if he was right. But it seems likely that the colonies would have sought some form of independence in the future, especially once westward expansion began. To paraphrase Tom Paine in his revolutionary tract *Common Sense,* released in early 1776, it is hard to imagine an island ruling a continent.

The Beginning of Resistance to British Rule

Every grade school student knows that the colonists fought the American Revolution over the issue of taxation without representation. And while there were certainly numerous reasons behind the break from Great Britain, the conflict that ensued came down to one of control. The British position was that Parliament had the authority to pass all laws and implement policies that affected the colonies in all cases, including taxation. The colonists, however, believed they should be governed by laws passed by their colonial assemblies. These two competing visions would ultimately lead the colonies to declare their independence.[22]

By 1763, the British believed that they had won a great victory over the French for control of North America, and that their empire stood at its apex. In the aftermath of the victory over the French, in what we call the French and Indian War, and what the Europeans called the Seven Years' War, the new King, George III, and his ministers, decided to rationalize the administration of their colonies in America. Great Britain had also accumulated a large debt from the four wars they had fought since 1689, including those in North America. They planned to station 8,000 soldiers in Canada and in the west to maintain the peace, secure their conquests, and keep the colonists from further encroaching into Indian Territory. For them, it seemed only reasonable that the colonists would pay their fair share of the costs for troops stationed on North American soil, so that the full burden would not fall on their own taxpayers. In addition, the British believed that the colonists had benefited immensely from the protection they provided. To be sure, Great Britain's motivation also included a perceived need to rein in the colonies, which they viewed as being too independent and to have grown distant from the British. British governance of the colonies was highly decentralized and barely penetrated into the countryside. Given this situation, the government of King George III, led by Lord Grenville, convinced Parliament to enact a series of laws designed to raise revenue and reduce the independence of the colonies, culminating in the Stamp Act.[23]

The colonists' view differed greatly. Having been lightly governed by Great Britain, they had become quite independent and were particularly sensitive over issues that involved their rights as British citizens. At the core of the colonists' view of their rights was the issue of taxation. With no representation in Parliament, many of the colonial leaders thought it illegitimate for a foreign power in which they had no input to levy taxes on them. Some even went so far as to consider the colonial assemblies the equal of Parliament, particularly in the areas of free speech and the ability to control their own internal financial affairs, a position soundly rejected in England, which believed that sole sovereignty rested in the Parliament.

The very nature of representation was in dispute between the British and their American colonies. By the 1760s, the English method of electing members to Parliament had diverged from a system of proportional representation tied to local districts. Some electoral districts were small, others large, and many areas had no representation at all. This included two of England's largest cities, Manchester and Birmingham. "The British justified this hodge-podge of representation by claiming that each member of Parliament represented the whole British nation and not just the particular locality he supposedly came from," writes historian Gordon Wood. The English maintained that this system of "virtual representation" covered the colonies as well, and gave Parliament the right to tax the colonists. The Americans rejected the notion of virtual representation. In electing members to local assemblies, the colonists had developed a system of "actual representation" in which the public voted directly for members of the legislature. They drew the legislative districts in proportion to population, and as populations changed, the districts were redrawn. The colonial system also favored tight control of elected officials by the people that voted for them. Since it was impractical for the public to make every decision through direct democracy, elected officials should be "tied down" as much as possible through short terms in office, a system of regular rotation, and direct instructions. The British attempted to defend their system of "virtual representation" by pointing to Manchester and Birmingham, which caused James Otis of Massachusetts to reply "If those now so considerable places are not represented, they ought to be."[24]

In 1765, Parliament approved the Stamp Act, which imposed a stamp tax "ranging from 1 shilling to 6 pounds on various commercial and legal documents such as wills, mortgages and college degrees, as well as on newspapers, almanacs, calendars, pamphlets, playing cards, and dice." While in theory the tax would fall primarily on lawyers and printers, colonists recognized that the tax would be passed on to them in the form of higher prices whenever they purchased a newspaper, bought and sold real estate, or otherwise needed legal services. The colonies were already experiencing an economic downturn that had set in after the war, and adding a new tax on top of this proved to be a combustible combination.[25]

Protests set in almost immediately, some even before approval of the Stamp Act. Led by the fiery Patrick Henry, Virginia was the first to act. In May of 1765, they approved the Virginia Resolves, which stated that the local assembly "HAVE the Sole Right and Authority to lay Taxes and Impositions." James Otis Jr., a Boston lawyer and member of the Massachusetts Assembly, authored a treatise entitled *The Rights of the British Colonies Asserted and Proved.* He argued that Parliament's powers were not unlimited, and that they did not have the right to tax the colonies without their consent. In 1765, no one publicly advocated for independence, and protests were pointed at the Parliament, with support for the King remaining strong. Even the popular Henry had to be careful of his words of protest against the King. In his speech supporting the Virginia Resolves, he concluded, "Caesar had his Brutus, Charles the First his Cromwell and George the Third" – amid cries of "Treason!" that arose from all sides of the room – "and George the Third," he continued artfully, "may profit by their example. If this be treason, make the most of it!"[26]

Protests took not only a political direction, but they also began to turn violent. Riots broke out in Rhode Island, Maryland, New Jersey, Pennsylvania, Connecticut, and New Hampshire. As a result, commissioners appointed to collect the stamp tax resigned and the British were unable to collect the tax. In response to the protests, Massachusetts proposed a meeting of all the colonies in New York in the fall of 1765. Dubbed the Stamp Act Congress, its intent was to compose a petition to the British to repeal the Stamp Act. Some historians suspect that certain individuals, since lost to history, orchestrated the violent protests to motivate the Stamp Act Congress to take a strong position against the British taxation measures. Nine colonies, mostly those represented at the Albany Conference, sent delegates. A majority were moderates, with a sprinkling of conservative members. The conservative element rejected any notion that the colonists had a natural right to exercise self-government. Instead, they protested the Stamp Act on the basis "that it is inseparable to the freedom of a people, and the undoubted right of Englishmen, that no taxes should be imposed upon them, but with their own consent."[27]

In March of 1766, Parliament repealed the Stamp Act, due in part to the difficulty of collecting the tax. Perhaps more importantly, the British merchant class had lobbied the government to end the stamp tax, since it had caused a reduction in trade with the colonies, due to the embargo of British goods implemented by the colonies. The respite would not last long, as the British maintained their sole right to legislate for the colonies "in all cases whatsoever" through passage of the Declaratory Act, which accompanied repeal of the Stamp Act. By 1767, the new Chancellor of the Exchequer, Charles Townshend, proposed a series of new, "indirect" taxes and other measures, which became known as the Townshend Acts. In his testimony before Parliament over the Stamp Act, Franklin had indicated the colonists saw a distinction between internal taxes (like the Stamp Act), which they opposed, and external taxes (those levied on imports), which he maintained they could support. Despite the distinction that Franklin had drawn on different methods of taxation, the Townshend duties led to a new series of colonial protests. They culminated in the Boston Massacre on March 5, 1770, when British soldiers, fearing for their lives, opened fire on an angry mob of protesters. Ironically, Parliament repealed the Townshend duties that very same day. The protests had not caused the removal of the duties, but once again Parliament reacted to pressure from English merchants, who were losing business due to the colonial embargo. For a time it appeared the crisis had passed, but the calm was not to last. The issue of who controlled the colonies remained unresolved.[28]

A Tea Party and the First Continental Congress

With the benefit of hindsight, it seems obvious there would be another clash between England and the colonists. Britain had repealed the Stamp Act and Lord North, the new head of the British government in 1770, had removed the Townshend duties. There remained a small tax on tea. But North did not recognize the colonists' position that Parliament had no right to tax them. "The properest time to exert our right to taxation is when the right is refused...a total repeal cannot be thought of till America is prostrate at our feet," said North. Or as General Gage asked at the end of the Stamp Act crisis, were the colonists "Subject to the Legislative Power of Great Britain?" In the colonists' view, Parliament lacked the authority to levy taxes without their consent. Few in America at that point were thinking of independence—the benefits of remaining in the empire were many. And the thought of taking on the greatest military force of the era was daunting. But British actions caused American resistance to continue to grow over time.[29]

From the repeal of the Townshend duties in 1770 to the 1773 Boston Tea Party, a period of relative calm ensued. For men like Samuel Adams, who had been at the forefront of the protests against the Stamp Act and the Townshend duties, this was cause for concern. Adams suspected that North was simply hoping that if enough time passed he could "unhinge the structure of radical protest that had come together in the two great protests."[30] And for most of the colonies that was true, though not in Massachusetts, where Samuel Adams lived.

Samuel Adams, born in 1722, had earned both a bachelor's and a master's degree from Harvard by the time he was twenty-one.[31] He worked as a brewer in his father's business, but his real interest was politics. His opposition to British rule may have originated in the problems his father, Deacon Adams, had in connection with a land bank that he helped start to assist farmers and workers in the 1730s. The bank's intent was to "issue large sums of money backed by the property owned by the subscribers." Creditors and other conservative leaders, however, considered the issuance of paper money by the bank inflationary. They believed it would lead to a rise in the price of goods and services, and that borrowers would attempt to repay their loans with paper money rather than in gold and silver currency. Although the Massachusetts Assembly approved the bank, the creditors managed to convince Parliament to dissolve it, and to make the board of directors, of which Deacon Adams was one, personally responsible for returning funds to those who had invested in the bank. This forced Samuel's father to face financial ruin and, upon his father's death in 1748, Adams found himself having to battle royal officials attempting to seize the estate he had inherited from his father. The ability of Parliament to overturn the decision of the local assembly showed Adams how little control the colony had over its own affairs.[32]

Adams could converse with farmers, workers, and the well educated. He also knew how to use the mechanisms of protest to achieve his ends. In the words of Ferling, Adams was "Tireless, understanding, intelligent, a good speaker and a better writer, persuasive, passionate and utterly fearless, and possessed every quality needed to lead the popular protest in Boston." His cousin, John Adams, was of the opinion that Sam was the indispensable figure in leading what would become the American Revolution. He was also a great organizer. He created the Sons of Liberty, a group of artisans, merchants, and tradesman, which he used to build a base for protest, and as a mechanism to ensure that those protests were orderly and did not lead to violence. Soon, chapters of the Sons appeared in other colonies. During the "quiet period" through 1773, he also organized "committees of correspondence," which linked together rural and urban residents. Soon committees were active in eleven colonies, providing them the means to collect and disseminate information on British activities, and an organized way for them to communicate.

The trouble began once again over tea. In 1773, the British East India Company was in deep financial trouble, and Parliament attempted to bail them out by passing the Tea Act, giving the company a monopoly on tea and reducing the tax that had remained after the repeal of the Townshend duties. This effectively reduced the price to the colonies. The reduction in the tax had two primary purposes: First, to stop the smuggling of contraband tea into the colonies. Second, it would make the legal tea cheaper than the contraband tea. The Tea Act would cause a new round of colonial protests, centered in the hotbed of Boston.

Why did the reduction in a tax and in the price of tea cause widespread protests in the colonies? There were several reasons. First, rumors had been circulating that the tea tax would be repealed completely, which some in Parliament had urged. Second, the colonists opposed allowing the East India Company to have a monopoly on the sale of tea. Third, and perhaps most importantly, a paradigm shift had occurred in the minds of many of the colonists and their leadership regarding their relationship with Great Britain. The period of resistance that had begun in 1763 had weakened the bonds between the British and the Americans. In part, the colonists wanted a return to the status quo prior to the French and Indian War, when they were lightly governed and the British Empire did not levy taxes on them.[33] Even a small tax on tea violated that principle. But the shift in thinking went beyond this, and extended to 1) the ability of the colonists to advance within the British system; 2) America's place in the world; and, 3) newly emerging ideas on self-government, the role and relationship between government and religion, and concerns over the threat to liberty that concentrated power represented. The fear of centralized power would prove one of the most difficult hurdles to clear when the colonists later declared independence and set out to form a new national government.

Nowhere was the paradigm shift clearer than in the way individuals gained social and economic advancement. In Britain, the ability to move up was strictly limited by membership in the aristocracy, which occurred at birth, or not at all. Though not a classless society, in the American colonies upward mobility was attainable—based on ability and hard work, as Franklin's life story showed. Yet, there existed definite limitations on how high one could rise under the British system in the colonies. As a young man, George Washington was denied a commission as an officer in the British Army, which forever colored his view of the British. He expressed his frustration in a 1769 letter to George Mason: "our lordly Masters in Great Britain will be satisfied with nothing less than the deprivation of American freedom."[34] John Adams said in 1776 that the high and mighty should be stripped of their position so that "the meritorious could rise as high as their industry and talent could take them."[35]

Thomas Jefferson went even further in questioning the relationship between the colonies and Great Britain, and America's place in the world, when he wrote *A Summary View of the Rights of British America* in 1774, in the aftermath of the Boston Tea Party. He stated, "Can any one reason be assigned why 160,000 electors in the island of Great Britain should give law to four million in the states of America, every individual of whom is equal to every individual of them in virtue, in understanding, and in bodily strength? Were this to be admitted … we should suddenly be found the slaves, not of one, but of 160,000 tyrants." Jefferson was giving voice to what Thomas Paine would later succinctly summarize in the question "Should an island govern a continent?"[36]

The various political writings in circulation starting in the early 1760s also colored the colonists' views and led to the development of an ideology that centralized power, as represented by the British, was a danger to the liberty of the colonists. Bernard Bailyn, in his book the *Ideological Origins of the American Revolution*, documents the multiplicity of available pamphlets, newspapers, and political tracks and the impact such writings had on the colonists' points of view. Many of these writings reflected the political philosophy of the Enlightenment writers, including, among others, John Locke. Locke believed that sovereignty resides in the people and that men voluntarily give up some of their innate freedom to create a political order that can protect their collective rights, often referred to as the "social contract."[37] For Locke, the basic rights that needed protecting were "life, liberty, and estate," words that Jefferson would soon echo in the Declaration of Independence. A government, to be legitimate, must be based on the consent of the governed. The leaders of the revolution were well aware of Locke's view that governments can be dissolved whenever they exhibit "Arbitrary Will" or "Arbitrary Power," a conclusion the colonists would eventually reach about King George and his government in July of 1776.[38]

Locke also called for a separation of church and state in his "Letter Concerning Toleration." "I esteem it above all things necessary to distinguish exactly the business of civil government from that of religion and to settle the just bounds that lie between one and the other."[39] The concept resonated with Jefferson, who would work to disestablish the Anglican Church in Virginia. The founders imbedded the concept of separation of church and state in the Bill of Rights as part of the Constitution of 1787, but the idea was alien in England, where the Anglican Church was the established state religion.

Bailyn argued that the political writing found in the 1760s in the colonies was heavily influenced by a group of thinkers who opposed the English aristocracy some 100 years earlier, during their own Civil War between 1642 and 1651. Historians sometimes refer to this group of writers as the "radical Whigs" or the "Countrymen." Chief among the radical Whig theorists widely followed in the colonies were two libertarians, John Trenchard and Thomas Gordon. Jointly they published a weekly newspaper, the *Independent Whig*, and a book called *Cato's Letters*. The libertarian ideal is based on individual liberty, limited government, free markets, and peace.[40]

The ideas of the radical Whigs had more impact on the colonial world of the 1760s and 1770s than they did in the England of their day.[41] The hallmark of their views was a fear of concentrated power in the hands of the few, especially if they controlled the military, which would ultimately result in a corrupt and despotic government. Trenchard believed that England could not be a republic because of its inequitable distribution of wealth, but was a limited monarchy in which the King, the Lords, and the Commons were in balance, which protected liberty. According to Trenchard, a republican government must be moored in a society where equality of property existed, and so England could not be considered a republic, since there was too much concentration of wealth.[42]

The ideas of the radical Whigs, as reflected in *Cato's Letters*, placed liberty at the forefront of values. In letter 62, Trenchard wrote, "By liberty, I understand the power which every man has over his own actions, and his right to enjoy the fruit of his labor, art and industry, as far as by it he hurts not the society, or any members of it…Indeed liberty is the divine source of all human happiness."[43] The loss of liberty was a grave concern to the colonists at the time of the Tea Act.

While the essays of *Cato's Letters* expressed a fear of too much concentrated power, it was not just about a fear of governmental power, but also about the relationship of power and wealth. Several essays developed the concept that an inequitable distribution of wealth was fatal to all governments, but especially to republican forms of government.[44]

"Very great riches in private men are always dangerous to states, because they create greater dependence than can be consistent with the security of any sort of government whatsoever...and as great riches in private men is dangerous to all states, so great and sudden poverty produces equal mischiefs in free government." In this letter, Trenchard was expressing a concern that governments can become too dependent on the wealthy, which will dominate the decision-making process. In fact, "liberty can never subsist without equality...In every country, and under every government, particular men may be too rich." Trenchard's view was that, while concern over the concentration of wealth exists within all forms of government, it is most acute in democratic governments. "An equality of estate will give an equality of power; and an equality of power is a commonwealth or democracy. An agrarian law, or something equivalent to it, must make or find a suitable disposition of property; and when that comes to be the case, there is no hindering a popular form of government." Though Trenchard expressed concern over wealth, power, and the stability of democratic government, he did not advocate an absolute leveling of society, but rather focused on excessive accumulations of wealth. In Trenchard's view, too great a concentration of wealth would result in the domination and corruption of a nation's political system by a wealthy elite class, allowing them to have great power over those without such wealth.[45]

The corrupting influence of concentrated power was worrisome to the colonists starting in the 1760s, and would become especially acute at the time of the Tea Act. By that time, many colonial leaders had concluded that a small group of men in England had thrown the English Constitution out of balance, the very balance that Trenchard argued was essential to maintain liberty. Writings of the period contain numerous references to the "overruling arbitrary power which controls the Kings, Lords, and Commons" to a "corrupt and prostituted ministry" and to the "fixed plan of the British administration to bring the whole continent into the most humiliating bondage." The view of the colonists, summarized by Bailyn, was that "the balance of the constitution had been thrown off by a gluttonous ministry usurping the prerogatives of the crown and systematically corrupting the independence of the Commons."[46] Colonists remained loyal to the King, and lay the blame on Lord North, who served in the role of prime minister, and his grab for power. Paraphrasing Sam Adams, Bailyn stated, "power always and everywhere had had a pernicious, corrupting effect on men. It converts a good man in private life to a tyrant in office."[47] Or as Lord Acton would later say, "Power tends to corrupt, and absolute power corrupts absolutely."

To control power and protect the liberty of the people, a balance of power among the elements of society and within the government was critical. Until the Stamp Act crisis, colonists had viewed the British Constitution as providing for such a balance: its separation of powers between the King, the House of Lords, and the House of Commons, representing the one, the few, and the many. The widely read *Cato Letters* made the point that liberty in Britain was preserved in this manner, but that the actions of a few officials bent on despotism could tip the balance. As events unfolded, beginning with the Stamp Act protests, the colonists saw the actions of the British government as a conspiracy to destroy the British Constitution and their liberty. The report of a Boston Town Meeting to its Assembly Representatives in 1770 succinctly summarized their view this way:

> *A series of occurrences, many recent events, … afford great reason to believe that a deep-laid and desperate plan of imperial despotism has been laid…for the extinction of all civil liberty… The august and once revered fortress*

> *of English freedom – the admirable work of ages – the BRITISH CONSTITUTION seems fast tottering into fatal and inevitable ruin.*[48]

In Charleston, New York, and Philadelphia, tea was either not offered for sale, or the ships carrying it were barred from port, due to protests by the colonists. But in Boston, the tea tax issue had reached its boiling point. Imperial Governor Hutchinson, spoiling for a fight, allowed the ships loaded with tea to dock. Radicals met at the Old South Church on December 16, and when it became apparent that tea would be unloaded the next day, crowds headed for the wharf, led by Sam Adams. Historian Ferling writes, "The defiant act of the night of December 16 was not spontaneous. It had been carefully planned for days, perhaps weeks." While a crowd of 2,000 watched, approximately thirty men dressed as Mohawk Indians boarded the ships and tossed crate after crate overboard. Adams counted more than 300 chests of tea floating in the harbor, at a value of perhaps up to $1 million.[49]

The British reacted (some would say overreacted) with a series of measures known as the Coercive or Intolerable Acts.[50] The Intolerable Acts suspended the Massachusetts charter (essentially disbanding their colonial government) and placed the colony under a military governor. The Acts also closed the port of Boston until the colony compensated the British East India Company for the dumped tea; it placed British officials outside of the colonial court system; and it required the colony to quarter British soldiers in their homes. The British government recognized Boston as the heart of the colonial resistance and assumed that if they could break Massachusetts, the rest would follow—a classic divide and conquer strategy, but it backfired. The other colonies saw the

British actions as a threat to themselves, especially the move to disband the Massachusetts charter. Washington, although he did not support the destruction of the tea, viewed the suspension of the charter as "an unexampled testimony of the most despotic system of tyranny that was ever practiced in a free government," and that "the cause of Boston ... now is and ever will be considered as the cause of America."[51]

The Intolerable Acts led to renewed calls for a continental-wide meeting of the colonies, though both radical and conservative factions opposed a congress. The radicals, led by Sam Adams, wanted an immediate boycott of British goods. The conservative factions in New York and Pennsylvania wanted to avoid participating in what they feared would be a defiant gathering. But those in the middle believed that convening a congress held the best hope for achieving reconciliation with Great Britain on terms that were acceptable to the colonists. Support for the idea of a Continental Congress also came from the committees of correspondence, the organizations that Samuel Adams had established during the prior period of resistance in the 1760s. The committees saw the Congress as embodying the "collected wisdom of the continent."[52]

The Continental Congress met in Philadelphia beginning on September 5, 1774. Philadelphia, the largest and most important city in all of the colonies, was also the busiest port, even though it was 100 miles from the ocean. "Visitors wrote in praise of its very exactly straight streets, its many fair houses and public edifices, and of the broad tidal Delaware, alive in every season but winter with a continuous traffic of ships great and small." The city had grown from a population of 10,000 people in the 1720s to over 30,000 by 1776.[53]

A group of accomplished and distinguished men served as delegates in Philadelphia. Of the fifty-four in attendance, half were lawyers and most had a college education.[54] Virginia sent George Washington, along with Patrick Henry and Edmund Pendleton. From Massachusetts came Samuel Adams and his cousin John Adams. Among the others, Pennsylvania sent Joseph Galloway, since Franklin was still living in England. Galloway played an important role—not so much for what he did, but for what he was unable to accomplish. Only Washington and Sam Adams were known outside of their own colony.[55]

In addition to providing a venue for unified action among the colonies, the Congress gave the delegates a chance to get to know one another and to exchange viewpoints and opinions. While a few had met previously, mostly they were strangers. John Adams first met Washington at the City Tavern, where the delegates went to unwind after their workday sessions. Later, Adams joined Washington at a Catholic mass. Delegates attended numerous social events, including one where attendees raised thirty-one toasts, and affluent members of Philadelphia society held additional receptions and dinners at their homes. Adams wrote to his wife, "I shall be killed with kindness in this place. We go to Congress at nine and there we stay, most earnestly until three in the afternoon, then we adjourn and go to dinner with some of the nobles of Philadelphia at four o'clock and feast on ten thousand delicacies, and sit drinking Madeira, claret and burgundy 'til six or seven."[56]

Perhaps it was the specter of war with the British Empire, but the unity of the colonies was of paramount importance to those in attendance. Patrick Henry said, "All America is thrown into one mass. Where are your landmarks—your boundaries of colonies? They are all thrown down. The distinctions between Virginians, Pennsylvanians, New Yorkers and New Englanders are no more. I am not a Virginian, but an American." This was a bit of hyperbole, since distinctions between the colonies would continue to dominate the decision-making process. But to achieve such unity, compromise would be needed. Through vociferous debate, they steered a middle course—between those who favored aggressive action and were unwilling to make any concessions, and those that wanted reconciliation with Great Britain so long as the colonists' rights were preserved.[57]

The first order of business was to determine how they would vote. Larger colonies wanted the vote proportioned based on population. Smaller colonies, fearful that their voices would be drowned out, held out for one vote per colony. They reasoned that unity was paramount, and speaking with one American voice was the key. In order to maintain unity, the larger colonies conceded the issue.[58] Later, this approach to voting would be reflected in the first American Constitution, the Articles of Confederation, with each state retaining its individual identity and sovereignty, and voting would be by state.

Next, the delegates took up the issue of a continent-wide boycott of British goods, as proposed by Virginia. New Englanders, led by Sam Adams, had come to the Congress hoping for such an action, but they knew that the other delegates viewed them as radicals, so they allowed Virginia to introduce the issue. The emerging alliance between Massachusetts and Virginia would prove to be incredibly powerful and convinced many that the Virginians were the true radicals. Joseph Reed, a lawyer from Pennsylvania and an observer of the Congress, said, "the Bostonians are mere Milksops" compared to the Virginians. Some southern colonies were concerned about the ability to continue to export, since they had rice and tobacco ready to be shipped. In the interest of unity, the New Englanders supported a ban on imports only, though the ban would be extended to exports in one years' time, if necessary.[59] The boycott of British goods was to be implemented through the Continental Association, and each city, county, and town was asked to elect a committee to enforce the embargo of British goods.

On September 16, Paul Revere galloped into Philadelphia with the Suffolk Resolves. Dr. Joseph Warren had composed them and Suffolk

County, where Boston was located, had approved them. Sam Adams and Warren had hatched a scheme to have the county approve the resolves in order to get Congress to support resistance to the British. The Suffolk Resolves included, among other items, a condemnation of the Intolerable Acts as unconstitutional and a call for a boycott of British goods. Congress approved them unanimously for two primary reasons: first, they wanted to show the British that they could not isolate Massachusetts, that the colonies were unified in their opposition to the Intolerable Acts. Second, many delegates hoped to "restrain the conduct of resistance…within the limits of the Suffolk Resolves" and maintain defensive measures against the British as a way to keep from escalating the crisis.[60]

Congress also adopted a series of rights and grievances, known as the Declaration of Rights, crafted by a subcommittee of twenty-one members, "to state the rights of the colonies in general…and the means most proper to be pursued for obtaining a restoration of them."[61] Members spent much time debating the various declarations, since they needed to reflect the common principles of the colonies. Even the source of the colonists' rights, whether by the laws of nature or based upon the English Constitution or the colonial charters, caused a fight. Ultimately, all three were included. The Declaration of Rights included numerous principles recognizable today. The first stated that the colonists were entitled to life, liberty, and property, which would later be enshrined in the Declaration of Independence in a slightly different form. The fourth raised the issue of the colonists' lack of representation in Parliament, and that taxation should be decided locally, subject only to the authority of the King. The eighth proclaimed the right of colonists to peaceably assemble.

The Declaration of Rights concluded by stating that the colonists intended to pursue "peaceable" measures, such as the boycott of British goods. The focus of the Declaration was on the colonists' grievances against Parliament. Most of the delegates did not want a complete break with the British, and continued to cling to the notion that they were loyal subjects of the King who had been aggrieved by the Parliament. The Declarations were to be presented to the King as a petition, along with a request that he resolve their grievances.

Though the First Continental Congress accomplished much (in a very short time), of equal significance is what it did not do. Joseph Galloway, a delegate from Pennsylvania and an ally of Benjamin Franklin, proposed a plan of union that resembled Franklin's Albany Plan. A member of the conciliatory wing of Congress, Galloway was looking for a way to reconcile with Great Britain. He proposed the creation of "an American national government that would consist of a unicameral assembly in which each colony was equally represented and a President-General who was to be appointed by the Crown." The plan appeared to have support, at least initially, but on September 28, the plan was tabled by a vote of six to five. During the next three weeks, Congress did not reconsider it and all references to the Galloway Plan were removed from the minutes.[62]

Why did the Galloway Plan fail? In part, this was due to the messenger. Galloway had not been a strong supporter of resistance to the British in the past and he lacked the trust of his fellow delegates. But most importantly, trying to build a national government was too divisive at that point: Massachusetts was under assault and the colonies needed to be united if they were to have any success at all. The colonists were pursuing a path of resistance to a strong central government represented by the British system. The ever-present suspicion of centralized power was a great disincentive to forming any type of national government, and it would continue to bedevil the leaders of the American Revolution over the ensuing decade.[63]

Nevertheless, the First Continental Congress was important for many reasons. Delegates had found a way to weave a path between two extremes: concede to British authority or adopt militant tactics against them. Congress demonstrated "that unified American resistance was possible." Not yet committed to a course of independence, they left the door open to reconciliation, but they placed the onus on the British to make the first set of concessions.[64]

On October 26, Congress adjourned and the delegates returned home. They agreed to meet again the following spring of 1775 if the crisis with Great Britain had not been resolved. Someone later asked Patrick Henry whom he considered the most prominent of the delegates. His answer: "If you speak of eloquence, Mr. Rutledge of South Carolina is by far the greatest orator; but if you speak of solid information and sound judgment, Colonel Washington is unquestionably the greatest man on the floor."[65] The colonists had found their first national leader.

George Washington[66]

Unlike the man of myth we all know, George Washington was a real person with weaknesses and strengths, as his biographers recognize. James Thomas Flexner, who authored a multivolume biography on Washington writes, "I found a fallible human being made of flesh and blood and spirit—not a statue of marble and wood. And inevitably…I found a great and good man."[67] Washington's role in the founding of the new nation was perhaps the single most important, he was truly the "indispensable man." In his life as a military officer and a planter, he was constrained by the British imperial system. Not being born into an aristocratic family made him ineligible for a commission in the regular British Army. As a planter, Washington experienced firsthand the disadvantages of the British mercantile system, which placed many of his peers in deep debt. This led him to see, earlier than most members of the colonial elite, the need for American economic independence.

He was born on February 22, 1732. We know little about his father, Augustine, who died when George was just eleven. His mother, Mary Ball Washington, was Augustine's second wife, and George was her oldest child. Mary was described as "a quite tall and physically strong woman who lived long enough to see him elected president but never extolled or even acknowledged his public triumphs."[68]

After the death of his father, George's half-brother Lawrence took him under his wing. Lawrence owned Mount Vernon, and had married into the influential Fairfax family. Young George got his start as a surveyor at the age of sixteen through connections with the Fairfax's. A surveyor's work required living in the wilderness and traveling in uncharted areas, skills and experiences George would use later. He was described as "a very tall young man, at least six feet two inches, which made him a head higher than the average male of the time. He had an athlete's body, well-proportioned and trim at about 175 pounds...His eyes were gray and blue and widely set. His hair was hazel brown...He was the epitome of the man's man: physically strong, mentally enigmatic, emotionally restrained."[69]

Tragedy struck the young Washington once again when Lawrence contracted tuberculosis. George traveled with his half-brother to Barbados where the tropical air was believed to offer a cure. While there, George contracted small pox, but he recovered and gained lifelong immunity to the disease that would be "the greatest killer of the American Revolution."[70] In 1752, Lawrence died and Washington eventually inherited the estate at Mount Vernon.

The death of Lawrence, who had been the adjutant general of the Virginia militia, gave Washington the opportunity to pursue the military career he had always wanted. Despite his lack of experience, George had the influence of William Fairfax behind him and Virginia's Governor Dinwiddie named Washington to replace Lawrence, at the tender age of twenty-one. For most of the next seven years, he saw war.

Given his lack of experience, it is not surprising that his first few military campaigns were less than stellar. In one incident that occurred in May of 1754, he helplessly watched as a local Iroquois chief named Tanacharison and his fellow warriors engaged in a massacre of French troops. Washington's next military encounter turned into a disaster for him and his men. He knew that a French expedition, known to number over 800 soldiers plus their Indian allies, were searching for him and his troops, who were about seventy-five miles southeast from Fort Duquesne. He built a fort, aptly named Fort Necessity, which was "an exercise in pure inexperience." The battle resulted in a humiliating surrender for Washington, who lost more than a third of his men. Over the course of his life, Washington maintained that the battle was a stalemate, and that the French had been the ones to call a truce, but the evidence does not match his account. On July 4, 1754, George Washington surrendered to the French, and was required to sign terms that indicated, "the British were responsible for the hostile action that launched the French and Indian War."[71]

In Great Britain, Washington was viewed as an "incompetent provincial officer." The view in the colonies was quite different, perhaps due to the efforts of William Fairfax, who framed Washington's efforts at Fort Necessity as a noble attempt to halt French influence in the Ohio Valley. The Virginia House of Burgesses, the colony's legislative body, officially recognized Washington for his bravery, and he was hailed as a hero on the home front. When the Virginia Regiment was disbanded and incorporated into the regular British Army, Washington was not offered a commission at the same level, a slight that reoccurred numerous times over the next several years. He decided to leave the army and resigned his commission in November 1754, returning to civilian life, though only briefly.[72]

It didn't take long for Washington to return to the military and achieve vindication on the battlefield. In the spring of 1755, the British sent General Edward Braddock to lead two regiments of troops with the intent to capture Fort Duquesne, thereby removing French military influence all the way to Canada. Braddock did not understand that the war he was to fight was distinctly different from the European theater of battle. Washington joined Braddock as an aide-de camp, and tried to warn him that the "Canadian French would not fight like the French in Europe, and that the Indians had their own way of fighting,"[73] but the General would not listen. The decisive battle occurred on July 9, 1755, in a clearing at the edge of a forest. While the British troops formed up as they would on a typical European battlefield, the French and Indians forces fired from the cover of the trees, and a massacre ensued. Of the 1,300-man British and American army, 900 were killed or wounded, while the other side had twenty-three killed and sixteen wounded. Braddock was one of the injured, and it was Washington that led the remaining troops in retreat in a display of uncommon military bravery. "Riding back and forth amidst the chaos, two horses were shot out beneath him and four musket balls pierced his coat, but he miraculously escaped without a scratch."[74] It would not be the last time that Washington would escape injury while others around him fell. For rallying the troops in an orderly retreat, he was praised and labeled a hero, despite the catastrophic defeat.

As a reward for his heroic actions in the campaign with Braddock, he was selected to command the newly reformed Virginia Regiment and held the position for the next four years, from 1755 to 1759. The main operations for the French and Indian War had moved north of the Ohio Valley to the Great Lakes and New England and the Virginia Regiment became responsible for protecting the Virginia backcountry, an area that stretched over 350 miles. Given the sheer size of the area and the number of men in the regiment, it proved to be an impossible task. Still, Washington used the opportunity to hone his leadership skills and learned many lessons that would serve him well later as commander in chief during the revolution, including the fine art of guerilla warfare, referred to at the time as "bushfighting." Promotions in the Virginia Regiment were based on performance, not bloodlines or connections, as in the regular British Army, and Washington resisted pressure from politicians to give out military commissions. He also learned to deal with lack of money and poor supply lines, good training for what was to come.

But Washington was still young and he lacked the sound judgment and ability to keep his temper in check, two characteristics he would hone to a fine level in the coming years. In the spring of 1758, the British assigned General John Forbes the job of removing the French from Fort Duquesne. More astute than General Braddock, Forbes accepted Washington's advice in numerous areas, including how to wage war against the New World French and their Indian allies. But in one area Forbes and Washington disagreed—which route was best to get the troops to Fort Duquesne. Washington wanted to use the road that he and Braddock had used "across northern Virginia and southern Maryland, then northwest across Pennsylvania to the forks of the Ohio."[75] Forbes and his engineers instead decided to cut a new road through Pennsylvania, since that was where they were stationed. Washington was vehemently and stubbornly opposed to the plan and predicted the entire campaign would fail. He attempted to go over Forbes' head by taking his complaints to the governor and then to the Virginia legislature. Washington was opposed to the plan because he wanted to retain Virginia's advantage for the future settling of the Ohio Valley.

He didn't want Pennsylvania to get the upper hand, with its new, direct road. He refused to see that the Forbes proposal was strategically superior to Washington's preferred road. At only twenty-six years of age, he didn't yet have the maturity to see the big picture. Biographer Flexner writes, "Not only did his inexperience make him sometimes militarily inept, but he never understood the wider implications of the situations in which he was involved. Although in moments of reflection conscious of his inadequacies, in action he could be rash, brash, impolitic, overly-self-confident."[76] As a young man, Washington was reportedly quite emotional and driven by great passion. He would later develop the self-control that he would become known for later in life.[77] Fortunately, twenty years would pass before his military skills would be needed to lead the colonies in the Revolutionary War, and by then he would be the mature leader that history remembers.

After the fall of Fort Duquesne, Washington resigned from the Virginia Regiment and returned to Mount Vernon to take up life as a planter. He had been greatly disappointed that he could not secure a regular commission in the British Army. In a 1757 letter to the new British commander, Lord Loudoun, Washington expressed this frustration, begging leave to say "had His Excellency General Braddock survived his unfortunate defeat, I should have met with preferment equal to my wishes. I had his promise to that purpose." He followed up the letter with a visit to Philadelphia in that same year to meet with Loudon, but received no further consideration for advancement in the regular British Army. He was outraged at the way in which he and his Virginia Regiment were treated as inferior, venting his frustration in a letter to Governor Dinwiddie: "We can't conceive that being American should deprive us of the benefits of British subjects, nor lessen our claim to preferment." By the time of his resignation from the regiment late in 1758, "he had acquired a powerful storehouse of grievances that would fuel his later rage with England," one of his biographers writes.[78]

In January 1759, he married Martha Dandridge Custis, a widow with two small children. Her former husband had been affluent, and Washington came to control the large Custis estate. In addition, he inherited Mount Vernon in 1761 when Lawrence's widow died. He was now a man of significant means.

Washington soon learned a further lesson on the limitations placed on a colonial planter under the British mercantile system. He was, like most of the planters in Virginia, a tobacco farmer, whose main crop was sold in England by a merchant known as a factor. Robert Cary, of Cary & Company, handled Washington's affairs. The factor would sell the tobacco crop and then purchase consumer goods from England for the planters. Washington ordered various goods, clothing, and furniture for Mount Vernon. The value of the various goods purchased over a five-year period may have exceeded $3 million.[79]

It was a system designed to put the planter into debt, and Washington soon learned he too was in debt to Cary, a common problem faced by the plantation owners in Virginia. It opened his eyes to the inequity of the British mercantile system, which placed all of the risk on the planters for bad weather, cargo lost at sea due to ship accidents, or declining market prices for tobacco. The system also provided substantial benefit to the mercantile establishments run by men like Cary. It soured his opinion of the relationship between the colonies and England. After he learned of the debt he had amassed, Washington set out to become independent from the factor system, and in 1765 he began to plant wheat and corn instead of tobacco. He also ceased ordering British goods, and began a process of paying down his debts. He had made his own personal declaration of independence from Great Britain.[80]

Tobacco is a labor-intensive crop, and Washington, like most Virginia planters, owned many slaves. It appears that the young

Washington had few qualms about slavery, viewing them less as people and more as a form of property. Some biographers have stated that Washington was an uncaring owner who provided scant clothing, minimal medical care, and flogged his slaves that attempted escape. Others described him as being relatively humane. He was unwilling to split up families, would not sell a slave without his permission if it meant breaking up a family, and provided medical care to his slaves. It seems likely that his views on slavery were typical of those of the planter class of this period.[81]

Gradually, he developed a more enlightened view of slavery. At the time of the revolution, he clearly saw slavery as degrading, and equated the policies implemented by England as an attempt to enslave the colonists. He wrote that the British "will make us as tame and abject slaves as the blacks we rule over with such arbitrary sway."[82] In 1786, he stated, "I never mean to possess another slave by purchase; it being among my first wishes to see some plan adopted by the Legislature, by which slavery in this Country may be abolished by slow, sure, and imperceptible degrees."[83] His will specified that after his death all the slaves he owned were to be freed.

During his time as a Virginia squire, Washington served as a member of the Virginia House of Burgesses, the colony's locally elected legislative body. His attendance was apparently spotty, and he remained quiet during most of the sessions he did attend. But by 1769, during the protests of the Townshend duties, Washington began to take a leadership role in Virginia's resistance to British rule. He advocated a total boycott of British goods, and he supported the actions taken as part of the Boston Tea Party [84] Due to his emerging leadership on the issue of resistance to the various taxation measures implemented by Parliament, he was selected to be a Virginia delegate to the First Continental Congress.

Endnotes

1 Benson Bobrick, *Angel in the Whirlwind* (New York, 1997), p.19

2 Bobrick, p. 18-19

3 For a discussion of this situation, see Walter Isaacson, *Benjamin Franklin An American Life*, (New York, 2003), p. 158; Brands,, p. 229; and Bobrick, p. 19-20

4 Isaacson, p. 158

5 John Ferling, *A Leap in the Dark: The Struggle to Create the American Republic*, (New York, 2003), p.8

6 Isaacson, p. 122

7 This section is largely drawn from the outstanding biographies of Franklin written by Isaacson and Brand as shown in footnote 3.

8 Isaacson, p. 7

9 Isaacson, p. 33

10 Isaacson, p. 37

11 Gordon Wood, *Revolutionary Characters: What Made the Founders Different*, (New York, 2007), p. 76; Isaacson, p. 113

12 Isaacson, p. 126-127

13 Isaacson, p. 209

14 Isaacson, p. 162-165; Ferling, p. 50; Isaacson, 151-153

15 Ferling, p. 26

16 Isaacson, p. 149 and p. 103

17 Quoted in Isaacson, p. 94

18 Ferling, p. 15

19 Ferling, p. 13-14

20 See Ferling, p. 18; Brands, p. 238; and Isaacson, p. 160

21 Quoted in Isaacson, p. 162

22 Jack Rakove (2012), "Rebel without a Cause: A Narrow Approach to the American Revolution," *New Republic*, retrieved 2/24/2013 from http://www.newrepublic.com/book/review/1775-american-revolution-kevin-phillis makes this point on core cause of the American Revolution

23 Ferling, p. 29-31; Bobrick,, p. 66-68 and Jack Rakove, *Revolutionaries: A New History of the Invention of America*, (New York, 2010), p. 25. See also Joseph J. Ellis, *Brotherhood of the Revolution: How America's Founders Forged a New Nation*, (New York, 2004), Lecture 2

24 For information on representation, See Gordon S. Wood, *The Idea of America: Reflections on the Birth of the United States*, (New York, 2011), p.181-183; On limitations of office in colonial America, see also Garry Wills, *James Madison*, (New York, 2002), p. 31

25 The quote is from Bobrick, p. 71; also see Ferling, p. 27

26 Bobrick, p. 73; Massachusetts adopted a resolution in 1764 that denied Parliament's right to tax the colonies. See Bobrick, p. 71; Ferling, p. 34 and p. 42

27 Quoted in Bobrick, p. 77; Ferling, p. 34-42; Bobrick, p. 74-75

28 Bobrick, p. 81-86; Ferling, p. 53-76

29 Ferling, p. 54; Bobrick, p.87

30 Ferling, p. 88

31 The outline presented for Samuel Adams over the next several paragraphs is from Ferling, p. 60-66

32 Ferling, p. 60-61

33 Rakove, *Revolutionaries*, p. 59

34 Quoted from the Papers of George Washington. Retrieved July 15, 2012 from http://gwpapers.virginia.edu/documents/revolution/letters/mason.html

35 Ferling, p. 101

36 Both quotes are from Fawn M. Brody, *Thomas Jefferson, an Intimate Portrait* (New York, 1974), p. 115

37 Stanley M. Honer and Thomas C. Hunt, *Invitation to Philosophy*, (Belmont CA, 1973), p. 170

38 Rakove, *Revolutionaries*, p. 173

39 Quoted from Jon Meacham, *American Gospel: God, the Founding Fathers, and the Making of a Nation*, (New York, 2006), p.62

40 This is how the Cato Institute views the principles of libertarianism on their website. Retrieved August 24, 2012 from http://www.cato.org

41 Gordon S. Wood, *The Creation of the American Republic 1776-1787*, (Williamsburg, 1998), p. 16

42 Eric Nelson, *The Greek Tradition in Republican Thought*, (Cambridge, 2006), p. 141-142

43 John Tranchard, *Cato's Letters*, No. 62, retrieved from http://press-pubs.uchicago.edu/founders/documents/v1ch16s4.html, August 24, 2012

44 Nelson, p. 141; and Jackson Turner Main, *The Anti-Federalists: Critics of the Constitution 1781-1788,* (Williamsburg, 1961), p. 10-11

45 The quotes are from Cato's Letter No. 91, No. 35; and 85

46 The quotes shown in this paragraph and the ideas expressed are from Bernard Bailyn, *The Ideological Origins of the American Revolution*, (Cambridge, 1992), p. 124-131

47 Bailyn, p. 60

48 Bailyn, p. 94

49 See Ferling, p. 101-106; and Bobrick, p.89-90

50 Brody says "…a foolish British government chose to regard the Tea Party not as mere mob

violence but as an act of insurrection."p. 115

51 James Thomas Flexner, *Washington – The Indispensable Man,* (New York, 1984), p.56; Ferling, p, 56 and 107

52 Jack Rakove, *The Beginnings of National Politics: An Interpretive History of the Continental Congress,* (New York, 1979), p. 30; Ferling, p. 108-111

53 David McCullough, *John Adams,* (New York, 2001), p. 78-79

54 McCullough, p. 83

55 Ferling, p. 112

56 McCullough, p. 81-85; Rakove, *Beginnings,* p. 43

57 Ferling, p. 113; Bobrick, p. 94

58 Ferling, p. 119; Rakove, *Revolutionaries,* p. 54

59 Ferling, p. 114-116

60 Rakove, *Beginnings,* p. 45-47

61 Rakove, *Beginnings,* p. 52-53

62 Rakove, *Beginnings,* p. 53-55; Ferling, p. 118

63 Ferling, p. 119 -120

64 Rakove makes both the point about the ability of the colonists to unite as well as placing the onus on the British in *Beginnings* on p. 61.

65 Quoted in Bobrick, p. 106

66 Flexner, p. 56.

67 Flexner, p. xiv

68 Ellis, p. 8

69 Ellis, p. 11-12

70 Flexner, p. 6

71 See Ellis p. 14-18; Ferling, p. 6-7; and Flexner, p. 15-16

72 Ellis, p. 18; Flexner, p. 16

73 Flexner, p. 21

74 Ellis, p. 22 for both the statistics on the dead and wounded and the quote on Washington's leadership

75 Ellis, p. 34

76 Flexner, p. 35

77 Ellis fleshes this view out more fully on p. 37

78 The discussion of Washington's disillusionment with his failure to obtain a commission in the British Army, including the quotes, are from Ron Chernow, *Washington: A Life,* (New York, 2010), p. 72-73 and p.92

79 Ellis, p. 49

80 Ellis, p. 49-53, Flexner, p. 43-48, and Ellis, *Brotherhood*, Lecture 4

81 James MacGregor Burns and Susan Dunn, *George Washington: The First President*, (Macmillan Audio, 2004), makes the case that Washington was a uncaring slave owner on disk 1, track 5; for a countervailing view see Flexner, p.53 and Chernow, *Washington*, p. 110-112

82 Chernow, p. 111

83 Quoted from Historynet, *George Washington: His Troubles with Slavery*, retrieved July 17, 2012 from www.historynet.com/george-washington-his-troubles-with-slavery.html

84 Ellis, p. 61

Chapter 3

The Beginning of War and the Move Towards Independence / 1775 to 1776

"We have it in our power to begin the world over again... The birthday of a New World is at hand."
– Thomas Paine, Common Sense –

When the First Continental Congress adjourned in October of 1774, many still hoped they could reconcile with Great Britain and avoid war. That hope would soon be dashed, as the conflict between the two sides entered a new and violent phase with the actions that would occur in early 1775 in Lexington and Concord. In the aftermath of those events, disagreements between the colonies kept them from declaring independence as soon as the fighting broke out. And once they did declare independence, they did so as thirteen separate states, not one American nation.

The War Begins

Just as the American colonists needed to find common ground among themselves, likewise the British were not unanimous about the actions they should take against their provinces. Some wanted to use force while others were willing to entertain the idea of reconciliation, including the sending of peace commissioners. They were also receiving reports of widespread resistance to British rule from their top General, Thomas Gage, who was also serving as the royal governor of Massachusetts.[1]

One British member of Parliament who wanted to find a path to reconcile the two sides was Edmund Burke. Burke, who was Irish, was a statesman, author, practical politician, and a known "friend of America," who would later be recognized as one of the intellectual architects of conservatism. Burke had been a member of Parliament since 1765, and had previously supported the colonists in their grievances over the tea duty. In March 1775, he made a stirring speech that warned the North government against using coercion against the colonists. Historian Jack Rakove has argued that Burke: "grasped the key fact that they (the Americans) were beginning to form a collective people – that is a nation." The colonists' resistance was rooted in their Protestant religion, a religion born in protest to a Catholic hierarchy in the old world. "The people are Protestants…a persuasion not only favourable to liberty, but built upon it," he argued. As such, Burke saw that the Americans would not back down either to the threat of force or its actual use. Burke also pointed out that distant provinces could not be expected to follow the rules as closely as those at home would.[2]

Unfortunately, those that mattered most ignored Burke's warnings, including the majority of the North government, the key members of Parliament, and the King, who all agreed that only force could bring the colonies back under British control.

They departed from Boston at 10 p.m. on the night of April 18, 1775, carried across the Charles River by the British navy, and then to Lechmere Point for their mission to Lexington and Concord. The road out would prove easier than the return trip for General Gage's troops. They had been sent to apprehend Samuel Adams and John Hancock, two of the key colonial leaders, who were in Lexington. They were then to seize the armaments stored in Concord in order to disarm the colonists.[3] The British government had made the decision to confront the Massachusetts colonists with a show of force. Despite the best efforts at British secrecy, the colonial spy network, of which Joseph Warren and Paul Revere were members, had become aware of the British troop movements. Revere set off on his horse, Brown Beauty, to warn Adams and Hancock of the approaching British troops. The two were able to escape from Lexington in the night, first to Woburn and then on to Worcester a few days later. Revere, on his famous midnight ride, alerted the town's people of Concord of the approaching danger they would soon confront.[4]

Meanwhile, an elite contingent of 800 British troops, reaching Lexington in the early morning hours, was confronted by a small group of minutemen. The minutemen had been formed to serve as the advance guard, ready at a "moments-notice." The British Major, Pitcairn, ordered the colonial troops to "Lay down your arms, you damned rebels, and disperse." It is unclear which side started the confrontation, but within minutes, eight colonists were dead and nine others wounded. Being greatly outnumbered, the minutemen scattered. Further fighting would erupt in Concord later in the morning, leading to Emerson's famous poem that included the line about the "shot heard 'round the world." In Concord, the regular British troops were the ones who broke and ran. The rebel troops and townspeople harried them all the way back to Boston. They returned to their barracks having lost sixty-five men, with an additional 207 wounded.[5] Any notion the British had that the colonists would cut and run at the first sign of regular troops had been dispelled.

With the outbreak of war, it would seem reasonable that the colonial political leaders would quickly move to declare independence during the Second Continental Congress that met in May 1775. But this was not the case, in large part due to different perspectives that the leadership from the various colonies brought forth, especially the views of the merchant class that inhabited the middle colonies of New York, New Jersey, and Pennsylvania. They wanted Congress to explore every opportunity to reconcile with Great Britain, so long as the rights of the colonists could be protected.

Historians have long argued over whether colonial America was an aristocratic society that emulated Europe, with a merchant class that was in conflict with populist agrarian interests; or whether it was a society similar in its viewpoints, a land of equality where liberty and democracy flourished, as Alexis de Tocqueville would later find in the post-revolutionary period.[6] In reality, the colonies were a bit of both, with a different mix of interests depending on the region, and these various interests affected the movement toward independence. The Second Continental Congress reflected these differences, as two major factions emerged. The moderate faction, drawn largely from the middle colonies, represented the merchant class of society. The middle colonies had always been the most diverse, representing a mix of religions, ethnic groups and languages. Entrepreneurship, finance, and nascent capitalism first began there. Also, class distinctions began emerging between the most successful merchants and the tenant farmers and artisans of the middle colonies.

The merchants saw little benefit from a total break with England, and also feared that independence would unleash democratic forces that they could not control. In their view, independence would not only be bad for their business interests, but a revolution could also threaten their elite position in society. They doubted that the British government would continue on its current course, and hoped that England "would abandon a mad policy that could be enforced only at great peril and enormous expense, and which was likely to destroy" what to them was a mutually beneficial relationship. This moderate group also feared the destruction that war would bring, and preferred a course of reconciliation with the mother country, if the rights of the colonists could also be protected.[7] When fighting broke out in Lexington and Concord, they supported the war effort, but continued to push for negotiations with the British to resolve the disputes without the need to take what they viewed as the rash step toward independence.

The moderate faction was led by John Dickinson, who, during the next twenty years, would hold political positions as a representative of both Pennsylvania and Delaware. Dickinson had become famous during the crisis over the Townshend duties in the late 1760s, when he wrote his *Letters from a Farmer in Pennsylvania*. In *Letters*, Dickinson argued that there was no real distinction between internal and external taxes, that it was "the purpose of the tax, not its form that mattered." If the duty was designed to raise revenue, as opposed to controlling trade, then he considered it illegal.[8] Dickinson grew up on an estate in Maryland, where his father owned slaves and raised tobacco. Sent to England to study law, he eventually returned and moved to Pennsylvania when he inherited his father's large land holdings. His immersion in the pacifist philosophy of Quaker society was a major influence on him and caused him to look first to peaceful alternatives for settling the conflict with Great Britain.[9]

The moderates had a justifiable fear of confronting the massive power of the British Empire. Dickinson would say that the colonies would need to be "so strong & united that … we should have nothing to fear from any other Power" before pursuing independence.[10] He also feared that America could never become a nation, that once the unifying influence of resistance to British rule was removed that the colonists would fall into conflict with each other.[11] Time would prove him right in some ways, since the United States would argue and disagree in the post-independence period over the form and structure of a centralized government, and would almost split into several smaller confederacies during the 1780s.

Dickinson and his group of moderates faced off against the leadership of the radical faction, drawn largely from members of the New England and the southern colonies, many of whom secretly favored independence in 1775. It seems obvious why the New Englanders felt this way, since it was in Massachusetts where the Intolerable Acts were implemented and where the first shots in the war were fired. The Southerners, specifically the Virginians, are somewhat harder to understand, but their pursuit of independence was largely tied to the twin issues of slavery in their midst and the dependence they felt on the British mercantile system.

As was discussed in Chapter 1, the society of the Virginian planters was largely aristocratic. By the 1750s, not more than 100 families owned the land and wealth of the colony. Life in Virginia had come to resemble that of the English gentry, with the role of the English country gentleman played by the Virginia planter.[12] So it is odd that the Virginian's would stand at the forefront of the revolutionary movement. As historian Daniel Boorstin writes: "the ways of history are obscure and even self-contradictory... May not the value they placed on their individual liberties have been increased by the sharp contrast with the slavery they saw about them? May not their aristocratic habit of mind ... and their belief that they could make judgments on behalf of their community have helped make them leaders of an American Revolution?"[13] Slavery did play a role in pushing the Virginians to join the radical faction, since they were quick to see that the actions of the British were an affront to their rights.[14]

The other major issue that seemed to push the Virginians to play a leadership role in opposing British rule was their economic dependence on the factor system. The planter class in Virginia was often in debt to their British agents (or factors) because they purchased English-made consumer goods with the money they earned from growing tobacco. Washington declared his own economic independence from England when he quit growing tobacco and set out to pay down his debt, but most of the Virginia elite were not in a position to do this.

By the time the Second Continental Congress met, leadership of the New England radical faction had fallen to John Adams. Adams knew the time was not right for independence, since his own colony had not given up on reconciliation. In a letter to the British people from the Massachusetts Provincial Congress in April 1775, the Congress maintained that they were "loyal and dutiful Subjects" of the King, ready to "defend his person, Family, Crown and Dignity" with their "Lives and Fortunes."[15] They blamed the outbreak of war on the ministerial government of Lord North for firing the first shots at Lexington and Concord. Adams understood that in 1775 the "idea of independence was as unpopular…as the Stamp Act itself" and that he and the other radicals would need to bide their time.[16]

John Adams

The Adams family came to the colonies to escape religious persecution as part of the Puritan migration from England in 1638. Henry Adams, John's great-great grandfather, settled in Braintree, Massachusetts. They were farmers, but due to the poor soil and short growing season, the Adamses would also pursue other endeavors as a way to prosper in the New World. His father John, in addition to his work as a farmer, was also a shoemaker and a deacon in the local church.

John Adams was born on October 30, 1735, the oldest son of Deacon Adams and his wife Susanna. John greatly admired his father and would later write in his autobiography: "In wisdom, piety, benevolence and charity in proportion to his education and sphere of life, I have never known his superior."[17] High praise indeed, since this was written after he had come to know Washington, Jefferson, and the other members of the founding generation.

While at Harvard, Adams fell in love with books and "was seldom ever to be without one for the rest of his days."[18] As with Franklin, he was originally slated to become a minister, but ultimately decided that he felt called to the law. To generate the money needed to join the office of a practicing lawyer, he moved to Worcester in the summer of 1755, and took a job as a schoolmaster in a one-room schoolhouse. He enjoyed the children, but found he was not particularly suited to life in the classroom, and dreamed of "more glorious pursuits."[19] Little did he know at the time that he would go on to become a revolutionary, a diplomat and the second president of the United States.

By the fall of 1758, Adams completed his studies and began his career as a lawyer. Upon the death of his father in 1761, he inherited most of the family estate, including the farm he was raised on. He combined his legal career with work on the farm, "building stone walls, digging up stumps, carting manure, plowing with six yoke of oxen, planting corn and potatoes."[20] John married Abigail in October of 1764, following a five-year courtship. David McCullough writes that his marriage to Abigail "was the most important decision of John Adam's life, as would become apparent in time. She was in all respects his equal and the part she was to play would be greater than he could possibly have imagined."[21] They had two children together, including John Quincy, who went on to become the sixth president of the United States.

Events would insert Adams into the middle of the colonial crisis starting with the Stamp Act in 1765. As a lawyer, Adams saw the crisis with the British from a legal and constitutional perspective. People have called him one of the most notable political thinkers and intellectuals of his time, but he was also a man of action, and his writing tended to be more in the form of letters and pamphlets than long discourses.[22] His political philosophy and writings mirror so much about the American frame of mind that it is worth delving into them in some detail.

Adams first major work on politics was "A Dissertation on the Canon and Feudal Law," published in the *Boston Gazette* in 1765. The piece established the principal that the British Parliament did not grant the colonists their rights, foremost liberty, but rather these were "original rights…inherent and essential, agreed on as maxims established as preliminaries even before a parliament existed." In "A Dissertation," Adams incorporated the rather paranoid style of the pamphlets of the era, a view that the actions of the British were not just a violation of the English Constitution, but a "deliberate assault launched surreptitiously by plotters against liberty both in England and America," according to historian Bernard Bailyn. In his rather paranoid views, Adams reflected "the prevalence of conspiratorial fears among the Revolutionaries." It was a view rooted in their fear of governmental power.[23]

In reaction to the Stamp Act, Adams wrote in his *Instruction of the Town of Braintree to their Representatives*, "we should (not) be subject to any tax imposed by the British Parliament, because we are not represented in that assembly in any sense."[24] Perhaps his most notable political work to appear prior to the Declaration of Independence was *Thoughts on Government*, written in 1776. Adams had spent an evening with George Wythe of Virginia discussing the need for the colonies to declare independence. Wythe had indicated that the great difficulty in declaring independence was the need to agree on a form of government for the colonies. Adams had volunteered that each colony "should form a government for itself, as a free and independent State."[25] Wythe then requested that Adams write down his ideas, which he did in *Thoughts on Government*, designed to guide each of the colonies in establishing "independent States" and not as a formula for developing an overarching national government. Interestingly, the form of government that Adams developed was similar to the Virginia Plan that would be unveiled in 1787 at the Constitutional Convention by James Madison, and that would form the basis of the Federal Constitution. *Thoughts on Government* would also be used by numerous states, including Massachusetts and Virginia, in establishing new constitutions beginning in 1776.

Adams began with a consideration of what the ends of government should be and stated: "Upon this point all speculative politicians will agree that the happiness of society is the end of government." He also argued what has become a core American belief "that there is no good government but what is republican" and that such a government must have as its principle foundation virtue. Virtue had both a private and a public connotation at the time. Private virtue meant that individuals must act in a moral way. But what precisely did Adams and others of his time mean by "public virtue"?

Adams and the other revolutionary leaders were facing a decision about what type of government should replace the British monarchy. The government's legitimacy would be derived from the consent of the governed—what we would describe as a democracy today, but a word they shied away from. Many of the leaders of the period equated democracy with mob rule, and preferred to refer to the new governments to be formed as republics where the people would elect representatives who would govern. The Tory critics, those who did not want to break with England, argued at the time that the loss of the monarchy would lead to anarchy, since the revolution was "clearly and literally against authority" and that "no society could hold together without the obedience of its members to legally constituted authority."[26] The more conservative minded also had concerns that independence would lead to a social revolution. As Maier writes, there were those who "saw a republican future in the threat of rebellion by poor whites, Loyalists... restive slaves who read their own meaning into the cause of liberty; mobs that freed debtors from jail, or the ordinary people who claimed seats in Virginia's provincial convention."[27]

Adams, himself a conservative, argued that a republican form of government would not lead to a loss of authority. Since no republican governments existed in the world at that time, Adams and other writers of the period referenced the ancient city-states of Athens and Rome as examples. Adams also dealt with the reality that republics in the past had been short lived and unstable. Finally, Adams and other supporters of a government grounded in popular sovereignty needed to demonstrate that a republican form of government was not antiauthority, but rather that the "revolution was designed to change the flow of authority but it was in no way intended to do away with the principal of authority," according to Gordon Wood.[28]

Adams and the other founders believed that governments, including the monarchy of Great Britain, derived their authority from the use of fear and coercion. A government based on the consent of the governed could not use such devices as a foundation. Wood writes: "In a republic there was no place for fear; there could be no sustained coercion from above. The state, like no other, rested on the consent of the governed freely given and not compelled."[29] If not fear, what would motivate compliance with the law? For Adams and others of the period, the answer would be found in public virtue. Adams, in a letter to Mercy Warren, described it this way: "Public virtue cannot exist in a Nation without private (virtue), and public virtue is the only foundation of Republics. There must be a positive passion for the public good, public interest...established in the minds of the people, or there can be no Republican government, nor any real liberty: and the public passion must be superior to all private passions." Public virtue, the need to voluntarily sacrifice individual interests for those of the greater good, was seen as the core of republican government and one of the essential foundations for freedom. Both individual liberty and the public good were of great importance to the founders, and these needed to be balanced with each other. The role of public and private virtue and the need to promote the public good were ideals to strive for, but they had not been achieved at the time of the revolution. Wood writes that it was "a vision so divorced from the realities of American society, so contrary to the previous century of American experience, that it alone was enough to make the Revolution one of the great utopian movements of American history. By 1776 the Revolution came to represent a final attempt...in which the common good would be the only objective of government."[30]

Neither Adams nor the other founders were naïve, and they knew that human nature would lead individuals to pursue their own self-interest and that man had the capacity for both good and evil. The founding generation shared a fear of concentrated power and the threat it posed to liberty, which were viewed as two ends of the spectrum. "Power is by its nature aggressive, encroaching, unstable; liberty is passive, exposed, subvertible," historians Stanley Elkins and Eric McKitrick write. [31] The founders also knew that society was made up of differing interests that needed to be balanced with one another. Adams wrote in his *Defence of the American Constitution* that was published in 1787 that "...power is always abused when unlimited and unbalanced." The structure of republican government would become increasingly important as a means to balance and restrain individual liberty in pursuit of the public good. Adams, in *Thoughts on Government*, laid out a concept for a multibranch set of governing institutions to do exactly that. James Madison would build on these ideas in helping to write the Constitution, a document which marries these two core American principles under an overarching national government designed to protect individual liberty and the rights of the minority through a government designed to achieve the public good.

For Adams, as with most of his generation, the first branch of government was the representative assembly. Adams argued: "It should be in miniature an exact portrait of the people at large. It should think, feel, reason and act like them. That it may be the interest of this assembly to do strict justice at all times, it should be an equal representation, or, in other words, equal interests among the people should have equal interests in it." As Jack Rakove has noted, this principal encapsulated the idea of one person, one vote.[32] Adams' concept that the legislature should be a mirror image of the public would come under withering criticism, as Chapter 4 discusses, from Madison, who wanted representatives to also act with independent judgment.

Adams too had concerns over the need to control the popular branch of government and, therefore, did not believe that a unicameral legislature was sufficient. He laid out six reasons why this was the case. They included the problem of "hasty results and absurd judgments"; the inability of the body to carry out and "exercise the executive power"; and its inability to carry out the judicial functions. Adams proposed that a separate branch be drawn from the assembly itself and be made up of a smaller number of representatives, in essence a body similar to the Senate. This body "would have a free and independent exercise of its judgment and ...a negative voice in the legislature." The executive would then be chosen by the two legislative branches, be a member of the legislature, and in order to maintain independence would have veto power over the legislature. The governor would serve a one year term and be the commander in chief of the army. Finally, the judicial branch "ought to be distinct from both the legislative and executive branch… so that it may be a check upon both." The judicial branch should be made up of "men of learning and experience in the laws, of exemplary morals, great patience, calmness, coolness, and attention." They should be appointed for life terms so they are not dependent on any man or body of men. Many states would use Adams' approach to governmental structure in preparing their constitutions, but the first American government, under the Articles of Confederation, did not use them.

John Adams played an important role in the Boston Massacre, agreeing to serve as the attorney representing the British soldiers because he believed "that no man in a free country should be denied the right of counsel and a fair trial, and convinced, in principle, that the case was of utmost importance." He also believed that it was better that many guilty people go free than that one innocent person should be punished. "The reason is, because it's of more importance to the community that innocence should be protected, than it is, that guilt should be punished." Although he was a revolutionary, Adams was a conservative revolutionary, one who had a fear of mob rule. While he pursued American independence, he did not want to see a breakdown in the social order, and believed that the rule of law must be maintained. Through Adams' defense, six of the eight soldiers were acquitted of all charges. Adams knew that in the short term his role would be unpopular, but his willingness to defend the British soldiers contributed over time to his reputation as a man of integrity.[33]

The Second Continental Congress

The Congress opened on May 10, 1775 in Philadelphia's State House, later renamed Independence Hall. According to McCullough, "it comprised a handsome main edifice, two stories tall with a bell tower and arcaded wings joining smaller offices at either end, all of it done in red brick." It would be the site of many of the most memorable events in the founding of the country, including the approval of the Declaration of Independence and the framing of the Constitution. The Congress met in the Assembly Room on the first floor.[34]

Most of the delegates knew each other this time, since of the sixty-five in attendance fifty had attended the first Congress.[35] During the early part of 1775 and into 1776, the Congress acted as a true national government, taking over the war effort, borrowing money, providing direction to the colonies in the formation of their governments, and in issuing a currency. But instead of the constraints provided by a written constitution, the delegates were limited by the written instructions they had received from their individual colonies, and by the need to achieve virtual unanimity in their actions, which gave Dickinson and the moderates a substantial amount of leverage early on. The need for unity also placed a strain on the members and their relationship to each other. Silas Deane of Connecticut wrote to his wife in June of 1775: "My time is all taken up and leaves me no spare time, and tires me effectually," adding that "no motion or resolution can be started or proposed but what must be subject to much canvassing before it will pass with the unanimous approbation of Thirteen Colonies whose situation and circumstances are various. And unanimity is the basis on which we mean to rise…"[36]

The first issue of substance was debated on May 16 over independence. John Rutledge insisted, "that previously some points must be settled, such as do We aim at independency? Or do we only ask for a Restoration of Rights & putting us on our old footing?"[37] Adams knew the time was not yet right to raise the issue of independence, and indicated that the goal should be independence from Parliament but a continued "dependence on the Crown." Dickinson proposed a twin track, recommending that the Congress move forward with plans for carrying forward the war effort, combined with fresh efforts at reconciliation with Great Britain. He recommended that the colonies yield the regulation of trade to Parliament, a position that had previously been rejected in 1774. This caused quite a stir, with Patrick Henry saying: "the Bill of Rights must never be receded from." In essence, Henry and the radicals were taking a stand against Parliament's right to regulate colonial trade.[38] Still, Dickinson succeeded in having a series of resolutions approved by Congress that would authorize further attempts at reconciliation and the preparation of a new petition to the King.

With the issue of independence settled for now, the need to establish a national army came next. Washington had arrived as a delegate to the Second Continental Congress in military uniform, perhaps to remind his colleagues of his availability to head the army. He was in great demand and was asked to serve on nine committees. Congress established the size of the army at 15,000 men and took steps to supply and fund it. Congress authorized ten companies of soldiers from Pennsylvania, Maryland, and Virginia to march north to reinforce the New Englanders, but a leader was needed to meld the troops together. John Adams nominated Washington for this role over his fellow New Englander, John Hancock. Adams considered Washington the most impressive man in Congress, but he also wanted to solidify the bonds that held the delegates from Massachusetts and Virginia together. Both he and Sam Adams considered "Washington's appointment as the political linchpin needed to bind the colonies together."[39] Adams would later write to Abigail that Washington was one of the most important characters in the world and that "the liberties of America depend upon him in a great degree." Washington, in his characteristic way, would downplay his own ability to lead the army: "I beg it may be remember[e]d by every Gent[leman] in the room that I this day declare, with the utmost sincerity, I do not think myself equal to the command I [am] honoured with." It was with good reason that he felt that way, as he faced the might of the British armed forces. "The misgivings he expressed in the wake of his appointment, then, were not affectations of false humility, but rather rigorously realistic assessments during an intense moment of self-evaluation in which he was mercilessly honest about his prospects for success," according to historian Ellis. Washington too saw that one of his great tasks was to nationalize the army, which until his appointment, was made up of separate colonial militias. His second set of orders to the troops stated that you "are now the troops of the United Provinces of North America: and it is hoped that all Distinctions of Colonies will be laid aside."[40]

Dickinson next put together a petition to the King, known as the Olive Branch Petition, which Congress had approved on July 8, 1775. The petition led to substantial tensions between Dickinson and Adams. In floor debate, Dickinson had warned the radicals that they would have blood on their heads if they blocked efforts to achieve peace. Adams' response was so vehement that Dickinson would later tell him: "If you don't concur with us in our pacific system, I, and a number of us, will break off from you in New England and will carry on the opposition by ourselves and in our own way." Adams backed down, knowing that maintaining unity required approval of the petition. But his frustration bubbled over in a letter to James Warren, when he wrote that he saw Dickinson as "a certain great Fortune and piddling Genius whose Fame had been trumpeted so loudly, [it] has given a silly Cast to our whole Doings." The letter became public when it was intercepted by the British, and General Gage was only too happy to publish it and add to the rift between two of the key resistance leaders. Adams came upon Dickinson in September on the way to Congress and recorded the following: "He passed without moving his hat or head or hand.

I bowed and pulled off my hat. He passed haughtily by…But I was determined to make my bow, that I might know his temper. We are not to be on speaking terms, nor bowing terms, for the time to come."[41]

To be fair, Dickinson was committed not only to attempts at reconciliation; he also supported a strong prosecution of the war effort. It was he and the recently arrived Thomas Jefferson, the newest delegate from Virginia, who were asked to prepare the *Declaration of the Causes and the Necessity for Taking Arms.* Jefferson had already achieved some degree of fame and recognition as a writer from his *Summary View of the Rights of British America*, and was asked to prepare the first draft. Dickinson objected to parts of it, and began to rework it. Jefferson, who had difficulty with criticism of his written work, would remark late in his life: "I prepared a Draught of the Declaration committed to us. It was too strong for Mr. Dickinson. He still retained the hope of reconciliation with the mother country, and was unwilling it should be lessened by offensive statements."[42] Historians would later debunk Jefferson's late in life recollections, and conclude that in fact Dickinson's redrafting had made the declaration stronger. Dickinson had, in his version added: "Our cause is just. Our union is perfect. Our internal resources are great, and, if necessary, foreign assistance is attainable." The Causes & Necessities would balance the need for reconciliation by indicating "that we mean not to dissolve that union which has so long…subsisted between us" with a strong statement of colonial intent to continue the struggle.[43] Congress approved the revised Causes & Necessities on July 8, 1775.

Congress then recessed for five weeks, returning in mid-September. They continued mobilizing for war, establishing a navy and providing direction to the colonies on the establishment of new governments. But external events would once again push the delegates toward declaring independence. On August 23, the King issued a proclamation that the colonies were in open rebellion against Great Britain. In September, the American diplomats to Great Britain, Richard Penn and Arthur Lee, learned that the King had refused to accept the Olive Branch Petition. They immediately sent a message to Congress, but due to the amount of time it took for correspondence to cross the Atlantic, it did not arrive until November. The King had also opened the new session of Parliament in October with an incendiary speech. He charged the colonists with waging an ever-widening war that "is manifestly carried on for the purpose of establishing an independent empire" and explained that the British would need "to put a speedy end to these disorders by the most decisive exertions." Even though the colonists could not agree among themselves on whether independence was their goal, the monarch had reached this conclusion. The King's speech would not reach the colonies until early January 1776. At roughly the same time, a pamphlet published by a little known author would ignite the movement toward declaring independence.

Common Sense

Thomas Paine authored *Common Sense* in late 1775. Published in January of 1776, this pamphlet made a deep impact on the thinking of many of the colonists, calling into question their continued loyalty to the King and urging them to move forward with independence. Historians agree that Paine's work had a profound influence on the future course of events.

Paine was born in Thetford, England in 1737, to a family of humble means.[44] He attended school for seven years, and then trained as a stay-maker for corsets, which was his father's business. Unhappy in that job, he went to work for the government as an excise tax collector. His duties took him to numerous towns in the English countryside, including Sandwich, Dover, and Lewes, all impoverished and suffering from economic distress. Paine identified with the masses of struggling people in England and he learned a great deal about the workings of the British government, much of which he disliked.

Paine's career was full of ups and downs. In 1774, at the age of thirty-seven, he decided to start over and moved to America. As Eric Foner writes: "The image of America in Paine's England...was of a land of abundance and equality, where individual merit, not social rank, set the limits of man's achievement."[45] Armed with letters of introduction from Franklin, whom he had met in London, Paine was hired as the editor of the periodical *Pennsylvania Magazine* in February of 1775. While working for the magazine, he met Benjamin Rush, a friend of John Adams, who was pushing for independence. In late 1775, Rush, along with others in the radical camp, suggested that Paine draft a pamphlet supporting American independence.[46] In *Common Sense*, Paine took on two of the major impediments holding back colonial independence: loyalty to the King, and the need for reconciliation with Great Britain, which the moderate faction supported.

Paine opened *Common Sense* with a concise argument on the reasons that governments are initially formed. Since human nature has the capacity for evil, individuals give up some of their liberty in exchange for the security which government provides, a view similar to that expressed by the political philosopher John Locke. "Here then is the origin and rise of government, namely, a mode rendered necessary by the inability of moral virtue to govern the world; here too is the design and end of government...freedom and security."[47]

Paine called into question the sanctity of the English Constitution with its checks and balances between the King, the aristocracy, and the Commons. Whereas other radical Whig writers in England believed that liberty survived due to the system of checks and balances, which resulted in a limited monarchy, Paine rejected this idea. He argued that two of the three branches of the British system were based on "two ancient tyrannies" in the King and the aristocracy. Only the Commons was republican in nature, "on whose virtue depends the freedom of England." Paine called into question the entire basis for the divine right of kings to rule. "And when a man seriously reflects on the idolatrous homage which is paid to kings, he need not wonder that the Almighty…should disapprove of a form of government which so impiously invades the prerogative of heaven." If hereditary rule resulted in a "race of good and wise men, it would have the seal of divine authority; but it opens the door to the foolish, the wicked and the improper" and is by nature an oppressive form of government.[48] In *Common Sense,* Paine called into question one of the major issues that impeded the colonies from declaring independence: allegiance to the King and to the British Constitution. Prior to Paine, as Maier explains: "reverence for the inherited institutions of British government inhibited the movement toward separate nationhood."[49]

Confronting the arguments of the moderate faction that still hoped to reconcile with Great Britain, Paine rejected the notion that there were any advantages to remaining within the empire. "I challenge the warmest advocate for reconciliation to show a single advantage that this continent can reap by being connected with Great Britain." He disputed the contention that England was either the "parent country" or that it provided protection to the colonies from outside forces since "she did not protect us from our enemies on our account but from her enemies on her own account." He found numerous disadvantages to reconciliation, including the possibility of being drawn into European wars on behalf of Great Britain. Paine rejected the contention that America was weak in relation to Great Britain, arguing, "there is something very absurd in supposing a continent to be perpetually governed by an island."[50]

One of Paine's primary purposes in writing *Common Sense* "was to bring forward and establish the representative system of government."[51] In this regard, he put forward a simple structure of government, with each colony having a unicameral legislature and a president elected from among their members. A Continental Congress would unite the colonies together, with a president chosen on a rotating basis from each colony. The newly independent nation would need to develop a constitution that would, among other things, secure: "freedom and property to all men, and above all things, the free exercise of religion."[52]

Common Sense concluded by stating that the time was right to declare independence. The country was in a position to field an army, could borrow sufficiently to build a navy, and had the resources to win a war. He no doubt understated the difficulty of the task of going against the greatest military power of its day, even concluding that, "With the increase of commerce, England has lost its spirit."[53] At a practical level, he also argued for the need to declare independence in order to secure the support of foreign powers like Spain and France, an issue that was also on the minds of many of the members of the Continental Congress.

Common Sense became one of the most highly read publications of its time. Paine's greatest influence came from the impact it had on the public. Its great strength lay in its title, a work of common sense written in a straight forward style that did not require a law degree or a college education to understand. John Ferling estimates that within six months of its release approximately 250,000 people read or heard it in the colonies, roughly one in two free adults.[54] Eric Foner writes that, "From up and down the thirteen colonies in the spring of 1776 came reports that the pamphlet was read by "all sorts of people" and that it made "innumerable converts to independence."[55] By April, Washington would comment that the pamphlet elicited "a wonderful change in the minds of many men."[56] Even John Adams, who despised Paine's plan of government, would say "all agree there is a great deal of good sense delivered in clear, simple, concise and nervous style. His sentiments of the abilities of America, and of the difficulty of reconciliation with Great Britain are generally approved. But his notions and plans of continental government are not much applauded."[57] While the pamphlet may have moved public opinion, which helped the radical cause in Congress, it would be another six months before the moderate faction would openly support independence, and some of their leaders never would.

Converting the Moderates

It would take time for *Common Sense* to become widely distributed. The first printing, which took place on January 9, 1776, consisted of only 1,000 copies.[58] A second edition came out near the end of January, followed by later editions. At the same time that *Common Sense* was first published, and before its impact could be felt, the moderates in Congress were able to garner the votes needed to appoint a five-member committee to prepare a response to the King's October speech, in which he claimed the colonists were pursuing a course of independence. While the response was to be provided to the colonies to clarify that independence was not their goal, its true audience was the King and his ministers, a last ditch attempt to forestall independence and restart negotiations. In early January, the radicals still lacked the votes to block the drafting of the moderates address.[59]

Ultimately, the moderates moved too slowly, and events would undermine their ability to delay independence. Washington's army lost a major battle when the invasion of Canada went badly at the end of 1775, news that reached Congress while James Wilson and Dickinson were drafting their response. The losses sustained in Canada were attributed by some, including Elbridge Gerry and General Charles Lee, to the lack of supplies and artillery, and the money needed to pay for the items could only come from foreign assistance. The realization was setting in that the colonists were in for a protracted war, one that could not be won without the assistance of France or Spain. Support from foreign governments would require a declaration of independence, since other nations were unlikely to engage in an act of war knowing that the colonists could still reconcile with Great Britain. Word reached the colonists in mid-February that Lord North was sending peace commissioners to America, but the proposal was made as part of the Prohibitory Bill. That bill not only cut off all trade with the colonies, but made all American ships and cargo subject to confiscation. As John Hancock said, "making all our Vessels lawful Prize don't look like a Reconciliation." When Wilson and Dickinson put forward their address in mid-February, opinion had shifted dramatically away from reconciliation, and Congress tabled the address they prepared.[60]

While the moderates would continue to hold out hope for the peace commissioners during the spring, and Dickinson would maintain this position even after the Declaration was approved, public opinion and the leadership of the various colonies moved in the opposite direction. In the spring of 1776, the southern colonies revised their instructions to their delegates and directed them to vote for independence. Most of the New England colonies had also taken this action. Only the middle colonies, the home of the moderates, continued to hold out.[61]

The actions of the British government ultimately drove the colonists toward independence. From the overreaction to the Boston Tea Party, to the King's speech claiming the colonists were seeking independence, to the cutting off of all trade and making colonial ships subject to confiscation, the policies of the British government contributed to the very thing they wished to head off: the loss of the American colonies. Further fuel was added in May 1776, when it became known that the King had hired German mercenaries, the feared Hessians, to fight alongside British troops. During the spring of 1776, the ministry of Lord North continued to ignore the Continental Congress, attempting to divide and conquer by breaking off individual colonies from the war effort. By the end of March, the moderate leader Robert Morris heard a report that the peace commissioners "can only Treat with the Colonies separately & will have nothing to do with the Congress. If this is the case, they may as well stay where they are." Both Morris and Samuel Adams were of the opinion that "British missteps, rather than American desires, had brought the colonies to the point of independence."[62] Benjamin Franklin also believed that the British were nudging the colonists to independence when he wrote in April: "our Enemies take continually every proper Measure to remove these Obstacles" to independence, daily providing "new Causes of increasing Enmity, and new reasons for wishing an eternal Separation."[63]

As summer approached, John Adams sensed that the time was right to move forward with independence. Adams, who outwardly seemed so firm in his views on independence, had his doubts as well, as he wrote in an April letter to James Warren, who had wondered why Congress was taking so long. "All great changes are irksome to the human mind, especially those which are attended with great dangers and uncertain effects. No living man can foresee the consequences of such a measure." Adams also had concerns over popularly elected government. "We may please ourselves with [the] prospect of free and popular governments. But there is a great danger that those governments will not make us happy…There must be decency and respect, and veneration introduced for persons of authority of every rank, or we are undone. In a popular government, this is our only way."[64] Adams believed that for a republican form of government to work, the public must be relied on to act with both public and private virtue. His *Thoughts on Government* had provided a roadmap for how to form new governments within the colonies. John Ferling writes, "Adams' objective that winter and spring, therefore, was to reassure his colleagues that a stable, enduring, and—from the conservative point of view—safe system of republican government could be instituted, one in which order, authority, and due subordination could be maintained."[65] For John Adams, the American Revolution was not a social revolution, one that would sweep away the existing social order, but rather a political revolution, one that would replace British rule over the colonies with self-government.[66]

Adams continued to exert significant leadership in Congress. Richard Stockton of New Jersey referred to him as the "Atlas of Independence." On May 10, Adams introduced a resolution that called on the colonies to form "such governments as shall…best conduce to the happiness and safety of their constituents in particular, and America in general." The resolution passed unanimously. A committee of three, including Adams, Edward Rutledge, and Richard Henry Lee were chosen to write a preamble to the resolution. The preamble concluded with the statement "it is necessary that the exercise of every kind of authority under the said crown should be totally suppressed, and all the powers of government exerted under the authority of the people of the colonies, for the…defence of their lives, liberties, and properties, against hostile invasions and cruel depredations of their enemies." With Dickinson absent attending to personal business, Congress approved the preamble on May 15. One of Adams' biographers writes: "When an exasperated James Duane told Adams it seemed 'a machine for the fabrication of independence', Adams replied that he thought it 'independence itself.'"[67] The resolution and its preamble led Pennsylvania to join the movement toward independence.

As the weather heated up in Philadelphia, so did the politics of independence. On June 7, Richard Henry Lee introduced a motion for independence: "*Resolved*, That these United Colonies are, and of right ought to be, free and independent States, that are absolved from all allegiance to the British Crown, and that all political connection between them and the state of Great Britain is, and ought to be, totally dissolved." Adams seconded the motion on the Lee resolution, and debate over it continued until June 11. At that point, the resolution was tabled for three weeks to allow the moderates a chance to send for new instructions. In the meantime, Congress appointed a committee made up of Adams, Jefferson, Franklin, Roger Sherman, and Robert Livingston to craft a declaration. It would fall to the 33-year-old Jefferson to write the first draft of the declaration.

Both the resolution and Jefferson's Declaration of Independence stated that the colonies were free and independent states. But the issue of sovereignty was left unresolved, and it was unclear if the actions that had been taken would result in the creation of one American nation. Historian Leonard W. Levy argues that "as the war continued into 1776, nationalist sentiment strengthened," and that "nationalism and centralism were twin causes." But that nationalist sentiment would not last, with leaders arrayed on both sides of the question. The colonies had united under the Continental Congress for the purpose of protecting their rights, and they would move forward to fight the war under a government formed by the Articles of Confederation that would ultimately be a "league of friendship," a compact of sovereign state governments. The national perspective did not survive the bickering among the states, and the colonist's fear of centralized power extended not just to the King and Parliament, but to a strong central government of their own making. The fear of a strong centralized power would ultimately overwhelm the sense of nationalism that had developed in the run up to independence.[68]

Endnotes

1 Ferling, p. 123

2 See Rakove, *Revolutionaries*, p. 67-69 for a fuller discussion of the Burke speech, which is where the quote can also be found.

3 Ferling, p. 128

4 Pauline Maier, *American Scripture: Making the Declaration of Independence*, (New York, 1997), p. 3-4

5 See Bobrick, p. 111-116 and Ferling, p. 132-135

6 See Gordon S. Wood, *The Idea of America: Reflections on the Birth of the United States*, (New York, 2011), p. 7-12 on how historians have seen this issue over time

7 Ferling, p. 136-137 and Rakove, *Revolutionaries*, p. 75-78 provide two somewhat differing views on the role of the moderates, with Rakove more sympathetic.

8 Rakove, *Revolutionaries*, p. 81

9 Rakove, *Revolutionaries*, p. 82

10 Ferling, p. 137

11 Rakove, *Revolutionaries*, p. 82

12 Boorstin, p 103

13 Boorstin, p. 140

14 Chernow, p. 111

15 Maier, p 8

16 Ferling, p. 140

17 McCullough, p. 32

18 McCullough, p. 35

19 McCullough, p. 38

20 McCullough, p. 53

21 McCullough, p. 57

22 Geroge A. Peek, Jr. (Ed.), *The Political Writings of John Adams*, (Indianapolis, 1978), p. x-xi

23 The quotes from *A Dissertation* are from Peek, p.19-20; the idea that Adams mimicked the paranoid style of the period is from Ellis, *Brotherhood*, Lecture 3 on John Adams; the quote at the end of the paragraph is from Wood, *The Idea*, p. 83

24 Peak, p. 23

25 Peak, p. 83

26 Woods, *Creation*, p. 66

27 Maier, p. 36

28 Woods, p. 67

29 Woods, p. 66

30 Woods, p. 54

31 Stanley Elkins & Eric McKitrick, *The Age of Federalism: The Early American Republic, 1788-1800*, (New York, 1993), p. 6

32 Rakove, *Revolutionaries*, p. 171

33 The quotes are from McCullough, p. 66 and p. 68; his fear of mob rule and the importance of the rule of law is from Ellis, *Brotherhood*, Lecture 3.

34 McCullough, p. 67

35 Ferling, p. 135

36 See Maier, p. 14-16 for detail on these points and as the source for the Deane quotes.

37 Rakove, *Beginnings*, p. 71-72

38 Rakove, *Revolutionaries*, p. 87-90 contains a more complete explanation of these debates

39 Chernow, p. 184-185

40 The importance of the appointment of Washington as commander in chief can be found in McCullough, p. 27-28; Ferling, p. 142-144; Chernow, p. 183-189; Ellis, *His Excellency*, p. 71 and Rakove, *Revolutionaries*, p. 123, which is where the Washington orders to the troops can be found.

41 McCullough, p. 95

42 Joseph J. Ellis, *American Sphinx: The Character of Thomas Jefferson*, (New York, 1998), p. 50-51

43 See Maier, p. 19-20; Ellis, *American Sphinx*, p. 50-51 and Ferling, p 45 on Dickinson's role in strengthening the draft of *Causes and Necessities*.

44 This section is largely derived from Eric Foner, *Tom Paine and Revolutionary America*, (Oxford, 1976), p. 1-17

45 Foner, p. 16

46 Foner, p. 73-74 and Ferling, p. 151

47 Nelson F. Adams (Ed.), *Common Sense and Other Political Writings of Tom Paine*, (Indianapolis, 1976), p. 6

48 The quotes are from *Common Sense* on p. 6 and 16 in Adams

49 Maier, p. 30

50 The quotes are from *Common Sense* on p. 22, 20 and 26 in Adams

51 Foner, p. 75

52 From *Common Sense*, p. 32

53 From *Common Sense*, p. 40

54 Ferling, p. 151

55 Foner, p. 79

56 Bobrick, p. 187

57 Bobrick, p. 189

58 See Special Collections & Archives Blog – *Common Sense* by Thomas Paine (1776), p. 3, retrieved 9/7/2012 from http://zsr.wfu.edu/special/blog/common-sense-by-thomas-paine-1776/

59 Ferling, p. 153-154 and Rakove, *Revolutionaries*, p. 97

60 Ferling, p. 154-156 and Rakove, *Revolutionaries*, p. 95-98

61 Ferling, p. 157-158

62 See Rakove, *Revolutionaries,* p. 97 and p. 102 for both quotes

63 Rakove, *Revolutionaries,* p. 100

64 McCullough, p. 105-106

65 Ferling, p. 161-162

66 Ellis, *Brotherhood*, Disk 3

67 McCullough, p. 109

68 Ellis makes the point that the revolution was not about nationhood in *Brotherhood*, Lecture 9; Levy, p. 4-5

Chapter 4

The Declaration of Independence: The American Creed / 1776

"We hold these truths to be self-evident..."
– Thomas Jefferson, July 1776 –

By June of 1776, the colonists were on the precipice of declaring independence, and Jefferson had been asked to prepare a document that stated the reasons why. Who was Jefferson, and why did the founders select him to write the draft? What did the document declare? And what core elements did it contain that would later become the American creed?

Thomas Jefferson

Thomas Jefferson is both the most interesting of the founders and the most difficult to know and understand, an elusive subject. A man of contradictions, he wrote the immortal words that "all men are created equal," yet he owned slaves his entire life. A Virginia aristocrat, he celebrated the common man. A believer in limited government, when he became president in the 1800s he acquired the Louisiana territory, a purchase that required an expansive use of presidential power from a man who wished to foster "an innocuous and almost invisible executive branch."[1] Given these contradictions, both liberals and conservatives often claim him as one of their own.

Jefferson was born on April 13, 1743, in what would later be Albemarle County on the edge of the Virginia wilderness. His father Peter was a third-generation Virginian who had built a modest home on property known as Shadwell, once owned by Thomas' grandfather. Peter Jefferson was a large man, reported to have immense strength. When three slaves failed in their attempt to pull down an old shed, Peter "bade them to stand aside, seized the rope, and dragged down the structure in an instant." One of his favorite sayings was "never ask another to do for you what you can do for yourself." Thomas would take this maxim to heart, and always believed in the importance of self-reliance.[2] Peter Jefferson was a remarkable man, a member of the Virginia House of Burgesses, a justice of the peace, sheriff of the county, and a lieutenant colonel in the militia. During his lifetime, he amassed a small fortune, mostly in land.

Jefferson, heavily influenced by his father, talked largely about the man's character. "My father's education had been quite neglected; but being of a strong mind, sound judgment, and eager about information, he read much and improved himself," Jefferson wrote in his autobiography.[3] Peter had a major influence on his son in a number of areas, including his great love of books, which Thomas would collect in great numbers. As a surveyor, Peter developed an interest in science and the natural world, which he would hand down to his son. As his wealth increased, Peter was able to expand the small house at Shadwell, spurring his son's interest in architecture and construction that would become a lifelong obsession in the construction of Monticello.

Tragically, Peter Jefferson died at the age of forty-nine. The cause is unclear, whether a slight illness made worse by the medicine of the day, or something more serious.[4] Tom, just fourteen years old, was crushed. His father, who did not believe in primogeniture (in which the eldest son inherits all), left half his estate to Tom; his sisters received healthy dowries, and his mother inherited Shadwell. Jefferson would later lead the effort to abolish the tradition of primogeniture in Virginia when he became governor.

It seems clear that Jefferson never had a close relationship with his mother. One of his biographers speculates that in his grief, he shifted the blame for his father's death onto his mother.[5] Except for his time at school, Jefferson lived with his mother at Shadwell until the age of twenty-seven. He believed that she controlled every aspect of his life, and carried hostile feelings toward her for most of his life.[6] When she died in 1776, the only mention in Jefferson's account book was a rather unemotional statement: "My mother died about eight o'clock this morning, in the 57th year of her age."

After his father's death, Jefferson spent his weekdays living at an academy run by James Maury, an Anglican minister. With Maury, he received a classical education, learning both Greek and Latin. He honed his writing skills and his appreciation for the precise use of language under his teacher's guidance. Jefferson was happy during this period, although it is unclear if this was due to Maury or to the friendships Jefferson developed. In 1812, looking back at his life, he wrote to Maury's son, who had been his friend during this period: "Reviewing the course of a long and sufficiently successful life, I find in no portion of it happier moments than these were."[7] He returned to Shadwell on weekends to assist his mother in running the household, time spent that was not as pleasant for him.

At the age of seventeen, Jefferson entered William & Mary College, where he studied for seven years. Jefferson had an insatiable appetite for learning and spent up to fifteen hours a day studying. He was fortunate to fall under the influence of two excellent teachers at the college. From William Small, he learned mathematics and science and would later credit his success as an architect and inventor "to the good foundation laid at college by my old master and friend Small."[8] Small also introduced him to the philosophers of the Enlightenment, including Montesquieu, Voltaire, and Locke, who had a great influence on Jefferson's political views. After two years of college course work, Jefferson decided to study law. Small arranged for him to serve as an apprentice under George Wythe, a very successful lawyer in Virginia, with whom Jefferson spent five years studying law, an unusually long time for that period. In letters to friends, he would refer to Wythe as a second father. Wythe influenced Jefferson's views on liberty, natural rights, equality, and religious tolerance.[9]

His role as a legal apprentice exposed Jefferson to the revolutionary fervor sweeping across Virginia in the mid-1760s in response to the British attempt to impose the Stamp Act tax. Jefferson's responsibilities included keeping track of the various activities of the committees that Wythe served on, and so Jefferson was present in the House of Burgesses in May 1765, when Patrick Henry made his famous speech that came close to charging the King with treason. Jefferson and Patrick were already acquainted, and the speech stunned Jefferson. "I well remember the cry of treason, the pause of Mr. Henry at the name of George III and the presence of mind with which he closed the sentence and baffled the charge vociferated."[10]

By April of 1766, at the age of twenty-two, Jefferson applied to practice law, splitting time between his career as a lawyer and his life as a Virginia planter. Rural life would forever influence Jefferson, who would place the ideal of the independent yeoman farmer at the center of his conception of American life. In the future, he would represent one end of that ideal, with Alexander Hamilton, among others, representing the polar opposite, seeing America's future in industry, finance, and commercial endeavors.

At the age of twenty-five, Jefferson began work on Monticello, on land that he had inherited from his father. This would prove to be a lifelong construction project. At about the same time, he also launched his political career with his election to the Virginia House of Burgesses in 1769. At twenty-five, Jefferson was tall (six feet two), ruddy of complexion, with red hair often tied in a ponytail. For a politician, he was also unusually quiet. Ellis writes of him: "Jefferson was a listener and observer, distinctly uncomfortable in the spotlight, shy and nervous in a distracted manner that was sometimes mistaken for arrogance."[11] Despite this, one of his first actions in the Virginia House was to propose a measure that allowed a slave owner to free slaves that he owned. The proposal would be defeated, but it showed that Jefferson, at a young age, had begun to question the morality of slavery. Given his contradictory nature, though, within a few weeks of this public action, he would advertise a reward for the return of one of his own slaves. In October of 1769, he represented Samuel Howell in court, a slave who was attempting to attain his freedom. In his presentation in court, Jefferson declared, "Under the law of nature, all men are born free," words that would be echoed in the Declaration of Independence seven years later.[12]

Jefferson was pulled into the politics of the revolution and supported various resolutions laid out by his Virginian companions, including one proposed by Washington for the non-importation of British goods in response to the Townshend duties. But in classic Jeffersonian style, he ignored the ban and ordered a piano from Britain just prior to his marriage to Martha Wales Skelton in December 1771. Martha, a recent widow, carried with her a dowry that doubled Jefferson's land and slave holdings. At age 23, she was reported to be quite beautiful, a graceful rider, and a fine dancer.

In July of 1774, Jefferson's tract *A Summary View of the Rights of British America* was published. It incorporated many of Jefferson's views on government, including that people are bestowed with certain natural rights; that the legislature is the supreme repository of power; and that ultimate sovereignty rests in the people.[13] The views he expressed, including that Parliament "has no right to exercise authority over us," went beyond the positions taken by other radicals in 1774. Jefferson also attacked the King, an unusual position in the mid-1770s when allegiance to the monarch was still the norm. As Ellis writes, Jefferson's "tone toward George III ranges between the disrespectful and the accusatory."[14] Jefferson's positions in *Rights* anticipated the views that would come to prevail in 1776. The tract also established his reputation as a fine writer once he joined the Continental Congress as a delegate in 1775.

The Declaration of Independence

Why did our founders select Jefferson to write the Declaration of Independence? Many years after its signing, Adams recalled that when Jefferson asked him why he should prepare the draft that he responded as follows: "Reason first: you are a Virginian and a Virginian ought to appear at the head of this business. Reason second: I am obnoxious, suspected, and unpopular. Reason third: You can write ten times better than I can." Jefferson remembered it differently, that the committee had simply asked him to prepare the draft, and so he did.[15]

We may never know the precise reason for Jefferson's selection, but it was certainly in part due to his reputation as a writer. Also, others on the committee demurred when asked to undertake the task. Benjamin Franklin, well known for his literary skills, was suffering from gout. He also told Jefferson, "I have made it a rule, whenever in my power, to avoid becoming the draughtsman of papers to be reviewed by a public body."[16] Jefferson, who was shy and a poor public speaker, made his contributions in Congress via his skill as a writer, and he had been drafted to serve on numerous committees that were assigned to prepare various resolutions.[17] One of his biographers argues that, "the genius of Jefferson's writing lay in his ability to take deep and complicated concepts of history, law and philosophy and clothe them in easy, graceful, direct and almost simple language."[18]

Many of Jefferson's colleagues considered the actual crafting of the declaration of secondary importance to the preparation of state constitutions, the urgent need to reach out for foreign assistance, and the monumental task of managing the floor debate over approval of the resolution declaring independence. Jefferson himself wished to be back in Virginia to assist in the drafting of its new constitution, and had recently completed a preamble for it.[19] Adams had been assigned to no fewer than twenty-three committees at the time, and took the lead in the debates over approval of the resolution and the declaration, and so he no doubt preferred to have Jefferson prepare the actual document. He also held Jefferson's writing in high esteem, due to his "peculiar felicity of expression."

The committee assigned to write the declaration met once before the drafting began and provided Jefferson with input into what the document should include. Jefferson then set out to draft the declaration alone, working "seated in an unusual revolving Windsor chair and holding on his lap a portable writing box, a small folding desk of his own design."[20] He later said that "he turned to neither book nor pamphlet" in writing the declaration, although he most assuredly referred to the preamble to the Virginia Constitution that he had been working on and the Virginia Declaration of Rights written by George Mason, which contained the statement that: "all men are born equally free and independent, and have certain inherent natural rights...among which are the enjoyment of life and liberty, with the means of acquiring property, and pursuing and obtaining happiness."[21] In a letter to Adams in 1813, Jefferson stated his goal in preparing the declaration as follows: "Neither aiming at originality of principle or sentiment, nor yet copied from any particular and previous writing, it was intended to be an expression of the American mind."[22] Jefferson wrote the draft over a two-day period, most likely between June 11 and 12.

The second paragraph would, over time, become the expression of the American mind that Jefferson referred to. Ellis has stated that those words are, perhaps, the most important fifty-five words written in American history, words that would inspire not only Americans but also people throughout the world.

> *We hold these truths to be self-evident; that all men are created equal; that they are endowed by their Creator with certain inalienable rights; that among these are life, liberty, and the pursuit of happiness; that to secure these rights, governments are instituted among men, deriving their just powers from the consent of the governed.*

While there would be extensive editing of the balance of the document, much to Jefferson's chagrin, this section underwent only two changes. The first was made by the committee members, who changed Jefferson's wording of "We hold these truths to be sacred and undeniable" to the more elegant "self-evident," which may have been added by Franklin.[23] The second was made by the Continental Congress, meeting as a Committee of the Whole, which changed Jefferson's wording from "inherent and inalienable rights" to "certain inalienable rights."

The declaration was heavily influenced by Jefferson's study of a number of English and Scottish Enlightenment writers, including John Locke, David Hume, Francis Hutcheson, and Henry St. John

Bolingbroke. Of these, Locke's contract theory of government was of particular importance in influencing Jefferson. Locke's political theory held that men are born with certain natural rights, including liberty and equality. In a state of nature, where no government exists, the natural rights of people can be trampled on. "To maintain their natural rights, men voluntarily give up some of their freedom and enter into a social contract to create a political power capable of preserving their collective rights and restraining transgressors," Locke writes.[24] Given the voluntary nature of the social contract, the legitimacy of a government must be grounded in the will of the people. When the government breaks faith with the governed, the people have the right to throw off an existing government and form a new one. Jefferson was declaring the right of the colonists to throw off the government of England, since it had infringed on their basic human rights, and to establish a new government.

What did these words mean at the time they were written, and what have they come to mean over time?

Equality

Two of the ideas that would animate America, indeed the world, from this date forward were the twin human rights of equality and liberty. But what did Jefferson and others of his time mean by "all men are created equal"? Historian Gordon S. Wood, first in a lecture delivered at the American Enterprise Institute in January 1995, and later in an expanded written version published by the Fordham Law Review in January 1996, provided an analysis of what equality meant in Jefferson's time.[25] The quotes attributed to Dr. Wood below are from the Fordham Law Review article.

The first element was social equality, based on the idea that people see each other as equals and expect to be treated as such. Wood uses a quote from Ronald Reagan to express what this means. "Whether we come from poverty or wealth...we are all equal in the sight of God. But as Americans that is not enough — we must be equal in the eyes of each other." In premodern times, certain people were viewed as being superior due to heredity. Wood argues that "people in the premodern world often assumed that a handsome child, though apparently a commoner, had to be the bastard offspring of an aristocrat."

Jefferson and many of the other founders rejected the notion that some are born superior, and they believed that distinctions between people occurred because of their environment, not due to bloodlines. Wood admits that today we no longer accept this, since we know that people are born with different talents and abilities. John Adams' view would more likely fit our modern conception: "Were there, or will there ever be a nation whose individuals were all equal, in natural or acquired qualities, in virtue, talents, and riches? The answer in mankind must be in the negative."[26] Still, Jefferson's view fits not only our compassionate side, but also is the bridge to our view of the need for equality of opportunity. If all people have equal worth, then we each have some responsibility for each other, and we need to cultivate the talents among all of us. As Dr. Wood writes: "Once the liberally educated came to believe that they could control their environment and educate the vulgar and lowly to become something other than what the traditional society had presumed they were destined to be, then enlightened elites like Jefferson began to expand their sense of moral responsibility for the vice and ignorance they saw in others and to experience feelings of common humanity with them...many of the revolutionaries concluded with Jefferson that all men were basically alike, that they partook of the same common nature." From this came our moral sense, our sympathetic instinct that made possible the natural compassion found in society.

Equality of opportunity means that people should be able to rise as far as their talents, abilities and penchant for hard work carry them.

Talent was not based on heredity but rather was distributed throughout the population, and society should encourage that talent. Tied to this is the concept of social mobility, that people should be able to move up the economic ladder based on their skills, abilities, talent, and hard work. Jefferson, who often wrote about a natural aristocracy, was referring to an aristocracy of skills and talent and not of bloodlines, a core American ideal.

Jefferson and many of the other leaders of the revolutionary period went beyond this and believed in a "rough equality of condition for a republican society — with every man an independent property owner."[27] This was not an attempt at social leveling, where everyone would have absolutely the same material conditions, but reflected a concern that too great a concentration of wealth and power would be inimical in a republican form of government. This would later prove a major source of division between Jefferson and Alexander Hamilton, since the latter had few concerns with great concentrations of wealth. In this, the writing of the radical Whigs discussed in Chapter 2 may have influenced Jefferson, especially the libertarians Trenchard and Gordon, who feared that concentrations of wealth would lead to the use of power in arbitrary ways. Jefferson also proposed governmental policies to deal with the problem of wealth concentration, in part by the elimination of primogeniture, which focused on reducing inequality caused by passing wealth from one generation to another. By eliminating primogeniture, Jefferson was attempting to eliminate an aristocracy of inherited wealth. He also proposed policies in the Virginia Constitution of 1776 that provided for the distribution of land to "every person of full age," which would include women as well as men. This proposal failed, indicating that policies involving redistribution may have been as controversial during the revolutionary period as they are today.[28]

One reason other members of the founding generation, including John Adams, may not have proposed or supported policies to ameliorate extremes of wealth is that parts of colonial America were relatively egalitarian already. This was certainly the case for Massachusetts, especially in comparison to the more hierarchal society of Virginia.[29] In 2011, economists Peter H. Lindert and Jeffrey G. Williamson completed a study of income distribution during the colonial period. They found that the colonists had a more equal distribution of income during the period from 1774-1800 than did the English, and that the middle colonies and New England were "more egalitarian than anywhere else in the measurable world," which was an outgrowth of their colonial founding by the Puritans and Quakers, who rejected great concentrations of wealth.[30] In an interview with the New York Times, Dr. Lindert said: "Compared to any other country from which we have data, America in that era was more equal. Today, the Americans are the outliers in the other direction." In fact, most working Americans during the colonial period did better than their European peers did. Only one group did worse, those at the top. As Lindert points out, today the situation is reversed: "The rest of the world can't come close to the 1 percent in America."[31]

Jefferson certainly understood the egalitarian nature of much of American society. In a letter from September 1814, he wrote "…first, we have no paupers who possess nothing…The great mass of our population is of laborers; our rich, who can live without labor…being few, and of modest wealth."[32] Despite his support for limited government, Jefferson was not afraid to recommend policies to alleviate great inequalities of wealth when he saw those existed. While serving as part of the American delegation to the French court in 1785, Jefferson wrote to James Madison about the extremes of wealth he saw in prerevolutionary France. He told about a conversation he'd had with a peasant woman who had difficulty finding work and often had no bread for her children. Jefferson lamented a situation in which "property is absolutely concentrated in a very few hands." He went on to say, "I am conscious that an equal division of property is impracticable. But the consequences of this enormous inequality producing so much misery to the bulk of mankind, legislators cannot invent too many devices for subdividing property...Another means of lessening the inequality of property is to exempt all from taxation below a certain point, and to tax the higher portions of property in geometrical progression as they rise."[33] In 1785, Jefferson was anticipating the graduated income tax that was implemented in the United States in the twentieth century.

Madison's response is also illuminating. "I have no doubt that the misery of the lower classes will be found to abate wherever the Government assumes a freer aspect & the laws favor a subdivision of property."[34] Madison's view, which Jefferson shared, was that a more republican form of government (freer as he expressed it) would lead to policies that fostered independent farmers and resulted in a better distribution of property. Madison, in January 1792, published an article on political parties in the National Gazette in which he made a further argument for a more egalitarian society. To combat the evil of parties (or factions as he referred to them in the Federalist Papers), and to allow a republican form of government to thrive, there first must be "political equality among all." Second, "by withholding unnecessary opportunities from a few, to increase the inequality of property...and especially an unmerited, accumulation of riches" requires "the silent operation of laws, which, without violating the rights of property, reduce extreme wealth towards a state of mediocrity, and raises extreme indigence towards a state of comfort."[35] Madison, a great defender of property rights, also believed that lessening inequality was essential to the survival of republican government.

Jefferson believed in minimal government and that the federal government should limit itself to foreign affairs and the relations between the states. He mistrusted all government power.[36] In his experience, government power and private wealth were one and the same in the Great Britain of his time. The aristocracy controlled both the wealth of the society and the instruments of government. He saw small government as a means to control the power of the wealthy elite, who in England used a strong central government to enhance their power. Lew Daly, in an article printed in *Dissent Magazine* in 2008, argues that "the ideal, simply, was a system (of limited government) that restricted the legal and political power of the wealthy, in order to prevent them from combining against independent smallholders and those without property."[37] Since both Jefferson and Madison wanted America to remain a nation of small, independent, yeoman farmers and were opposed to the development of cities and industry, they may have expected that small government would suffice to achieve a roughly equal society.

The Jeffersonian view of government would, from the very beginning, compete with an alternative vision of the need for a robust central government in order to promote the development of industry. As I discuss later in this volume, Madison supported the creation of a strong federal government through his role as one of the primary authors of the American Constitution. One of his main partners in this endeavor was Alexander Hamilton, who put forward the alternative idea of a country with a robust manufacturing base, supported by a strong financial sector. Hamilton championed the need for strong federal government action to create his vision, which he, Madison, and Jefferson would fight over in the 1790s. In the post-Civil War era, Hamilton's vision would shift into overdrive, with industrialization creating large and powerful centers of private power in the form of modern corporations and a corresponding increase in the concentration of wealth. This would animate progressives like Theodore Roosevelt and Franklin Roosevelt to use the power of the federal government to balance and regulate such private power and achieve a greater distribution of wealth.

Liberty / Freedom

Liberty is at the core of what it means to be an American. Louis D. Brandeis, the Supreme Court justice, said, "Liberty has knit us together as a people."[38] Not only is liberty found in the Declaration as a right granted by the Creator, but American school children recite it every day in the Pledge of Allegiance when they say we are: "one nation, under God, indivisible, with liberty and justice for all." When Americans disagree with each other, the argument may end with a reminder that it is a free country, a shorthand way of recognizing that everyone is entitled to their own opinion. Our concept of freedom has developed and changed over the last 236 years of our existence, and Americans have often disagreed over its meaning and its place among multiple rights, but it has always played a central role in American life.

Even before the Declaration of Independence, the colonists had viewed themselves as having certain rights as Englishmen, including the right to liberty and property. Many of the colonists that had come to the New World, including the Puritans, had done so in pursuit of religious freedom. And part of what spurred independence was a perceived notion that the government of Great Britain was attempting to deny the colonists their rights, including the right to liberty.

The components of freedom at the time of the revolution were as numerous as they are today. One was individual liberty as expressed by John Locke, who believed that men are equal and free and that governments are instituted to protect the individual's right to "life, liberty and estate." Locke's view is at the heart of classical liberalism, in which government's role is strictly limited. This differs from the liberalism that developed in the twentieth century in which government is viewed as having a positive effect on life and liberty. Today's conservative political philosophy squares most closely with classical liberalism in terms of individual liberty. Individual liberty also has embedded within it the idea that there is a private sphere of life separate and distinct from the public sphere. The private sphere includes, among other things, decisions about where to live; what career to choose; whether to get married and to whom; whether to have children; and what religion to practice, if any.

A component of individual liberty that deserves discussion is economic liberty. According to the *Concise Encyclopedia of Economics*, the key ingredients of economic freedom are personal choice, voluntary exchange, the freedom to compete in markets, and the protection of property. Private property, the ability to own and use property, is of fundamental importance in economic freedom, and the government plays a key role in providing a legal structure that protects private property rights.[39] Over time, economic freedom would be integral to the establishment of a free market capitalist system in the United States.

The founders were interested in the promotion of economic freedom and unleashing the talents of Americans on the world stage. They believed in the protection of property rights and were opposed to schemes that would result in the massive redistribution of wealth. But they also knew that economic freedom was one of many competing rights and values, including the need for a degree of equality. They also feared that a republican government, one grounded in popular sovereignty, could not survive in a society where wealth was overly concentrated. Republicanism, which required a virtuous citizenry and greater equality, and classic liberalism, which valued natural rights and individualism, could sometimes be at odds with each other.

The extent of economic freedom in the United States has been the subject of a long debate that began at the country's birth and continues to this day. On one side stand those who believe in an absolutely free market capitalist system and prefer little government involvement in the economy, a system sometimes referred to as laissez-faire economics (literally from the French it means "let it do its own thing"). On the other side stand those who favor a mixed economy, one in which "private economic freedom is combined with government regulation, social protections, and the maintenance of public goods." The idea of a mixed economy developed in the late nineteenth and the twentieth centuries in response to problems associated with free market capitalism, including "frequent depressions, workplace dangers, low wages, assaults on labor rights, mass unemployment, environmental negligence, and public health issues."[40]

Both of these approaches to economic freedom occurred after the founding generation, although Adam Smith first outlined the case for laissez-faire economics in 1776, in *An Inquiry into the Nature and Causes of the Wealth of Nations*. But the American economy in the 1770s was primarily based on agriculture and operated under a mercantilist system, one in which raw materials from the colonies were shipped to England to be manufactured into consumer goods. A modern capitalist economic system was still in the future, and the founding generation could not have foreseen the changes to come. In the 1790s, Alexander Hamilton would become the great proponent of an industrial future for the United States. However, his was not a laissez-faire approach to economics, but rather a collaboration between government and the private economy as a means to spur economic growth.

Another important component of liberty was political freedom. This is the right to participate in public life, to influence government through voting and/or serving as an elected official. Historians and others sometimes refer to this as republicanism, and as we have seen, the founders believed that a republic needed to be grounded in the public virtue of the people. By public virtue, they meant the need to voluntarily sacrifice individual interests for those of the greater good, which was at the heart of republican government and one of the core foundations for freedom.

These two concepts of liberty, political and personal (economic) liberty, existed side by side at the time of the revolution. As historian Eric Foner writes: "In the colonial era, 'liberty' stood as a meeting point between liberal and republican understandings of government and society. There seemed no necessary contradiction between the personal freedom central to liberalism and the public liberty of the republican tradition."[41] Part of the reason these two ideas could coexist, at least for a time, was due to the widespread egalitarian nature of colonial society. Wealth was more evenly distributed than in Europe, and in the colonies, the majority of farmers owned land. Widespread property ownership was also considered a precondition for liberty. Sir William Blackstone, the English judge and a Member of Parliament, had said that men without property would fall "under the immediate domination of others."[42] Individual liberty and the republican ideal of the public good embedded in political liberty would eventually clash and lead men like Madison and Hamilton to push for a stronger national government as a means to balance the two.

Journalist and author E.J. Dionne makes the point that we are a nation conceived in argument. Dionne writes that in our contemporary debates each side insists that one value (liberty, equality, the public good) "overrode all others in the judgment of the organizers of our revolution and the authors of our Constitution." But, in fact, the founders themselves held contradictory views on these issues, and were attempting to balance "liberty, equality, republicanism, democratic sovereignty, and the common good," values that were not always easy or even possible to completely reconcile.[43]

Pursuit of Happiness

Historians have long puzzled over why Jefferson removed from the Declaration the reference to property, which were the words that Locke had used, and substituted instead the words "pursuit of happiness." George Mason, in preparing the Virginia Declaration of Rights, had included both "the means of acquiring property, and pursuing and obtaining happiness." But Jefferson completely removed the reference to property in the Declaration. Some have speculated this may have been a subtle means of supporting the end of slavery, an institution that Jefferson knew was immoral and inconsistent with the principles proclaimed in the Declaration.[44]

Jefferson never fully explained what the phrase meant, but in 1819, he wrote a letter to William Short in which he stated he was a follower of Epicurus, the Greek philosopher whose focus was on living a happy life. Jefferson, in summarizing the philosophy of Epicurus, wrote, "Happiness (is) the aim of life, virtue the foundation of happiness, (and) utility the test of virtue." For Jefferson, happiness needed to rest on something larger than just material gain, something beyond just the right to pursue prosperity. Kathleen Kennedy Townsend, the daughter of Robert Kennedy, has argued that the founders believed "that you attained happiness, not merely through the goods you accumulated, or in your private life, but through the good you did in public." She quotes President Kennedy as defining happiness as the Greeks did, in "the full use of one's talents along the lines of excellence."[45] Perhaps Jefferson would have liked the modern phrase "money won't make you happy."

Writer Jon Meacham, in an article in *Time* magazine entitled "Free to Be Happy," states that Jefferson was influenced by Aristotle, who writes that happiness is "the end of action." For Aristotle, Meacham writes, happiness was "an ultimate good, worth seeking for its own sake." Many of the founders thought that the pursuit of happiness was either the "first law of government," or the "end of government." Ultimately, Meacham insists that the pursuit of happiness was "the pursuit of the good of the whole, because the good of the whole was crucial to the genuine well-being of the individual."[46]

God and Religion

Religion has always played an important role in American life. Three colonies were founded based on the pursuit of religious freedom: Massachusetts by the Puritans; Pennsylvania by the Quakers; and Maryland by the Catholics. In 1630, John Winthrop writes to the Puritans in his sermon *A Model of Christian Charity*, "…we must consider that we shall be as a City upon a Hill," a metaphor Ronald Reagan often used to refer to America's special place in the world. The founders, too, were heavily influenced by their views of God, religion, and morality.

What did Jefferson mean when he wrote in the Declaration that men "*are endowed by their Creator with certain inalienable rights*"? Jefferson formed his views on religion at a very young age, most likely by the age of twenty-two. He was heavily influenced in his thinking by Henry Saint-John Bolingbroke, an English deist.[47] Deists believed in a God that had created the universe and then allowed it to operate according to its own principals. Since God was perfect, the machine was perfect and there was no need for him to interfere with the operation of the universe.[48] The Deist's God might be equated with a watchmaker who builds a watch, winds it up, and then walks away and allows it to operate on its own.[49]

Jefferson's Creator God in the Declaration is not the God of any particular religion. Jefferson espoused the view that people should be free to choose to worship God in their own way, or not to worship at all. For this to occur, government should refrain from interfering in religious life. Correspondingly, no one religion should be allowed to dominate the government. Jon Meacham writes, "In the public business of the nation…it was important to the Founders to speak of God in a way that was unifying, not divisive. 'Nature's God' was the path they chose, and it has served the nation admirably."[50]

Jefferson's work as a lawyer had further influenced him, as he saw the corrupting influence that the Anglican Church had on the governments of both England and Virginia. Neither Quakers nor Presbyterians were allowed to freely practice their religion in Virginia prior to 1784 and could be charged with heresy and burned at the stake if they tried. Jefferson would conclude, as he later wrote in an 1802 letter, on the need for a "wall of separation" between government and religion. Starting in 1774, he and Madison worked to repeal Anglicanism as the official religion of Virginia. In 1779, he proposed "An Act for Establishing Religious Freedom" in Virginia. It would be five years before the bill would finally pass, and Jefferson would list it as second only to the Declaration of Independence as one of his greatest accomplishments.[51]

As for the other Founding Fathers, they placed a great deal of importance on God and religion, in large part because religion could instill a greater sense of morality in individuals, which was needed in a republican form of government. The revolutionary generation thought that the success of a republic would be dependent, in part, on both private and public virtue. Private virtue, grounded in morality, could be advanced by religion. Washington said, "And let us with caution indulge the supposition that morality can be maintained without religion." Adams echoed this view in a letter to Jefferson: "Without religion this world would be something not fit to mention in polite company, I mean Hell." Jefferson was not certain that religion was the wellspring of all morality, and believed that atheists could be moral, but he also thought that morality was a gift from God. In 1816, he told John Adams that: "the moral sense is as much a part of our constitution as that of feeling, seeing or hearing; as a wise Creator must have seen to be necessary in an animal destined to live in society."[52]

The one thing many of the founders agreed on was the need for tolerance of all forms of religion. One of Franklin's biographers writes: "he was a prophet of tolerance. Focusing on doctrinal disputes was divisive, he felt, and trying to ascertain divine certainties was beyond our mortal ken." Franklin would comment that the moral improvement project he had set out on as a young man had "no mark of any of the distinguishing tenets of any particular sect" so that "it might be serviceable to people in all religions." Franklin was practical and pragmatic in his view of religion.[53]

Washington too was tolerant of different religions. As a vestryman in his local Anglican Church, he took on such duties as overseeing the finances of the church and helping to pay the minister. He did not, however, kneel during prayer or take communion, and he had irregular attendance. Ron Chernow writes of Washington that his "religious style probably reflected an Enlightenment discomfort with religious dogma...He was sober and temperate in all things, distrusted zealotry, and would never have talked of hellfire or damnation."[54] As such, he was opposed to religious fanaticism and issued numerous statements on religious tolerance. "We have abundant reason to rejoice that in this Land the light of truth and reason has triumphed over the power of bigotry and superstition, and that every person may here worship God according to the dictates of his conscience."[55]

Adams too shared the views of Jefferson, Franklin, and Washington on both the importance of religion and the need for tolerance. "I hate polemical politics and polemical divinity. My religion is founded on the love of God and my neighbor," Adams said.[56] In 1779, he assisted in the preparation of a new constitution for Massachusetts. Part of the Declaration of Rights included in the Constitution stated that no one was to be "hurt, molested, or restrained in his person, liberty or estate for worshipping God in the manner most agreeable to the dictates of his own conscience."[57]

Consent of the Governed

Jefferson grounded the legitimacy of government in the "consent of the governed," in the principal of democracy. The founder's theory of government was that political liberty was equivalent to democracy, to government by the people, although they did not often refer to democracy, since they equated it with mob rule.[58] Initially, voting was restricted to property-owning white males in the newly drafted state constitutions. Given the widespread distribution of property in 1776, voting rights were fairly expansive, especially for the period. The revolutionary generation feared that those without property would too easily fall under the domination of others. In the words of James Iredell, a future member of the first Supreme Court, "there must be some restriction as to the right of voting; otherwise the lowest and most ignorant of mankind must associate in this important business with those who it is presumed, from their property and other circumstances, are free from influence, and have some knowledge of the great consequence of their trust."[59]

Not all of the founders believed that voting should be restricted to property owners or those that paid taxes. Jefferson's view on voting was more expansive, favoring people that either "having resided (for) a certain time, or having a family, or having property, and or all of them."[60] Between the time of the signing of the Declaration in 1776 and the drafting of the Constitution in 1787, voting rights would be further expanded within the states among white males to largely eliminate property ownership as a qualification. Part of this was spurred by Madison, who would expand the definition of property beyond physical possessions to a man's "opinions and free communication of them." "The idea that property included ownership of one's self helped to democratize the political nation. If all persons had a property in their rights, then there was no logical reason why all should not participate in government," historian Eric Foner writes. Over time, voting would gradually come to be seen as an entitlement, as a right unto itself.[61]

It is important to remember that the grand sentiments expressed in the preamble to the Declaration of Independence were ideals to be pursued, but they did not reflect the condition of the colonies in 1776. Over the course of American history, the ideals would animate Americans, lead to numerous disagreements over their meaning, and require the struggle of many people to have the blessings of equality, liberty, and democracy extended to all. Certainly, at the time of the revolution, such rights were denied to a large portion of the population, including, most glaringly, slaves, women, and native people. Women would not receive the right to vote until 1920, when the country approved the Nineteenth Amendment to the Constitution. It would take the Civil War to finally free African Americans, and another 100 years beyond this before civil rights would be fully extended to people of color. Jefferson's statement that all men are created equal would animate some of the northern states to free their slaves, including New York in 1799, and New Jersey five years later. Still, many in the South continued to support slavery, and denied the claim made in the Declaration that all men are created equal.[62]

Martin Luther King, Jr., in his "I Have a Dream Speech" delivered in front of the Lincoln Memorial in 1963, reminded the nation that it had fallen short of its founding ideals when he said:

> *In a sense we have come to our nation's capital to cash a check. When the architects of our republic wrote the magnificent words of the Constitution and the Declaration of Independence, they were signing a promissory note to which every American was to fall heir. This note was a promise that all men, yes, black men as well as white men, would be guaranteed the unalienable rights of life, liberty and the pursuit of happiness. It is obvious today that America has defaulted on the promissory note insofar as her citizens of color are concerned. Instead of honoring this sacred obligation, America has given the negro people a bad check, a check which has come back marked "insufficient funds." But we refuse to believe that the bank of justice is bankrupt.... Now is the time to make justice a reality for all of God's children.*

Some leaders, including Dr. King in the 1960's, would see positive governmental action as necessary to expand the rights illuminated in the Declaration. The use of government to expand rights has always been controversial, dating back to the founding, when conflicts arose between individual liberty and republican values of the public good. The Jeffersonian ideal was that limited government would marry these two concepts together. As one historian writes: "In the absence of governmental favoritism, the natural workings of society would produce justice, liberty and equality...A limited government would allow citizens both to achieve economic independence and to become virtuous, thus reconciling order and freedom, equality and liberty."[63] This expected outcome would almost immediately run into problems in the aftermath of the Revolutionary War in the 1780s, and lead Madison and Hamilton to propose a stronger national government, albeit one with limited powers.

The tension between the need for strong governmental action to fully implement the promises of the Declaration of Independence and the importance of individual freedom has continued throughout American history, with American's struggling to find ways to balance the two. Almost immediately upon the implementation of the Constitution, Jefferson and Hamilton disagreed over whether Congress had the right to establish a national bank. Washington sided with Hamilton, and the bank was formed. Henry Clay and other Whigs in the early 1800s argued for strong national action to construct "internal improvements," and for active governmental involvement in the fledgling economy. But both the Federalists of Hamilton's day, and later the Whigs that Clay represented, had a strain of elitism about them. Jefferson and Andrew Jackson would strive for a greater role for the common man in politics and the expansion of democracy, at least for free white males, but would pursue these policies by limiting government.[64] Lincoln continued in the Whig tradition and provided federal subsidies to foster the transcontinental railroad, and land grants to settle the West. He also freed the slaves as part of the Civil War, which was fought over the issue of slavery. In the aftermath of the Industrial Revolution in the United States, when large and monopolistic corporations developed, President Theodore Roosevelt would use federal power to break up such organizations. Franklin Roosevelt expanded federal power in the face of the Great Depression through his New Deal. He also proposed his Four Freedoms as a goal for all human societies in 1941, just prior to the United States entering World War II, including freedom of speech, freedom of worship, freedom from want, and freedom from fear. Later in the twentieth century, Ronald Reagan would celebrate the private economy and the need to limit government, views that would change the terms of the debate in the United States. To this day, Americans struggle with the relative merits of individual liberty versus joint action through government to expand rights and solve societal problems. This is also part of what it means to be an American, a nation born in argument.

Adoption of the Declaration

The largest part of the Declaration was dedicated to the list of indictments and grievances against the King. It summarized "the past twelve years of colonial opposition to British policy designed to make the king responsible for all of the trouble," written from the perspective of the colonists, and was intended to help join the colonies into one coherent unit for purposes of challenging the British Empire.[65] That would be the section of Jefferson's draft that the Congress would debate and edit the most, since it provided the justification for independence.

July 1 dawned hot and humid, a typical summer day in Philadelphia. One can imagine that the room at the State House where the Congress met must have been oppressive, especially given that the windows were closed and the shades drawn in order to maintain secrecy. John Hancock, the president of the Congress, opened the session that day by returning to Lee's resolution declaring the colonies free and independent states.[66]

John Dickinson spoke first, and made one last impassioned plea to put off a decision on independence. He spoke for two hours, reiterating many points he had previously raised. When he finished, no one rose to speak in opposition, until Adams finally assumed the mantle of leadership. McCullough writes, "He wished now as never in his life...

that he had the gifts of the ancient orators of Greece and Rome. For he was certain that none of them ever had before him a question of greater importance." Almost on cue, a summer storm erupted as Adams began to speak. It was his finest moment, as he made the case for independence. Jefferson remarked that he spoke "with a power of thought and expression that moved us from our seats." After Adams concluded, others would also speak, with the debate raging for nine hours as the thunderstorm continued unabated. By the end of the long afternoon, they took the vote, with nine of the thirteen colonies voting for independence — not the unanimous vote that the supporters had hoped for. Dickinson kept Pennsylvania from voting yes, New York still did not have clear authorization to support the resolution, and Delaware was missing one of its key supporters for independence, Caesar Rodney. South Carolina also voted no, but their delegate John Rutledge indicated they might change their vote, and so Congress deferred the decision to the next day.

John Dickinson and Robert Morris did not attend the session on July 2. It is unclear why, although it was perhaps an act of statesmanship on their part, allowing the Pennsylvania delegation to vote with the majority and Congress to speak with one voice. South Carolina changed its vote, and Rodney broke the tie for Delaware. The final tally was 12-0, with all voting in the affirmative except New York. The colonies were now independent, at least on paper. Adams wrote to Abigail: "The second day of July 1776 will be the most memorable epocha in the history of America… It ought to be solemnized with pomp and parade, with shows, games, sports, guns, bells, bonfires, and illuminations from one end of this continent to the other from this time forward forever more." Other than missing the actual date by two days, Adams foresaw the future annual celebrations of independence.

Congress next turned its attention to Jefferson's draft of the Declaration of Independence, debating and editing it over the next two days,

July 3 and 4. The preamble would largely remain intact, with Congress making one change, from "inherent and inalienable rights" to "certain inalienable rights." Most of the Declaration, made up of an indictment of the King, laid out the justification for the colonists break with Great Britain, and provided the support needed to undertake the revolution. They would delete fully one-quarter of the draft, and strengthen other sections. Since no record survived of the process Congress used to edit Jefferson's version, historians can only speculate over the process they used. In the end, the work of Congress strengthened the draft prepared by Jefferson. Perhaps the most noteworthy deletion was the reference that the King was responsible for the slave trade in America. Jefferson would later write that this reference was deleted at the insistence of South Carolina and Georgia. But as David McCullough writes: "Very possibly there were many delegates from North and South, happy to see the passage omitted for the reason that it was patently absurd to hold the King responsible for horrors that, everyone knew, Americans...had brought upon themselves."[67] Always thin skinned, Jefferson chafed at the extensive changes made by Congress. Franklin, noticing his displeasure during the congressional session, leaned over and told him the story of a hat maker who had made up a sign that said: "John Thompson, hatter, makes and sells hats for ready money," with a picture of a hat next to the words. He decided to show the sign to some friends to get their input. One by one, they suggested changes. When they had finished, all that was left was his name, and the picture of the hat. We don't know if Franklin's story provided any solace, but Jefferson sent friends a copy of the original declaration so they could compare it to the copy that was finally approved by Congress on July 4. At some point later in his life, Jefferson must have gotten over the editing job (mutilation as he called it), since he listed the Declaration as one of the three great accomplishments in his life.[68]

Endnotes

1 Joseph J. Ellis, *American Creation,* (New York, 1997), p. 210

2 Brody, p. 20

3 Brody, p. 21

4 Willard Sterne Randall, *Thomas Jefferson: A Life,* (New York, 1993), p. 17

5 Randall, p. 18

6 Randall, p. 21 and Brody, p. 37

7 Randall, p. 23-24

8 Randall, p. 39

9 Randall, p. 47-48

10 Randall, p. 70-77

11 Joseph J. Ellis, *American Sphinx: The Character of Thomas Jefferson,* (New York, 1996), p 32

12 Randall, p. 142-147

13 Randall, p. 214

14 Ellis, *American Sphinx,* p. 35

15 McCullough, p. 119

16 Isaacson, p. 310

17 Ellis, *American Sphinx,* p. 56-57

18 Randall, p. 273

19 See Ellis, *American Sphinx,* p. 55-58 for a fuller discussion of the drafting of the declaration as being of secondary importance.

20 McCullough, p. 120

21 For the sources that Jefferson may have referred to in writing the declaration, see Randall, p. 272; Maier, p. 104; McCullough, p. 121; and Ellis, *American Sphinx,* p. 64-65

22 McCullough, p. 121

23 McCullough, p. 122 and Isaacson, p. 311-312

24 Honer and Hunt, p. 170

25 Gordon S. Wood, *Thomas Jefferson, Equality, and the Creation of Civil Society,* 64 Fordham L. Rev. 2133 (1996), http://ir.lawnet.fordham.edu/flr/vol64/iss5/1

26 McCullough, p. 377

27 Wood, *Thomas Jefferson,* p. 2140

28 Rakove, *Revolutionaries,* p. 305-307

29 Rakove, *Revolutionaries,* p. 305

30 Peter H. Lindert and Jeffrey G. Williamson, "American Incomes Before and After the

Revolution," National Bureau of Economic Research, July 2011 retrieved from http://www.nber.org/papers/w17211

31 Freeland C., *America, Land of Equals*, New York Time (2012, May 3), retrieved 8/28/2012 from http://www.nytimes.com/2012/05/04/us/o4iht-letter-o4.html?pagewanted=all

32 Adrienne Koch & William Peden (Ed.), *The Life and Selected Writings of Thomas Jefferson*, (New York, 1972), p. 649

33 Thomas Jefferson letter to James Madison, October 28, 1785, retrieved from http://press-pubs.uchicago.edu/founders/print_documents/v1ch15s32.html I became aware of this quote from an article published by Daly L. (2005), "Equality of Property is the Life of a Republican Government," *New Social Democrats*, retrieved 8/24/2012 from http://www.socialdems.com/page.asp?pid=1513

34 James Madison letter to Thomas Jefferson, June 19, 1786, retrieved from http://press-pubs.uchicago.edu/founders/print_documents/v1ch15s33.html

35 Madison J. (1792), "Parties," *National Gazette*, retrieved September 21, 2012 from http://www.constitution.org/jm/17920123_parties.txt

36 Wood, *Thomas Jefferson*, p. 2135

37 Daly, Equality of Property

38 Eric Foner, *The Story of American Freedom*, (New York, 1998), p. xx

39 Robert Lawson," Economic Freedom," *The Concise Encyclopedia of Economics*, 2008, retrieved May 7, 2013 from http://www.econlib.org/cgi-bin/printcee.pl

40 Ruy Teixeira and John Halpin, *The Origins and Evolution of Progressive Economics*, March 2011, retrieved May 7, 2013 from www.americanprogess.org

41 Foner, *Freedom*, p. 9

42 Foner, Freedom, p. 9

43 E.J. Dionne Jr., *Our Divided Political Heart*, (New York, 2012), p. 130-134

44 Ellis, *Brotherhood*, raises this point in lecture 6

45 Kathleen Kennedy Townsend, "The Pursuit of Happiness: What the Founders Meant – and Didn't," *The Atlantic*, June 2011, retrieved April 22, 2013 from http://www.theatlantic.com/business/print/2011/06/the-pursuit-of-happiness-what-the-founders-meant

46 Jon Meacham, "Free to Be Happy," *Time Magazine*, July 8 / 15, 2013, p. 40

47 Randall, p. 85

48 Honer and Hunt, p. 88

49 Chernow, p. 131

50 Jon Meacham, *American Gospel: God, the Founding Fathers, and the Making of a Nation*, (New York, 2006). P. 23

51 See Randall, p. 137-139 and 291-292 for more information on Jefferson's views on the relationship between religion and government.

52 All quotes are from Meacham, p. 28-29

53 Isaacson, p. 93-94

54 Chernow, p. 131-133

55 Meacham, p. 26

56 Meacham, p. 17-18

57 McCullough, p. 222

58 Woods, *Creation,* p. 24

59 Woods, *Creation,* p. 168

60 Woods, *Creation,* p. 169

61 Foner, *Freedom,* p. 17-18

62 See Maier, p. 198-200 on this point.

63 Foner, *Freedom* p. 20

64 See Dionne, p. 173-185 for a more complete discussion on these points.

65 Ellis, *American Sphinx,* p. 59; see also Ellis, *Brotherhood,* lecture 6 for the importance of the grievances section of the declaration.

66 The account in these paragraphs is drawn from McCullough, p 125-129 and Ferling, 172-175

67 Maier, p. 143-150 and McCullough, p. 134

68 Randall, p. 278-279

Chapter 5

The Failure of the First American Government / 1776 to 1783

"For, without certain revenues, a Government can have no power. That power which holds the purse-strings absolutely must rule."
– Alexander Hamilton, September 1780 –

The colonies had declared themselves free and independent states, but the question of nationhood was far from settled. The resistance to British taxation and the struggle for independence had arisen first in opposition to Parliament and then to central rule by the King and his various governments. It should not surprise us to learn that the first American government under the Articles of Confederation was weak, lacked the power to tax, and excluded an executive branch to carry out the policies of Congress. The states were not yet willing to give these elements of power over to a national government. Over the seven-year period from 1776 to 1783, the weakness of the central government resulted in financial catastrophe, endangered the war effort, and almost resulted in the destruction of the republic and the establishment of a military dictatorship.

Drafting the Articles of Confederation[1]

Although there had been early attempts to develop a plan of union during 1774 and 1775, none was comprehensive or dealt with the relationship between the central government and the colonies. Both Silas Deane and Ben Franklin put forward plans in 1775 that attempted to change the method of apportioning votes in Congress and for raising money. As previously discussed, voting in the Continental Congress was based on one vote per colony. Deane and Franklin's recommended approach was to switch to a system under which votes and expenses would be apportioned based on population, with larger colonies having a greater number of votes and more of the common expenses. The small colonies opposed this, fearing that the interests of larger colonies would dominate the national government. This contentious issue was finally resolved at the Constitutional Convention in 1787, when the large and small states developed a compromise.[2]

At the same time that Jefferson was assigned to a committee to prepare the Declaration of Independence, a separate committee headed by John Dickinson drafted the Articles of Confederation in the summer of 1776. The initial Dickinson draft reflected his concern that the colonies needed a strong national government to win the war and ensure that the colonies did not fall into disunion after independence was achieved. He proposed a national government with greater power than Congress would ultimately agree to. Rakove writes that Dickinson established a framework under which the confederation "would enjoy clear precedence over the rights of the states; that would be empowered to interfere in some of aspects of their internal police; and that would limit their ability to exercise powers inimical to the union." The draft provided for religious toleration in all of the new states, a provision that other members of the committee quickly removed, since not all of the new states shared the middle colonies' penchant for religious freedom. Dickinson also proposed that the central government have power over western lands and be given the ability to settle border disputes between the colonies. This was a divisive issue between those states that had claims to lands west of the Alleghenies, like Virginia, and those that did not, like Maryland.

The Dickinson plan did not give the confederation government the power to levy taxes directly on the people. Rather, Congress would requisition money from the states to fund the war effort and the cost of the union, an approach that would prove wholly inadequate for meeting the needs of the army. The proposed Articles required that at least nine states approve the use of any of its major powers, and that all states approve amendments. The Dickinson plan was more expansive than the Articles that were eventually approved, which underwent major modifications by the Congress as a whole. It would also prove difficult to get the final product ratified by the states.[3]

Congress debated the committee's draft of the Articles of Confederation in the summer of 1776 in the absence of Dickinson, who had resigned his position as a delegate. While they would accept the Committee's recommendation that voting be by state, and that expenses incurred in running the central government would be apportioned based on population, Congress would remove the central government's control of western lands. In addition, Dickinson had included a provision that prohibited one state from adopting measures that would discriminate against the residents of other states. This provision was also removed. Delegates to the Congress were beginning to realize that even this stripped down version of Confederation was unlikely to prove popular with the states. Disputes over voting remained, with the large states unhappy with the concept of equal voting, given they would pay the largest share for the costs of the war effort based on their larger population. Southern delegates also protested including slaves in the population numbers for purposes of taxation, threatening to end the confederation if they were included, and so the northern delegates capitulated on this issue. The topic of western lands continued to prove problematic as well. As Rakove writes, "During the debate of 1776 threats of disunion flowed freely. James Wilson warned that Pennsylvania would never confederate if Virginia clung to its western claims. The Virginia delegates replied that those claims were inviolable."[4] Given the problems of representation, expenses, western lands, and the overarching concerns of the war effort, Congress placed further discussion of the Articles of Confederation on hold for the next eight months.

In October 1777, the American Army, under General Gates, had won a major victory over the British at Saratoga, New York, forcing the surrender of Burgoyne's army of 6,000 troops. Congress saw an opportunity to capitalize on the victory and secure a formal alliance with the French, who had already been providing supplies and money toward the war effort. Congress also needed to deal with the serious problem of inflation caused by issuing continental currency without sufficient backing of tax collections from the states. Delegates to the Congress felt that both of these efforts would be strengthened once they approved a draft of the Articles.[5] In November of 1777, Congress finally approved a draft of the Articles of Confederation. One issue that was finally resolved was where sovereignty would be located, whether in the states, in the national government, or in some combination of the two (which would be the case for the Constitution of 1787). A newly arrived member of Congress, Thomas Burke, made a strong argument that the states should be considered sovereign, and an article was added to that effect. It was the final death knell for any attempt to make the central government a true national endeavor, but it was the most that proponents could achieve given the fractious nature of the relationship between the states.

Virginia was the first state to approve the Articles, in December of 1777. By February 1779, with Delaware's approval, twelve states had ratified the plan of confederation. Unfortunately, Maryland refused to ratify the Articles because they had not provided Congress with the power over western lands. Maryland, which had no claims to such lands, wanted its residents to have the same ability to purchase land west of the Alleghenies as the residents of other states, like Virginia. The war effort would continue without a formal structure of government until 1781, when Virginia removed its claims to western lands and Maryland finally ratified the Articles of Confederation.

Why did the first American Constitution result in such a weak central government? First and foremost, the majority of people still viewed their nation as being the state that they came from and not America, which did not yet elicit any sense of overarching national loyalty as Great Britain had prior to the war. As historian Forrest McDonald observed, when Patrick Henry said, "I am not a Virginian, but an American," everyone knew he was engaging in rhetoric. When Jefferson said, "Virginia, sir, is my country," everyone knew he meant it.[6] A small number of the elite had gotten to know one another from their service in the Continental Congress, but this did not extend to the mass of people, who had never traveled outside their state or even their region, and did not have any identification with other states or the United States as a whole. Even among the elite, there was only a small group, primarily the merchant class from the middle colonies that Dickinson came from, along with Washington and others from the Virginia planter class that had a nationalist point of view. In order to preserve the unity needed to win the war, the nationalists, who were outnumbered, chose not to pursue a stronger national government that could fracture what little consensus existed. [7]

The second major reason is that the colonies were essentially fighting a war against a strong central government represented by the British. Many Americans did not want to see the strong British government replaced by a strong American one. Although the Continental Congress had acted as a true national government for the colonies, taking over the war effort, borrowing money, providing direction to the colonies in the formation of their governments, and issuing a currency, the support for this approach began to wane as individual state rivalries began to reemerge in 1777. Some of the founders, like Richard Henry Lee of Virginia, were early supporters of states' rights, with sovereignty located in the states and the central government serving more as a "league of friendship" than as a true national government. To these men, centralized power was never to be trusted, since it led to despotic government and the loss of liberty. Lee would later oppose the ratification of the Constitution because it shifted too much power to the federal government.[8]

The fear of centralized power was deeply rooted in the American psyche, and was one of the core ideological elements that fostered resistance to British rule. Many of the founders were influenced by the writings of the radical Whigs of England, also known as the Countrymen, as they have been referred to by historians. [9] The radical Whigs believed that liberty was endangered by the government of Robert Walpole, who acted as the first British Prime Minister for a span of twenty years beginning in 1722. One of the hallmarks of Walpole's rule was the use of patronage to influence Parliament, which led to charges of corruption by his opponents.

The radical Whigs believed that Walpole's government had brought the mixed Constitution of England, under which the King, the aristocracy and the commons were represented, out of balance. This balance kept any one group from becoming too powerful and endangering liberty. While the views of the radical Whigs held little sway in Great

Britain, they were widely read in the colonies. As Chapter 2 discusses in greater detail, the colonists viewed the taxation policies of the British government as "a deliberate conspiracy by ministers of the Crown to take away their liberties, step by step, and reduce them to slavery."[10] Given this, the colonists distrusted the type of centralized power, which the British system represented, and lodged more of their power in state governments as opposed to the national government. They also stripped their state governors of most power, placing it in the hands of the legislature, which was thought to be most responsive to the people. To some in the founding generation, controlling and dispersing power as a means to protect liberty was the true lesson of the spirit of 1776.

But the fear of centralized power came with its own drawbacks. The weakness of the central government would result in extensive problems that would hamper the war effort. The most important of these were the inability to finance the war, and the lack of a strong executive under the Articles, which meant that no one was in charge of administering the war.

Major Problems – Money and Administration

In the absence of a constitutionally approved national government, the Congress needed to address the financing of the war effort. Even had the Articles been approved, Congress would have lacked the ability to levy taxes, and would have needed to rely on requisitions to the states to pay for the war, funding not readily forthcoming. In addition, the Articles had not provided for an executive to implement congressional policies. Both of these deficiencies led to serious problems with national finances, causing major hardships in the everyday lives of average people and in providing supplies and pay to the army.

As an introduction to this section, which deals with the financial problems facing the United States during the Revolutionary War, I have included a brief primer on money.[11] Money began as a medium of exchange. In a barter economy, farmers, for example, could trade a certain volume of wheat for clothing or other finished products. However, it was not always convenient for a farmer to carry bushels of wheat to market, so a desirable commodity such as gold or silver was introduced as a medium of exchange. Gold or silver coins were easily portable and had an intrinsic value that made them desirable. This was the earliest stage of money. Those forms that someone can exchange into a valuable commodity are sometimes referred to as hard currency or specie.

Later, governments and banks became the main source for the creation of money. Governments initially assumed the job of the coinage of precious metals, and the printing of paper money or notes that were often redeemable for a certain amount of hard currency. Banks created money through the process of loaning other depositors money. The person who deposits money in a bank continues to have the right to withdraw his money at any time, while the borrower can access the loan to make purchases, thereby increasing the supply of money. This arrangement works so long as the bank maintains a certain level of cash reserves and the depositors do not attempt to withdraw their funds at the same time, often referred to as a bank run. This can occur when depositors fear for the solvency of a bank and everyone tries to withdraw their money at the same time. Classic bank runs happened during the Great Depression of the 1930s and during the financial crisis of 2008. To avoid bank runs, governments since the Great Depression have typically insured a certain level of deposits, providing assurance to depositors that their money is safe. In the United States today, the federal government insures up to $250,000 per individual deposit.

Money in modern economies is no longer redeemable in gold or another precious commodity. The global gold standard only lasted from the mid-1860s until the Great Depression. The United States totally abandoned the gold standard in 1971, when President Nixon no longer allowed foreign governments to exchange dollars for gold. In the modern world, central banks, such as the Federal Reserve in the United States, control the supply of money and they require that banks maintain certain levels of cash reserves. A central bank also controls the money supply through the short-term interest rates they charge other banks for lending. In the modern world, money is backed by the economic activity of an individual country, and not by an artificial amount of a precious metal. So long as the government only allows the money supply to grow in relation to economic activity, inflation can be kept in check.

A government can foster inflation, a general rise in prices, by printing too much money too quickly. A precious metal standard, in which paper money can be redeemed for a certain amount of gold and silver, can limit the amount of money in circulation. But inflation can occur even under a hard currency system, which occurred in Europe in the 1500s when explorers found silver in Mexico and Peru, causing a general rise in prices. During the phase when money was convertible into a commodity, inflation could also occur during emergencies or war. Governments had to borrow more money than their metal reserves would support, so they would go off the gold standard. Inflation was often the result. Or during an emergency, a government might borrow more than their ability to repay (based on levels of taxation and the size of the economy), thereby causing inflated prices for goods and services and depreciation in the currency. This is what happened during the Revolutionary War.

Prior to the revolution, the colonies had very little in the way of hard currency, and no banking system. The money supply was inadequate for the economic activity taking place. To deal with this, the colonies printed paper money, called bills of credit, and loaned these out at a low interest rate. The loans were typically secured by a mortgage on real property. These notes often ended up in circulation, as the borrower used them to purchase various goods and services, so they were often considered legal tender. (The term "legal tender" means currency that must be lawfully accepted as payment for a debt.) The money issued by the colonial governments was not convertible into gold or silver, but was limited by the amount of taxes that the government could collect within a reasonable time. For example, if taxes produced $5,000 a year, then the colony would redeem $20,000 in bills of credit over the following four years. As historian E. James Ferguson stated, "Since the money was created and upheld solely by political acts, confidence in the government was essential to its value. The holder had to be confident that withdrawals would be continuous and the future governments would have both the will and the ability to collect taxes." Prior to the war, governments issued only the amount of paper money that could be redeemed with the taxes that would be collected within the next few years.[12] During the Revolutionary War, the inability to collect taxes, combined with the extraordinary costs of the war, caused the value of the currency to depreciate and prices to escalate rapidly.

In order to fund the war, Congress printed paper money. Given the lack of financial backing in the form of taxes for the paper money issued, and a British blockade that resulted in the loss of trade, the currency quickly depreciated and inflation became rampant. Initially, the issuance of debt and the emission of paper money to fund the war worked well, since Congress issued only a relatively small amount. The first bills of credit (paper money) they issued, in the face amount of $25 million, produced $23 million for the war effort. This was near the limit of what the economy could absorb without causing inflation, but Congress had no ability to redeem any of the paper money then in circulation. The war effort still needed funding, and by 1778, Congress issued bills with a face value of $66 million that would only yield $24 million in real purchasing power, as inflation exploded and investors lost confidence in the ability of Congress to ensure repayment. From 1775 to 1779, Ferguson estimates that the Continental Treasury disbursed a total of $263 million to pay for the war, although due to depreciation of the currency, it purchased only $80 million in needed goods and services. Though figures vary from different sources, Congress issued somewhere over $200 million in paper money to cover the war and other incidental expenses during this period.[13]

They covered the balance of expenses by issuing governmental bonds, called loan certificates, and borrowing from foreign governments. The bonds carried an interest rate initially set at 4 percent. When this proved insufficient to raise enough money, Congress raised the rate to 6 percent. By the end of the war in 1783, the public debt of the United States stood at $43 million. Merchants in the middle colonies held most of this debt. Foreign aid also helped fund the war, although the government used most of these loans to directly purchase needed weapons and supplies overseas.[14]

The war expenses far exceeded anything the colonies had experienced before. In 1779 alone, the cost of the war effort exceeded $100 million. While the states could levy taxes and should have been withdrawing currency as they did so, they also struggled to raise sufficient revenue to support the Continental paper being issued. Meanwhile, inflation was running rampant, making life miserable for ordinary people. By 1779, prices were eight times higher than they had been in 1776. To provide some context, this would be the equivalent of a gallon of milk rising from $3.40 in 2013 to $27 by 2016. Wages for artisans and laborers could not keep up, and even many congressmen felt the pain and were forced to share lodgings and dine at boarding houses. Meanwhile, the most affluent members of society managed to avoid any of the hardships experienced by the great mass of people. Washington was shocked when he went to confer with Congress in Philadelphia in the winter of 1778-1779. "Having watched helplessly for more than a year as his hungry, unpaid, ill-clad, and poorly housed soldiers suffered, and sometimes died of deprivation, he was aghast at the sumptuous lifestyles of the affluent in this city. The rich wore the finest clothing, rode in elegant carriages attended by servants in livery, and dined at tables laden with every conceivable delicacy," according to one historian.[15]

Given the runaway inflation that occurred, and the extraordinary costs of the war, Congress was unable to meet the demands of the army for supplies and pay. In 1777, Congress requisitioned $5 million from the states to be paid into the Continental Treasury. The states raised some of the needed money, but not in the amount requested. The states also retained much of what was raised for their own needs rather than distributing it to Congress. Congress had also requested that the states begin to remove some of the currency in circulation, which did not occur, and for a brief time attempted to implement a system of price controls. Since Congress lacked the power either to raise taxes on its own or to compel the states to follow its demands, the financial system of the country began to collapse. As Rakove argues, "It is certainly true that the states would never have ratified the Articles had they contained such provisions, and that during the 1780s the absence of these powers contributed substantially to the growing weakness of the confederation."[16]

In addition to the lack of money and rampant inflation, no executive branch existed to implement the policies that the Congress did approve. The government had no president in place with the authority to execute policy, and no Treasury Secretary or Federal Reserve chairman to rescue the financial system of the country. In addition, the system for procuring supplies for the army was in disarray, leading to inadequate food and clothing, and no pay for the soldiers. There was also a sense that the purchasing agents charged with procuring supplies for the army, primarily merchants who also continued with their private business affairs, were corrupt and engaged in graft. The purchasing agents were paid through a fixed commission rather than given a salary, and their incomes were derived from the amount of expenditures they incurred, giving them no incentive to reduce the costs of supplies.[17]

Since the Articles of Confederation had still not been ratified by 1780, and Congress was essentially bankrupt, it devolved even more power to the states, requiring them to provide supplies and to pay the army directly. Congress also devalued the currency at a rate of 40 to 1, reducing the $200 plus million in circulation to $5 million, and stopped printing the Continental currency, which was essentially worthless, giving rise to the term "not worth a Continental." But the states, too, were near bankruptcy, and lacked the ability to respond to the new demands being placed on them. They had already levied $85 million in taxes on their citizens, a figure almost 100 times that which had been levied prior to the war. The states could not tax at any greater rate, and most began to seize and sell the property of loyalists to Great Britain. The removal of price controls at the state level, done as a means to alleviate food shortages, led to another rapid increase in prices. By 1780, the United States had reached the low point of the revolution, both in terms of its financial affairs and in terms of the war effort.[18]

The Confederacy might have avoided financial collapse if Congress had been given the authority to levy taxes. They could not have raised taxes to a level sufficient to cover all of the expenses of the war, since that level of taxation would have exceeded the wealth generated by the American economy at the time of the revolution. But the cost of war is almost always too high to be paid from current taxes and governments typically borrow to fund such extraordinary costs. In the late 1600s, England was involved in the Nine Years War. To fund ever rapidly growing military expenditures, Great Britain borrowed heavily, and interest payments on its debt utilized almost one-third of its revenues.[19] The United States has also financed its major wars through borrowing. The following chart shows governmental debt as a percent of Gross Domestic Product (GDP) in the years before and after the Civil War, World War I, and World War II.

	Debt to GDP %
Civil War	
1860	1.9%
1865	31.0%
World War I	
1916	2.7%
1919	33.4%
World War II	
1941	43.5%
1945	112.7%
Source: Congressional Budget Office, December 2005	
Long Term Budget Outlook	
http://www.cbo.gov/publications/21728	

If the United States had been generating a steady flow of taxes during the revolution, it might have been able to borrow a larger portion of the money needed to fight the war, or, in the alternative, been in a position to remove more of the paper money in circulation, thereby avoiding the worst elements of price inflation and currency depreciation. If investors and foreign governments had the confidence in the federal government to repay them, debt financing may have been feasible. As economists George A. Akerlof and Robert J. Shiller argue, much of economic activity is driven by "animal spirits," non-economic motives that compel human behavior. Chief among these animal spirits is confidence. "In good times, people trust... But then when the confidence disappears, the tide goes out."[20] By 1780, there was no confidence left in the American economy or in the ability of the Confederation Congress to manage the financial affairs of the country.

One of those who saw the financial problems of the country clearly was young Alexander Hamilton, who by the early 1780s argued for the creation of a modern financial system for the United States. Hamilton had served as Washington's aide since early in the war and he saw first-hand the problems a weak national government had wrought. In a letter to Robert Morris, named by the Congress as the new superintendent of public finance in 1781, Hamilton argued that they needed to restore the public credit of the new country. Historian Richard Sylla writes that Hamilton saw the need for "sound public finances (tax revenues to pay public expenses including the army, as well as interest on old public debts, which would make it possible to borrow more money), a stable currency, a banking system, a central bank he called the 'Bank of the United States,' securities markets, and corporations."[21] Congress would make various proposals to stabilize the country's financial system during the 1780s, including amendments to the Articles that granted Congress the power to levy taxes, but none proved successful, largely due to the requirement that all amendments be approved by all thirteen states.

Washington and the Continental Army

Ellis, in his book *Revolutionary Summer: The Birth of American Independence*, provides an account for how the "political and military experiences were two sides of a single story."[22] And indeed, the political decisions being made had a significant impact on the war and the Continental Army, which somehow found a way to survive despite the continuing shortages it faced. Washington's army had forced Howe to abandon Boston in the spring of 1776 when they took the high ground of Dorchester Heights and pointed their artillery at the British army. Howe then moved on to New York, and Washington followed. The American Army suffered a major defeat there and was forced to abandon New York, but Howe inexplicably allowed the Continental forces to escape to New Jersey in November of 1776. Washington won a small victory with his crossing of the Delaware on Christmas night, surprising the Hessian troops camped at Trenton, which lifted the spirits of the Continental forces.

The first major victory in the war was not Washington's however, but belonged to his main rival, General Horatio Gates. Gates surrounded the British forces under the command of General Burgoyne in the summer of 1777 and forced the surrender of what remained of Burgoyne's troops at Saratoga. The victory led to attempts by Gates and his supporters to undermine and replace Washington, an effort that would prove unsuccessful. While Washington had made many military mistakes in the battle of New York, he was still the clear leader of the Continental Army.

Unlike many of the political leaders, whose perspective remained parochial, the soldiers were beginning to develop a national identity. As Washington biographer Ron Chernow writes, "The Continental Army was the purest expression of the new, still inchoate country, a working laboratory for melding together citizen soldiers from various states and creating a composite American identity." Washington and his army were the first to recognize that the Revolutionary War was not just about independence, but also about bringing into existence a new and unified nation.[23] While the winter pauses in the war caused some of the greatest hardships, they also demonstrated the great perseverance of the men that made up the Continental Army. In December 1777, Washington made camp at Valley Forge, twenty miles from Philadelphia. On the road there, he spotted bloody footprints from those men who were barefoot. "To see men without Cloathes to cover their nakedness, without Blankets to lay on, without Shoes, by which their Marches might be traced by the blood from their feet is a mark of Patience and obedience which in my opinion can scarce be paralle'd," Washington observed.[24] The troops constructed over two thousand small log cabins, measuring just over 200 square feet that a dozen men lived in during the harsh winter. Food was in short supply, with the men sometimes eating "fire cakes," which consisted of a combination of cooked flour and water. A doctor who was there described it as follows: "Poor food---hard lodging---cold weather---fatigue---nasty clothes---nasty cookery---vomit half my time---smoke out of my senses---the devils in it---I can't endure it." Disease was rampant, and some 2,000 men lost their lives.[25] All suffered equally, both enlisted men as well as the officers. Washington did not return to Mount Vernon, choosing to stay with his men, although he did live in a nearby home owned by Isaac Potts.

It is peculiar that the Continental Army would suffer such deprivation when they were camped in a fertile area considered America's breadbasket. From the perspective of the twenty-first century, we often think that the American Revolution was universally popular, but the local farmers were a patchwork of loyalists, patriots, and those who were simply indifferent, and their first priority was to feed their own families. Those farmers with surpluses preferred to sell their supplies to the British, who could pay in pounds sterling, rather than the American Army, who could only offer worthless Continental paper. The lack of supply was further exacerbated by the collapse of the quartermaster system in late 1777, when its head, Thomas Mifflin, resigned and his replacement proved to be incompetent.[26]

The rank and file soldiers mostly consisted of the poorest members of society, indentured servants, immigrants, and the working class. Many of them enlisted for the duration, not so much from a commitment to a revolutionary ideal but because they had few other opportunities. The officers were different, acting as a band of brothers. "They had come to see themselves — and Washington encouraged this perception — as the chosen few who preserved and protected the original ethos of 1775-76 after it had died out among the bulk of the American citizenry," according to Ellis.[27] Washington had grown disillusioned by the lack of support from the population, and the inability of the Congress and the states to provide for the army. He also fulminated against those who made a profit at the expense of his beloved troops, and thought it the intent of "the speculators — various tribes of money makers — and stock jobbers of all denominations to continue the war effort for their own private emolument, without considering their avarice and thirst for gain must plunge everything…in one common ruin."[28]

It is surprising that the Continental Army did not simply mutiny given the harsh circumstances during the winter of 1778 at Valley Forge. Some did leave, but by March 1778, reenlistments had increased the size of the force that would leave the winter encampment to around 12,000 men. The French also supported the American war effort, signing the Franco-American treaties in February of 1778. Although the French supported the American forces, the extraordinary costs of supplying and paying the army continued throughout 1778. During a two-month period alone in that year, the army used 4.5 million pounds of beef and flour, while their horses required 253,000 bushels of grain and 2.5 million pounds of hay.[29]

Washington and his officers faced a choice as they left Valley Forge that spring. Should they confront the British Army in either New York or Philadelphia in a full frontal assault, or turn the war into a defensive struggle designed to deny the British control of the countryside. The officers preferred the offensive strategy, even though Washington knew that he would need an army of 40,000 plus men to successfully pursue such a strategy. Washington, who also preferred the offensive option, decided to wait on events, which was another means of adopting a defensive strategy. It would prove over time to be the correct choice.[30]

During the summer of 1778, Washington followed and harassed the British Army as they moved from Philadelphia back to New York. The British retreat to New York was a precursor for their new strategy of focusing the war effort in the South late in 1778, a move that would finally force Maryland to ratify the Articles of Confederation. In June, a portion of the Continental troops engaged the retreating British Army at Monmouth in New Jersey. It was an indecisive battle, the last major one for Washington for the next three years.[31] The war had been full of ups and downs, but the period from the battle at Monmouth in 1778 to the decisive victory at Yorktown in 1781 proved to be a very trying time for Washington, a man of action who would have preferred to confront the enemy more directly. As Ellis writes: "The thirty months between the fall of 1778 and the spring of 1781 felt to Washington like one long downward dip, the most frustrating and difficult period of his life, the true testing time for both himself and what he believed he was fighting for."[32]

Washington had come to the realization that the government established by the Articles of Confederation was inadequate. He saw that the British spoke and acted as one nation, had the authority to levy taxes, and could raise an army and navy designed to fight a sustained war. Washington became one of the earliest advocates for an expanded national government, in large part because he did not believe the war was winnable given the political conditions that existed under the Articles. "Certain I am that unless Congress speaks in a more decisive tone; unless they are vested with powers by the several States competent to the great purposes of War, or assume them as a matter of right…that our Cause is lost. We can no longer drudge on in the old way. I see one head gradually changing into thirteen," Washington wrote in 1780.[33]

The Articles of Confederation Approved

The southern strategy adopted by the British placed not only Washington but Congress and the southern states under great pressure. Washington was not alone in thinking that the period from late 1778 until 1781 was the low point for the war. The mood among the political leadership and the general population was much the same. The young country was financially bankrupt, the economy depressed, runaway inflation a major problem, and the war effort was stalled. Congress had tried to turn over the needs of the army to the states, but they too were unable to raise sufficient revenue to meet those needs.

The British used their occupation of New York as the jumping off point for a series of military operations against the South. In May of 1780, Charleston fell, and an invasion of North Carolina appeared imminent. The political leadership in Virginia knew it would soon suffer the same fate. James Madison, who had recently joined the Congress, and Thomas Jefferson, who was the governor of Virginia, both agreed on the need to ratify the Articles. Virginia finally relinquished its claims to western lands, so long as Congress also rejected all private claims. Maryland, with its long coastline and large inward waterways along the Chesapeake Bay, felt threatened by the British navy. They reached out to the French for naval assistance. In return, the French insisted that they ratify the Articles, which Maryland did in February

1781. The long-stalled Articles of Confederation finally went into effect on March 1, 1781.[34]

By this point, some in Congress already believed that the Articles provided too little power to the central government. The Articles described the union as a "league of friendship," an alliance of sovereign states. In early 1781, many feared that the weakness of the United States would cause France to seek an end to hostilities. John Adams informed the Congress of French concerns that it was involved in an unwinnable war, and that other European powers were considering a peace conference to mediate the conflict. If the United States were forced to end the war at this point, the British would hold New York and most of the South and stand in the way of the future settlement of the west.[35] With this in mind, Congress began to consider ways and methods to strengthen the central government.

A number of recommendations came out of the various congressional committees, some of which were implemented and others that were ignored. A committee led by Madison, that also included James Duane and James Varnum, suggested that Congress had "implied powers" to compel the states to act, and proposed that a new article be added allowing Congress to use military force as necessary to "compel…States to fulfill their federal engagements." Varnum, who had served as a general officer in the war, was one of a number of former soldiers who had joined the Congress and saw the need for a strong national government. Congress never enacted his proposal, nor a variety of other measures designed to strengthen the central government. While a group of nationalists in Congress was interested in strengthening the government, a majority of the delegates still opposed such actions, believing it was inimical to the purposes of the revolution.[36]

Congress did agree to establish four executive departments: Foreign Affairs, Finance, War, and Marine. They also finally proposed an amendment to the Articles that would allow for the collection of a 5 percent tax on all imports, known as the impost. Robert Morris, then 47, was appointed Minister of Finance, an office he assumed in May 1781.

Robert Morris was born in England in 1734 and immigrated to America with his father when he was thirteen years old. A successful businessman, he made a fortune through military contracts during the French and Indian War. By 1776, he may have been the wealthiest man in America. He settled in Pennsylvania and as the Revolutionary War approached, he became allied with Dickinson and the moderate faction in the Continental Congress, preferring a path of reconciliation with the British. But when that proved impossible, he signed the Declaration of Independence. In his role in Congress, Morris also provided great personal financial assistance to the Continental Army during the early phases of the war, procuring supplies and arms that helped Washington in his capture of the Hessian troops at Trenton.[37]

Morris was a controversial figure despised by some because he continued his private business affairs during the war while serving in Congress. A large man who stood over six feet tall, he was arrogant and overtly ambitious during a time in history when most people considered it unseemly to act in this way. Although he had a strong reputation for financial acumen, some saw his business practices as self-serving and at times dishonest. During the war, he sold food to the French Army, since they had hard currency, even though American troops were starving. Thomas Paine thought he was corrupt, a war privateer, although a congressional committee absolved him of any wrongdoing. The Virginian's distrusted him due to his business background with the largest mercantile house in Philadelphia, a position they saw as akin to the British factor system that had placed so many of them in debt. Despite the controversies that swirled around him, Congress asked Morris to serve as Superintendent of Finance, since many believed he was the one man who could tackle the major financial problems facing the country. He drove a hard bargain, requesting power not just over finances, but also over other aspects of government. As historian Richard Beeman phrased it, he was the closest thing to a "prime minister, British style, America ever had."[38]

Morris proposed a multistep financial program to rescue the country's finances. First was the establishment of a national bank, the Bank of North America. Morris was able to convince the Congress to charter the Bank in 1781. He opened the Bank in January 1782 with an initial capital investment of $400,000, most of which came in the form of a loan of hard currency from France, with the balance from wealthy investors. Notes issued by the Bank could be used to pay both state taxes and congressional requisitions, and were intended to, over time, provide a stable currency that would replace the now worthless Continental paper. We should not confuse the Bank's role with that of a modern central bank like the Federal Reserve, which issues the official currency of the nation and controls the money supply. The notes issued by the Bank were not considered legal tender for the payment of private debts.[39]

The heart of the Morris plan was the assumption of a portion of the state's debt, to be funded with the impost and other new taxes. Morris estimated the total debt to be held at the national level at around $25 million. (This figure is based on the estimate that Morris made at the time, and varies from the official $43 million figure that the U.S. Bureau of the Public Debt reports on its Web site). The impost tax would cover approximately 25 percent of the annual debt payments of $2 million, with the balance expected to come from a land tax of $1 per 100 acres and other excise taxes. The Morris plan, if adopted, would have provided the new national government with the means to pay down its debt and to provide for a stable currency, but it was never approved. Ellis writes that "Morris was attempting, on his own, to impose a national economic architecture on a political foundation that vested sovereignty in the states." The final act of the war was taking place at about the same time as Morris announced his plan, thereby lessening the perceived sense of urgency for an already unpopular national tax.[40]

The War Comes to an End

Washington had long been obsessed with retaking New York, thinking it would be the final and decisive battle in the war. He had hesitated attacking the British Army there because he simply lacked the manpower. But Count Rochambeau, who was in charge of the 6,000-man French Army, disagreed. Due to the inability of Congress and the states to provide the supplies and men needed, Washington's army was too small to take on the British in New York, even with French assistance. Rochambeau directed that the French navy, which was moving north from the Caribbean, instead sail for the Chesapeake. The French navy, under the command of Admiral de Grasse, had a fleet of twenty-nine ships and an additional 3,200 troops that were due to arrive off the Chesapeake by September 3, 1781. The British Army, under the command of Lord Cornwallis, had created havoc in the Virginia countryside. The French saw an opportunity to confront the British in Virginia.[41]

Washington finally realized the great opportunity the arrival of the French fleet would provide for a major American victory. He requested from Morris a fleet of thirty double-decker transport vessels to move the army south. Because the government had no means of borrowing money, Morris engineered loans based on his personal credit, ensuring that the troops would be adequately supplied and transported to Virginia.[42]

In August of 1781, Cornwallis moved his army of 9,000 men to the eastern tip of the Yorktown peninsula, ultimately getting them trapped between the French navy and the armies of Washington and Rochambeau, which totaled over 19,000 men. The battle would ensue as a typical European siege, with the French Army leading the way. Washington and his men were not experienced in this type of warfare, as Rochambeau noted when he said that the Americans conducted themselves with zeal and courage but were "totally ignorant of the operations of a siege." Cornwallis was forced to surrender his entire army on October 19, 1781. This was the first and only time Washington negotiated the surrender of an opponent. Yorktown would prove to be the final and decisive battle in the war, although at the time it was unclear that this was the case, and Washington worried that the King would continue with the war, despite reports from London and Paris that the British were conceding that their American colonies were lost. Finally, in the spring of 1782, the North government collapsed, and was replaced by one willing to negotiate a peace agreement.[43] While the land war was largely concluded at Yorktown, the British continued operations at sea as peace negotiations moved forward, and American trade continued to suffer for much of 1782. The British also continued to occupy New York and other parts of the United States, which meant that the Continental Army remained in the field. But the British calculus had changed, and they no longer believed they could completely defeat the Continental Army or conquer and subdue the United States.

As the war gradually came to a close, the political battle to find a way to fund the central government continued. During 1781, eight states approved the impost. Morris had achieved some success in stabilizing the American financial situation, aided by a $2 million loan from Holland that John Adams had secured. Morris also strongly lobbied the states for approval of the impost. By the end of the legislative session in 1782, all states had approved the impost with the exception of Rhode Island and Georgia, which was still under British occupation and did not have the ability to vote.[44]

As 1782 unfolded, the victory at Yorktown and the ensuing round of peace negotiations that took place between the British and the Americans made it more difficult for the Morris plan of finance to receive unanimous state approval. The first setback occurred when tiny Rhode Island rejected the impost at the end of 1782. For Rhode Island, this was largely an economic issue. The state was heavily dependent on the importation of goods, and needed to retain the taxes it generated from imports to pay for its own sizable debt. Congress decided to send a delegation to see if they could get Rhode Island to reconsider, but they soon cancelled the delegation's journey upon learning that Virginia, which had previously voted to approve the tax, had rescinded their approval of the impost. With the war essentially concluded, the main rationale for a stronger national government imbued with the power to tax was beginning to run into significant opposition. The sense that the war had been fought against a strong central power began to once again strengthen. Many of the arguments brought forward in opposition to the impost would foreshadow those used to protest the Constitution. It would pit those who favored the development of a strong national government against those who preferred that power be focused at the state level.[45]

Morris became increasingly desperate, since without the impost the government had no means to pay the obligations that the Congress had incurred to foreign and domestic creditors, not to mention a way to pay the soldiers. At the end of 1782, a three-member army delegation arrived in Philadelphia to prod Congress to make good on a commitment it had made in 1780 to provide half-pay pensions to officers for life. The army delegation also lobbied for the payment of long-delayed salaries for the troops, some of whom had not been paid in over six years. Washington and his army were encamped in Newburgh, New York, spending another cold and snowy winter without pay or adequate supplies. "The army, as usual, are without pay and a great part of the soldiery without shirts. And tho(ugh) the patience of them is equally threadbare, the states seem perfectly indifferent to their cries," Washington wrote in a letter to Major General John Armstrong. The discontent of the army was palpable, and Washington was becoming increasingly concerned that the officers who had been able to suppress previous mutinies may themselves choose to lead a rebellion. In fact, a letter in May 1781 from one of Washington's officers had urged him to seize power and install himself as king so that the army could receive justice, advice that he rejected.[46]

Alexander Hamilton, who had been Washington's aid-de-camp, was now a member of Congress. He, along with Gouverneur Morris and Robert Morris, decided to fan the flames by using the threat of a military coup by the army as a means to place pressure on Congress to approve the overall plan of finance. Hamilton, in a letter to Washington in February of 1783, wrote, "The claims of the army, urged with moderation but with firmness, may operate on those weak minds which are influenced by their apprehensions rather than their judgment...But the difficulty will be to keep a complaining and suffering army within the bounds of moderation." Although Washington agreed with the need to strengthen the central government and provide a stronger financial system, he also immediately saw the danger that could ensue from attempting to use the army in this way, responding to Hamilton that the army was "a dangerous instrument to play with."[47]

Washington must have sensed the danger that Hamilton's proposal would cause. On March 11, radicals led by General Horatio Gates, Washington's longtime rival, called a meeting in Newburgh to plot a potential military coup. Washington learned of the meeting and had it cancelled, and then scheduled a meeting for all officers for March 16. At this meeting, Washington solidified his position as one of the unique figures in history, a man who did not allow his own ambitions to overshadow the needs of the newly emerging nation. A lesser man may have used the events at Newburgh to declare himself military dictator or King and assumed all power. But Washington's commitment to a republican form of government was clear, based on the speech he delivered at Newburgh. Ellis writes, "His central message was that any attempted coup by the army was simultaneously a repudiation of the principles for which they had been fighting and an assault on his own integrity. Whereas Cromwell and later Napoleon made themselves synonymous with the revolution in order to justify the assumption of dictatorial power, Washington made himself synonymous with the American Revolution in order to declare that it was incompatible with dictatorial power."[48]

In his speech at Newburgh, delivered before 500 assembled officers, Washington emphasized how he had always stood with the army: "If my conduct heretofore has not evinced to you that I have been a faithful friend to the Army, my declaration of it at this moment would be equally unavailing and improper. But as I was among the first who embarked on the cause of our common country. As I have never left your side one moment, but when called from you on public duty. As I have been the constant companion and witness of your Distresses, and not among the last to feel and acknowledge your Merits. As I have ever my own Military reputation as inseparably connected to the Army...it can scarcely be supposed...that I am indifferent to its interests." He went on to indict those who were attempting to promote a coup, cautioning against "this dreadful alternative, of either deserting our Country in the extremist hour of her distress, or turning our Arms against it…has something so shocking in it, that humanity revolts at the idea." He recommended that the officers show patience, that Congress would ultimately do what was right. Washington sensed that although the speech was powerful, some officers remained unconvinced. He ended his remarks to the officers by reading a letter from Congressman Joseph Jones, who was sympathetic to the plight of the army. Washington struggled seeing the words, which were barely legible. Donning a pair of glasses, something none of them had ever seen him wear, he said: "Gentleman, you will permit me to put on my spectacles, for I have not only grown gray, but almost blind in the service of my country." Many of the officers began to weep, and the threatened military coup ended, both by Washington's speech, but also by this small but important gesture.[49] Historian Richard Beeman writes that Washington's performance at Newburgh was one of those seminal moments in American history, on par with the Constitutional Convention and Lincoln's Gettysburg Address, and proved decisive for the future direction of the nation.[50] Washington's assurance to the troops that Congress would do what was right ultimately proved correct when the officers received five years of full pay in lieu of half pay for life.

In March of 1783, a draft peace treaty with Great Britain, which American envoys Adams, Franklin, and John Jay had negotiated, reached Congress. The trio had ignored the instructions they had received from Congress in June 1781 to follow the lead of the French in the negotiations, recognizing that France would be only too happy if the United States were its vassal state. The Treaty of Paris, as signed in September of 1783, achieved all that the young country had hoped for. Not only did the British recognize American independence, but also the boundary of its territory would extend to the Mississippi River in the west, with a northern boundary established where Congress had wanted it. British forces were required to leave American soil, and loyalists received no compensation.[51]

The arrival of peace would further split those who favored a stronger central government from those who preferred to keep power at the state level. Those who preferred a weak central government had prevailed in the debate over the Articles of Confederation, establishing a "league of friendship" among the states rather than a strong national government. Those who opposed a stronger central government had some powerful arguments on their side. The debate over the impost revealed many of these arguments and was, in many ways, a rehearsal for the great debate that would ensue in 1787 over ratification of the Constitution. The main fear of those opposed to the impost was the abuse of power that could result from providing Congress with the power to tax, with some equating that power as an instrument of tyranny. There were also concerns that power would be concentrated in too few hands, leading to the development of an aristocracy. While the public could control the power of the state legislatures, there were concerns over whether the people could control a distant Congress. While the opponents of the impost believed the government should honor the debt created during the war, they thought that it should find other means to do this. The alternatives they proposed included having the states pay off the debt under the requisition system established under the Articles; the sale of public lands in the west; and having each state pay off a share of the debt themselves.[52]

Washington stood on the other side of this argument, and had no qualms about the need for a stronger central government. His experience during the war had shown him that a weak national government was dangerous, and made him a vigorous supporter of national unity. In March 1783, Washington wrote to the Governor of New York the following: "I am decided in my opinion that if the powers of Congress are not enlarged, and made competent to all *general purposes*, that the Blood which has been spilt, the expence that has been incurred, and the distresses which have been felt, will avail in nothing; and that the band, already too weak, which holds us together, will soon be broken; when anarchy and confusion must prevail."[53] Washington also believed in the need for a stronger executive function at both the state and the national level. He did not share in the fear of centralized power that the opponents of the impost exhibited.

By June of 1783, Washington chose to speak out in a circular to the states, which laid out explicitly his views on the need to strengthen the federal union. He had been reticent about becoming too involved in politics, given his role as commander in chief and his firm belief that the military should be subordinate to civilian authority. He also wanted to protect his reputation as a virtuous leader, and not appear overly ambitious, so he prefaced the circular by making it clear that he "would not take any share in public business hereafter." In preparing the circular, Washington felt the need to maintain his standing as a leader that acted in the public interest, and not be seen as promoting his own personal interest or ambition.[54]

Of the four things that he considered most important to the well-being of the country, the most crucial was "an indissoluble Union of the States under one Federal Head." He feared that a weak federal government would lead to the United States falling under "the sport of

European politics, which may play one State against another" in order to advance their own interests. He concluded by stating his view that tyranny can also arise from anarchy, and "that arbitrary power is most easily established on the ruins of Liberty abused to licentiousness."

In December of 1783, Washington resigned his commission as commander in chief and retired to Mount Vernon. It was an act reminiscent of Lucius Cincinnatus, who had saved Rome in war and then retired without seizing power. In fact, one of Washington's generals, Henry Knox, had formed the Society of Cincinnati for former officers of the army, and Washington became the president. On December 22 in Annapolis, where the Congress was housed temporarily, at a formal dinner in his honor, Washington gave a toast that reminded those in attendance about his view of the need for a stronger union. After all the other toasts, thirteen in total, Washington rose and said: "Competent powers to Congress for general purposes." The next day, he surrendered his commission, an act that led King George III to call him "the greatest man in the world." With Washington headed off for retirement from public life, at least temporarily, the battle for a stronger national government would fall to new leadership. Two of those who would assume this role, and pull Washington back into the middle of the movement for a stronger national government, were James Madison and Alexander Hamilton.[55]

Madison and Hamilton

James Madison was perhaps the greatest American political theoretician. Along with his ability as a legislator, he developed the ideas that framed the American Constitution, which gave him the richly deserved title of Father of the Constitution. Madison, along with Hamilton and the ever-important presence of Washington, would push through a new political system that would allow nationhood to take root. Hamilton would later become his political enemy, when they split over the direction the new nation would take. But in the 1780s, the two men moved in unison in the pursuit of a stronger union.

Madison's motivation as a nation builder was multifaceted. Two important influences on his thinking were his experiences working at both the state and national level of politics. His experience at the state level was sandwiched in between his work in Congress. It brought to his attention the inadequacies of having the states voluntarily provide the resources needed to both meet the war effort and pay off the debts of the United States after the war. At the national level, he saw firsthand how enfeebled Congress was in solving the problems it confronted, and led him to propose amendments to the Articles of Confederation designed to strengthen the national government. He also saw at the state level how petty politics and the self-interest of local legislators led them to act in ways opposed to the larger public good.[56] His view that only an "extended republic" could provide legislators with the independence of judgment they would need to enact public policies that transcended their self-interest grew out of his experience at the local level. This view led him to support a new Constitution that he believed could achieve these ends.

The Madisons were one of the oldest and most established of the aristocratic Virginia planter families. John Maddison came to America in 1653, and immediately received 600 acres of land when he paid the way for twelve other immigrants who were to be indentured servants. John's great grandson, Ambrose, changed the spelling to Madison and eventually settled in Orange County, southeast of the Blue Ridge Mountains in an area known as the Piedmont, a region with fertile soil. By the time Ambrose's son, James Madison Sr., took over the plantation, it had grown to over 4,000 acres with dozens of slaves.[57]

James junior was born on March 16, 1751, the oldest of ten children that his mother Nelly bore. Seven of the children lived to adulthood, and Nelly reached the age of 97. When James was nine years old, his father built the home, known as Montpelier, that he would live in for his entire life. Historians know little about Madison's early life, other than a few old age recollections he left us. He apparently had a good relationship with both of his parents, and was intellectually curious. At the age of eleven, his parents sent him to a boarding school run by Donald Robertson. Under Robertson, he studied Latin and Greek, along with logic, philosophy, math, and French. Madison would later say of Robertson: "all that I have been in life I owe largely to that man." He spent five years with Robertson, and then two years back at Montpelier under the tutelage of the Reverend Thomas Martin. Martin lived with the Madisons and served as the family teacher. Martin had also attended the College of New Jersey (present day Princeton), and convinced the family that young James should attend school there. The reputation of the College of William and Mary was in tatters at the time and the family had concerns for James living in the lowland area of Williamsburg, since he was a sickly youth. At the age of eighteen, James junior set off for the College of New Jersey.[58]

John Witherspoon, a Scottish clergyman and philosopher well steeped in enlightenment thought, had recently taken over as the president of the College. His students learned Milton, Algernon, Sidney, and Locke and they read the writings of Trenchard and Gordon, the co-authors of the Cato Letters. Witherspoon believed that justice and virtue should be part of the foundation of government, and that these were more important than simple majority rule, a concept that would influence Madison's own political philosophy. As with Jefferson, Locke's writings had a significant impact on Madison's views, and his college education gave him the intellectual foundation upon which he would later develop his own approach to government.[59]

Madison, who worked hard and was disciplined in his approach to school, graduated in two years. Witherspoon later said that Madison never did or said anything improper during his time in college, something he later told Jefferson, who never failed to needle Madison about this. After graduating, he stayed on for an additional year of study with Witherspoon, and then considered law as a profession. In a letter to his friend from college, William Bradford, he wrote, "I intend to read Law occasionally and have procured books for that purpose." But his interest in the field may have only been a means for understanding politics and government better.[60] Madison was at a bit of loss for what to do with his life after graduating from college, and he had to confront the fact that he was often sick. In another letter to Bradford, Madison indicated he did not "expect a long or healthy life." Bradford responded by writing that he worked too hard at his studies, and this is what caused him to be in poor health.[61]

As with so many from the founding generation, the coming of the Revolutionary War provided Madison with the opportunity to participate in public life in a meaningful way. In all likelihood, Madison would still have become involved in politics. But in the words of historian Jack Rakove, "there was a world of difference between entering a legislature charged with overseeing the parochial concerns of a provincial society or finding oneself thrust into politics in the midst of revolution."[62]

In December 1774, Madison, along with his father, was elected to the Orange County Committee of Safety. These committees were being formed throughout the colonies based on the advice of the First Continental Congress and were designed to enforce the trade embargo on British goods. The following October, Madison was named a colonel in the Orange County militia, under the command of James senior. Although he drilled with the militia, his poor health would keep him from being a soldier. He did show great zeal in the politics of revolution and assisted his father in procuring supplies and readying the militia for a possible war with England.[63]

In the spring of 1776, as the decision for independence neared, Orange County elected twenty-five-year-old Madison to represent it at the Virginia Provincial Convention, which served as the governing body of the colony. One of the prime tasks for the delegates was to write a new constitution for Virginia, a job that Jefferson had wished he could be involved in, rather than serving at the Continental Congress. Madison, both shy and brilliant, was a political novice with little to contribute, at least initially. The main job of writing the new constitution fell to George Mason, considered the ablest political theorist of his day. The Declaration of Rights that Mason drafted contained the words "all men are born equally free and independent, and have certain inherent natural rights...among which are the enjoyment of life and liberty," words that Jefferson would echo, in more stirring prose, as part of the Declaration of Independence.

Madison had a great interest in the subject of religious freedom and he ultimately had a major influence on the wording of the Declaration of Rights in this area. The Anglican Church was still the established religion in Virginia, and other religions faced discrimination and their adherents were banned from openly expressing their beliefs. In January of 1774, Madison had written to Bradford in a rage about the imprisonment of several Baptist ministers that Culpeper County had jailed for preaching without a license. "There are at this time in the adjacent county not less than 5 or 6 well-meaning men in close Gaol for publishing their religious Sentiments which in the main are very orthodox. I have neither the patience to hear talk or think of anything relative to this matter..." Madison believed that all people should have the fundamental human right to believe or not believe as their conscience dictated.[64]

Mason's original draft had stated that all men should "enjoy the fullest Toleration in the Exercise of Religion," but toleration did not bestow a fundamental right to religious freedom, it simply meant that the state would tolerate alternative views. What the state could tolerate, the state could also choose not to tolerate. Madison proposed an amendment that read: "all men are equally entitled to the full and free exercise of religion according to the dictates of Conscience." This change recognized that religious freedom was a right and not a privilege, and as adopted in its final form stated, "all men are equally entitled to the free exercise of religion." Madison had made his first significant mark in the world of public policy.[65]

Madison learned a valuable lesson in practical politics when he was defeated in his bid to earn a seat in the new Virginia House of Delegates in April 1777. Elections were a social event, with the planters gathering at the county seat to vote. The candidates for office typically bought the voters drinks, a practice that Madison refused to do. He felt that the "personal solicitation" of voters and the serving of alcoholic beverages were inconsistent with "the purity of moral and republican principles." His opponent, a planter and tavern keeper, felt no so such compunction and defeated Madison. James would spend the next six months at home, before a new opportunity opened for him.[66]

In November 1777, he was appointed a member of the Council of State, an eight-member advisory board to then Governor Patrick Henry of Virginia. His time on the Council was consumed with the problem of supplying the army, given the financial problems that confronted both Virginia and the Continental Congress. Madison saw firsthand the problems the country faced from printing too much paper money without the adequate backing of taxation. "As a member of an executive body charged with implementing the assembly's vague will, he began to recognize the limits of legislative supremacy," one historian writes, which would later lead to his support for a strong executive as part of the Constitution.[67]

Madison's abilities impressed many of the older men he worked with, especially Jefferson, eight years his senior, who had been elected governor in June of 1779 to replace Henry. They had met before, but now they developed a collaboration that would extend until Jefferson's death. As biographer Richard Brookhiser writes, "Madison and Jefferson were bound by their differences as by their similarities." Both were from aristocratic backgrounds, but shared a vision for liberal political reforms. Jefferson was a tall redhead, a dreamer, a man with immense talents in many areas, and a gifted writer. Madison was diminutive (perhaps 5 feet 6 inches), practical, studious, and a good writer. They both loved books, and in 1783 would unveil plans for a congressional library containing over 1,400 books. Jefferson came to rely on Madison's judgment and practical advice in many areas of public policy.[68]

In December of 1779, after his service on the Council of State, Madison was selected to represent Virginia at the Continental Congress. There had been numerous complaints that the new delegates to Congress were a mediocre lot, a complaint that no one could level against Madison. Due to heavy snows, Madison did not arrive in Philadelphia until March 1780. During the intervening months, he prepared a paper entitled "Money" in which he delved into the financial problems facing Congress and the states. He rejected the notion that the problem was the quantity of paper money in circulation, but rather argued it was the inability of the government to redeem the money at a fixed date in the future for gold or silver. He would also soon learn that the inability of the government was due less to the ability to redeem the money in specie, since there was little of that available, but due to the lack of the power to tax.

Madison's first year in Congress was taken up with ratifying the Articles of Confederation. Virginia continued to make extensive claims to western lands, which kept Maryland from ratifying the Articles.

When New York finally ceded its claims to Congress, Madison saw an opportunity to have Virginia do the same, and Congress worked out a compromise for a national domain.

In 1781, Madison served on a committee to determine how to strengthen the national government. The committee, with the full support of Madison, proposed that Congress had the "implied power" to coerce states to fulfill their financial obligations to the union. Even though Madison believed that the powers were implied, he and the committee recommended that Congress amend the Articles to reflect this provision. As historian Jack Rakove notes, Madison and the other members of the committee saw this amendment as "fulfilling rather than subverting the Articles." The use of implied powers was a response to the situation of a country at war, a means to provide funding to Congress so that it could support the army. At this point, Madison still supported the government established under the Articles, and was looking for ways improve its operations and financial solvency. His support for "implied powers" revealed a certain naiveté on his part, the first of several instances in his life where he became enamored of an idea that had no possibility of passage. Congress tabled the recommendation.[69]

Madison also supported many of the goals that Robert Morris put forward to stabilize the nation's finances, although he did vote against the charter for a national bank proposed by Morris, a vote that later foreshadowed his opposition to the bank bill proposed by Hamilton in 1790. He became a key figure in support of the impost and other measures to raise revenue for the central government, and was a member of the congressional delegation that met with the army's representatives dispatched from Newburg in January of 1783. He was joined at that meeting by another up-and-coming young man, Alexander Hamilton, who had recently been appointed to Congress to represent New York. Hamilton was an even stronger supporter of national union than

Madison, and the two would go on to collaborate in this effort in the years that followed.[70]

We live in a nation that is part Jeffersonian and part Hamiltonian. From the aristocratic Jefferson, we cherish liberty, equality, democracy, and the importance of the ability of the average person to fully participate in government. Jefferson also believed in limited government. From Hamilton came the vision that America's economic future lay as a capitalist country, and he did much to lay the foundation for this. Hamilton was also a major supporter, nay shaper, of a stronger central government designed to create one nation. As Ron Chernow writes, Hamilton would go on to develop the "machinery of a modern nation-state — including a budget system, a funded debt, a tax system, a central bank, a customs service, and a coast guard."[71] From Hamilton, we inherited our deep tradition of an active government that supports the economic development of the nation, a position that in our time is identified with the more liberal Democratic Party.

While Madison came from one of the most powerful families in Virginia, Hamilton came from a humble background.[72] His mother, Rachel Faucette Lavien, had escaped from the island of St. Croix and her abusive husband. She landed in Nevis, where she met James Hamilton. James, a descendent of a powerful Scottish family, had made his way to the Caribbean to try his hand at business. He and Rachel formed a common law marriage, since she was unable to obtain a divorce from her husband. They had two sons together, James Jr., and Alexander, who was born in 1755. Hamilton's illegitimate birth would later be a target for his political enemies. John Adams once referred to him as "the bastard brat of a Scottish peddler."

Alexander inherited his intelligence and will power from his mother. His father, who was the black sheep of his family, was unsuccessful in almost every endeavor he undertook. We know little about Hamilton's early life. He may have had a tutor at a young age, and learned French from his mother. At the age of eleven, his father abandoned the family, with Hamilton later claiming that his father left because he was unable to support the family. Two years later, his mother died from an unknown illness in a bed next to Alexander, who survived the same illness. The two boys were placed under the guardianship of their first cousin, who shortly thereafter committed suicide. "Such repeated shocks must have stripped Alexander Hamilton of any sense that life was fair, that he existed in a benign universe, or that he could count on help from anyone," according to one of his biographers.

The fate of the two brothers would diverge, perhaps due to their disparate abilities. James was apprenticed to a carpenter, while Alexander was taken in by a successful merchant, Thomas Stevens, whose son bore a striking resemblance to Hamilton, so much so that it has been speculated that Stevens was Alexander's real father. Hamilton worked as a clerk at a mercantile house, where he learned about business, including the importance of a stable currency and access to credit. The mercantile house also traded in slaves, a practice Hamilton grew to detest. He later became a lifelong supporter of the abolition of slavery. At the age of eighteen, his cousin assisted him to immigrate to America.

Hamilton had a unique ability to impress important people, and through contacts he made, attended Kings College (present day Columbia) in New York in early 1774. There he was exposed to the views of those still loyal to Britain, specifically from the President of the College, Myles Cooper. But he also absorbed the revolutionary ferment sweeping through New York, and identified with the rebel cause. At a rally sponsored by the Sons of Liberty in July 1774, Hamilton gave a speech fully in support of the Boston Tea Party and the ban on importing British goods. He also began writing in support of the patriot cause, producing two well-regarded pamphlets. In one, "The Farmer Refuted," Hamilton anticipated the type of guerilla warfare that Washington would be required to adopt as his strategy during the war.

In March of 1776, Hamilton parlayed his budding fame as a writer and received a commission as a captain in the New York artillery regiment. He was popular with his men, and a brave soldier. In his role helping to defend New York City from the British in the summer of 1776, he caught the eye of General Washington. Hamilton was one of the last men to leave New York as the Continental Army retreated. The Americans would not return to New York City for seven years.

Despite being ill, Hamilton and his artillery regiment were part of the army that crossed the Delaware with Washington on Christmas night in 1776 in order to spring a surprise assault on the Hessian troops camped in Trenton. In early 1777, Washington invited Hamilton to join his staff as an aide-de-camp with the rank of lieutenant colonel. From this position, he met Eliza Schuyler, the daughter of the rich and powerful New Yorker, Phillip Schuyler. They married in December 1780, when Hamilton was twenty-five and Eliza twenty-two. As Chernow notes, the wedding "ended his nomadic existence and embedded him in the Anglo-Dutch aristocracy of New York." His relationship with Phillip Schuyler helped to move his career forward, and the two men shared a conviction that the national government under the Articles of Confederation needed strengthening.

While Hamilton served as one of Washington's chief aides for over four years, he always yearned to return to the battlefield. Washington, however, passed him over for several promotions as a battlefield commander, since full colonels stood waiting for similar promotions. Washington also feared losing the man who proved to be his most able assistant, who had a unique ability to serve as his alter ego. No doubt Hamilton resented being passed over for promotion, and this would lead to their ultimate falling out. On February 15, 1781, Hamilton made Washington wait for ten minutes on a flight of stairs, causing Washington to lose his temper and say "I must tell you sir, you treat me with disrespect." The impetuous Hamilton resigned on the spot, and no amount of pleading from Washington would get him to change his mind. It reflected one of Hamilton's great weaknesses, his outsized ego, and a moment of poor judgment in being unwilling to accept the commander in chief's apology. He did remain on the staff until they found a replacement, and, ultimately, Washington would arrange for him to command a light infantry battalion from New York. Hamilton was part of the assault on Yorktown, bravely leading a night attack on a British position there.

After the battle of Yorktown, Hamilton returned to the Schuyler home in Albany, New York, to spend time with his wife and son Phillip. He also began an intensive period of legal studies, and in just six months passed the bar exam in New York in 1781. In November of 1782, he was selected as a delegate to Congress. He had been thinking and writing about the problems of government under the Articles of Confederation, and was one of the earliest proponents for developing a revised and more powerful structure for a national government. He particularly worried that the central government had no direct authority over the people of the United States, but only operated as a league of friendship among the states. He wished to see a government with a strong executive, the ability to tax, and with a separate judicial branch. At this point, Hamilton's views went beyond other nationalist supporters, like Madison, who still thought the Articles could be revised and made to work. Perhaps Hamilton was such a proponent of a strong and independent nation, since as an immigrant he felt no overriding allegiance to any one state, but rather identified with the United States. Before long, his views would begin to hold sway with an important group of leaders in the post-war world.

Endnotes

1 This section is largely drawn from Rakove, *Beginnings*, p. 139-164

2 Rakove, *Beginnings*, p. 143-144

3 Rakove, *Beginnings*, p. 152 and p. 157-158; Ferling, p. 177

4 Rakove, *Beginnings*, p. 158-162; Ferling, p. 181

5 Rakove, p. 163; Ferling, p. 203

6 Forrest McDonald, *E Pluribus Unum: The Formation of the American Republic 1776-1790*, (Indianapolis, 1965), p. 32

7 Washington's central role as a member of the nationalist camp is explored more fully in Ellis, *The Quartet*. As previously noted, that work was released after this chapter was initially drafted in 2013 and so his insights were not available to this author other than as after the fact reflections.

8 Ferling, p. 177-179

9 See especially Bernard Bailyn's *The Ideological Origins of the American Revolution* and Gordon Wood's *The Creation of the American Republic*. A useful summary of these two works and the influence of the Countrymen is found in Elkins and McKitrick, p. 4-29.

10 Elkins and McKitrick, p. 7

11 This section is largely drawn from John Kenneth Galbraith & Nichole Salinger, *Almost Everyone's Guide to Economics*, (Boston, 1978), p. 74-80

12 E. James Ferguson, *The Power of the Purse: A History of American Public Finance 1776-1790*, (Chapel Hill, 1961), p. 4-8

13 See McDonald, p. 44-45 and Ferguson, p. 28

14 Information on bonds is from Ferguson, p. 35; the size of the debt in 1783 from Bureau of the Debt retrieved 1/11/2013 from http://www.publicdebt.treas.gov/history/1700.htm ; information on foreign loans from Ferguson, p. 40

15 Ferguson, p. 29-30 and Ferling, p. 219-221

16 Rakove, *Beginnings*, p. 205-208

17 Ferguson, p. 70; Rakove, *Beginnings*, p. 209

18 Rakove, *Beginnings*, p. 212-213; Ferling, p. 224-225; McDonald, p. 46-47

19 Taylor, p. 289

20 George A. Akerloff and Robert J. Shiller, *Animal Spirits: How Human Psychology Drives the Economy and Why It Matters for Global Capitalism*, (Princeton, 2009), p. 12-13

21 Richard Sylla, "Hamilton and the Federalist Financial Revolution 1789-1795," *The New York Journal of American History*, from http://www.alexanderhamiltonexhibition.org/about/Sylla%20-%20Federals%20Revolution.pdf

22 Joseph J. Ellis, *Revolutionary Summer: The Birth of American Independence*, (New York, 2013), p. xviii

23 The quote is from Chernow, *Washington*, p. 121; Ellis, *His Excellency*, p. 112 makes the case that the army was the first national institution

24 Ellis, *His Excellency*, p. 112

25 Chernow, *Washington*, p. 325-327

26 Joseph J. Ellis, *American Creation*, (New York, 1997), p. 64 and 78

27 Ellis, *His Excellency*, p. 114

28 Chernow, *Washington*, p. 329

29 The troop numbers are from Ellis, *His Excellency*, p. 118; the needs of the army are from Ferling, p. 217

30 This is the major argument of Ellis, *Creation*, Chapter 2.

31 Ferling, p. 216

32 Ellis, *His Excellency*, p. 121

33 Ellis, *His Excellency*, p. 126-127

34 Ferling, p 231-232; Rakove, *Beginnings*, p. 287-288

35 Ferling, p. 233

36 Ferling, p 234; Rakove, *Beginnings*, p. 290-291

37 Ferling, p. 235-237

38 Ferling, p. 238; Ellis, *The Quartet*, p. 41-47; and Richard Beeman, "*Plain, Honest Men: The Making of the American Constitution*", (New York, 2009), p. 10-11

39 Rakove, *Beginnings*, p. 290-291; Elizabeth M. Nuxoll, *The Bank of North America and Robert Morris's Management of the Nation's First Fiscal Crisis*, from www.thebhc.org/publications/BEHprint/vo13/po159-po170.pdf

40 Rakove, *Beginnings*, p. 290-291; McDonald, p 51-52; Ellis, *The Quartet*, p. 44

41 Ellis, *His Excellency*, p. 133-134; Chernow, *Washington*, p. 406-407

42 Chernow, *Washington*, p. 406; McDonald, p. 50

43 Chernow, *Washington*, p. 413 for Rochambeau quote; Ellis, *His Excellency*, p. 137; Ferling, p. 242

44 Jackson Turner Main, *The Anti-federalists: Critics of the Constitution 1781-1788*, (New York, 1961), p. 73; McDonald, p. 54; McCullough, p. 271; and Beeman, p. 11

45 McDonald, p. 55; Main, p. 88; Rakove, *Beginnings*, p. 316

46 Chernow, *Washington*, p. 431 for quote; Bobrick, p. 473

47 Chernow, *Washington*, p. 433 for quote from Hamilton letter; Rakove, *Beginnings*, p. 318; Ellis, *His Excellency*, p. 141

48 Ellis, *His Excellency*, p. 142

49 The account of Washington's speech at Newburg is drawn from copies of the speech itself, and also from accounts provided in Ellis, *His Excellency*, p. 144; Chernow, *Washington*, p. 435-436 ; Bobrick, p. 475

50 Beeman, p. 6

51 Ferling, p. 252-254

52 See Main, p. 75-84 for a complete discussion of those opposed to a stronger national union.

53 The quote is from Ellis, *His Excellency*, p. 140

54 For a more complete discussion on the issue of Washington's concern for reputation, see Gordon Wood, *Revolutionary Characters: What Made the Founders Different*, (New York, 2006), p. 43

55 Chernow, *Washington*, p. 444 for Cincinnatus reference; Ellis, *His Excellency*, p. 146 for toast; Ferling, p. 255 for George III quote

56 Wood makes this point in regards to Madison in *Revolutionary Characters*, p. 147-150

57 Ralph Ketcham, *James Madison: A Life*, (Charlottesville, 1990), p. 3-10

58 Jack N. Rakove, *James Madison and the Creation of the American Republic*, (New York, 2007), p2-3; Ketcham, p. 19-23

59 Ketcham, p. 38-43 and p. 48-49

60 Ketcham, p. 55; Rakove, *Madison*, p. 6

61 Richard Brookhiser, *James Madison*, (New York, 2011), p. 19

62 Rakove, *Madison*, p. 8

63 Ketcham, p. 63-64

64 Ketcham, p. 57-58

65 Ketcham, p. 72-73; Rakove, *Madison*, p. 15

66 Rakove, *Madison*, p. 17

67 Rakove, *Madison*, p. 17-19

68 Ketcham, p. 84; Brookhiser, p 29-30

69 Rakove, *Madison*, p. 24-25 and *Beginnings*, p, 294-295; on Madison's sometimes naïve point of view, see Garry Wills, *James Madison*, (New York, 2002), p. 21-23

70 Rakove, *Madison*, p. 27-28; Chernow, *Washington*, p. 432

71 Ron Chernow, *Alexander Hamilton*, (New York, 2004), p. 4

72 This section is drawn primarily from Chernow, *Hamilton*, p. 1-161

CHAPTER 6

The Postwar Years / 1783 to 1787

"We are either a United people, or we are not. If the former, let us, in all matters of general concern act a nation; which have national objectives to promote and a National character to support. If we are not, let us no longer act a farce by pretending to it."

– GEORGE WASHINGTON, NOVEMBER 1785 –

The years from 1783 to 1787 were pivotal, a period when a small group of dedicated nationalists were able to design, through thoughtful analysis and intense political debate, a whole new structure of government, one that would be the essential ingredient in allowing one American nation to emerge. They accomplished this despite the fact that in 1783, most people saw no need for a stronger federal government, and in fact opposed the idea. What changed? And why?

The Best of Times, the Worst of Times

When Dickens opened *A Tale of Two Cities* with: "It was the best of times, it was the worst of times," he may just as easily have been writing about America of the 1780s instead of France. On the one hand, the tenor of the times seemed good. The country had achieved a great victory over the British; democratic governing institutions had been approved in all of the states; and the limitations imposed by the old aristocratic systems of Europe no longer applied to the United States. Farmers and planters looked forward to selling tobacco and wheat outside of the British mercantile system, and manufacturers hoped for expanded trading partners. Immigrants and citizens looking for new opportunities were settling the frontier area beyond the mountains. Historian Bernard Bailyn writes that, "despite depressions, doubts and fears for the future, and despite the universal easing of ideological fervor, the general mood remained high through all of these years. There was a freshness and boldness in the tone of the eighties, a continuing belief that the world was still open..." The sense of good times was especially true for the early postwar years, when the economy was growing and the country's public debt appeared to have stabilized. The states had assumed much of the debt, which lessened the perceived need to grant the central government the power to tax, although this would prove to be a temporary solution that would prove to be inadequate. Many Loyalists had fled to England, opening up numerous opportunities in public service and the professions. New schools and universities were opening and some states began to invest in infrastructure, including new canals and roads to connect east and west.[1]

In 1785, Benjamin Franklin returned to the United States after spending almost nine years as the chief diplomat to the French court. He had been instrumental in securing an alliance with France during the Revolutionary War, and in negotiating the peace treaty with the British that ended the war. Upon returning to Philadelphia in September of 1785, "he found the people of Pennsylvania enjoying peace and prosperity." He observed that farmers "have had plentiful crops, their produce sell at high prices and for hard money...Our working-people are all employed and get high wages, are well fed and well clad..." Even though Franklin saw good times at home, his experience in Europe had convinced him that the United States needed a stronger central government in order to survive in the world.[2]

While the tenor of the times was good, that did not last for more than a few years.[3] As the 1780s unfolded, problems began to mount that would allow the nationalists to coalesce and call for a convention, ostensibly to recommend amendments to the Articles. Three interrelated problems arose that the central government was powerless to contend with: continued financial problems, trouble in the realm of foreign affairs, and festering issues with interstate commerce among the states.

In terms of the continuing financial problems, the measures Madison had shepherded through Congress in 1783, including the impost, had still not received the unanimous approval of the states. By 1786, New York finally approved the impost, but placed so many restrictions on it that it was effectively dead. The failure of the impost made clear one of the major weaknesses of the Articles: the need for unanimity in order to approve any major change. At one time or another, all states had approved some form of the impost, but the measure never went into effect. Given the differing interests of the states, their own rivalries, and their parochial interests, attaining unanimous consent was almost impossible. The failure of the impost meant that Congress still had to rely on requisitions to the states to fund its obligations, which primarily consisted of foreign debts. Since the states had largely taken over responsibility for servicing the domestic debt, payments to the central government were generally not forthcoming. Left without a source of funding to meet repayment on foreign debts, Congress consequently failed to make interest payments to France in 1785.[4]

Some states would struggle more than others to repay debts they had assumed. The amount of debt also varied from state to state, from a low of $387,500 in New York to a high of $5.4 million in

Massachusetts. By 1785, Virginia had retired most of its debt, however, the debt level in Massachusetts would cause a multitude of problems for that state, including an outright rebellion in 1786 by some who could not afford to keep up with the taxes the state levied in order to meet its payments.[5]

By 1786, even those who had opposed the Morris financial program, as amended by Madison's various proposals, had begun to see the problems associated with the failure to provide a stable funding source to Congress. When Morris left office in 1784, Arthur Lee and Samuel Osgood formed the majority of a new Board of Treasury. Both men, who had been opponents of Morris and his financial program, initially thought that the opening of western lands would provide sufficient resources to retire the foreign debt. But by 1786, they too had become exasperated by the unwillingness of the states to provide needed funding. Osgood wrote in a letter to a friend "that the united states must be entrusted with Monies other than the scanty Pittance that they obtain from the annual Requisitions...either be vested with coercive Powers as to the Collection of Money or with the Impost...or cease to be a Congress of any Consequence to the Union."[6]

Foreign policy problems also mounted, and Congress lacked the resources and authority to deal with them. The treaty with Great Britain required that the states provide payments to British citizens and loyalists for property confiscated during the war and for prewar debts, much of which was owed by Virginia planters. When the states refused to make such payments, the British used this as a pretext to continue to occupy their forts in the Ohio River Valley. From here, they armed the local Indian tribes, who harassed settlers in the area. The federal government had no standing army (one that is maintained in peacetime and consists of full-time, professional soldiers), which it could dispatch to protect the settlers. During the revolutionary period, colonists felt a strong ideological aversion to maintaining a standing army, with many of the founders seeing it as a threat to liberty and an "instrument of tyranny," as Madison stated in 1787. The fear of standing armies had existed during colonial times, particularly during the protests over British taxation measures, when some of the colonies, particularly Massachusetts, had experienced occupation under the British army.[7]

In 1783, the British closed their ports in the West Indies for trade with the United States, but continued to flood the American market with their own goods. The British would allow no American products to be shipped within their empire, except those carried on British ships. John Adams, serving in the role of diplomat to Great Britain, urged Congress to adopt retaliatory measures. But the Articles did not provide Congress with the power to regulate foreign trade. The restrictions on trade that the British implemented soon led to a commercial depression that spread to fishing, shipbuilding, and other industries in the 1780s. The maritime industries of New England were especially hard hit, but all of the northern states suffered, as did New York City. Fishermen found themselves idle, and the situation for skilled and unskilled workers in the northeast became increasingly desperate. Farmers in the North, who had expanded their production during the war in order to meet the needs of other regions, now found insufficient demand for their products.[8]

Trade problems between the states were a further source of tensions in the 1780s. Each state not only issued its own currency, causing problems with exchange rates, but states levied tariffs on the products of neighboring states. New York, for example, had a tariff on farm products from New Jersey and Connecticut. Pennsylvania also had duties on products coming into its state, causing James Madison to remark that New Jersey was like "a cask tapped at both ends," since it was caught between the much stronger states of New York and Pennsylvania. The problems of trade restrictions between states were not restricted to just the North, as Virginia and South Carolina both levied tariffs and restricted trade with North Carolina.[9]

In response to these problems, a committee of Congress proposed in 1785 that the Articles be amended to provide the central government with the power to regulate both foreign and interstate commerce and to levy duties on imports. The duties would be returned to the states where they were collected. The committee report received no support in Congress, with the southern states fearing that the proposal was designed to help northern business interests. Even more importantly, the proposal stoked the fear of placing too much power within the federal government. James Monroe of Virginia, a principle supporter of the report, summarized the views of the opponents that "it was dangerous to concentrate power, since it might be turned to mischievous purposes."[10]

Foreign relations with Spain also suffered when that country closed off the Mississippi River to American use in 1784. Congress asked John Jay, who was serving as secretary for foreign affairs, to negotiate with the Spanish government to open the river, but they refused to yield. After a year of frustrating and fruitless negotiations, Jay told Congress that the best the United States could hope for was a treaty that opened up Spanish trade in return for a twenty-year ban on American navigation of the Mississippi. Jay assumed that the Spanish were a declining power and that the loss of the Mississippi was inconsequential since settlers would not reach it for at least twenty-five years. The proposed terms of the treaty split the northern members of Congress from their southern brethren. The North wanted the advantages of the commercial treaty, which it hoped would help end the depression caused by Britain's ban of American products in its markets. The South saw the treaty as threatening their ability to settle the western lands in the Mississippi Valley, including Kentucky and Tennessee. Southern Congressmen thought that without access to the river and New Orleans, settlers would be unable to obtain needed supplies and could not trade their goods, thereby closing the area to further westward expansion. The allegiance of those that did choose to settle in the west would also not be toward the United States, an issue of primary concern to Washington.[11]

Ultimately, Congress split along sectional lines, with the vote eight to five in favor of the proposed treaty terms. Since nine votes were required to approve it, the proposal failed. But the defeat left bitter feelings between the North and South, and showed that no consensus existed over what best served the national interest. The failure of the treaty also led to speculation that the union was about to be dissolved. James Monroe told both Jefferson and Madison that the North was considering breaking off from the Confederation to form its own nation.[12]

The problems continued to mount, to the point where an atmosphere of crisis had settled in among some in the elite. John Quincy Adams, in a speech to his fellow graduates of Harvard in 1787, called it the "critical period when the country was groaning under the intolerable burden of … accumulated evils." Historians, dating back to the early 1800s, have long argued over whether post-war conditions in the country warranted the creation of a new central government eventually embodied in the Constitution. Historians sympathetic to the government created by the Articles of Confederation have tended to downplay the problems, instead seeing the Constitution as a conspiracy of the wealthy few designed to protect their status and property, and as a movement that undermined the very ideals of the revolution. On the other side are those historians who see the ideals of the revolution as being rooted in the movement to create a stronger national government through constitutional reform. "The core revolutionary principle in this view is collectivistic rather than individualistic, for it sees the true spirit of '76 as the virtuous surrender of personal, state and sectional interests to the larger purpose of American nationhood," according to one historian.[13]

Despite the problems that existed in the realm of finances and foreign affairs, the weak government under the Articles was popular with the public. Historians with differing perspectives agree on this. John Ferling writes, "No evidence existed of widespread popular sentiment on behalf of altering the Articles of Confederation and strengthening the national government." Rakove writes that "few American leaders believed that the new nation was actually poised on the brink of a crisis" and that "most Americans showed little interest in public affairs." And Ellis opined that "the very weakness of the federal government under the Articles of Confederation [was] the ideal expression of revolutionary intentions."[14]

Most Americans in the 1780s generally ignored the workings of the Congress, newspapers wrote few articles about it, and there was little by way of widespread debate over the weakness of the national government. Perhaps this was because Congress could achieve little, and had difficulty reaching decisions. Attendance was sporadic, with Congress often unable to achieve a quorum to conduct business. Given the weakness of the central government, few politicians wanted to be a member. The reputation of Congress had gone from embodying the "collective wisdom" of the continent to one held in extremely low regard by the public.[15]

In the absence of the unity enforced by the war, with little public support for a stronger central government, little held the country together in the 1780s; citizens had no sense of national unity or identity, and there was much to split the new country apart. While we can't know what might have happened in the absence of the Constitution, people at the time, including Madison, thought that the states would split into "two or more Confederacies."[16] The question is, Why didn't this happen? How did the United States choose a different path than disintegration, one that resulted in a wholly new structure of government framed at the Constitutional Convention held in Philadelphia in 1787?

One compelling and succinct answer has been posited by Ellis, who makes the case that "a tiny minority of prominent political leaders from several key states conspired to draft and then ratify a document designed to accommodate republican principles to a national scale." Ellis goes so far as to call the actions of the nationalists a coup d'état, since they represented only a small elite group that wanted fundamental changes made in the federal government. He argues that either the vast majority of the public found the creation of a stronger government irrelevant to their daily lives, or they were hostile to it.[17]

The nationalists were, no doubt, a small and elite group in 1787, and they did not represent the population as a whole. But the use of the term coup stretches the definition a bit far. Merriam-Webster defines a coup as a sudden exercise of force in politics, especially the violent overthrow or alteration of an existing government by a small group. Historically, coups have involved the use of violence or force, often by the military, in the overthrow of governments. From Napoleon seizing power in France in 1799 backed by the army, to Lenin's overthrow of the government of Russia in 1917 through force of arms, to Castro's takeover in Cuba in 1959 with his guerilla army, coups have involved the use of force. Compare those events to the nationalists of 1787, who used the power of ideas and debate to achieve fundamental changes to government. Ultimately, the people, acting through special conventions convened in each state, ratified the Constitution.

In my view, the nationalists set off on a second phase of the American Revolution, one that would give birth to one nation. They had two major advantages: First, even though public opinion did not support a complete revamp of the Articles of Confederation, the elites of the society, even those that would later oppose the Constitution, generally agreed that the central government needed strengthening. Given the difficulty of amending the Articles due to the unanimous consent required of the states, the nationalists began to contemplate a complete revision of the constitutional arrangement through the calling of a convention. Some would call this extra-legal approach an act of treason, since Congress had only authorized the holding of the convention to consider amendments to the Articles and not the creation of a wholly new Constitution. The second element was a breakthrough in the intellectual sphere, where Madison developed a theory that liberty could best be preserved in a larger republic like the United States. Until Madison, "the received wisdom…held that republican governments could exist only in small, relatively homogenous societies," according to Jack Rakove. Events would also help push forward their effort, most importantly an armed rebellion that broke out in the western area of Massachusetts, and brought forward the specter of anarchy. The main characters on the road to the convention were Washington and Madison, with an assist from Hamilton.[18]

Washington and the Conference on the Potomac

During the 1780s, Washington continued to feel dismayed by the failures of the national government, just as he had during the war. Not only was he concerned for his country, but those issues also affected him personally; the closure of trade to the West Indies reduced his income from Mount Vernon at the same time that those who owed him money paid in depreciated currency. In addition, he had grave concerns over whether Congress could manage the settlement of western lands. Washington owned nearly 60,000 acres spread over the Shenandoah Valley, western Pennsylvania, and large tracts on the Ohio and Great Kanawha Rivers, a tributary of the Ohio. He looked to the income from rents and the sale of those western properties to backfill for the losses he was experiencing from his plantation. He foresaw a gradual settlement taking place, supported by a series of internal improvements, a process he felt could only be undertaken by a strong national government, and not the current one under the Articles. He also worried about the continued presence of British forts in the west, and that without internal improvements and a strong American military, the settlers "would in a few short years be as unconnected to us, indeed more so, than we are with South America."[19]

From a broader perspective, Washington feared for the future of his country. In a 1785 letter, he wrote, "We are either a united people under one head…or we are thirteen independent sovereignties, eternally counteracting each other." His criticisms of the government under the Articles are familiar: a weak executive; the inability to tax; and the lack of a strong army and navy. Washington's concerns over the weakness of the military covered not only its inability to protect western settlers, but also extended to the sphere of international relations. Barbary pirates had begun to prey on American merchant ships, and without a navy, the Congress was helpless to respond. "Would to Heaven we had a navy to reform those enemies to mankind or crush them into non-existence" Washington told his former military partner, the Frenchman Lafayette.[20]

Washington was also troubled over the issuance of paper money by many of the states, given his experience with the inflation that occurred during the war and the hardships experienced by the army. The United States had little by way of gold or silver, and so hard currency was scarce. The situation was reversed for a short time in the immediate aftermath of the war due to spending by both the British and French armies. But Americans longed for luxury items from Europe, and so specie soon flowed out of the country, leaving a shortage of currency in circulation. The shortage of money caused hardships to farmers and merchants who had gone into debt, making it difficult for them to raise enough cash to pay their creditors. Some states, to pay their own debt burden, began to levy ever-higher taxes, which placed further burdens on the merchants and farmers, many of whom began to lose their farms and businesses to foreclosures. Washington was personally sympathetic to those who found themselves in such a bind, and was in fact lenient to those who owed him money. But he opposed the response of seven of the thirteen states, which issued paper currency to ease the burden. He believed that such an approach would only provide a short-term benefit to debtors, lead to another round of currency depreciation, and aid speculators. "An evil equally great is the door it (paper money) immediately opens for speculation, by which the least designing and perhaps most valuable, part of the community are preyed upon by the more knowing and crafty speculators," Washington wrote. He was also apprehensive about those states that gave relief to debtors by invalidating contracts, seeing that such actions would "ruin commerce, oppress the honest, and open a door to every species of fraud and injustice."[21]

Many might see Washington's views on paper money and debtor relief as self-serving, designed to protect those like himself who were creditors. But his own statements indicate that he believed that all would eventually suffer from inflation and a depreciating currency. "The wisdom of man, in my humble opinion, cannot at this time devise a plan by which the credit of paper money would long be supported." Whatever benefit was achieved for those short on cash would soon be lost, since "depreciation keeps pace with the quantity of the emissions" of paper money. Washington's view was that state legislators were acting in the short-term needs of the public, but ignoring the long-term problems they were creating.[22] Standard republican ideology in 1776 had assumed a virtuous public, that individuals would voluntarily sacrifice their own short-term interest to promote the larger public good. But Washington was a realist who knew that reform of the central government was needed to promote the public interest. Ellis writes of Washington that:

> *Making voluntary sacrifice the operative principle of republican government had proved to be a romantic delusion. Both individual citizens and sovereign states often required coercion to behave responsibly, which meant that the federal government required expanded powers of taxation and ultimate control over fiscal policy.*[23]

But Washington was reticent to lead the effort to reform the federal government. He took seriously his promise to retire from public life, and saw that he had enhanced his reputation by giving up power at the end of the war. At the age of fifty-five, Washington was also feeling the effects of rheumatoid arthritis. He understood that the public was not ready to overturn the government under the Articles, and that his own views were out of step with popular thinking. He feared becoming involved with an effort that might be doomed to fail.

He did take one step in the direction of returning to public life when he hosted a conference on the navigation of the Potomac River in 1785 at Mount Vernon. Washington had long dreamed of a series of internal improvements to the river, including locks and canals, which would allow it to flow all the way to the Ohio River. Internal improvements to the Potomac River would knit together Washington's private interest in developing his western lands with the larger public interest of tying those who were settling in the west to the United States. Such a venture required the cooperation of both Virginia and Maryland, since both shared rights to the Potomac. At the conclusion of the conference, Virginia proposed a meeting of all the states "to consider how far a uniform system in their commercial regulations may be necessary to their common interest and their permanent harmony." Out of this came the Annapolis Convention.[24]

Madison, Hamilton and the Annapolis Convention

Madison had gradually changed his mind. Always a supporter of a stronger national government, he initially believed that amending the Articles of Confederation could achieve this purpose. By the late 1780s, he had concluded that the federal union needed more-radical changes if it was to survive. His experiences serving as a legislator in Virginia, along with the events of the period, were the key turning points that led him to this conclusion.

In 1783, Madison was one of the first victims of term limits. The Articles of Confederation restricted individual members from serving more than three one-year terms consecutively in the Congress, and so Madison returned home to Montpelier. Despite his political career, he still had found no means to support himself, since holding political office during this period was an unpaid position. "A politician dependent on his salary would, many felt, be tempted to sacrifice the public good to his own needs," Madison biographer Ralph Ketchum writes. Jemmy, as his family called him, was still dependent on his father and the income from the plantation to support him, but life as a planter did not appeal to him. He did some minor speculation in western lands with his friend and neighbor James Monroe, and once again read the law, but he had no real intention to become a practicing attorney. His need for independence from life as a planter had a moral as well as financial dimension. As with Jefferson and Washington, Madison "saw the incongruity between slavery and the professed ideals of the revolution." He wrote to Edmund Randolph that he wished "to depend as little as possible on the labor of slaves." But also, as with Jefferson and Washington, he could never find a way to be free of the system of slavery without bringing financial ruin on his own family and the economy of his native Virginia.[25]

Politics once again rescued him. During the spring elections of 1784, Orange County elected him to serve as its representative in the Virginia House of Delegates. He met with some success in the legislature, pushing forward an Act for the Establishment of Religious Freedom, in 1785. This had been a cherished goal that he shared with Jefferson, to institute the free exercise of religion in the state and eliminate Anglicanism as the established religion. In 1784, the legislature had considered a bill, supported by Patrick Henry, to levy a tax to support religious teachers. Madison opposed it since it would involve the state in the establishment of religion. Through a series of maneuvers, including the circulation of a petition protesting the bill that garnered over 10,000 signatures, Madison and his supporters were able to defeat the measure in 1785. Madison then introduced Jefferson's bill for the establishment of religious freedom. After passage of the religious freedom Act, he wrote to Jefferson, "I flatter myself [that we have] in this Country extinguished forever the ambitious project of making laws for the human mind."[26]

But in other areas, particularly the reform of the state's laws, the repayment of pre-war debts to the British, and the expansion of national power, he met major opposition at the state level.

Both Madison and Jefferson wanted to strengthen the Virginia Constitution of 1776. While minor bills passed easily, attempts to reform the court system and the penal code failed. Madison believed that a comprehensive revision of the legal code could have been completed "with great ease...if the time spent on motions to put it off...had been employed on its merits." An attempt to establish a public school system also failed to pass the legislature. Madison also wanted Virginia to meet its obligations under the Paris peace treaty, which required the states to allow British citizens and loyalists to sue to recover payments owed to them from their pre-war debts. He saw that state barriers to enactment of these provisions had allowed the British to use this as a pretext to continue to occupy its forts in the Ohio Valley, thereby forestalling western expansion. Madison's attempts to pass legislation in this area failed and heightened his "conviction that the states, left to their own devices, would never display the harmony, integrity, and stability required if the United States was to achieve domestic solvency and international respect."[27]

Concerns over financial matters also weighed on him by late 1785, specifically the move to issue paper money, the same issue that concerned Washington. As Rakove writes, "the proposals for paper money and debtor relief that were now appearing had a more sinister intent, Madison thought: to deprive creditors of their rightful property by forcing them to accept payment in the depreciating currency the states were likely to emit." Madison's fear in this area was partially self-serving, since he was attempting to fight off measures that were "inimical to wealthy families" like his own. Yet, it also reflected a deeper dilemma that Madison was facing over the proper balance between majority rule in a democracy and the protection of the natural rights of individuals and the minority from the tyranny of the majority. To Madison, unjust measures that denied a minority of the people their rights, even if approved by a majority of the public, were no more just than rule by a dictator. The protection of minority rights from majority factions was at the center of Madison's reflections on, and development of, the Constitution.[28]

He was further disillusioned in his attempts to increase the power of Congress and push forward pro-federal government policies at the state level. Madison pressed for the revenue plan of 1783 that he had helped fashion while in Congress, along with state compliance with requests for funding the central government. Madison and fellow legislator Patrick Henry, the state's most popular politician, stood opposed on issues involving the expansion of federal power. While Henry approved altering the formula contained in the 1783 revenue plan for allocating expenses among the various states, he wanted a one-year delay in raising the taxes needed to pay these expenses.

Given the foreign policy challenges presented by Great Britain and Spain, Madison, by 1785, supported allowing Congress to regulate both foreign and domestic trade, a power that "appears to me not to admit of a doubt." Madison achieved no greater success in this attempt when Congress watered down his proposed resolution and he became disillusioned that any measure increasing congressional power would ever pass.[29]

The proposed Jay Treaty with Spain in the spring of 1786 further undermined his attempts to have Virginia pass measures designed to strengthen the Congress under the Articles. Madison thought that the Jay Treaty "would be a voluntary barter in time of profound peace of the rights of one part of the empire to the interests of another part," as he wrote to fellow Virginian James Monroe. He believed that Spain was attempting to divide the states from each other and "to foment the jealously between the eastern and southern states." Passage of the treaty, or even failure by a narrow margin, would "be fatal...to the augmentation of the federal authority."[30]

All of these failures made Madison gravely concerned about the quality of decision making at the state level. He saw that the Virginia legislators were "unaccustomed to consider the interests of the state as they are interwoven with those of the confederacy." One historian has observed of Madison's view of state politics that: "The Virginia legislators seemed parochial, illiberal, small minded, and most of them seemed to have only a particular interest to serve... They often made a travesty of the legislative process and were reluctant to do anything that might appear unpopular." Madison's concerns were not just isolated to Virginia, but extended to decision making taking place in other states. By 1786, New York had failed to pass the revenue measures of 1783, and New Jersey refused to pay its federal expenses so long as New York refused to ratify the tax scheme. The two states were also engaged in a trade war. And the proposed Jay Treaty divided northern interests from southern ones, threatening to break the confederation into multiple parts. By 1786, Madison had concluded that a "strategy of gradually strengthening the Confederation...seemed risky." He began to consider other, more radical, means to create a strong federal government. The Annapolis Conference gave him his first opening.[31]

The Annapolis Conference, which opened on September 11, 1786, was a flop in terms of attendance; only twelve delegates showed up, representing Virginia, Delaware, New Jersey, Pennsylvania and New York. But while small in number, all those who attended were ardent nationalists, and the conference gave them an opportunity to discuss the problems and shortcomings of the federal union. In addition to Madison, Alexander Hamilton of New York and Edmund Randolph, then governor of Virginia and Madison's friend, also attended. So did John Dickinson of Pennsylvania, whose original draft of the Articles had provided for a much stronger confederacy. The meeting had been called for the express and limited purpose of improving commercial relations between the states, but the final communiqué of the conference would go well beyond this.

Madison and Hamilton, the one-time collaborators in Congress for a stronger national government, were quite the pair. Hamilton was a dashing figure, full of charisma and brashly self-confident, a man born to rule. He had come a long way from his humble beginnings, and through his own skills and abilities, and the help of some powerful patrons, he now stood at the apex of American society. Madison, on the other hand, was from one of Virginia's most established and aristocratic families. Always dressed in black, he came across as a somber figure, to the point of being viewed by some as a "gloomy stiff creature." Ellis writes of Madison that he was a man who "seemed to lack a personality." Another historian has referred to Madison as "a queer mixture of intellectual assurance, bordering on conceit, and social timidity and awkwardness" who could also be "funny and a superb raconteur among warm companions, even telling the occasional bawdy tale."[32]

Together, Hamilton and Madison made a formidable team. Hamilton, after leaving Congress in 1783, had become a lawyer and a member of elite New York society. He had been out of politics for three years, but still had the same concerns over the weakness of the Congress. Hamilton had written in response to an inquiry from James Duane that, "The fundamental defect [of our present system] is a want of power in Congress." Hamilton built on these themes in a series of articles published in the summer of 1781 entitled the "Continentalist," where he further described the problems with government under the Articles of Confederation and expressed fear that the "states would amass progressively more power until the union disintegrated." After leaving the army, he worked as a tax collector for Robert Morris in New York in 1782. In that role, Hamilton was able to convince the state legislature to issue a call for a national conference to amend the Articles of Confederation. And just before he left Congress in 1783, he drafted a resolution calling for the same type of convention to fix the problems of government under the Articles.[33]

By 1785, Hamilton expressed grave, if overstated, concerns over a potential uprising of the have-nots, triggered by the economic depression that New York and many other states were experiencing. He sensed a crisis on the horizon and warned that "those who are concerned for the security of property...must endeavour to put men in the legislature whose principles are not of the leveling kind." Hamilton's fear of the have-nots has sometimes been viewed as placing him in support of the establishment of an American hereditary aristocracy, and some of his writings on government lend themselves to such a critique, as when he wrote that government should combine "the continuity of a monarchy... with the liberties of a republic." Later, while at the Constitutional Convention, he supported a president that would serve for life, essentially an "elective monarch." As his biographer, Ron Chernow, notes, "However atrociously misguided the idea was, it fell short of proposing a real monarchy," since the president would be elected and subject to recall.[34]

A better description of Hamilton is that he favored merit, and wanted to promote those, like himself, that possessed superior skills. Hamilton, who was a member of the Society of the Cincinnati, opposed the group's policy that the eldest sons inherit their father's membership. That particular provision had been quite controversial, spurring opposition from Franklin, Adams, Jay, and Jefferson. Hamilton, in a speech to the Society in 1786, expressed his opposition to the policy. He likened it to primogeniture since it "refers to birth what ought to belong to merit only, a principle inconsistent with the genius of a society founded on friendship and patriotism." Hamilton, as the second son, could hardly be expected to favor any form of primogeniture. While he often showed a lack of sympathy for the poor and downtrodden in his writings, and equality was not of major concern to him, he was not a supporter of government by a hereditary monarchy.[35]

Despite the poor turnout, the Annapolis Convention attendees decided to salvage something from the meeting. The New Jersey delegation's instructions had allowed them to discuss matters beyond commerce, which the group used as pretext to invite all of the states to attend a general convention to be held in Philadelphia in May of 1787. Hamilton drafted the initial communiqué, which was so provocative in its indictment of the current shortcomings of the central government that Edmund Randolph asked him to rewrite it. Always prickly, Hamilton flared up, and it took Madison to convince him to amend the statement, since Randolph could ensure that "all [of] Virginia will be against you." The core point of the final Address of the Annapolis Convention was "that the power of regulating trade is of such comprehensive extent" to "require a correspondent adjustment of other parts of the Federal system." By such means, Hamilton, with an assist from Madison, was able to enlarge the scope of the Philadelphia Convention. Their intent was clear: to craft a completely new government to replace the Articles.[36]

On his way home from Annapolis, Madison went to Mount Vernon to begin the process of lobbying Washington to attend the Philadelphia Convention. Madison knew that what he, Hamilton, and the other committed nationalists intended to do could be viewed, by at least some, as treason, a charge they could be inoculated from if Washington attended. In addition, any attempt to restructure the federal government would flounder without the active backing and participation of

Washington. But Washington demurred, believing at this point that the chances of a successful convention were slim; he did not want to tarnish his reputation as the American Cincinnatus, especially because he too saw that the convention could be seen as treasonous. But Madison was not easily discouraged. He returned to the Virginia legislature that fall and sponsored a resolution that placed Washington's name at the top of the list of delegates to attend the convention. He was attempting to gradually box in Washington.[37]

Events in western Massachusetts would prove to be a major catalyst in bringing Washington around and leading to widespread state participation at the Philadelphia Convention. The trouble had begun in the fall of 1786, at about the same time that the Annapolis Convention was meeting. With Massachusetts awash in debt from the war, the government began to raise taxes at the same time that farm prices and wages were shrinking. Farmers in the western part of the state lacked the hard currency to keep up with both the rising tax burden and mortgages on their farms, and foreclosures skyrocketed. The farmers, many of whom were veterans of the Revolutionary War, began to organize with the goal of closing the courts that were processing the foreclosures. Daniel Shays was one of their leaders, a man who had fought at the battles of Bunker Hill and Saratoga, and the movement became known as Shays Rebellion. The Confederation Congress sent Henry Knox, one of Washington's former generals, to investigate the situation. He overreacted to the rebellion, both in terms of the numbers of those that supported it and of their ultimate intent. Knox estimated that the rebels had over 15,000 men under arms, when there were probably no more than a few thousand. He also concluded that the rebels were "determined to annihilate all debts public and private." Henry Lee, a neighbor of Washington's, received the report from Knox and informed the general that "anarchy" could ensue and that the rebels intended to redistribute all property. What the rebels really wanted was relief from court ordered foreclosures, and their main tactic was to close the courts so that they could not act.[38]

The Shaysites overreached when they attempted, in the winter of 1787, to take over the arsenal at Springfield, a move that scared many of the Massachusetts elites "out of their wits." Since the Congress had no money, nor an army to confront the rebels, Governor James Bowdon borrowed 20,000 dollars from private interests and gathered a force of 4,400 men. The rebels were quickly routed, ending the insurrection. While the rebellion was largely a tempest in a teapot, the fears it engendered left a lasting mark.

Washington's response to Shay's Rebellion was one of concern. He wished to know if the rebels had real grievances, and if they did, why the government had not acted to deal with them. But he was also greatly concerned over the reaction in Europe, where the rebellion might be viewed as an indication that the Americans were incapable of self-government. "I am really mortified beyond expression that, in the moment of our acknowledged independence, we should by our conduct verify the predictions of our transatlantic foe and render ourselves ridiculous and contemptible in the eyes of all Europe." Washington now feared "that mankind left to themselves are unfit for their own government" and wrote to Madison on the need to overhaul the government under the Articles of Confederation:

> *What stronger evidence can be given of the want of energy in our governments than these disorders? If there exists not a power to check them, what security has a man of life, liberty or property?... Thirteen Sovereignties pulling against each other, and all pulling at the federal head, will soon bring ruin on the whole; whereas a liberal, and energetic Constitution, well guarded & closely watched,*

to prevent incroachments, might restore us to the degree of respectability & consequence to which we had a fair claim.[39]

Other members of the founding elite also expressed major concerns over Shays Rebellion. For Madison, it was just more proof of the need for a stronger national government. The states were without federal help and thus "prey to internal violence and subversion." Hamilton feared that disorder would engender further disorder. John Adams, from his position as the ambassador to the court of St. James, began work on a book describing the need to reform the government of the United States. Only Jefferson, in Paris serving as the American diplomat to France, seemed unfazed. "The spirit of resistance to government is so valuable on certain occasions that I wish it to be kept alive...I like a little rebellion now and then," he wrote to Abigail Adams in 1786. Later, in 1787, he wrote: "The tree of liberty must be refreshed from time to time with the blood of patriots and tyrants." But Jefferson's views on Shays Rebellion were outside of the mainstream of elite opinion.[40]

Shays Rebellion helped convince Congress to finally support the call for a convention. Congress had received the Annapolis Address in September of 1786, but no action was taken until the following February. In part, the delay was caused by the inability of the Continental Congress to achieve a quorum during this period. In part, it was due to opposition to the idea of a convention, especially from the New England delegates, who thought Congress lacked the authority to take this action. Shays Rebellion caused the New England representatives to rethink their position and withdraw their opposition to the proposed meeting. Finally, on February 21, 1787, the Congress adopted a resolution supporting the Convention, albeit solely for the "purpose of revising the Articles of Confederation," and stating that any proposed changes would be reported to and approved by the "Congress and confirmed by the several states."[41] In other words, Congress and all of the states would need to unanimously approve any changes to the Articles of Confederation, an approach that would most likely fail, just as all other attempts to modify the Articles had.

This was obviously much less than what Madison, Washington, and Hamilton had in mind, and they and others would soon ignore the mandate provided for in the congressional resolution. By the spring of 1787, Madison was finally able to convince Washington to attend the convention. According to Ellis, "[Madison] informed Washington that his canvas of the roster of state delegations revealed an impressive array of talent heavily weighted in favor of much more than tinkering, indeed disposed to a thorough transformation of the existing political system. This piece of intelligence tipped the balance." Washington now felt that the convention had at least a fighting chance of making a real difference, and he agreed to attend.[42]

Mr. Madison Prepares

James Madison was an odd person to lead a second revolution. He was exceedingly shy in meetings, "with a voice so weak" that people had trouble hearing him in public debates. Yet his style may well have been perfectly suited for the Constitutional Convention since "his arguments during debates tended to arrive without the rhetorical frills or partisan edges, but rather with the naked power of pure thought."[43] By 1787, Madison was also experienced in the practice of politics, a realm where compromise and the ability to count votes were at a premium, and so part of his effort was outward looking, trying to determine the views of the various state delegations that would attend the convention. Finally, Madison was always the most prepared person in any political meeting. In the months preceding the Philadelphia Convention, he focused his vast intellectual talents upon the problems of government.

We see examples of his ideas prior to the Convention in two political tracks and in letters he sent to Washington, Jefferson, and Edmund Randolph. He prepared the first of these, called "Of Ancient and Modern Confederacies," in the summer of 1786, prior to the Annapolis Convention. In it, he analyzed the problems and weakness inherent in confederacies, from ancient Greece, through the Roman Empire, to the Swiss Confederations, and the United Provinces of the Netherlands. From this study, he concluded that confederacies were doomed to fail since they lacked a strong central government. In the words of the historian Ellis, Madison believed that: "Either the confederated republic of the United States came together as one nation or it suffered the sad fate of its European predecessors, which was a combination of civil war, anarchy, and political oblivion."[44]

In *Vices of the Political Systems of the United States*, written in April 1787, Madison laid out the major problems facing the country. He began with a litany of how the states had failed to meet their responsibilities to the central government and to each other. His most persuasive and cogent example of state failures looked back at the Revolutionary War, "when external dangers supplied in some degree the defect of legal & coercive sanctions, how imperfectly did the States fulfill their obligations to the Union?" In other words, if the states would not comply with federal requests for financial assistance during a time of existential danger, why would they comply during a time of peace?[45] His view was an outgrowth of the sum of his political experiences to date, from service at the state level as part of the executive council in Virginia, to his time as a delegate to the Continental Congress, and then to his role as a state legislator in Virginia. He had seen how the states had ignored federal requests for funding, and how this had endangered the war effort. He also saw that the lack of federal power in the post-war era had led to a lack of common purpose among the states. His experience in the Virginia legislature had brought him to the conclusion that representatives acted primarily on their constituent's short-term interests, or even worse on their own short-term interests, without regard for the broader public interest.[46]

To Madison, part of the problem lay in the very structure of the governments that had been framed in 1776. Too much power was vested in the legislative branch, with little power given to the executive or the judiciary to allow them to undertake their own duties and to serve as a check on the popular passions of the legislative branch. This had been a natural outcome in 1776, when the break from Great Britain had occurred as a reaction to a strong and distant central authority and to colonial experience with abusive power from royal governors. But, Madison argued, the country had learned much since that time. As one historian writes: "events since 1776 had revealed that inexperienced legislators confronting the staggering problems the war created, and subject to intense pressures from their constituents, could not act with the 'wisdom and steadiness' the situation required."[47]

Madison had reached the conclusion that the solution lay in a stronger and more viable government at the federal level, one that would have the ability to adopt laws that were binding directly on the American people themselves, and not based on the voluntary compliance of the states. From the perspective of American nationhood, this was a key intellectual breakthrough. If properly empowered, the federal government could knit the United States into one American nation. To do this would require the authority to act on behalf of the American people, who would elect representatives and hold them directly responsible for their actions, with the laws of the federal government directly binding on the people.

Madison reached this conclusion based on some truly radical thinking on the nature of republican government. Prior to Madison, political theorists like Montesquieu had believed that a republic could only exist in small and homogenous geographic areas. Madison flipped this theory on its head, showing that small republics suffered from the problems of factions. "All civilized societies are divided into different interests and factions," Madison wrote in *Vices*, whether "creditors or debtors—Rich or poor—husbandmen, merchants or manufacturers—members of different religious sects—followers of different political leaders—inhabitants of different districts—owners of different kinds of property." His concern was with a majority faction since, "what is to restrain them from unjust violations of the rights and interests of the minority, or of individuals?" Madison's answer was that a national republic, an extended republic, could provide better protections for the rights of the minority against the "tyranny of the majority." He thought this would occur because such factions "will be unlikely to unite a majority of the whole number in an unjust pursuit"[48] at the national level:

> *If an enlargement of the sphere is found to lessen the insecurity of private rights, it is not because the impulse of a common interest or passion is less predominant ... but because [it] is less apt to be felt and the requisite combinations less easy to be formed by a great than by a small number. The Society becomes broken into a greater variety of interests, of pursuits, of passions, which check each other, whilst those who may feel a common sentiment have less opportunity of communication and concert.*[49]

In trying to protect the rights of minorities from majority factions "he was not thinking so much of protecting the civil rights of the poor and propertyless, but rather the rights of creditors from paper money schemes that allowed debts to be repaid with nearly worthless currency" Ellis writes.[50] This is the Madison, a self-interested person trying to protect the affluent, that Charles Beard, the Progressive era historian, writes about in his work on the economic motivation of the founders. But while part of his motivation may have been self-interest that was far from the whole story. The principle of protecting the rights of individuals and minorities in a democratic society would prove to be essential and would cover issues ranging from freedom of speech, religion, conscience, to due process of law and equal protection under those laws, and later extend to civil and women's rights. In a letter to Jefferson in October 1787, Madison recognized this as it applied to religion, writing: "The same security seems requisite for the civil as for the religious rights of individuals. If the same [religious] sect form a majority and have the power, other sects will be sure to be depressed."[51] Ellis also makes the case that Madison was "trying to rescue the American Revolution, not so much from democracy as from a fatal aversion to government itself." [52] The role of government is another of those ongoing debates in American society.

Madison also believed that a national government in an enlarged republic would produce an additional benefit by allowing for the election of more capable men, those like himself, to serve in the legislature. While serving in the Virginia legislature, he had seen the impact when inexperienced men were elected as legislators, men who failed to operate in the larger public interest. Government at the national level would create "a process of elections as will most certainly extract from the mass of the society the purest and noblest characters which it contains."[53] Madison wanted representatives at the national level who could act with independent judgment and be less beholden to those who elected them. "An individual is never to be allowed to be a judge or even a witness in his own cause," Madison wrote to Jefferson in 1787. The great need is for a government that "may be sufficiently *neutral* between different parts of the Society to controul one part from invading the rights of another." In other words, government should act as an independent arbitrator between interests in society, and in the process, can ensure the public interest. In order to achieve this, the Constitution would eventually give elected officials longer terms in office than those provided for under the state constitutions of the time, remove the power of recall, and eliminate term limits, all to ensure that elected officials could act in as disinterested and fair a fashion as possible.[54] Madison was grappling with the age-old problem in democratic governments of whether elected officials should act purely as delegates who simply follow the wishes of their constituents, or whether, as Madison preferred, they should exercise independent judgment, voting based on their conscience and a broader conception of what is in the public interest.

In some ways, Madison was attempting to "perfect" politics. But this was not an attempt to perfect human nature. Madison was a realist who understood that a republic could not survive on civic virtue alone, on the complete sublimation of self- interest, as those in 1776 thought. He had also concluded that no society "could attain the homogeneity and uniformity that previous writers demanded of republics," even small republics.[55] Rather, it was a perfection that would be grounded in an extended republic, where interests would compete over a larger area, and where elected officials would act as the umpire, resolving disputes.

In *Vices*, Madison did not spend much time on how the new government was to be structured. But in an April 16, 1787 letter to Washington, Madison lays out his thoughts in this area. His approach, unlike that of Hamilton, recognizes that the states cannot be eliminated, but rather "some middle ground" must be found "which may at once support a due supremacy of the national authority, and not exclude the local authorities wherever they can be subordinately useful."

Madison was proposing an early version of federalism, in which federal power would be enumerated and limited but, within those areas, the national government would have clear and direct authority over the people without the states acting as intermediaries.[56] Representation would need to be based on population, or some other equal scheme, and not on voting by individual states, as the Articles of Confederation required. The national government would be supreme in all areas "which require uniformity" like regulation of trade and the taxation of imports.

The federal government, in his mind, would consist of three branches, a legislature, a judiciary, and an executive. Just as the states and the federal government would provide for checks and balances on each other, so too the three branches would result in a separation of powers under which each would check the other. The legislature would be further split into two branches, "one of them chosen every [few] years by the people at large…; the other to hold their place for longer term, and to go out in such a rotation as always to leave in office a large majority of old members." Madison also thought that this upper house, what would become the Senate, should have the power to veto state laws. In this, he retained some naiveté, since a veto of state laws had very little chance of being approved at the Constitutional Convention. The federal veto was Madison's ultimate answer for controlling majority factions at the state level, since the national government would have the "negative in all cases whatsoever on the legislative acts of the States" a power that could be used to invalidate laws, like the issuance of paper money and debtor relief, that Madison found so troubling. The new national government would therefore be in a position to act as a "disinterested & dispassionate umpire in disputes between different passions & interests in the State." Given this, the Senate would play a very large role in Madison's constitutional scheme "as the branch best suited to control the passions of the people, to secure a place for wisdom and stability in the great republic," and to slow down the popular passions that could dominate an elected assembly.[57]

While Madison had given great thought to many elements of the new national government, he had given little consideration to the role and structure of the executive. "I have scarcely ventured to form my own opinion either of the manner in which it ought to be constituted or of the authorities with which it ought to be cloathed." At the Constitutional Convention, he and the other delegates would grapple with how to structure the presidency.

Madison closes his letter to Washington by stating: "To give a new System its proper validity and energy, a ratification must be obtained from the people, and not merely from the ordinary authority of the Legislatures." This was Madison's way of bypassing the unanimous consent required of the states to amend or change the Articles. The Convention would, as we shall see, follow Madison's advice and choose to have the Constitution ratified by special, popularly elected conventions.

Endnotes

1 Carol Berkin, *A Brilliant Solution: Inventing the American Constitution*, (Boston, 2003), p. 12-13. The Bailyn quote is from Rakove, *Beginnings*, p. 333. Information on economic growth is from Wood, *Creation*, p. 394 and Ferguson, p. 336. See also Ferling, p. 257 for westward expansion and infrastructure improvements.

2 Beeman, p. 38-39

3 See for example John Kaminski on post-war America in the 1780s, retrieved 6/4/2012 from http://www.pbs.org/wgbh/aia/part2/2i1624.html and Berkin from Chapter 1.

4 Rakove, *Beginnings*, p. 338; See also U.S. Department of State Office of the Historian, "U.S. Debt and Foreign Loans, 1775-1795," retrieved 5/12/2014 from https://history.state.gov/milestones/1784-1800/loans

5 Beeman, p. 15; Rakove; *Beginnings*, p. 338-339; Ferguson, p. 180-182

6 Rakove, *Beginnings*, p. 340-341

7 Berkin, p 20-21; Ellis, *The Quartet*, p. 86; On the fear of standing armies, see Christopher

Hamner, *American Resistance to a Standing Army*, retrieved 3/1/2013 from http://teachinghistory.org/history-content/ask-a-historian/24671

8 McCullough, p. 350; Rakove, *Beginnings*, p. 345-346; Ferling, p. 263; Berkin, p. 14

9 Berkin, p. 15

10 Rakove, *Beginnings*, p. 348-349

11 Rakove, *Beginnings*, p. 350; Ellis, *The Quartet*, p. 88; Ferling, p. 265-266

12 Ferling, p. 266

13 Joseph J. Ellis, *Founding Brothers: The Revolutionary Generation*, (New York, 2001), p. 14; The disagreements among historians date all the way back to the founding era. In 1888, John Fiske wrote a book entitled "The Critical Period of American History" in which he argued that the adoption of the constitution saved the country from disaster. The Fiske view was largely accepted until the twentieth century, when the Constitution as a conspiracy of the elite was depicted in Charles A. Beard's "An Economic Interpretation of the Constitution," published in 1913. Beard saw the founders who attended the convention in Philadelphia as an undemocratic and self-interested minority that personally gained from the establishment of a new system of government. Beard's work was built on by Merrill Jensen, who argued that those who supported the Articles of Confederation were the true embodiment of the spirit of the revolution.

The Beard/Jensen conspiracy view was challenged by a number of historians, most forcefully Forrest McDonald in 1957, who argued that the Constitution was the work of principled men who were not motivated by their own self interest. McDonald found that the seven men with most at stake in terms of ownership of Continental debt either left the Convention or refused to sign the Constitution, a fact at odds with the idea of self interest as the primary motivator of the drafters of the Constitution.

The Jensen view of the Articles of Confederation and the events leading up to the Philadelphia Convention were countered by Jack Rakove in "The Beginnings of National Politics: An Interpretive History of the Continental Congress," a seminal work of history that has been relied on in this book as a source of information. Rakove is of the "nationalist interpretation of the origins of the American union," and rejects the simplistic notion put forth by Jensen that the politics of the era were largely dictated by a clash of radicals (who supported the Articles) versus conservatives (who supported the Constitution).

14 The quotes are from Ferling, p. 278; Rakove, *Beginnings*, p. 365-366; and Ellis, *His Excellency*, p. 169

15 Rakove, *Beginnings*, p. 354-355

16 The Madison quote and the idea of the breakup into multiple confederacies is from Joseph J. Ellis, *American Creation*,(New York, 2007), p. 93

17 See Ellis, *Founding Brothers*, p. 8-9; *Brotherhood*, Lecture 8; and *American Creation*, p. 107

18 Jack N. Rakove, *The Road to Philadelphia: 1781-1787*, p. 99, in Levy (Ed.).

19 Chernow, *Washington*, p. 465. The quote is from Ellis, *His Excellency*, p. 155-156, as is the information on the number of acres of western land that Washington owned.

20 Chernow, *Washington*, p. 514

21 James Thomas Flexner, *George Washington and the New Nation: (1783-1793)*, (Boston, 1970), p. 92-94

22 Flexner, *New Nation*, p. 94, which is also where the quotes are from.

23 Ellis, *His Excellency*, p. 168-169

24 Chernow, *Washington*, p. 500; Flexner, *New Nation*, p. 90; on Washington's health problems, see Beeman, p. 31

25 Ketchum, p. 144 for the quote on income from politics and p. 148-149 on his views on slavery.

26 From Rakove, *Revolutionaries*, p. 351

27 The quote is from Rakove, *Revolutionaries*, p. 351; see also Ketcham, p. 161-162 for problems Madison encountered in passing legislation at the state level and p. 171 for the quote at the end of the paragraph on his experience at the state level in complying with the peace treaty.

28 The quote is from Rakove, *Revolutionaries*, p. 352; see also Ketcham, p. 181 on Madison's concern with majority rule.

29 The quote is from Rakove, *Madison*, p. 44

30 The quotes are from Ketcham, p. 177-178

31 The Madison quote is from Rakove, *Madison*, p. 43; the historian referenced is from Wood, *Revolutionary Characters*, p. 148; gradual strengthening is Rakove, *Revolutionaries*, p. 352

32 See Chernow, *Hamilton*, p. 174 for descriptions of Hamilton and Madison; the Ellis quote is from *Founding Brothers*, p. 53.

33 On the Duane letter, see Rakove, *Revolutionaries*, p. 405; the quote in the sentence on the "Continentalist" is from Chernow, *Hamilton*, p. 158; on lobbying the New York legislature and the drafting of resolutions in Congress, see Rakove, *Revolutionaries*, p. 409 and 412-413.

34 Chernow, *Hamilton*, p.219 and p. 232

35 Chernow, *Hamilton*, p.217-218

36 Chernow, *Hamilton*, p.223-224; Address of the Annapolis Convention, retrieved March 8, 2013 from http://oll.libertyfund.org

37 Wills, p. 25; Rakove, *Revolutionaries*, p. 358

38 Ferling, p. 279; Beeman, p. 16-17

39 Chernow, *Washington*, p. 518; George Washington to James Madison letter of November 5, 1786, retrieved April 4, 2013 from http://gwpapers.virginia.edu/docments/constitution/1784/madison2.html

40 Ketchum, p. 186; Chernow, *Hamilton*, p. 225; Ellis, *American Sphinx*, p. 118

41 Beeman, p. 20-21

42 Ellis, *His Excellency*, p. 175

43 Ellis, *American Creation*, p. 100

44 Ellis, *American Creation*, p. 103

45 James Madison, *Vices of the Political System of the United States*, April 1783, retrieved March 26, 2013 from http://teachingamericanhistory.org/library/index.asp?

46 See Rakove, *Madison*, p. 49-50

47 Rakove, *Madison*, p. 50

48 Madison letter to Thomas Jefferson, October 24, 1787, retrieved April 21, 2013 from http://press-pubs.uchicago.edu/founders/documents/v1ch17s22.html

49 Madison, *Vices*

50 Ellis, *American Creation*, p. 105

51 Madison letter to Jefferson, October 24, 1787

52 Ellis writes this as footnote 16 on page 267 of *The Quartet.*

53 Quoted from Rakove, *Madison*, p. 56

54 This point on the need for independent judgment is from Wills, *Madison*, p. 33.

55 Rakove, *Madison*, p. 56

56 See Lance Banning, "The Practicable Sphere of a Republic: James Madison, the Constitutional Convention, and the Emergence of Revolutionary Federalism," p. 171-174, in Beeman, *Beyond Confederation.*

57 Banning, p. 176

Chapter 7

The Delegates Gather: The Virginia Plan Unveiled / May 3 to June 5, 1787

Catching many delegates unprepared, the well-formulated Virginia Plan gave large states the initiative, and they dominated the Conventions early stages.[1]

– Winton Solberg –

Carpe diem may have been the watchword for Madison and his fellow Virginia delegates when they put forward their plan for a new national government. They knew achieving success at the Convention would prove difficult, but they also understood that the individual or group that put forward the first coherent proposal for constitutional reform would control the agenda. The Virginians found willing accomplices in the host delegates from Pennsylvania.

The Virginia and Pennsylvania Delegates Prepare

James Madison was the first of the out-of-town delegates to arrive in Philadelphia, taking the stagecoach from New York on May 3, 1787, where he was serving as a member of the Continental Congress. The Convention was not scheduled to open until May 14, but he had urged the other members of the Virginia delegation to arrive early so they could prepare.[2]

Madison stayed at a boardinghouse run by Mary House, a block away from the Pennsylvania State House (today's Independence Hall), where the Convention would be held. The boardinghouse was familiar ground for Madison, his home away from home during his last term in Congress from 1780 to 1783 and the place where he had first fallen in love with the sixteen-year-old Kitty Floyd in 1783. Kitty was the daughter of another member of Congress, William Floyd, who also stayed at the boardinghouse in 1783. She and Madison were engaged to be married in the spring of 1783, but Kitty called it off when she fell in love with a nineteen-year-old medical student. Perhaps their age difference ultimately decided her, since Madison was thirty-two at the time. Jefferson, who also had stayed at Mrs. House's, had seen how happy Madison had been in the company of Kitty and attempted to assuage his friends broken heart when he wrote: "I sincerely lament the misadventure which has happened from whatever cause it may have happened. Should it be final however, the world still presents the same and many other resources of happiness, and you possess many within yourself."[3]

Madison may well have awakened on the morning of May 13 to sounds of cannon fire and the noise of cheering crowds when Washington arrived in Philadelphia. The local newspaper noted, "The joy of the people on the coming of this great and good man was shown by their acclamation and the ringing of bells." Washington and Franklin were the only true national figures in 1787, and Madison had spent a good deal of time and effort ensuring that Washington would attend the Convention. Given his plan to replace the Articles of Confederation, a goal that extended beyond the limited congressional authorization to simply propose amendments to them, Madison knew he needed men of great reputation to be involved at the Convention. As historian Garry Wills writes, "members of the convention would have been denounced for treason had not 'great names' given them cover—Franklin's name and, especially, Washington's. It would take great temerity to call them *enemies* of their country."[4]

Washington had intended to stay at Mrs. House's also, but Robert Morris convinced him to instead stay with him. Morris owned a grand mansion in the city, including a "beautiful walled garden, an ice house, a hothouse, and a stable with room enough for twelve horses."[5] In addition, Morris' wife and Martha Washington were good friends, although Martha did not travel to Philadelphia with her husband. Rather than unpack, Washington immediately paid a courtesy call on Franklin, where they enjoyed a dark beer together. We have no record showing what they spoke of, but both had long been supporters of the need to strengthen the federal government. Washington had only agreed to attend the convention when it became apparent that the delegates would consider more than halfway measures, and would "probe the defects of the Constitution to the bottom, and provide radical cures, whether they are agreed to or not."[6] Franklin, who had made proposals to create a strong union in the past, was also influenced by his many years abroad, including the previous eleven years in Paris as the American ambassador. He had concluded that the United States needed a stronger central government if it was to hold its own in the world with the great nations of Europe.[7]

Washington revered Franklin, and referred to him by the same title, "Your Excellency," that others bestowed upon him. Franklin was the only other person who could be considered a rival to Washington in serving as the chairman of the convention. But Franklin was in poor health, and in fact was unable to attend the opening day of the convention, which did not occur until May 25. He requested that Robert Morris place Washington's name into nomination as the presiding officer, and the delegates appointed Washington by acclimation to the position.[8]

The convention was supposed to open on May 14, but poor weather delayed many of the delegates from arriving on time. Heavy rain along the eastern seaboard during late April and early May had made many roads impassable. One historian writes, "The crude and hazardous state of America's roads stood as a sharp reminder to men like Madison of the way in which America's infrastructure—whether roads, bridges, schools, or public agencies capable of promoting economic development—had suffered because of the frailty of government at every level of American society."[9] In addition to poor weather, delegates also needed time to prepare instructions to those who would cover their farms, businesses, or law practices during what would prove to be an extended absence. Washington, who prided himself on being on time, complained in a letter home that the late arrivals were "highly vexatious to those who are idly and expensively spending their time here."[10]

But the delay actually worked to Madison's advantage. By May 17, all of the members of the Virginia delegation had arrived in Philadelphia, and Madison was able to lobby his fellow state delegates on his plan of government. In addition to Madison and Washington, the Virginia delegation included Governor Edmund Randolph, George Mason, John Blair, James McClurg, and George Wythe. Randolph, a lawyer and only thirty-four years old in 1787, was from one of the wealthiest families in Virginia and had been involved in politics since his early twenties. He had also been an aide-de-camp to Washington during the war. He would vacillate on the Constitution, first supporting Madison's approach, later unwilling to sign the document, and then finally supporting its ratification in Virginia. Mason, then sixty years of age, was widely considered one of the leading constitutional theorists of his time and had drafted both the Virginia Constitution and the Declaration of Rights in 1776, which had influenced Jefferson in his preparation of the Declaration of Independence. Mason was a homebody, having hardly left his family estate since 1776. He had agreed to attend the Convention out of a sense of duty, and initially supported the nationalist agenda out of deference to Washington. He too later refused to sign the document and fought against its ratification, largely because it lacked a bill of rights.[11]

The Virginia delegation found a strong ally for fundamental reform in the delegates from Pennsylvania, which included nationalists such as Franklin, Robert Morris, Gouverneur Morris (no relation to Robert), and James Wilson. Both Wilson and Gouverneur Morris would play critical roles in the Convention. Gouverneur Morris was a lawyer and an experienced politician, having served in both the Continental Congress and as an assistant to Robert Morris in his role as Superintendent of Finance in the Confederation Congress. A large man who stood over six feet tall, he had lost a leg in a carriage accident and walked with an oak peg attached to his leg. Originally from New York, he had stayed in Philadelphia following his defeat for a second term to the Continental Congress. His experience in the Congress and working for Robert Morris made him an ardent nationalist. He was also an elitist "who made it abundantly clear that he believed that only people such as himself should be entrusted with political power."[12] Morris would speak more than any other person at the convention, and would draft the final document.

James Wilson, another outspoken member of the Pennsylvania delegation, was originally from Scotland. He emigrated to American in 1765, and studied law under John Dickinson, which placed him in the middle of the emerging revolutionary crisis. Selected as a member of the Second Continental Congress, he was a signer of the Declaration of Independence. He was also greatly influenced by Robert Morris, whom he served as a legal advisor. His service in the Congress had taught him that the country needed a stronger national government, and he would be the most outspoken proponent of a strong role for the people in the new government.[13]

Each morning, Washington and Madison would make their way to the Pennsylvania statehouse, only to find an insufficient number of states present to form a quorum and open the convention for business. The Virginia delegation would then meet among themselves to prepare a plan of action for the convention. In the afternoon, they often joined the Pennsylvania delegation to share their thoughts and ideas. On May 16, Franklin hosted a large dinner party for the Virginians. Historian Richard Beeman writes that it was this dinner that "enabled the delegates most committed to a dramatic overhaul of the Articles of Confederation to coalesce. It helped that the two titans of America's Revolutionary experience—Franklin and Washington—made clear their support for a reinvigorated continental government."[14] Out of the numerous meetings held between the two delegations would emerge what delegates referred to as the Virginia Plan, an ambitious fifteen-point plan that carried Madison's imprint.

One of the major issues that the Virginians and the Pennsylvanians knew they would face was getting the small states to yield on the issue of equal representation in the Congress. Both Robert and Gouverneur Morris wanted to confront the issue head on, arguing that, "the large states should unite in firmly refusing to the small States an equal vote" in the Convention itself. In other words, voting at the Convention would be in proportion to population, which would allow the large states to ramrod through the issue of proportional representation. Madison feared that such a move would result in the potential collapse of the Convention before it could even begin its work, preferring to convince the small states "in the course of the deliberations, to give up their equality for the sake of an effective Government." Madison's approach won the day, and the Pennsylvanians agreed to defer a confrontation over the issue of representation.[15] But equal state voting in the Convention would incorporate into the entire proceedings the need for compromise between the large and small states.

The Convention Opens

On May 25, 1787, a cool and rainy day, the Convention finally achieved the requisite quorum of seven states and opened for business. They quickly nominated Washington and unanimously selected him to serve as presiding officer. Madison selected a seat "in front of the presiding member, with the other members on my right and left hand," he later wrote.[16] From this position, he could observe the proceedings and take copious notes, which formed the basis for much of what we know of the proceedings at the Convention. The Convention secretary was Major William Jackson of South Carolina, whose primary role was to take the minutes of the meetings, a job which he failed to do in a competent manner.

The delegates also decided to hold the meeting in secret, agreeing that, "nothing spoken in the House [shall] be printed, or otherwise published or communicated without leave." This may seem unduly secretive in an age where we hold transparency and open public debate in high esteem, but the delegates believed that the candid exchange of ideas could only occur in private. They may also have had a concern that the actions some planned to undertake, to completely dismantle the Articles of Confederation, which exceeded the mandate the Continental Congress had authorized, would be stopped dead in their tracks if the public became aware of the deliberations before they could come to any final conclusions.[17] The Convention would proceed that hot summer behind closed doors with the windows shuttered and the shades drawn.

In addition, the Convention rules permitted any delegate to request reconsideration of an item. The Convention met as a Committee of the Whole, which allowed for open debate and the recording of votes, but these decisions were not final, since they could be brought back for further consideration later. In other words, the Convention operated under parameters that meant that until everything was decided, nothing was decided.

Political scientist Robert Dahl has persuasively argued that "Framers" is a better term for those who attended the Convention, since many of the founders were not present. Both John Adams and Thomas Jefferson were serving overseas in England and France respectively. Patrick Henry refused to attend, stating that he "smelt a rat," and feared that the Virginia delegation planned to exceed their authority in constructing a new national government. Those like Henry that opposed the creation of a stronger central government largely boycotted the Convention. That group, which later became known as the antifederalists, stood opposed to the new Constitution. Samuel Adams was not invited to attend, and, as one historian writes, "as a decentralist with democratic leanings, there had been less likelihood that the Massachusetts Assembly would add him to the state's delegation than there was that Boston would be struck by a July snowstorm."[18]

Who were the fifty-five men that did attend the Convention? Jefferson called them a group of "demi-gods" and John Adams referred to them as men of "Ability, Weight, and Experience." They were clearly the elite of society. Most were well educated, with thirty-one having attended college at places such as Harvard, Princeton, and William & Mary. Twenty-nine were lawyers, although not all of them practiced law. Others were businessmen, merchants, land speculators, and southern planters. Many were born to wealth. There were also a few, such as Franklin and Hamilton, that had risen to positions of prominence from humble origins, but "there was no one in the room who might properly be called a man of ordinary means, a yeoman farmer, a shopkeeper, a sailor, or a laborer."[19] Twenty-four of them had served in the military during the Revolutionary War, which gave them a broader and more continental perspective than others. Almost all of them were experienced politicians who had served either in the Continental Congress or in their state legislatures. They were also relatively young, with an average age of forty-four and a median age of forty-two. Twenty-five slave owners attended, and they fought to protect the peculiar institution, although the Constitution never mentions the word slavery.

Some of the delegates would dominate the debates to come, while others remained silent. While twenty-five would take an active part, only about a dozen became the leaders. In addition to Madison and Franklin, this group included Roger Sherman, Gouverneur Morris, James Wilson, Elbridge Gerry, William Paterson, John Dickinson, Charles Pinckney, Edmund Randolph, and George Mason. Alexander Hamilton, who had done so much to bring about the Convention, would play a somewhat diminished role. This was in part because the other members of the New York delegation were opposed to strengthening the central government. It was also because Hamilton's views were too far outside of the mainstream of thought in comparison to the other delegates. He supported life terms for legislators; believed that the executive should be modeled on a monarch; and wanted to completely eviscerate the states.[20] None of these positions would win him many friends or influence his fellow delegates.

The Virginia Plan

Edmund Randolph rose to unveil what would become known as the Virginia Plan on the morning of May 29. Perhaps out of respect for

John Dickinson of Delaware, the main author of the Articles of Confederation, Randolph expressed his great respect for the men who had written the Articles. But he also indicated that they simply could not foresee, "in the then infancy of the science of constitutions and confederacies" the problems they now faced. Randolph outlined those problems, including the inefficiency of requisitions, commercial discord among the states, foreign debts, the problems of paper money, the violation of treaties, and the inability of the federal government to deal with these problems.[21]

Randolph next laid out a vision for a national government. The most important branch to the Framers was the legislature, the body that represented the people and the one where power must predominately reside. According to one historian "It was this conviction that the legislature was the core and all else was periphery that separates them from modern Americans, who look to the president for leadership and policy making."[22] The lower house would be elected by the people in proportion to population or based on financial contributions to the government. The upper house would be selected by the lower house from among a slate of candidates that would be nominated by the state governments. The Senate was designed to provide a check on the power of the people's house, since the Framers did not fully trust those elected directly by the public to consistently act in the broader public interest and protect minority rights. They equated direct democracy with mob rule and political parties with factions, as Madison described them. As Randolph and many others in the room saw it, the problems in the state governments arose "from the democratic parts of our constitutions" and the fact that those state constitutions had failed to provide "sufficient checks against democracy."[23] The national legislature would also have the power to veto all laws passed by the state governments.

The legislature, had it been approved in this form, would select an executive. This would have established a parliamentary system similar to what would later evolve in England. Under such a system, the executive (called the prime minister) is the party leader for the majority that controls the legislative branch. Much debate would ensue over this issue during the summer, including whether there should be one or several executives; the powers the office should hold; and how the executive was to be elected, with many fearful of direct election. A national judiciary would also be created, and a small number of its members would also serve, along with the executive, on a council of revision that would have the power to review all state and national laws before they became effective and reject them as necessary. Once the various proposals were prepared and approved by the Convention, they would be submitted to an "assembly or assemblies of Representatives, recommended by the several Legislatures to be expressly chosen by the people" to decide on the amendments.[24] In other words, state legislatures would not vote on the new Constitution, but rather special ratifying conventions would be held. All of this was as Madison had envisioned it, with certain changes made by Mason, Randolph, and Washington.

It is important to stop here and ponder the Framers' views on democracy and the importance they placed on private property rights. Randolph was not alone in his skeptical view on the subject. Elbridge Gerry believed "the evils we experience flow from the excess of democracy." Roger Sherman hoped that "the people...have as little to do as may be about the government." Hamilton wanted the new government structured to protect against the "imprudence of democracy."[25] And Madison, as already discussed, had an abiding fear of majority factions that could pass laws that deprived individuals of their rights, particularly the right to property.

We may attribute part of these concerns to the way the Framers defined democracy. Madison distinguished between a direct democracy and a republic, as he discussed in *Federalist* No. 10. The Federalist Papers were a series of newspaper articles written primarily by Hamilton and Madison as a means to defend the new Constitution during the ratification debate in New York. By a direct democracy, Madison was referring to "a society consisting of a small number of citizens, who assemble and administer the government in person," whereas a republic is a "government in which the scheme of representation takes place." "The two great points of difference between a democracy and a republic are: first, the delegation of the government, in the latter, to a small number of citizens elected by the rest; secondly, the greater number of citizens and greater sphere of country over which the latter may be extended."[26] As Dahl points out, the Framers recognized that in a proposed new nation as large as the United States, with "thirteen existing states with more to come, 'the people' could not possibly assemble directly to enact laws, as they did at the time in New England town meetings."[27] There was a need for a republican form of government in which the people delegated their authority to representatives.

Part of the Framers' criticism of democracy was class based and derived from their concern for protecting the status of the elites in society. The men who gathered in Philadelphia were realists who viewed human nature as it was, and who were under no illusions that they could perfect mankind. They had "a vivid sense of human evil and damnation," as historian Richard Hofstadter writes, and as such distrusted rule by the common man.[28] They wanted to place limitations on popular government to protect property rights and their own place in society. Their experience with democracy in the states, where laws allowing for debtor relief and the printing of paper money were approved, along with the threat posed by Shays Rebellion, had led them to conclude that too much democracy could also cause problems and needed to be reined in. As one historian writes, "an excess of power in the people was leading not simply to licentiousness but to a new kind of tyranny, not by the traditional rulers, but by the people themselves...The people, it seemed, were as capable of despotism as any prince."[29] In 1776, when many of the states had prepared their constitutions, few people had clearly recognized the danger that too much democracy posed, a danger the Framers intended to control.

The Framers' goal of protecting private property rights would be a key component for the future economic growth of the United States, and would provide for a more equitable distribution of income than in Mexico or the countries of Central and South America. In a book entitled *Why Nations Fail*, economists Daron Acemoglu and James A. Robinson argue that what separates rich from poor nations is the establishment of a set of political and economic institutions that distribute power widely, ensuring that citizens can control their leaders so they act in the public interest, and provide incentives for individuals to work hard to get ahead. The authors write that, "political institutions ensure stability and continuity" and protect the individual against the risk of "a dictator taking power and changing the rules of the game [and] expropriating their wealth."[30] As the Framers knew, not only dictators but also democratic governments without adequate checks could lead to the taking of one's wealth or property. In a society built on a concept of basic natural rights and the importance of individual freedom, such actions by the government would put a chill on the motivation for people to invest, save, and start new businesses or farms if one's possessions could easily be taken by government fiat. Although Jefferson had changed the words of the Declaration of Independence to "life, liberty and the pursuit of happiness," his original source, Locke, had referred to "life, liberty and estate," as being essential human rights. Jefferson himself wrote, "That the true foundation of republican government is the equal right of every citizen, in his person and in his property...

in the American States…every one may have land to labor for himself if he chooses."[31] Jefferson tied the right to property to his concept of equality. In Virginia, he proposed that all people be given a minimum of fifty acres of land. In America of the 1780s, the majority of white men were farmers who owned their own land, which made the protection of private property essential, and "the social precondition of freedom."[32]

As we saw in previous chapters, concerns about individual rights were derived from John Locke's theory of government, "with its conception of an isolated, materialist individual" who enters into society to protect those rights. In the Lockean worldview, individualism was of paramount importance. But scholars have noted another viewpoint present among the founders, classical republicanism. Garrett Ward Sheldon succinctly defines this as the view that man is "naturally social, with a need to participate in political life" and that man has "capacity for public virtue."[33] All of the founders subscribed to some elements of classical republicanism, but to differing degrees, from Jefferson and Paine on the liberal side to Hamilton and Adams on the conservative side. Depending on where the lines were drawn, the concepts of classical republicanism could clash with a Lockean worldview, since it assumed that all people in society had a group responsibility to each other. "The sacrifice of individual interests to the greater good of the whole formed the issue of republicanism," according to Gordon Wood, who goes on to write that the ideal of true liberty was "natural liberty restrained in such manner, as to render society one great family; where everyone must consider his neighbors happiness, as well as his own."[34]

Given the competing notions of individualism and community needs, the Framers' fear of too much democracy was not the whole story, since they also knew they had few other options for creating a legitimate government other than one grounded in popular sovereignty and the consent of the governed. They had already rejected the divine right of kings to rule through a monarchy. Some of them may have wished for an aristocratic government under which the most affluent would govern, but once again, such a government would lack any claim to being legitimate unless it was grounded in the popular will. At the Convention, Madison told the delegates: "It seems indispensable that the mass of citizens should not be without a voice in making the laws which they are to obey, and in choosing the magistrates who are to administer them." James Wilson would repeatedly argue that, "the ultimate power of government must of necessity reside in the people."[35]

The structure of the new government was intended to balance the need for a system of government grounded in popular sovereignty, while slowing down the impulses of the will of the people, and to ensure that one interest or another would not dominate. At the Convention, even Alexander Hamilton would say: "Give all power to the many, they will oppress the few. Give all the power to the few, they will oppress the many."[36] Perhaps hearing the voice of Hamilton, Richard Hofstadter succinctly summarized it as follows:

> *If, in a state that lacked constitutional balance, one class or one interest gained control, they believed, it would surely plunder all other interests. The Fathers, of course, were especially fearful that the poor would plunder the rich, but most of them would probably have admitted that the rich, unrestrained, would also plunder the poor.*[37]

The Framers were hoping that a well-constructed constitutional system could foster a government responsive to the long-term needs of the public. Much of the debate that would ensue over the legislative branch would revolve around trying to find the correct balance between the role a legislator must play in representing the public and the importance of passing laws that may, in the short term, be unpopular, but which would work to advance the long-term public interest. The Framers also wanted to defend against politicians acting in their own personal interest, in aggrandizing themselves. Rather than elected officials being simply a mirror of their constituents, they wanted to motivate such officials to view issues from a broader perspective. In both the House and especially in the Senate, "the Federalists wanted a body that would promote deliberation, discussion, and compromise," writes one historian. "In the best situation, deliberation would transcend constituents' immediate concerns and be based at least in part on the members' own views about what would be good for the nation." The Framers attempted to achieve this by structuring the Constitution with longer terms of office than most of the state constitutions of the day allowed for. They also created a House of Representatives with larger districts, all in an attempt to give legislators more independence and the ability to act with a broader view of the public good.[38]

Journalist Fareed Zakaria, in a 1997 essay, coined the term "illiberal democracy," which is a political system that holds free and fair elections, but the results of the democratic process do not result in a "good government," since the winners in such elections often ignore constitutional limits on their own power and deprive their citizens of basic rights and freedoms. What the Framers were grappling with was how to form a liberal democracy, which Zakaria defines as a "political system marked not only by free and fair elections, but also by the rule of law, a separation of powers, and the protection of basic liberties of speech, assembly, religion, and property."[39] The Convention would spend much time in grappling with the best method of achieving this balance, one that had not been previously tried on such a scale anywhere in the world.

Randolph's speech had gone on for a long time, and when he finished the Convention adjourned for the day. The scope of the Virginia Plan was breathtaking, and gave many of the delegates cause for concern. Were they really going to ignore the directive of the Congress to only amend the Articles of Confederation, and truly embark on a complete reworking of the national government? Although the plan itself was couched in the language of amending the Articles, the men of the Convention were all experienced politicians and recognized that the Virginia Plan went well beyond making small changes to the government. Instead, it proposed a national government, one that would act directly upon the people instead of the states. Perhaps most importantly, the method of voting in the legislature, as proposed in the Virginia Plan, would no longer be based on an equal vote of the states, but rather on a proportional system tied to population that would favor the large states. And the proposal to veto state laws could have the impact of reducing the state governments to little more than administrative units for the new national government. Many of the small state representatives recognized this, with William Patterson of New Jersey writing in his notes that Randolph was pursuing "a strong consolidated union in which the idea of states should be nearly annihilated."[40] Patterson, as one of the main spokesmen for the small states, would have much more to say in opposition to certain elements of the plan in the coming weeks.

Each of these proposals would undergo significant changes, especially the issue of proportional representation in the legislature and the role that the states would continue to play. The veto of state laws would not survive, which would be a great blow to Madison. But the underlying principal that the United States would have a national government would prevail, as indicated by the vote that took place the next day, when Randolph once again addressed the Convention. Rather than open debate on the specifics of the Virginia Plan, he proposed three resolutions that would establish the general principal that the national government should be supreme. Two of the three were deferred, but the third one, which stated "that a national Government ought to be established consisting of a supreme Legislative, Executive & Judiciary," was then debated. As Madison's notes indicate, the focus of the discussion was "less on the general merits than on the force and extent of the particular terms *national & supreme.*" According to one historian, "the strategy of the Virginia Plan's advocates was to get the delegates to accept the basic principle of a 'supreme national government' before getting bogged down in the details of the plan itself."[41]

Charles Pinkney of South Carolina asked of Randolph whether his intent was to abolish the state governments altogether. His second cousin, General Charles Cotesworth Pinkney, questioned whether Congress had given the Convention the authority to discuss a national government that was so distinctly different from that under the Articles of Confederation. Gouverneur Morris responded by describing what he saw as the difference between a federal and a national government. To Morris, a federal government was simply a compact that rested on the good faith of the parties, whereas a national government had complete and compulsive power. Morris argued that, "in all Communities there must be one supreme power, and only one."[42] His core point was that if the United States was to be one nation, then power must be placed in the national government.

Roger Sherman of Connecticut, who had just arrived, was very concerned that the Convention was moving too fast. A man with no formal education, he had passed the bar, was a successful businessman, and an experienced politician. He had served in the Continental

Congress and been part of the committee that drafted the Declaration of Independence and the Articles of Confederation. William Pierce of Georgia described Sherman as "the oddest shaped character I ever remember to have met with, he is awkward, un-meaning, and unaccountably strange in his manner."[43] But Sherman was an effective debater and would emerge as one of the leaders of the small states, a man who would be in the middle of some of the major compromises crafted at the Convention. His concern, that the Convention was making too many "inroads on the existing system," was echoed by George Read of Delaware and General Pinckney, who moved a much weaker resolution that "a more effective Government consisting of a Legislative, Executive and Judiciary ought to be established." A tie vote ensued on this resolution. Pierce Butler of South Carolina then moved the original resolution, which surprisingly passed on a vote of six states in favor, one opposed, and one state divided. Only Sherman and his fellow Connecticut delegates voted no, and New York split its vote, with Hamilton voting yes and Yates voting no.

Historians have puzzled over why this resolution passed so easily, since it meant the delegates were now committed to overturning the Articles of Confederation. The most compelling answer is that the Convention was largely made up of dedicated nationalists, and this allowed them to so easily and quickly achieve a major breakthrough. This is not to say that there were not major disagreements that would soon emerge over the extent of establishing a national government and the role of the states.[44] But ultimately these differences would be a matter of degree, since those who opposed major change had stayed home. Of equal importance on this early vote was that many of the delegates that represented the small states had not yet arrived, including those from New Hampshire, New Jersey, Maryland, and Georgia. While many of the small state delegates were less nationalist in their outlook than Madison, Washington and Hamilton, they would ultimately support a stronger central government so long as the interests of the small states were protected.[45] While Madison was happy with the results of the vote, he also knew this was but one small step and that much debate would ensue on a variety of issues, including the form and powers of a new government; the issue of representation; the role of the states; and the issue of slavery. He was also aware that even within those delegations that had supported the resolution were men who would protest the reduction of state power and protect their parochial interests, including Mason and Randolph from his own home state. "But it was a vitally important step," Richard Beeman writes, because "it put the delegates on a course to abandon…the definition of federalism embodied in the Articles of Confederation."[46]

First Attempts at Creating the Legislature

The Convention next moved to the issue that would preoccupy them for many weeks of debate: the nature, form, and method of electing Congress. On May 31, the principle of a bicameral legislature was resolved quickly in the affirmative without any real debate, other than a protest lodged by Franklin, who was still wedded to the idea of a single house legislature, modeled on the one he helped author for Pennsylvania's Constitution. By this point, most of the Framers supported a political system that included a series of checks and balances, and a two-house legislature was a core component of such a system. The Massachusetts Constitution, written by John Adams in 1780, had pioneered a system of government that included a two-house legislature, a strong executive, and a separate judiciary. Adams had also recently published his *Defence of the Constitution of Government of the United States of America*, excerpts of which appeared weekly in the *Pennsylvania Mercury* as the Convention met. The new Federal Constitution would eventually follow certain elements of the Massachusetts model, including increasing the power of the executive and judicial branches and incorporating a bicameral legislature.[47]

A single versus a bicameral house legislature was not the key issue, since the Framers all agreed that legislative power needed to be filtered through two institutions. The key issue was whether the new national government would operate directly on the people, and whether those same people would elect the government in direct proportion to population, or whether the government would continue under a confederation model where the states would directly control the government. "Whether the government should represent states or people—whether the United States should be a nation or a confederation—was seen by most of the delegates as being the most important issue before the convention."[48] This issue of representation would split the Convention between large and small states, and between different sections, specifically the North and South over slavery. During debate on May 30, Madison had proposed that, "an equitable ratio of representation ought to be substituted" for the "equality of suffrage established by the Articles of Confederation." The delegates postponed his motion when Delaware threatened to leave the Convention over the issue, the first but not the last such threat by one state delegation or another. The instructions they had received from their legislature prohibited them from approving any changes to the one-state-one-vote rule from the Articles of Confederation.[49] Madison's notes on the debate of May 30 indicate some wishful thinking on his part, when he wrote, "the proposed change of representation would certainly be agreed to" since only Delaware was opposed. The future outcome of the debates on this issue would prove Madison wrong.

During the May 31 session, the delegates went on to discuss the fourth resolution contained in the Virginia Plan, "that the members of the first branch of the National Legislature ought to be elected by the people of the several States." That branch would later become known as the House of Representatives. Debate over this issue would pit those who opposed a strong democratic element to the new Constitution against those who saw this as essential. And the players on each side of the debate were not what one would have expected. Roger Sherman, son of a shoemaker and a self-made man, opened the debate by stating his view that "the people...should have as little to do" with the government as possible. Elbridge Gerry of Massachusetts followed Sherman and argued that "the evils we experience flow from the excess of democracy." Gerry was the son of a successful merchant and sea captain, a Harvard graduate, and an experienced politician who had served in the Continental Congress. He was a supporter of strengthening the national government, in part based on his experience during the war when he was responsible for supplying the troops. A small man with a hawk-like nose, he spoke with a stammer and made many enemies during the Convention due to his unpredictability on key issues. He would ultimately refuse to sign the document and became a vocal opponent of ratification of the new Constitution. His opposition to a strong role for the people in the new government emanated from his experience with Shays Rebellion. Gerry equated democracy with mob rule, and while he maintained that he still supported a republican form of government, he had "been taught by experience the danger of the leveling spirit." Butler of South Carolina joined them in opposition, but his resistance to electing the House by popular vote stemmed from a need to protect slavery. He wanted the elections based on the amount of property a person owned, with slaves counted as part of that property. Such a scheme would favor the most affluent, himself included.[50]

Historian Daniel Boorstin has observed that the ways of history are sometimes obscure and contradictory, and so it was with those who defended a strong role for the people in the new government, some of whom were clearly part of the elite of society. George Mason, a first-rate constitutional scholar who had drafted Virginia's Declaration of Rights, spoke in defense of democracy. Mason, who was "born to privilege" and who had increased his wealth during his life, argued strongly for the election of the House by the people. While he admitted, "we had been too democratic," he feared that the Convention would go too far in the other direction, and that the new government "ought to attend to the rights of every class of the people," from the lowest to the highest order of citizens. His lifelong friendship with Washington would later be tested when Mason ultimately refused to sign the Constitution because it did not contain a bill of rights.[51]

James Wilson, another member of the natural aristocracy, spoke next. He would prove to be one of the strongest supporters of democracy at the Convention. Wilson, like Madison, had a strong underpinning as a political theorist. A conservative man by nature, he had stood opposed to the liberal Pennsylvania Constitution of 1776, which had a single legislative chamber and a weak executive. He had allied himself with the merchant class from the middle states, and during the run up to the vote for independence in 1776, had joined with Dickinson and Morris in urging a go-slow approach. Due to this, he was suspect in the eyes of the more radical Pennsylvanians. His biographer described him as a man who took "such pride in his intellect that he was often unable to hide his feelings of superiority over those ordinary citizens around him,"[52] and the French chargé d'affaires, Louis-Guillaume Ottos, described him as "haughty" and "aristocratic." While Wilson was a strong supporter of the role of the people in the new Constitution, his faith in democracy came more from his theoretical views rather than a natural love of people or an optimistic view of human nature. Nonetheless, he saw clearly that to gain popular support, the new government would need to be established based on the will of the people, and he wanted the new federal government to be established on "as broad a basis as possible."[53] In his response to Gerry and Sherman, he indicated that, "no government could long subsist without the confidence of the people."[54]

Madison joined the debate next, indicating that "popular election of one branch of the National Legislature [w]as essential to every plan of free Government." Even though Madison had concerns that democracy could lead to the oppression of minority rights by the will of the majority, he also maintained that the public had to have a strong role in the selection of representatives to fill the first branch of the Congress. He also favored the appointment of the second house of the legislature by the first branch, and the executive appointment by the second branch.[55]

When the delegates cast the vote on whether the election of the House of Representatives should be by the people, it passed on a six-to-two vote, with two states divided. So far, Madison's approach of presenting a broad framework for the type of government he hoped to see, as outlined in the Virginia Plan, was working, but it would not last. The small states had not yet organized their resistance. And the vote on this matter, as with many other items, would shortly be reconsidered.

The debate next turned to how to form the second branch of the legislature, which would become the Senate. The Senate would be modeled after the British House of Lords, which represented the aristocratic element of English society. Since America had no hereditary aristocracy, the Framers viewed the Senate as an institution that would "be drawn from the upper levels of society, to be higher in place than ordinary citizens and, above all, [be] more knowledgeable and more deliberative," according to one historian.[56] As Randolph explained during the debate on the subject on May 31, "the general object was to provide a cure for the evils under which the U.S. labored," which included an excess of democracy. The Framers viewed the Senate as the chamber that would slow down the passions of the House, and provide greater stability to the government.

The Virginia Plan called for the House of Representatives to choose the Senate based on a slate of candidates put forward by the state legislatures. Such a proposal, if combined with the direct election of the House based on proportional representation, would mean that the large states would dominate both chambers of the legislature. Richard Spaight of North Carolina, along with Sherman and Butler, proposed that the state legislatures should choose the members of the Senate. Wilson wanted the people to directly elect both the Senate and the House, "because the second branch...ought to be independent of both" the House and the state legislatures. They then put the original proposal as contained in the Virginia Plan to a vote and lost, with only three states voting yes. Madison had finally lost a major vote, causing him to remark that, "A chasm [was] left in this part of the plan."[57]

On May 31, the Framers debated one last major element of the Virginia Plan that dealt with whether the Congress would be provided with the power "to legislate in all cases to which the separate States are incompetent" and "to negative all laws passed by the several States" where such laws were found to be in violation of "the articles of Union."[58] Several members protested that the language of the resolution, specifically the word "incompetent" was too vague. Both Randolph and Madison indicated they did not intend to give unlimited power to the national legislature, and that the new government would be one of enumerated and limited powers. This seemed to assuage the Convention members, and they approved the first part of the resolution on a vote of nine to zero, with Connecticut divided. Surprisingly, the proposal to allow the national legislature to veto state laws passed without debate and dissent, a decision that they would ultimately overturn later in the Convention. They decided to postpone a final element of the sixth resolve, which would have allowed for the use of force against a delinquent state, when Madison indicated he was having second thoughts about such an approach. The delegates then adjourned for the day.

The Convention met every day except Sunday, from 10 o'clock in the morning until 3 o'clock in the afternoon. Discussions continued in the taverns and at private dinners in the homes of Franklin, Morris, and other members of the Pennsylvania delegation. There were more than 100 taverns in the city, and one can imagine the delegates debating the various issues from that day's session over a glass of wine, a stein of beer, or a cup of tea. One dinner for twelve included an order for sixty bottles of Madeira.

The delegates all stayed within walking distance of the State House. Mrs. House hosted six delegates, including Madison and, for a time, Randolph. George Mason stayed at the Indian Queen, while Hamilton and Gerry were at Miss Daley's boardinghouse. Others were located at Mrs. Marshall's boardinghouse, or, like Washington, stayed in private homes. They would normally have a light breakfast before setting out for the State House, and the big meal of the day would be served in the late afternoon around 3:30, generally at one of the taverns in the city, or in the boardinghouses. In the evening, many of the delegates would first catch up on their correspondence, and then join each other for evening tea.[59]

Washington was much in demand in his time away from the Convention, socializing with the other delegates at the City Tavern and

Indian Queen, attending dinners with the Irish American Sons of St. Patrick or the Society of Cincinnati when they held their annual session in the city on May 15. He also attended mass at the local Catholic Church on at least one Sunday. For entertainment, Washington received a private tour of the local Anatomical Museum, and attended plays at the Southwark Theatre outside the city. In early July, Washington went trout fishing with Robert Morris near Valley Forge. While Morris fished, Washington toured the place where the Continental Army suffered so much. He was only able to find remnants of "the encampments in the woods where the grounds had not been cultivated."[60]

Madison also socialized with his fellow delegates at the taverns of the city and at dinners at Mrs. House's place. But he spent most of his hours away from the Convention writing his notes from that day's session. He had been frustrated in his own research on the history of confederacies with the lack of documentation, and he intended that his own notes from the Convention would ensure that no such void would occur and that he would "preserve as far as I could an exact account of what might pass at the Convention." He would recall later in life that the job almost killed him, but as he wrote to Jefferson, he intended "to go on with the drudgery, if no indisposition obliges me to discontinue it."[61]

The Executive Branch – First Discussions

When the Convention met on June 1, the delegates turned to the subject of the executive, rather than continue the difficult discussions between the large and small states over the issue of representation. Although the delegates had hoped to move beyond the particularly divisive issue of representation in the Congress, a new set of divisions would arise over the executive. It would pit those who continued to fear the power of a strong executive against those nationalists who had experienced the problems the central government faced during the war and in its aftermath due to the lack of a separate and independent executive branch. Most of the delegates to the Convention were not as reticent about executive power as those who would form the antifed-eralist camp during the ratification debates over the new Constitution. But some of the influential members, including Randolph, Mason, and Franklin, feared placing power in the hands of one man. And both sides had concerns that they not create a new form of monarchy out of the executive branch. Ultimately, the Framers would create a powerful executive, the office that would become the presidency, but it would take most of the summer to determine the final outlines of this branch of government.

Those who feared a strong executive continued to be influenced by the experiences of the colonists in the 1760s and 1770s, during the buildup to the eventual break with Great Britain. During that time, royal governors, appointed by the King, had often dissolved local colo-nial assemblies when they disagreed with their decisions. They also vetoed bills on a regular basis.[62] The opponents of a strong executive feared the return to monarchy, which they had fought to overturn during the Revolutionary War. The concerns they held, which focused largely on the concentration of power in the hands of one individual, had led to the weakening of executive power at the state level in the constitutions approved in the years immediately following the Dec-laration of Independence. Pennsylvania had gone the furthest in this regard, when they eliminated the office of governor and replaced it with a twelve-member executive council. Other states made the executive dependent on the legislature, which elected the governors. Eight states required the annual election of the governor and limited the number of terms that any individual could serve in that role, all in an attempt to limit the power of the office.[63] And the Articles of Confederation did not even include an executive officer among its provisions.

On the other side from those who feared a strong executive stood those men—such as Washington, Hamilton, Robert Morris, James Wilson, and Gouverneur Morris—who supported what they referred to as energy in the executive. They wanted to provide leadership to the system. As one political scientist has observed "the ship of state cannot do without the pilot who sets the course, who knows where the shoals and reefs lie, and who can direct all hands."[64] At the state level, the allure of having a weak executive had waned somewhat, with both New York and Massachusetts strengthening their governor's office in certain limited ways.[65] But the central government totally lacked an independent executive office, which had contributed to the mismanagement and inefficiency in both the prosecution of the war effort and in the failures in the economy caused by runaway inflation and the calamitous depreciation of the currency. These failures had led to the creation of several executive departments in the 1780s, including the Office of Superintendent of Finance headed by Robert Morris. But in some ways, Morris had also poisoned the well with his attempt to use the army to push forward his policies on taxation, actions that had culminated in Washington putting down an attempted coup in Newburg, New York. Morris' actions "reminded his detractors of the dangers of allowing ambitious ministers to manipulate legislative deliberations."[66]

As the discussions on the executive opened on June 1, these various positions informed much of the debate that followed. Unlike the positions the delegates staked out over congressional representation, which tended to follow the interests of their particular states, the discussions over the executive did not follow such a neat and consistent pattern.

The initial debates that took place from June 1 through June 4 focused on three core issues: whether the new Constitution should center all of the executive functions in one individual or rather in a committee; the method for electing the executive; and the issue of the veto.

The Convention began the June 1 discussions by taking up resolution number 7 from the Virginia Plan, which called for the legislature to choose a national executive for a set term of years, and that would possess all of the executive powers of government. Charles Pinkney expressed his support for a strong executive, but feared giving the power of war and peace to the office, "which would render the Executive a monarchy." Wilson then moved that the executive be a single person, which Pinkney seconded. A long period of silence ensued, and the chair asked if they should put the question to a vote. At this point, Benjamin Franklin "observed that it was a point of great importance and wished that the gentleman would deliver their sentiments on it before the question was put."[67] This opened the floodgates, and the delegates began to express their wide-ranging views on the subject.

Roger Sherman stated that the executive should be "nothing more than an institution for carrying the will of Legislature into effect," and as such should be appointed by the legislative body. Edmund Randolph, himself a governor, was opposed to having a single person in the role of the executive, arguing that it would be the fetus of monarchy. Wilson quickly responded that having a single executive, "instead of being the fetus of monarchy, would be the best safeguard against tyranny." The delegates moved on to issues surrounding the method of selecting the executive and the term of office, since they had reached no consensus on the issue of one versus a multiple person executive.[68]

The debate over the method of selecting the executive carried over to June 2. Wilson had, the day before, indicated his support for direct election of the executive. As Richard Beeman notes, "Wilson believed that a president, elected directly by people, was essential as both the symbol and the executor of 'we the people'...only the president stands above region or state and only the president can claim to represent the will of all of the people."[69] The Framers were attempting to establish the only truly national office of the central government. On this issue, Wilson largely stood alone, although Morris and Madison supported the principle of direct election of the president. The other delegates to the Convention had two main concerns with direct election. First, they feared that the public would have insufficient information to judge candidates from other states, which would lead them to prefer candidates from their own state, making it difficult to achieve a majority for any one candidate. At this point, the concept of national parties that would run under the banner of a presidential candidate was unknown, and the Framers disparaged parties as factions. Second, to the extent that a national majority did form, Madison and others from the South worried that the larger free population of the North would favor its candidates over southern contenders for the presidency.[70]

Wilson attempted to deal with these concerns in his proposal of June 2 that would later become the electoral college system. Under his proposal, the voters would elect a certain number of temporary electors that would then select the president. The Convention instead voted to have the national legislature appoint the executive by a vote of eight states to two, with a term limited to seven years. Despite the large vote in support of the motion, this decision would later be revisited. Many still had concerns that having the legislature choose the president would place too much power in its hands and produce a pliable official without independent judgment. The delegates were attempting to find a middle ground that would ensure "that the executive could function with a reasonable amount of independence from the legislature while at the same time preventing him amassing too much power for an extended period of time."[71]

The issue of creating a unitary executive, which had been postponed on Friday June 1, came to a vote the following Monday. Wilson indicated that he was not convinced of the need for multiple men in the role of the executive, and that, in fact, all of the states had agreed "to place a single magistrate at the head" of the state governments in the office of governor. Wilson went on to argue that, "among three equal members, he foresaw nothing but uncontrolled, continued, and violent animosities" that would ultimately poison the entire government. When the vote was called, seven states supported a single man in the position of president, and three states voted no. The no votes included New York, Delaware, and Maryland. Three members of the Virginia delegation (Randolph, Blair, and Mason), voted no, but the balance of the state delegation supported the motion, including Washington.[72]

Perhaps Washington's presence had led to this result. Franklin, who also opposed a single executive and preferred some form of an executive council, seemed to allude to this when he said, "The first man put at the helm will be a good one. Nobody knows what sort may come afterwards." Pierce Butler of South Carolina wrote in a 1788 letter that, "many of the members cast their eyes towards General Washington as President, and shaped their ideas of the powers to be given to a President by their opinions of his virtue." It was clear that most members of the Convention, although concerned about placing too much power in the hands of any one man, would also place much more power in the new office of president because of their great respect for Washington. One historian has argued: "had Washington been absent, it is entirely possible that the Framers of the Constitution would have created a multiple executive," or at least have created an office that the legislature would select, as Sherman had proposed. Such a system would have resulted in the United States having a parliamentary system for selecting its national leader, rather than a presidential system.[73]

Washington was sitting through a variety of discussions for what would become his new job description, his biographer Ron Chernow has observed. And some of the debates may well have embarrassed him and other delegates. On June 2, Franklin had asked Wilson to read a paper he had prepared, which contended that the executive should serve without pay. Franklin, who could usually be found on the side of the common man, did not seem to understand that if the executive served without pay that only the most affluent could be president. Although Franklin's motion, seconded by Hamilton for discussion purposes only, went no further, it was still an awkward moment for Washington, since it raised the question of whether he could be "trusted with a salary from the people." Madison later wrote to Jefferson that he thought the issue "was peculiarly embarrassing."[74]

The Convention next turned to whether the president should be given some form of veto power over legislation, which would once again raise the issue of the abuses the colonists had suffered at the hands of royal governors. The Framers also grappled with a strong countervailing concern about the need to place a check on the legislature to prevent the passage of ill-considered or unconstitutional laws. Madison had originally proposed placing the veto power in the hands of the Senate, although he had also envisioned some form of a council of revision. The Virginia Plan built on this concept, with a council of revision that would include the executive plus an as-yet-unspecified number of members of the new national judiciary. It would have a limited veto power, since the national legislature would be able to override the veto of the council of revision.

Elbridge Gerry opened the discussion by questioning whether the judiciary should have any role in wielding the veto power, "as they will have a sufficient check against encroachments on their own department by their exposition of the laws, which involved a power of deciding on their Constitutionality." His remarks indicate that Convention members envisioned some form of judicial review of the laws passed by the Congress. Whereas today we are accustomed to the Supreme Court's role in evaluating the constitutionality of laws, the Framers were still grappling with this notion, along with other elements about how to achieve a system of checks and balances among the branches of government.[75]

James Wilson built on Gerry's concerns and made the case that the three branches of government should be "distinct and independent," and that both the executive and the judiciary should have an absolute veto. Hamilton seconded this motion, which stirred up opposition from those in the room who opposed a strong executive. "The absolute veto is a royal prerogative," as one political scientist has argued, since it "rests on a principle antithetical to republicanism—the superiority of one man."[76] Madison then proposed a compromise under which "a proper proportion of each branch should be required to overrule the Executive." Gerry inserted into his motion that a two-thirds vote of each branch of the legislature would be required to overrule the president's veto. The motion passed on a vote of eight states in favor, with only two opposed. It was a major breakthrough, especially when combined with the concept of a unitary executive. The Framers were in the process of forming an executive branch with powers that exceeded those of any of the state governors of 1787.

As they were gradually adding significant powers to the president's job, it was inevitable that the Framers would need to develop some means to remove him from office. Two days before the issue of the veto power was resolved, John Dickenson of Delaware made a motion "that the Executive be made removable by the National Legislature on the request of a majority of the Legislature of the individual States." His motion was defeated, with only his home state approving it, but the issue of executive removal from office would reappear later in a different form. As part of Dickinson's speech on June 2, he made a strong and impassioned defense of maintaining the power and integrity of the state governments, and he charged that some of his fellow delegates were attempting to abolish the states totally. He also made a plea "that each State would retain an equal voice in at least one branch of the National Legislature," a proposal that would foreshadow the Grand Compromise that would ultimately be reached between the large and small states on the issue of representation.[77]

The Convention would review the Virginia Plan on June 5 without reaching further consensus over how to select the judiciary and whether the new Constitution should be ratified by special conventions of the people. During the first week of the Convention, Madison and his allies had cause for celebration. Seizing the initiative, they had managed to accomplish many of their major goals, including that: 1) the national government would be supreme; 2) the new Congress would have the power to legislate in all cases where the states were not competent; 3) the House of Representatives would be elected by the people; 4) the Congress would have the ability to veto State laws; and 5) a strong executive branch would be established. The small state counterattack had not yet materialized, but it would, once deliberations returned to the method of electing the national legislature.

Endnotes

1 Winton Solberg, Editor, *The Federal Convention and the Formation of the Union of the American States*, (Indianapolis, 1976), p. 74

2 Berkin, p. 31-32; Beeman, p22-23

3 Beeman, p. 24-25; Ketchum, p. 108-110, including the quote from Jefferson

4 The quote from the newspaper, the *Pennsylvania Packet*, is from Chernow, *Washington*, p. 526; Wills, p. 26

5 Beeman, p. 34-35

6 Ellis, *His Excellency*, p. 175

7 Beeman, p. 38

8 Beeman, p. 68

9 Beeman, p. 23

10 See Berkin, p. 36-37 on the need for extensive preparations for those who attended the convention; the Washington quote is from Chernow, *Washington*, p. 527

11 Beeman, p. 44; Berkin, p. 244-246

12 Beeman, p. 45-48, including the quote on his elitist tendencies , which is from p. 48; also see Berkin, p. 230

13 Beeman, p. 49-51; Berkin, p. 232-233

14 Beeman, p. 53

15 Rakove, *Madison*, p. 62

16 Catherine Drinker Brown, *Miracle at Philadelphia*, (Boston, 1986), p. 30

17 Rakove, *Madison*, p. 62; Ferling, p. 284

18 Robert A. Dahl, *How Democratic is the American Constitution*, (New Haven, 2001), p. 4; Ferling, p. 283

19 Berkin, p. 49; The descriptions of the delegates are largely drawn from the biographical sketches provided by Berkin on pages 211-261 and also from Beeman, p. 64-68.

20 Berkin, p. 51 and 41-42

21 Solberg contains a summarized version of Madison's "Notes of Debates" and has been used in this chapter. The above quote is from p. 75.

22 Berkin, p72-73

23 Beeman, p. 89

24 Solberg, p. 79

25 The quotes are from Solberg, p. 85; Richard Hofstadter, *The American Political Tradition*, (New York, 1948), p. 4; and Ferling, p. 290

26 Alexander Hamilton, James Madison, John Jay, Introduction by Clinton Rossiter, *The Federalist Papers*, (New York, 1961), p. 81-82

27 Dahl, location 1243 in the Kindle version

28 Hofstadter, p. 4

29 Wood, *Creation*, p. 404 and 410.

30 Acemoglu and Robinson, p. 79 in the I Books version

31 Bowen, p. 72

32 Foner, *Freedom*, p. 12

33 Both Wood and Bailyn were instrumental in developing the concept of the importance of classical republicanism during the founding period. Another seminal work was J.G.A. Pockock, *The Machiavellian Moment*, (Princeton, 1969). The quotes are from Garrett Ward Sheldon, *The Political Philosophy of Thomas Jefferson*, (Baltimore, 1991) p. 3-4 and p. 5, which has a useful summary of Pockock.

34 Wood, *Creation*, p. 53 and 60.

35 Hofstadter develops these ideas on p. 5-6 and the quotes are from his book. Ellis writes that the founding period was predemocratic in *The Quartet*, p. xviii, but I would argue it was more a time of evolution toward democracy, a period where democracy was beginning to emerge, even though there were many elites who distrusted the masses.

36 Quoted in Michael P. Federici, *The Political Philosophy of Alexander Hamilton*, (Baltimore, 2012), p. 79

37 Hofstadter, p. 8

38 For an excellent discussion of the need to foster the long-term views of the legislative branch, see Michael J. Malbin, "Congress During the Convention and Ratification," in Levy & Mahoney (Ed), p. 185-208.

39 Fareed Zakaria, "The Rise of Illiberal Democracy," retrieved 7/27/13 from http://fareedzakaria.com/1997/11/01/the-rise-of-illiberal-democracy/

40 Beeman, p. 89

41 Beeman, p. 100

42 Solberg, p. 81

43 Beeman, p. xix; and Berkin, p. 218

44 Berkin, p. 71 makes this case

45 Ellis, in *The Quartet*, makes the case that these men were confederationists. I would argue that in fact the 39 members who ultimately signed the Constitution were all nationalists in one form or another, but were separated by the need to protect either their role as small state representatives or to protect slavery. Those who failed to sign the Constitution and who later joined the Antifederalists were the true confederationists. But I do find Professor Ellis' view compelling that the small state representatives forced the more extreme nationalist to scale back their agenda and that in order to get agreement at the Convention the issue of sovereignty needed to be obscured. My own views have been heavily influenced by Ellis in this area, as this book shows.

46 Beeman, p. 102-103

47 See Akhil Reed Amar, *America's Constitution: A Biography*, (New York, 2005), p. 58-60 for a more detailed discussion of the systems of checks and balances; the publishing of Adams work during the Convention is from David O. Stewart, *The Summer of 1787: The Men Who Invented the Constitution*, (2007, New York), p. 38

48 Malbin, p. 186

49 Berkin, p. 45

50 Solberg, p. 84 for the quotes from Gerry; see also Beeman, p. 111-114; Berkin, p. 213

51 Solberg, p. 85 for the quotes from Mason; see also Beeman, p. 118; and Berkin, p. 244

52 Quoted in Beeman, p. 131

53 Beeman,p. 118

54 Solberg, p. 85

55 Solberg, p. 85-86, contains Madison views and quotes are from that source.

56 Beeman, p. 119

57 Wilson's quote is from Solberg, p. 87; the Madison quote from Beeman, p120

58 Solberg, p. 77-78

59 See Beeman, p. 72-79 and Drinker, p. 50-53 for more information on how the delegates spent their off hours in Philadelphia

60 The quotation is from Flexner, *New Nation*, p.132; other information on how Washington spent his time is from Chernow, *Washington*, p. 534-535

61 Ketchum, p. 196 and p. 207

62 Jack N. Rakove, *Original Meanings: Politics and Ideas in the Making of the Constitution*, (New York, 1997). P. 249

63 Wood, *Creation*, has a discussion on p. 137-143 of the weakening of executive power in the constitutions approved in the immediate aftermath of independence.

64 Judith A. Best, "The Presidency and the Executive Power," in Levy & Mahoney (Ed), p. 210

65 See Rakove, *Original*, p. 252-253 for more detail on how these states did this.

66 Rakove, *Original*, p. 254

67 Solberg, p. 89- 90

68 Solberg, p. 90-91

69 Beeman, p. 129

70 Rakove, *Original*, p. 259 and Amar, p. 155

71 See Rakove, *Original*, p. 259 for the delegates concerns about focusing too much power in the legislature, especially the quote from Morris. The quoted information is from Beeman, p. 136

72 Solberg, p. 96-97

73 The Franklin quote is from Drinker, p. 60. The Butler quote from Flexner, *New Nation*, p. 134. The quote from the historian is from Beeman, p. 128

74 Drinker, p. 61

75 Solberg, p. 97. See Beeman, p. 138 for a more extensive discussion of the issue of checks and balances.

76 Best, p. 217

77 Solberg, p. 93-95

Chapter 8

Conflicts and Compromises / June 6 to July 16, 1787

"...that in one branch the people ought to be represented; in the other the States"
– Samuel Johnson, June 29, 1787 in Convention –

"Mr. Wilson did not well see on what principle the admission of blacks in the proportion of three fifths could be explained...[but] these were difficulties...which he thought must be overruled by the necessity of compromise..."
– James Wilson, July 11, 1787 in Convention –

From the perspective of the early twenty-first century, some people view the creation of the Constitution as a quasi-religious act, equivalent to Moses coming down from Mount Sinai with the tablets that contained the Ten Commandments. The 2012 Republican candidate for president, Mitt Romney, described the Constitution and the Declaration of Independence as follows: "They're either inspired by God or written by brilliant people, or perhaps a combination of both." But the Constitution, far from being pre-ordained, was really an act of political compromise among the various interests represented at the Convention. Chief among these compromises were those between large and small states and between sectional interests, specifically the protection of slavery by the South. The fate of the Convention hung in the balance over the outcome of these disputes. The compromises that emerged would cause some of the biggest supporters of a stronger federal government, including Madison and Washington, to question whether the final product was sufficient to warrant their support, although ultimately they chose to sign the document. And the compromises the Convention agreed to came at a cost, particularly the protection of slavery, which later an abolitionist called a "covenant with death."

The Small States Regroup

On June 6, 1787, the debate returned to the issue of proportional representation when Charles Pinkney made a motion for the states to appoint the members of the House of Representatives. Gerry, who, as we have seen, was no friend of democracy, surprisingly sided with those who favored election by the people, although "his idea was that the people should nominate certain persons in certain districts, out of whom the State Legislatures should make the appointment." Wilson opposed the motion and stated that he "wished for vigor in the Govt, but he wished that vigorous authority to flow immediately from the legitimate source of all authority," by which he meant the people. Mason too supported this position, since the new government would represent the people and not the states, and the people "ought therefore to choose the Representative."[1]

Madison used this occasion to make his longest speech yet on his overarching theory for protecting minority rights through an extended republic in which the "sects, factions and interests" would be divided into a larger community with "so great a number of interests & parties, that …a majority will not be likely at the same moment to have a common interest separate from that of the whole or of the minority." The idea was so novel that it likely swayed few delegates. Hamilton observed that "there was truth in his principles but they do not conclude as strongly as he supposes." While the idea of the extended republic went beyond the ability of many of the delegates to grasp, Madison's delivery also subtracted from his bold ideas. He was a poor speaker, and one delegate observed that, "the warmest excitement of debate was visible in [Madison] only by a more or less rapid and forward seesaw motion of his body." Regardless, the motion to have the states appoint the members of the House was defeated in a vote of eight to three.[2]

Madison's first major setback occurred on June 7, over the issue of electing the Senate, when Dickenson proposed having the state legislature select its members. Dickenson was beginning the counterattack of the small states that would culminate within the week in a rival plan. While the motion did not include an equal state vote in the Senate, Madison immediately recognized the danger of this proposal, since that would be the likely outcome. "Moreover, the upper house would lose its character as a small, highly select institution even if legislative election and proportional voting were both honored: give Delaware one senator, and Virginia would need sixteen," writes Jack Rakove. Madison would need to rethink how to apportion votes in what he had envisioned as a small and elite body that acted "with more coolness, with more system, and with more wisdom" than the House. "Enlarge their number and you communicate to them the vices which they are meant to correct," Madison had argued, although he had not completely reconciled the combination of proportional representation with a diminutive second branch.[3]

Ultimately, the delegates approved the motion on a vote of ten to zero. One historian argues that it was George Mason who ultimately persuaded the other delegates to support the motion, when he observed that, "the State Legislatures also ought to have some means of defending themselves against encroachments of the National Governments." Even the large-state representatives saw the wisdom of this argument.[4] But the core of the debate remained as to whether the small states should have an equal vote in the Senate.

Madison and the nationalists would suffer their second major setback over the issue of the congressional veto of state laws. Pinckney moved that "the National Legislature should have authority to negative all laws which they judge to be improper," since "the States must be kept in due subordination to the nation." Madison seconded the motion and reiterated the problems that had occurred under the Articles of Confederation, when "experience had evinced a constant tendency in the States to encroach on federal authority; to violate national Treaties; to infringe the rights and interests of each other; to oppress the weaker party within their jurisdiction." He went on to state that if the national government had no veto power, then the use of force against recalcitrant member states would be the only other alternative. In the previous day's debate over the Senate, Dickenson had compared the new national government to the solar system, with states as planets that "ought to be left to move freely in their proper orbits." Madison referred to the metaphor, indicating that without congressional veto power the states "will continually fly out of their proper orbits and destroy the order & harmony of the political System."[5]

Wilson too stood in support of the motion. He reminded his fellow delegates of how they had been "one nation of brethren" in the First Continental Congress, and that they did not view themselves as Virginians or Pennsylvanians or members from any individual colony but as one, united whole. But then "the tables at length began to turn," as the Articles of Confederation were weakened and resulted in "the want of an effectual controul in the whole over its parts," with the national interest "continually sacrificed to local interests."[6]

Opposition to the congressional veto was strong and came from a variety of sources, including the South, which wanted to protect slavery. Gunning Bedford of Delaware made the most compelling case for why the small states should oppose placing a veto power within the national government. Bedford had been Madison's classmate at the College of New Jersey and had finished at the top of their class. Overweight, handsome, and well-liked by the other delegates,[7] he observed that the veto power would injure Delaware, since both Virginia and Pennsylvania would control 1/3 of the votes in the Congress, compared to Delaware's 1/90. The national veto of state laws was defeated on a vote of seven to three, with the delegation from Delaware divided when Dickinson and Read voted yes, but Bedford and Basset voted no.[8]

Catherine Drinker Bowen opens her classic work on the Convention, *Miracle in Philadelphia*, by describing how "the air lay hot and humid" over the city and "old people said it was the worst summer since 1750." This was the typical description of the weather surrounding the Convention, and much of what we know about it comes from the diaries and records of the delegates themselves. Major Butler's wife left town because she "could not support the excessive heat of that climate," while Paterson of New Jersey described Philadelphia as "the warmest place I have been in." While this is the standard account, other documentary evidence indicates that the city enjoyed a cool summer in 1787. Regardless of average temperatures, no doubt there were some very hot days. William Samuel Johnson recorded in his diary that thirty-three of eighty days of the Convention fell into this category. The heat was made worse by the delegates keeping the windows and doors to Independence Hall closed due to the secrecy of the meetings. Plus, most of the delegates dressed in wool suits, and the buildings of the time tended to trap heat within them.[9]

Whether or not the temperature outside was warming up, the temperature inside the Convention became heated on June 9. Up until that point, as John Dickinson had written to his wife, the Convention was "very busy," but the debates were "of excellent temper."[10] It would not remain so, as William Paterson of New Jersey led the small state coalition in opposing proportional representation.

Paterson was a diminutive man, no more than five feet two inches, whose family had emigrated from Ireland when he was two years old. His father had done well as a merchant and had sent his son to the College of New Jersey, where he earned a master's degree, and then studied law and began a legal practice. As attorney general for New Jersey, he had become known for prosecuting people for fornication and adultery, had advocated legislation that would outlaw billiards and that would reduce the number of taverns in the state. As one historian writes, "everything about…Paterson, from his neatly placed wig to his spotless attire to his mild manner, seemed to signal his hatred of controversy, his love of order, and his devotion to a life of rules and regulations. He was, to put it bluntly, a prig." He was also a supporter of a stronger national government, including an energetic executive, and he had a strong fear of disorder. Above all, he wished to protect the interests of New Jersey, a small state.[11]

Paterson asked that the issue of "suffrage in the National Legislature be taken again," a motion seconded by his fellow New Jersey delegate, David Brearly. At forty-two, Brearly was already the chief justice of the New Jersey Supreme Court. He supported giving the national government "energy and stability," but "he was astonished, he was alarmed" when the Convention had proposed destroying the equal vote that each state enjoyed under the Articles of Confederation. He believed the only way such a plan would work would be to draw thirteen new and equal states; otherwise, the large states "will carry everything before them." Paterson asked that the Massachusetts delegates read the instructions they had received from their state, which included a provision that they were there "For the sole and express purpose of revising the Articles of Confederation." He was raising one of the major problems that the nationalists faced, the charge that they were exceeding the instructions of both the Congress and their individual states. "We are met here as the deputies of thirteen independent, sovereign states, for federal purposes. Can we consolidate their sovereignties and form one nation, and annihilate the sovereignties of our states who have sent us here for other purposes...We have no power to go beyond the federal scheme and if we had, the people are not ripe for it." He then threw down the gauntlet: "Let [the large states] unite if they please, but let them remember that they have no authority to compel the others to unite. New Jersey will never confederate on the plan before the Committee."[12]

Madison does not record in his notes the reaction of the delegates, but there must surely have been a sense that the goodwill so far exhibited between the delegates, and any movement toward consensus, was illusory. It became even clearer when Wilson defended the system of proportional representation "stating for his first position that as all authority was derived from the people, equal numbers of people ought to have an equal number of representatives, and different numbers of people different numbers of representatives. This principle had been improperly violated in the Confederation, owing to the urgent circumstances of the time." He concluded by stating that "If the small states will not confederate on this plan, Pennsylvania and he presumed some other States, would not confederate on any other."[13] It was midday, and Paterson requested that they defer the motion, since so much was at stake. The Convention adjourned until the following Monday to allow for a cooling off period.

When debate reopened on June 11, a new and equally divisive issue surfaced: slavery. This issue not only divided the Convention, but in the future it would also split the American nation more deeply than any other, with impacts that would later cost over 600,000 lives and with implications that continue to reverberate today. Of all of the differences that existed between the states, those that separated the northern from the southern were the greatest. Pierce Butler of South Carolina had written home that the interests of the two regions were "as different as the interests of Russia and Turkey." Jefferson had used adjectives like cool for the North and fiery for the South, laborious for the North and indolent for the South. And the further South one went, the more stark were the differences, causing Madison to comment that of the affairs of Georgia he knew as little of as those of Kamchatka.[14]

The Framers would ultimately compromise on the issue of slavery, with the northern states conceding additional protections and powers to the South, even though the word slavery is not mentioned anywhere in the document. Perhaps this was because many of the Framers knew that slavery was their great failure, that a nation dedicated to the proposition that all men are created equal cannot also condone the ownership of one human being by another. In the North, slavery was indeed on the road to extinction by 1787. Vermont and New Hampshire had both made it illegal in their state constitutions of the late 1770s. A state Supreme Court decision had ended the practice in Massachusetts in 1783, and Pennsylvania, Rhode Island, and Connecticut had all passed laws ending slavery by the mid-1780s. Only pockets of slavery remained in New York and New Jersey. Even the Virginians felt uncomfortable with slavery. Washington had written a year before the Convention that, "there is not a man living who wishes more sincerely than I do to see a plan adopted for the abolition of slavery." Madison had written in *Vices*, that, "where slavery exists the republican theory becomes still more fallacious." Randolph had contemplated moving to Philadelphia, where he would free his slaves and "thus end my days without undergoing any anxiety of holding them." And Mason was a supporter of abolition who said that slave owners were "petty tyrants."[15] It would be left to the states of the Deep South, South Carolina and Georgia, to defend slavery at the Convention.

Future abolitionists would call the Constitution a "covenant with death," although the document would be less than explicit in its views on slavery, perhaps because of the hostility of the Northerners and the ambivalence of the Virginians. "It was neither a "contract with abolition" nor a "covenant with death," Ellis has argued, "but rather a prudent exercise in ambiguity…Any clear resolution of the slavery question one way or the other rendered ratification of the Constitution virtually impossible," and would have ended any hope for nationhood.[16] But even given the ambiguity of the document, the southern slave owners were able to win some major concessions, especially on representation, that would enhance their power in the new government and provide them with the protections for slavery they required to support the new Constitution.

⸻

The debate of June 11 opened with a compromise put forward by Roger Sherman, when he "proposed that the proportion of suffrage in the 1st branch should be according to the respective numbers of free inhabitants; and that in the second branch or Senate, each State should have one vote and no more." His idea was similar to that which the Convention would agree to thirty days later, and would be known as the Connecticut or Grand Compromise. But, Madison, Wilson, and their allies were not ready to compromise on the issue of representation, which was so central to their views for how the new government should work.

John Rutledge of South Carolina used the opening created by Sherman to propose that, "suffrage should be according to quotas of contribution," which meant according to the wealth found in each state, which would include the value of slaves. By doing so, the southern states would increase their number of representatives. After much debate, Wilson offered an alternative in which representation would be "in proportion to the whole number of white & other free Citizens & inhabitants of every age sex & condition including those bound to servitude for a term of years and *three fifths of all other persons* not comprehended in the foregoing description, except Indians not paying taxes in each State." Charles Pinckney of South Carolina seconded the motion. The reference to three-fifths of all persons meant black slaves, a formula originally proposed by the Congress in 1783 as means of measuring how much each state should contribute to pay for the central government. It was not meant to indicate that a black person was only worth three-fifths of a person, but rather as an estimate of the amount an individual slave contributed to the economy and thus to wealth. The proposal put forward by Wilson was that this methodology, which had been proposed as a means to raise revenue, should be extended to representation. As the constitutional scholar Amar Reed writes: "The more slaves the Deep South could import from the African continent—innocents born in freedom and kidnapped across an ocean to be sold on auction blocks—the more seats it would earn in the American Congress."[17]

It is ironic that Wilson would be the one to make such a motion, since he was the most ardent supporter of democracy in the new government, a man who had told the Convention that he wanted to "raise the federal pyramid to a considerable altitude," which meant it had to have "as broad a basis as possible." Some have speculated that he was willing to give extra representation to the southern states in exchange for their support of proportional representation in both branches of the legislature. Wilson thought that Southerners would be open to proportional representation since they believed that their states would grow faster in the future due to their warmer climates and greater availability of land. Only minimal records exist of the events that occurred in the evenings after the Convention adjourned, so we have no way to document the deal making that took place between individuals. Given this, we will never know whether Wilson made such an explicit bargain with Rutledge, although it is certainly a logical conclusion.[18]

Only Elbridge Gerry spoke against the Wilson motion. He questioned why one type of property, slaves, should be favored over other types "in the rule of representation more than cattle and horses of the North." But the motion passed on a vote of nine to two, with only New Jersey and Delaware voting no, and then largely because they were opposed to proportional representation and not on the basis of opposition to slavery. It may have been the absence of Gouverneur Morris of Pennsylvania, who missed all of June and who was the staunchest opponent of slavery at the Convention, which resulted in the delegates approving the motion with so little debate. When he returned, the anti-slavery forces would bring the issue up for further consideration, although his opposition was largely based on protecting the commercial interests of his state and not opposition grounded in the immorality of slavery. Ultimately, the three-fifths rule would stand—an odious compromise that would haunt the nation until slavery was finally eliminated.[19]

Back and forth the Convention went, with the debate now returning to representation in the Senate. It was becoming clear that the battleground would be over the Senate, where the small states would hold out for an equal vote. Before compromise would occur on this issue, the Convention would almost fail.

On June 13, the Report of the Committee of the Whole was presented, which included nineteen provisions that the Convention had agreed to thus far—a triumph for Madison and his allies from the large states, albeit a temporary one. The Convention agreed to allow delegates to make handwritten copies of the report so they could review it. What happened next illustrates both the importance of the secrecy rule the Convention had adopted and the power Washington had over other men.

The General had been silent for much of the Convention. He would open the meeting and then return to his seat with the Virginia delegation once the Convention met as a Committee of the Whole. Washington was clearly not a constitutional scholar like Wilson, Madison, or Mason. Still, he was a firm supporter of a stronger national government, and had thrown his support behind the Virginia Plan and the creation of a strong executive. Without his support, it is unlikely the Convention would have met at all.

One delegate mislaid his copy of the report, which someone brought to Washington. Clearly angry, Washington addressed the Convention:

"Gentleman, I am sorry to find that some one member of this body has been so neglectful of the secrets of the convention as to drop in the State House a copy of their proceedings...I must entreat [the] gentleman to be more careful, lest our transactions get into the newspaper and disturb the public repose by premature speculations." Tossing the paper onto his desk, he stalked from the room with these words: "I do not know whose paper it is, but there it is—let him who owns it take it." Washington's words placed William Pierce of Georgia, who related the incident, into a state of terror when he realized his own copy was missing. He crept up to the table and was relieved to find that the document was in someone else's handwriting. No one ever claimed the document. Chernow writes: "the vignette shows how [he] functioned as the conscience of the convention and could make this room full of dignitaries feel like guilty schoolboys, summoned to the headmaster's office for a reprimand."[20]

The New Jersey and Hamilton Plans

The Convention now entered into its most dangerous phase, as delegates submitted rival plans, and the chances of success for the entire endeavor appeared less and less likely. William Paterson opened the session on Friday, June 15, with the New Jersey Plan. It proposed amending the Articles of Confederation to provide additional powers to Congress over taxation, and included a provision to create an executive board, which would consist of an unspecified number of individuals appointed by the Congress and removable by them based on "the applications by a majority of the several States." The taxing power would be limited to the levy of taxes on imports, and the burden of paying federal expenses would be apportioned based on population, including three-fifths of all other persons. The federal government would have the authority to ensure compliance through force. Carol

Berkin writes, "the large states would thus be saddled with more taxes but deprived of any extra power," since voting in Congress would continue to be by states in a unicameral legislature. Also, the Framers would never enhance the power of the national government, as proposed in the Virginia Plan, if there were only one branch of Congress. To do so would violate the systems of checks and balances they were struggling to establish. Overall, the New Jersey Plan was biased toward the small states, much as the Virginia Plan was to the large states. Some question whether the small states really did intend for the delegates to take their plan seriously. Pinckney would raise this later in the debates over the New Jersey Plan when he said: "The whole comes down to this, give New Jersey an equal vote, and she will dismiss her scruples, and concur in the National system."[21]

John Dickinson, who had been pushing for a compromise between the large and small states, pulled Madison aside after Paterson finished his presentation. "You see the consequences of pushing things too far," he told Madison. The small states favored many of the elements of the Virginia Plan, "but we would sooner submit to a foreign power" than "be deprived of an equality of suffrage, in both branches of the legislature." Dickinson, originally from Pennsylvania, had since moved to tiny Delaware, and could see both sides of the issue. He was looking to fashion a compromise position where the national government and the states would share sovereignty. But Madison and his allies were still not ready to compromise on the issue, and the debate between the large and small states over proportional representation would go on for the next two weeks in an intense and often hostile fashion. While Madison and his allies would have the better of the debate, they would ultimately fail in their attempt to convince the small states to accept proportional representation in both houses of Congress.[22]

Until now, Alexander Hamilton had been unusually quiet. Perhaps because he was outvoted by the two other New York delegates, John Lansing and Robert Yates, who were unalterably opposed to a strong national government. But on June 18, Hamilton rose to propose his own plan of government in a speech that would last for six straight hours. The Convention knew that Hamilton was a nationalist, a continentalist, and that he desired a government "tuned high," a strong central power that would pervade the whole. "Yet, what he proposed [that day] outdid in audacity any former statement," Catherine Bowen Drinker writes.[23]

Hamilton began by stating that he opposed both previously presented plans, but he focused his criticism primarily on the New Jersey Plan, "being fully convinced that no amendment of the Confederation leaving the States in possession of their Sovereignty could possibly answer the purpose." He made a broad appeal to shift power to the national government, since the people were so strongly attached to their states that they "would retain a commanding political advantage over Congress." In the process, his plan would all but eviscerate the states. Unlike Madison, he despaired "that a Republican Government could be established over so great an extent," although he shared Madison's view of the great divisions of society between "the few and the many" and that both groups needed to have a check on the power of the other. He then went into a very impolitic discussion extolling the virtues of the British system of government and his fear of democracy. Under most of the state constitutions then in effect, representatives served very short terms in office. Hamilton's plan envisioned both a Senate and an executive that would serve "during good behavior," in essence a life term. Despite his suspicion of democracy, even Hamilton proposed that members of the House of Representatives be elected by the people to serve three-year terms, and the power of that body be checked by a Senate that would represent the elite of society. The executive, which Hamilton did not believe "could be established on Republican principles," would have an absolute veto on the legislative branch. In a very poor use of words, Hamilton alluded to the fact that there would be opposition to so much power being placed in an "elective monarch," a phrase that would come back to haunt him many times in the future and lead to charges that he wanted an aristocratic government. While Hamilton clearly favored a government composed of the elite few, it was an elite whose membership would be based on ability and not heredity.[24]

"Alexander Hamilton at the Federal Convention cuts a disappointing figure, at odds with his previous and subsequent magnificent performance in support of the Constitution. His long speech was out of tune, unacceptable to both sides," one historian writes. Why did the brilliant Hamilton put forward a plan he knew had no chance of being seriously considered? Some have argued that it simply reflected what he believed, and perhaps that is the whole story. But was there more going on than that? Perhaps Hamilton put forward a plan that extolled the virtues of the British system of government and that resembled a new form of monarchy in order to make the Virginia Plan look more moderate, to help the other delegates see that if that plan failed that a more extreme nationalist plan could one day be implemented.[25]

We will never know the answers to these questions, and there exists no documentary evidence, no letters or journals from Hamilton, that tells us what he was thinking. His enemies would use the speech against him later in life, attacking him as a supporter of monarchy. Hamilton would defend himself, saying the speech had been made based on "propositions without due reflection," an interesting admission from a man who usually considered himself to be right. Some historians have argued that Hamilton's speech made Madison uneasy. But when Madison began to speak the next day, he never mentioned Hamilton's speech. If he felt so uncomfortable with Hamilton's views on government, one would think that Madison would indicate this in his speech that day. Since there was no support for Hamilton's plan, Madison may have felt no need to make a case against it, or perhaps he secretly knew that Hamilton's real intent was to place the Virginia Plan in a more favorable light.[26]

Madison instead spent his time on June 19 rebutting the New Jersey Plan. He did this by posing a series of questions on the problems that the United States faced, then showing how the New Jersey Plan fell short of meeting those problems. Would it prevent violations of the law of nations that will result in foreign wars? No, he answered, the "existing Confederacy does not sufficiently provide against this evil." Would it prevent encroachments on the federal authority? No, since the states would ratify the amendments to the Confederation and not the people themselves, and so the acts of Congress would not be paramount to the acts of the states. On he went in his criticism of the New Jersey Plan, and concluded by admitting that the real issue "lies in the affair of Representation; and if this could be adjusted, all others would be surmountable." However, he did not offer up any compromise on this issue to placate the small states. When he was finished, so was the New Jersey Plan, and the delegates voted seven to three to turn the debate back to the Virginia Plan. But even with this victory, New Jersey, New York, and Delaware voted no, and Maryland was split. The Convention would continue to struggle to find consensus over the issue of proportional representation, since the small states intended to hold out until they received an equal vote in at least one branch of the legislature, which was the true intent of the New Jersey Plan.[27]

Large States, Small States, and Sectional Differences

For the next week, the Convention skirted around the real issue, which was whether there would be proportional representation in only one or in both houses of Congress. On June 27, as the heat and humidity rose in Philadelphia, so too did the temperature inside Independence Hall, as the Convention entered into its most dangerous phase. The chances for success began to wane, as it appeared that one or more states would bolt from the Convention if they did not get their way on the crucial issue of proportional representation. Luther Martin took the floor on behalf of the small states and delivered a two-day "lengthy harangue," in the words of one delegate.

Martin, a graduate of the College of New Jersey and a highly successful lawyer and supporter of the revolution, had served as Maryland's attorney general. Others described him as a man "of medium height, broad shouldered, near sighted, absent minded, shabbily attired, harsh of voice...with a face crimsoned by the brandy he continually imbibed." Martin was reported to have a drinking problem, and some historians have speculated that he may have been drunk during the two-day tirade when he presented his opposition to equal representation in the Congress.[28]

Martin believed that the central government was meant to preserve the states, not to govern individuals, which in his view was the responsibility of the states. Given this, the central government's "powers ought to be kept within narrow limits." He was unalterably opposed to the Virginia Plan, and believed that "an equal vote in each State was essential to the federal idea." By the second day of Martin's speech, Madison stopped taking detailed notes and recorded that the balance of "his discourse was delivered with diffuseness and considerable vehemence." Martin's speech, described by some as bombastic, was even denounced by those who generally agreed with him. Oliver Ellsworth of Connecticut would later write that the speech "might have continued two months, but for those marks of fatigue and disgust you saw strongly expressed on whichever side of the house you turned your mortified eyes."[29]

Madison responded with his most direct challenge to the small states by demonstrating that, in fact, the large states did not have a common interest. "In point of situation they could not have been more effectually separated from each other by the most jealous citizens of the most jealous State. In point of manners, Religion, and the other circumstances which sometimes beget affection between different communities, they were not more assimilated than the other States." In fact, their economic interests were quite different, with Massachusetts dependent on fishing, Pennsylvania on flour, and Virginia on tobacco. It was more likely that the large states would be rivals rather than partners, Madison argued. Wilson supported his colleague on June 30, with a speech that pointed out how unfair it would be for a minority of the people to control the majority. "Such an equality [of votes in the second branch] will enable the minority to control the majority... It would be in the power then of less than 1/3rd to overrule 2/3rd whenever a question should happen to divide the States in that manner."[30]

After Wilson had finished speaking, Madison tried a new argument, one that posited that the divisions of the country were not between the large and small states, but rather were sectional in nature, with the states divided between North and South based on their "having or not having slaves." Madison indicated that, "he was so strongly impressed with this important truth" that he had been "casting about in his mind" for some solution. Perhaps one branch should be represented based on the number of free inhabitants, and in the other "according to the whole number counting the slaves as if free." But Madison never put this forward as a motion, perhaps because it undercut his rationale for a veto of state laws, since the veto might one day endanger the peculiar institution. As one historian writes: "How could the South ever accept a national veto over laws affecting slavery?"[31]

The debate had become extremely overheated, to the point where Franklin had suggested that the Convention should open each day's session with a prayer led by a local clergyman. His motion lacked support, and as Franklin noted at the bottom of his speech, "the Convention, except for three or four persons, thought prayer unnecessary!" Perhaps they should have listened to him before Gunning Bedford of Delaware began the speech on June 30 that one historian has called "one of the most ill-tempered and bellicose speeches of the Convention." He dug his heels in, largely in response to Madison and Wilson, and "contended that there was no middle way between a perfect consolidation and a mere confederacy." In a thundering voice, he shouted: "I do not, gentleman, trust you." If the large states dissolved the confederation, then "the small ones will find some foreign ally of more honor and good faith, who will take them by the hand and do them justice." This was the first time that any delegate had threatened the assistance of a foreign power if they did not get their way, and it led to an immediate response from Rufus King of Massachusetts, who was "grieved that such a thought had entered into his heart. He was more grieved that such an expression had dropped from his lips."[32] At that point, the Convention adjourned until Monday July 2. The delegates faced the very real prospect that the Convention would collapse.

Taking a step back from the abyss, the Convention appointed a committee to meet over the July 4 recess to come up with an acceptable plan. Both Wilson and Madison opposed the committee idea, but the other delegates knew, as Hugh Williamson of North Carolina expressed it, that compromise was now the only answer, or the Convention would fail. "If we do not concede on both sides, our business will soon be at an end...As a Committee would be a smaller body, a compromise would be pursued with more coolness."[33]

Compromise is never easy. In today's world, people chastise politicians for failing to work together in a bipartisan manner, but the Framers, too, struggled with finding common ground. So when Gerry delivered the committee's report on July 5, he indicated that the members "were of different opinions...and agreed to the Report merely in order that some ground of accommodation might be proposed," and that those opposed to an equal state vote in the Senate "have only assented conditionally." During their recess meetings, the committee had agreed to a proposal put forward by Franklin, his major substantive contribution at the Convention. Franklin proposed that in the House, each state would receive one member for every 40,000 inhabitants. He didn't mention the three-fifths clause, although one historian has argued that the members of the committee assumed that this would be a part of any method of apportioning votes, and that the lack of specificity in the Franklin proposal was designed to spare him embarrassment, since he was a member of the Pennsylvania abolition society. In the Senate, each state would have an equal vote. Franklin threw a bone to the large states by requiring that all bills for raising or appropriating money would originate in the House of Representatives.[34]

Madison immediately saw that the proposal for originating money bills in the House was of little value, since the Senate could simply reject any proposal it did not like. Gouverneur Morris attempted to appeal to larger purposes, stating that he had come to the Convention "as a Representative of America" and wished that the members would "extend their views beyond the present moment." While couched in broad rhetoric, his views were really a self-serving way to defend the large state position. Gerry, who indicated he too had "material objections" to the proposal, made an astute observation when he said, "We were neither the same Nation nor different Nations. We ought not therefore to pursue the one or the other of these ideas too closely," since the result would be the breakup of the United States into numerous smaller confederacies.[35]

Although the large states clearly had the better of the argument from an intellectual perspective, given that the small states could not provide a compelling reason for why they would be harmed from a combination of the large states, there was simply no way to achieve a new and stronger union without recognizing the small states claims. "In the end, the framers could not avoid treating the states as constituent elements of the polity; nor could they deny that simple residence in a state would establish the most natural bond of civic loyalty," Rakove writes.[36] The Framers were struggling with a new and untried version of federalism, one in which the states and the new central government would share sovereignty more equally. The strengths of such a system, in a nation as large and diverse as the United States, are obvious today. Matters that involve foreign policy, disputes between the states, and those that involve a common national interest (such as interstate commerce) would be resolved at the national level. Other problems would be left to the states, which would have the freedom to implement different solutions that best matched local conditions.

None of the Framers, with the exception of Hamilton, wanted to eliminate the states. Instead, the issue was over equality of voting, and on this issue, there was a price to be paid in that the Senate would forever more be an undemocratic institution, in terms of voter equality. The equal state vote encompassed in the compromise meant that voters from small states were over-represented in the Senate, while voters from large states were under-represented. To take just a few examples, a voter in Nevada, with a population of 2.8 million people, has, in the Senate, fourteen times the voting strength of a voter in neighboring California, with a population of 38 million. The ratio between New York and Connecticut is 5.4 to 1. The most absurd ratio of all is the one between Wyoming, the least populous state (population 583,000), to California, where it works out to 70 to 1. As one political scientist writes, "surely the inequality in representation [in the Senate] reveals a profound violation of the democratic idea of political equality among all citizens."[37]

The large state representatives, including Madison and Wilson, were still not ready to concede an equal state vote in the Senate, even in the aftermath of the committee report, and so the Convention moved back once again to the issue of proportional representation in the House of Representatives. Between July 9 and July 16, this issue would reopen the discussion of how to count slaves, another enduring division blocking the path of the delegates toward the formation of a "more perfect" union. The small states felt compelled to maintain their political identity as the price of nationhood, and the southern states defended slavery as essential to their way of life and its protection as the price for them to support a new Constitution. At one point the debates became so contentious that Washington wrote to Hamilton, who had left the Convention, "I almost despair of seeing a favorable issue to… the convention and do therefore repent having had any agency in the business." The back-and-forth between the two sides eventually led to a final decision to incorporate the three-fifths rule into apportioning representatives.

Two other issues of importance were decided during this period. First, the future number of representatives in the House would be adjusted based on a census of the country that would take place within six years after the seating of the first Congress, and every ten years thereafter. Second, new states would be admitted to the union on an equal basis with the existing thirteen states.[38]

To the modern reader, the debate over slavery that took place the week of July 9 to the 16 lacks any sense of its immorality, of the stain that it left on a country dedicated to the proposition that all men are created equal, and instead reflected hard political bargaining on the part of the northern and southern states to protect their interests. While some, like Franklin, opposed slavery because it was wrong, other critics at the Convention opposed the counting of slaves because it would disadvantage their region. Gouverneur Morris was a prime example, railing against including slaves in the apportionment of legislative seats largely because he feared that commercial interests would suffer. "To our way of thinking this fateful compromise was both a moral blot on the Constitution and a crude index of the perceived racial inferiority of African Americans," Rakove writes. "To northern delegates at Philadelphia it was merely a political bargain."[39] John Dickinson, who had been involved in so many of the debates and decisions that had led to the independence of the United States, a man who had written the draft Articles of Confederation, wrote the following in his notebook at one point during the debate on slavery:

> *Acting before the World, What will be said of this new principle of the founding a Right to govern Freemen on a power derived from Slaves…[who are] themselves incapable of governing yet giving to others what they have not. The omitting [of] the WORD will be regarded as*

an Endeavour to conceal a principle of which we are ashamed.[40]

Final Compromises on the Issue of Proportional Representation

The weather had turned cool and cloudy over the weekend preceding the fateful vote of Monday, July 16. On that day, the Convention considered "the question for agreeing to the whole Report as amended & including the equality of votes in the 2d branch." The report referred to was the Franklin committee's compromise proposal, which is sometimes referred to as the "Grand Compromise" or the "Connecticut Compromise" by historians. The Grand Compromise won approval on the closest of votes, with five states in support, four opposed, and one divided. The states in support included the small states of Connecticut, New Jersey, Delaware, Maryland, and North Carolina. North Carolina had changed its vote, most likely because the strong nationalist William Blount from that state had left the Convention and returned to the Confederation Congress that was meeting in New York. Massachusetts split, when Gerry and Strong supported the motion, while their colleagues King and Ghorum voted no.[41]

Randolph, who had introduced the Virginia Plan and supported its provisions on proportional representation, moved for an adjournment. Paterson immediately seconded the motion, but this was not a measure of support from him but rather a threat. Sensing that the large states intended to regroup and counterattack, he indicated "that it was high time for the Convention to adjourn, that the rule of secrecy ought to be rescinded, and that our constituents should be consulted" and that adjournment be made permanent. To make his position perfectly clear, he also added that, "no conciliation could be admissible on the part of the smaller states on any other ground than that of equality of votes in the second branch." Fortunately, cooler heads prevailed. Rutledge of South Carolina, though he had lost on the issue of proportional representation in the Senate, urged his fellow delegates "that although we could not do what we thought best, in itself, we ought to do something." Pinkney asked Randolph to clarify whether he really wanted a permanent end to the Convention, or simply an adjournment for the day, and Randolph indicated that a temporary adjournment was all he sought. He did close the conventions business for the day on an ominous note, saying that, "in case the smaller states should continue to hold back, the larger might then take such measures…as might be necessary."[42]

The next morning, the large state delegations met to discuss their options. To ensure that the small states did not feel excluded and to prove that the large states were not colluding against them, they made the meeting open to small state delegates as well. Madison, in his notes, does not indicate exactly what took place at this meeting, other than his comment that "the time was wasted in vague conversation on the subject [of an equal state vote in the Senate], without any specific proposition or agreement." He does indicate that two sides emerged, one that wanted the large states to now go their own way and propose a government based purely on proportional representation. But apparently, his side did not have the votes to push such a scheme through, since the other side preferred to keep the thirteen states together by yielding to the small states.

The Grand or Connecticut Compromise prevailed. William Samuel Johnson of Connecticut, one of its main supporters, had earlier made the argument that "On the whole he thought that as in some respects the States are to be considered in the political capacity, and in others as districts of individual citizens, the two ideas embraced on different sides, instead of being opposed to each other, ought to be combined;

that in one branch the people ought to be represented; in the other the States." As Ellis writes, the Connecticut Compromise, "essentially declared the theoretical question of state versus federal sovereignty politically unresolvable except by a split the difference structure that neither camp found satisfactory. The only workable solution was to leave the sovereignty question unclear."[43]

Sovereignty can be divided, in a theoretical sense, and that is what the Framers did, considering it the only way to preserve the union of all thirteen states. But ultimately, when disputes would arise, the locus of decision making would need to reside somewhere. Future divisions in the nation would not involve the small states versus the large states, but rather would be sectional in nature, with the North and the South squaring off against each other. It would take the next sixty-plus years, a Civil War, and the death of many Americans to finally resolve the issue that the new national government was supreme and eliminate the curse of slavery. "In reality, the delegates had deferred rather than solved the problem of political sovereignty," one historian writes.[44]

Endnotes

1 Solberg, p. 106-107

2 Solberg, p. 108-109 for quotes from Madison; the Hamilton quotes are from Rakove, *Original Meanings*, p. 61; the description from the delegate on the Madison speaking style is from Stewart, p. 68

3 See Rakove, *Madison*, p. 67 and *Original Meanings*, p. 62-63

4 Rakove, *Original Meanings*, p. 62

5 Solberg, p. 116-117

6 Solberg, p. 118

7 Beeman, p. 145 and Berkin, p. 235

8 Solberg, p. 118-119

9 Bowen, p. 3; Stewart, p. 81-82; the documentary evidence for a cool summer in Philadelphia can be found at http://www.consource.org/document/appendix-the-weather-during-the-convention-1787/

10 Quoted from Berkin, p. 96

11 See Berkin, p. 100; Beeman, p. 147-148; and also *A Biography of William Paterson 1745-1806*, retrieved August 4, 2013 from http://www.let.rug.nl/usa/biogaphies/william-paterson/

12 Solberg, p. 120-122; Bowen, p. 84-85

13 Solberg, p. 123

14 The quotes are from Bowen, p. 92

15 See Ellis, *Founding Brothers*, p. 89-90 for the information on which states had outlawed slavery; the quote from the Virginia delegates is from Stewart, p. 70

16 Ellis, *Founding Brothers*, p. 93

17 Solberg, p. 125-126; Beeman, p. 156; Reed, p. 90

18 Stewart makes this case in Chapter 6, which is where the quote from Wilson is also taken. But Stewart admits at the beginning of Chapter 7 that he does not know who actually proposed the deal, whether it was Wilson, Rutledge, or perhaps even Franklin. Beeman makes a similar observation on p. 153.

19 Solberg, p. 126; Beeman, p. 155 for why New Jersey and Delaware voted no on the motion.

20 Chernow, *Washington*, p. 530-531

21 Berkin, p. 102; the Pinkney quote is from Rakove, *Original Meanings*, p. 63

22 The quote is from Rakove, *Revolutionaries*, p. 370; Beeman raises the issue of Dickinson being able to see the issue of proportional representation from both sides on p. 162

23 Bowen, p. 112

24 All quotes are from Solberg, p. 140-147

25 Bowen, p. 114. Stewart, p. 94-96, does not believe that Hamilton had any other motives than to put forward what he believed and points to the fact that the Virginia Plan was well on the way to being adopted when he made his speech. This does not seem persuasive, since the Convention was just as likely to break up at this point as it was to approve the basic outline of the Virginia Plan.

26 Bowen, p. 115 for the Hamilton quote and for the unease of Madison with what Hamilton had said. Beeman makes a similar remark on page 170.

27 Solberg, p. 152-155

28 Beeman, p. 174-175; Berkin, p. 239-240

29 Solberg, p. 179-182

30 Solberg, p. 184 and p. 193

31 Solberg, p. 194; the historian referenced is Rakove, *Madison*, p. 71

32 The Franklin quote is from Beeman, p. 181; the description of the Bradford speech is from Beeman, p. 184, and the quotes are from Solberg, p. 197-198

33 Beeman, p. 188-189

34 Solberg, p. 201-202; Beeman, p. 201-204

35 Solberg, p. 204

36 Rakove, *Original Meanings*, p. 78

37 The ratios have been updated based on population figures in 2013 but were originally taken from Dahl, location 393, as was the quote.

38 Beeman, p. 211-212

39 Rakove, *Revolutionaries*, p. 374

40 Quoted in Beeman, p. 215

41 Solberg, p. 222; Beeman, p. 219

42 Beeman, p. 220-221; Stewart, p. 124-125

43 Solberg, p. 187; Ellis, *American Creation*, p. 110

44 Beeman, p. 225

Chapter 9

We the People / July 17, 1787 to September 17, 1787

"In all our deliberations on this subject we kept in our view, that which appears to us the greatest interest of every true American, the consolidation of our Union..."

–From the letter of transmittal of the Constitution signed by George Washington, September 17, 1787 –

The mood of the Convention had changed after July 17, when the delegates agreed to the Grand Compromise. They had accomplished a major goal of moving toward a new and stronger national government by protecting the small states and slavery, although the issue of slavery would undergo one more round of intense debate. The Framers had been meeting for over two months, and for those that had stayed the entire time, fatigue and homesickness had set in. Still, much work remained to transform the numerous decisions into a coherent document. Increasingly, the Convention turned to a series of committees to complete their work.

Ellis has said that chronology is the last refuge of the feeble minded, but the only refuge of the historian. But some subjects are better analyzed when completed in their entirety, like the presidency, so this chapter will move away from a purely chronological approach. In addition, I have selected those subjects that best illustrate the importance to the Framers of building one new American nation, or that are at the core of our constitutional system. Numerous books, many of them referenced here, provide a more detailed version of the events that took place over the last two months of the Convention.

When the Convention reconvened on July 17, delegates began briefly debating the powers the new Congress should have. For such a monumental decision, they spent precious little time on the issue, less than a day. The delegates ended up deadlocked over whether the legislature should have plenary (i.e. full and complete) power, or should be limited to a list of enumerated powers. This deadlock would remain until the Committee of Detail, charged with preparing a first draft of the new Constitution, released their report on August 6.[1]

On July 17, Madison's proposal to give the Congress the power to veto state laws was also once again defeated. Luther Martin, not always the most judicious of men, asked an important question: whether all of "the laws of the states [would] be sent up to the general legislature before they shall be permitted to operate?" Such a process would be cumbersome and would have required Congress to spend a great deal of time reviewing state laws, "rather than tending to the business of the nation at large," as Beeman writes.[2] Martin did propose a resolution that included a provision "that the legislative acts of the U.S.…shall be the supreme law of the respective States," which was passed without dissent. Out of this was born the supremacy clause of the Constitution.

Debating the Presidency Once Again

Beginning on July 17, and continuing for most of the next nine days, the Convention debated the presidency. The delegates had previously decided there would be a single executive that would be elected by the legislature for a single seven-year term and that the president would have a limited veto power over the laws passed by the Congress. The Convention would revisit each of these elements multiple times before adjourning. The ensuing debates generally centered around three major issues: 1) the method to be used to elect the executive; 2) the length of term for the office; and, 3) whether the incumbent should be eligible for re-election. They also considered the method for removal from office.[3]

Who should elect the president? The Convention delegates considered three basic choices: election by the legislature, election by the people, and a middle position that would eventually become the electoral college. They concluded that each of these alternatives had major weaknesses. If the legislature elected the president, the fear was that "the Nat. Executive would be rendered subservient to them," as Madison observed on July 25. If the people were to elect the president, the delegates had major concerns that no candidate would command a majority, since the public was likely to only vote for those from their home state that they were most familiar with. The delegates simply could not envision that individuals with a national reputation, other than Washington, would emerge in the future. This is understandable, given that "sources for information were sparse: the nation's few weekly newspapers were located in urban areas, mail delivery was erratic and expensive, and the cost of books was prohibitive for most farmers and artisans," as one historian writes. Some of the delegates also did not think the public capable of making a sound selection for president. Mason spoke for this group when he said, "it would be as unnatural to refer the choice of a proper character for chief Magistrate to the people, as it would, to refer a trial of colours to a blind man." The delegates also found the electoral college system to be deficient, in part due to the expense and inconvenience of bringing together in one place electors from widely separated states.[4]

How long should a president serve and should the incumbent be eligible for re-election? The method of election would affect the issue of how long a president could serve and his eligibility for re-election. If Congress were to elect the president, then many felt he should have a reasonably long term, to ensure independence, but that the incumbent should not be eligible for re-election, since his re-election would be the "work of intrigue, of cabal, and of faction," with the result that the president would be a toady, a "willing tool of his supporters," as Gouverneur Morris argued.[5] Many of the delegates wanted an executive that would serve a long term and be eligible for re-election, since this would ensure "energy," provide the incumbent with the time to master the job, and ensure the president would have the ability to fight off legislative encroachment. Still others feared a powerful executive that would become a new monarch and would repudiate all they had fought against in 1776.

The delegates tied themselves into knots over the executive branch. On July 26, Mason observed that, "in every Stage of the Question relative to the Executive, the difficulty of the subject and the diversity of the opinions concerning it have appeared. Nor have any of the modes of constituting that department appeared." So it was no surprise that when the Convention voted on this subject, they ended up right back where they had begun nine days earlier—a single executive who would serve a seven-year term, be appointed by the legislature, be ineligible for re-election, be subject to impeachment, and have a limited veto over legislation. This would not be the last word on the presidency.[6]

Final Decisions on the Presidency

Following the futile debate that occurred between July 17 and July 26, the Convention moved on to other matters, including the establishment of a Committee of Detail to prepare an initial draft of the Constitution, which I discuss in the next section. The delegates deferred the issue of the executive for a time, briefly discussed it on August 24, and finally assigned it to an eleven-member committee on Postponed Parts that met on August 31. The committee comprised one representative from each of the eleven states that were still in attendance at the Convention.

The major change the committee made was to substitute election by Congress for a revised form of an electoral college as the mode for electing the president. John Dickinson had raised the issue before the committee, stating his concern about the election by the legislature. Since the presidency would be such a powerful office, he was concerned that the people would never accept the office "unless they themselves would be more immediately concerned in [the president's] election." Madison then set about drafting a new and complicated proposal for consideration. Each state's legislature would appoint electors based on the method of their own choosing, with the number of electors equal to the total membership in the House and Senate. A state could choose to have the legislature appoint the electors, which would satisfy those concerned that the public would not make a well-informed choice. According to some of the delegates, appointment by the legislature offered an alternative that would result in better informed and less parochial electors. Alternatively, the people of that state could directly elect the electors, thereby satisfying those like Dickinson and Wilson who wanted a more inclusive role for the people. The electors would meet in their own states, rather than as one group, which reduced the concern over the cost and difficulty of bringing all of the members together at one time. The electors would vote for two people, one of whom could not be from their home state. The individual who had the greatest number of votes would be elected president. The person with the second most votes would be elected vice president, an office that the Convention had recently added. If no candidate received a majority, the Senate would choose the president.

The electoral college would prove to be of great benefit to the slave owners of the South. Madison, who had ultimately decided to support the direct election of the president in his speech on July 25, had admitted that such an approach would work to the disadvantage of the South, since there was a "disproportion of qualified voters in the" South compared to the North. Madison thought this disadvantage would evaporate over time, since he believed that the southern states would grow more rapidly in the future than the northern states. He was willing make such a sacrifice, at least in the short term, since "local considerations must give way to the general interest." Few of his fellow southern delegates felt the same way. Election of the president through the electoral college mechanism would mean the three-fifths rule for counting slaves would come into play, since the number of electors would largely equal the number of House seats each state was assigned. Virginia would particularly benefit from the additional electors they would receive by including slaves in their allocation of House seats and the corresponding number of electors. After the first census in 1790, Virginia would receive six more House seats than Pennsylvania, even though both states had roughly the same number of free inhabitants. "For thirty-two of the presidency's first thirty-six years, a (slaveholding, plantation-owning) Virginian would occupy the nation's highest office," observes Amar Read, due to the impact of the electoral college.[7]

The Committee of Detail also made three other changes to the presidency. First, the president would serve a four-year term and be eligible for re-election. The House would have the power of impeachment, and the Senate would try an impeached president. Third, the president would have the power to make treaties and appoint ambassadors and judges to the Supreme Court, with the advice and consent of the Senate.[8] These powers had originally been assigned solely to the Senate, largely because the small states wanted to have greater control over these matters. But with this change, the committee made them a shared responsibility between the two branches of government as a further means to strengthen the checks and balances the Framers were striving for. The Convention had previously assigned the power to declare war to the Congress, and the role of commander in chief to the executive, and now the two great elements of foreign policy, the war-making power and the power to make treaties, would be in "joint possession" of the president and Congress.[9]

When the Convention delegates received the committee report on September 4, they expressed a concern about having the Senate select the president if no candidate emerged with a majority. Most of the delegates assumed that, other than Washington, no candidate would achieve a majority, placing the Senate in a position to regularly select the person who would hold the office of the president. James Wilson articulated most clearly the concern of having the Senate make the selection, indicating that this would have a "dangerous tendency to [move the government toward an] aristocracy." The Senate would not only be in control of the executive branch, but through its role of advice and consent on Supreme Court nominations, "the Legislative, Executive & Judiciary powers [would] all be blended in one branch of Government," thereby violating one of the core tenets of the separation of powers. Randolph, Mason, Rutledge, Pinckney, and Williamson all agreed with Wilson on this point. Wilson then proposed that the House of Representatives rather than the Senate select the president. This motion was defeated, in large part because the small states believed it gave the large states too much sway over the selection of the president. Not only would the electoral college be weighted toward the large states, since their number would largely be drawn from the number of members of the House, but that same House would then select the president in cases where no candidate received a majority. Hugh

Williamson and Roger Sherman came up with an ingenious solution to the problem under which the House would make the selection, but the voting would be by state and not per capita. The compromise proposal won the endorsement of the Convention on a 10-1 vote.[10]

The Convention also made a few other changes to the proposals affecting the presidency. They included a provision that the president must be a natural born citizen of the United States or a citizen of the country at the time of adoption of the Constitution. They added this provision due to a concern "that a foreign earl or duke might cross the Atlantic with immense wealth" and try to buy the presidency, as Akhil Reed Amar noted. The minimum age for the president was set at thirty-five years, and a requirement added that a presidential candidate must have been a resident of the United States for at least fourteen years. Finally, Mason added the words "high crimes and misdemeanors" to the list of reasons for impeaching a president. While the terms were still rather vague, the delegates approved them in order to move on to other matters.[11]

The Convention had created an executive officer who was far more powerful than any state governor was. One individual would occupy the office, and the method of selection of the presidency was separated from the legislative branch. Those that supported a powerful executive had won the day by reminding their fellow delegates that "it was imperative for the President to be truly independent if the separation of powers was to work," and for the "executive to serve as check on the legislature." The Framers also largely left the definition of the powers of the office ill defined. "The ambiguity...provides the system with flexibility and responsiveness to emergencies but also makes the office a kind of a blank canvas on which each incumbent can paint his own colors, and some have chosen to paint it with bright, bold ones," according to the political scientist Judith Best.[12]

Fatigue had set in, and it began to affect some of the decisions made in September. For those delegates that had attended for the entire time, they had been away from their jobs and loved ones for over three months. Speeches became shorter, and even the indefatigable Madison was wearing down, in part due to illness. His note taking lessened noticeably as the Convention dragged on. Later in life, Madison indicated that the method of electing the president "was not exempt from a degree of the hurrying influence produced by fatigue and impatience…"[13] In addition to the restlessness of the delegates, two other factors contributed to the creation of the electoral college. One was the Framers' views of political parties, and the second was the lack of any acceptable alternatives.

Why the Electoral College? – The Problem of Parties

As we have seen, part of the Framers' hesitancy about having the people directly elect the president came from their concern that no candidate would receive a majority. They could not foresee the role that political parties would play in the future, and many of them opposed parties. Jefferson, in a 1789 letter, had written: "If I could not go to heaven but with a party, I would not go there at all." Adams, likewise, had written in 1789 that, "there is nothing which I dread as much as a division of the republic into two great parties, each arranged under its leader, and concerting measures in opposition to each other." While neither man had attended the Convention, many of the delegates shared their perspective. As discussed in Chapter 5, Madison's theory of republican government included the fear of factions and the need to control them. While today we view a faction as a splinter group within a political party, the founders used the terms faction and party interchangeably. Washington was opposed to political parties during his entire eight-year term as president, and warned the nation of the dangers of parties in his farewell address, when he talked of "the baneful effects of the spirit of party generally."[14]

The founders' anti-party perspective grew out of their sense that parties acted out of a narrow sense of their own interests or ideology, and as such, did not serve the public interest. This is what Washington referred to in his farewell address when he stated that parties "serve to organize faction, to give it an artificial and extraordinary force; to put, in the place of the delegated will of the nation the will of a party." Yet the founders also resigned themselves to the fact, as Madison wrote in *Federalist* No. 10, that "the latent causes of faction are…sown in the nature of man," that they were the price of living in a free society. Adams too believed that "All countries under the sun must have parties. The great secret is to control them." Part of the objective of the constitutional arrangements that the Framers were designing at the Convention was to control the deleterious effects of parties.[15]

What the founders had difficulty seeing was the positive role of political parties in a democratic system, especially one built on divided power and checks and balances. For such a system to work, parties would ultimately need to play a key role in organizing the will of the majority, creating a legitimate opposition, and tying the president and legislature together to accomplish public policy objectives and pass laws. According to historian Richard Hofstadler, the Convention "had framed a Constitution which, among its other ends, was meant to control and counteract parties, and yet they gradually began to realize that they could not govern under it without the help of such organizations…the new Constitution which they had so ingeniously drawn up could never have [worked] if some of its vital deficiencies, not the least the link between the executive and legislature, had not been remedied by the political parties."[16]

The founders would eventually realize that parties were more than just a necessary evil, that they could indeed be a force of good in a free society, a way to "organize social conflict and political debate." Madison's views on party would evolve over time, as Robert Dahl has noted. In 1787, Madison was primarily concerned with the protection of minority rights from the threat of overbearing majorities. By the 1790s, he began to see that the real problem was the threat of minority factions. Dahl argues that Madison began to see the need for organized political parties as a way to protect the rights, liberties, and entitlements of the majority from minority factions. Madison and Jefferson would form a national political party, the Republicans (not to be confused with the modern Republican Party), that would later be called the Democratic-Republicans, and ultimately, under Andrew Jackson, would become simply the Democrats. Both Madison and Jefferson believed that the only way to combat the policies of Hamilton and the Federalists in the 1790s was to organize a political party that could command the loyalty of a majority of citizens. Each future president would ultimately become not only the nation's political leader, but also the leader of a party whose membership extended to the Congress and the people.[17]

Why the Electoral College? – Lack of Alternatives

"The United States came within a hair's breath of adopting a kind of parliamentary system," writes Robert Dahl. Under such a system, as is found in Great Britain and many other countries in the world, the legislature elects the executive, who is usually a member of the legislative body. The executive, often called a prime minister, is also the head of the party with a majority in the legislature, and he or she forms a government. In a parliamentary system, the legislative and executive branches are more fully tied together. The Virginia Plan had proposed that the legislature elect the executive, and the Convention voted numerous times for this proposal. Yet, the Framers feared that the president would be too weak, a creature of the legislative branch, and so they moved toward the electoral college alternative, almost out of a sense of desperation, since they knew of no other alternatives. "Had Britain progressed further toward the norms of cabinet government and strong party connections between executive and legislature that emerged in the next century, the framers might have reasoned differently about the political dimensions of executive appointment and leadership," Jack Rakove writes. But at the time the Framers were drafting the Constitution, the British parliamentary model did not yet exist.[18]

After ratification, one major flaw became apparent in the electoral college system. The Constitution called for each elector to cast ballots for two people, as a means to compel electors to cast a vote for at least one candidate who was not from the elector's home state. In this way, they hoped candidates with national credentials would emerge. Once political parties began to form, the candidates for president and vice president could end up in a tie vote, throwing the election to the House. This occurred in the election of 1800, when the Republicans nominated Jefferson and Burr to run as a ticket for president and vice president respectively. President Adams stood for election as the Federalist candidate. Both Jefferson and Burr ended up with seventy-three electoral votes, and it took thirty-six ballots before Jefferson emerged as the winner in the House. The Twelfth Amendment eventually fixed this problem by eliminating the requirement for double balloting and allowing for a separate vote for president and vice president.

Gradually, the American system for choosing a president through the electoral college would become more grounded in the popular will. The Framers' chief fear that no national candidates would emerge, or that none would receive a majority, proved false, largely due to the formation of political parties. Abraham Baldwin of Georgia, a little-known delegate to the Convention who was generally silent during the debates, had predicted that "the increasing intercourse among the people of the states, would render important characters less and less unknown." Wilson agreed, believing that "continental characters will multiply as we more and more coalesce."[19]

Over time, states would change their rules so the electors would vote for the candidate that won the popular vote. When Jefferson was elected president in 1800, electors were chosen by the state legislatures in ten of the eighteen states. By the time of Andrew Jackson's election in 1832, only one state (South Carolina) had the legislature select the electors. The rest of the states chose their electors based on the candidate that won the popular vote in the election. Though there is no constitutional requirement that the electors vote for that candidate, generally they are selected by and are members of the political party whose candidate wins the election, and they pledge to support their party's candidate. To further strengthen this requirement, twenty-six states have passed laws that require the electors to cast their ballot for the winner of the popular vote.[20]

Today in the United States, forty-eight of the fifty states also assign their electors on a winner-take-all basis. In other words, all of the electors from a state vote for the winner of the popular vote, regardless of how close that vote may be. By way of illustration, George W. Bush won all twenty-five of Florida's electoral votes in 2000, even though he won the popular vote in the state by less than 600 votes. The shift to winner take all began in 1824, and by 1836, all but South Carolina used this system. The change occurred primarily to enhance the influence of state political leaders, who "concluded that by concentrating all of the state's electoral votes in a single slate, they could enhance their weight in the electoral college and thus their influence on the elections."[21] As the election of the president became tied ever closer to the popular will, the occupant of the office began to see himself as embodying the will of a majority of the nation, since he was the only person elected by all of the people.

The compromise that finally created the electoral college came with a cost, as most compromise does. Because the number of electors are equal to the number of House and Senate seats that each state receives, small states have proportionally more voting leverage. Although not as pronounced as the disparity in the Senate, "the vote of a Wyoming resident...is worth four times the vote of a California resident in the electoral college."[22] Prior to the Civil War, the electoral college worked to the advantage of the slave-owning South, due to the three-fifths rule.

But the most pernicious result of the electoral college system is that the candidate with the most popular votes does not always win the presidency. This has happened four times in our nation's history, in 1824, 1876, 1888 and most recently 2000. Al Gore received 450,000 more popular votes that year, but George W. Bush prevailed in the electoral college in large part because he won all of Florida's electoral votes by the narrowest of margins. Attempts to amend the Constitution to implement the direct popular election of the president have proved controversial. Robert Dahl has indicated that over seven hundred proposals have been introduced in the House to change the electoral college system. In 1993, a proposal actually passed the House with 83 percent of the vote, but then died in the Senate.[23]

Proposals to eliminate the winner-take-all provisions that most states follow date back to Madison's time. In an 1823 letter to George Hay, Madison favored assigning electoral votes in a proportional manner, rather than based on the winner-take-all approach that had become increasingly common by that time. Recent proposals to change this method surfaced in the aftermath of the 2012 election, in which the Democratic candidate Barack Obama won with 51 percent of the popular vote and 332 electoral votes. Some Republican strategists, frustrated in their attempts to win the White House, proposed changes to the winner-take-all approach, but only for selected states that typically vote Democratic in the presidential election but which are controlled by Republicans at the state level. Under one of these proposals, electoral votes would be awarded to the winner of each congressional district, with the two statewide electors given to the candidate that wins the popular vote. As the "National Journal" notes: "rewriting the rules would dramatically shrink or eliminate the Democratic advantage, because of the way House districts are drawn. The decennial redistricting process has dumped huge percentages of Democratic votes into some urban districts, while Republican voters are spread over a wider number of districts, giving the party an advantage." In addition to the demographic shifts that have focused Democratic voters into urban areas and Republicans into rural and suburban areas, gerrymandered districts (named for Elbridge Gerry) further contribute to the problem. In 2012, Democrats won one million more votes than the Republicans did for House seats, yet the Republicans garnered an additional thirty-three seats. Depending on how changes to the electoral college system are made, it could result in the candidate who wins the popular vote actually losing the election, worsening the problem with the present system. One analyst has estimated that if electoral votes were allocated on the district basis, Obama would have lost the election despite receiving five million more votes than his opponent, Mitt Romney, a result that is difficult to justify in the world's oldest democracy.[24]

The Committee on Detail

In addition to reaching some major conclusions on the mode of electing the president and his term, the Convention had much other work to do to complete the Constitution. On July 23, Elbridge Gerry made a motion to refer all of the proceedings and decisions that the Convention had made to date to a Committee of Detail that would prepare a report on the Constitution. The Convention unanimously adopted Gerry's proposal, and formed a five-member committee that included John Rutledge, Edmund Randolph, Nathan Ghorum, Oliver Ellsworth, and James Wilson. Randolph prepared the initial draft of the document, which the committee amended, with portions of it re-written by Wilson. The Convention adjourned until August 6, when the committee revealed its work.[25]

In preparing the draft, Randolph indicated that he was guided by two great principles. The first was that the Constitution should be based on broad and essential elements "lest the operations of government be clogged by rendering those provisions permanent and unalterable, which ought to be accommodated to times and events." In other words, they would need to state the document in broad terms so that future leaders would be able use it and not be hindered by it. The second was to "use simple and precise language" so that all would understand its meaning. This second principle would prove to be more difficult to attain, as the delegates themselves would disagree over the meaning of some of the provisions included in this first draft of the Constitution.[26]

We the People – How to Ratify the Document?

The draft report opened with the words "we the people," words that indicated the new Constitution was to be the product of the people themselves and not a compact among sovereign states. The Convention had made this possible, in part, by the decision they had reached on July 23 that the proposed Constitution would be ratified by the people through special ratifying conventions, rather than through the process laid out in the Articles of Confederation, under which the

Confederation Congress and all thirteen states would be required to approve the new document.

There were both practical as well as theoretical reasons for referring the Constitution to special ratifying conventions. At the practical level, many delegates had substantial concerns that obtaining the support of all thirteen states for the proposed Constitution was an impossible hurdle to clear. Rhode Island had not even sent a delegation to the Convention, and two of New York's three representatives had left early due to their opposition to the creation of a strong national government. Nathan Ghorum put forward the case on practical grounds when he stated that the state legislatures should be avoided because they were the ones "who are to lose power which is to be given up to the Genl. Govt." He also expressed concerns that the other states should be forced to "suffer themselves to be ruined if Rho. Island should persist in her opposition to general measures."[27]

Mason raised the theoretical problems, arguing that the state legislatures had no power to ratify the new federal Constitution, since they were "mere creatures of the State Constitution." The only body with the power to approve the document, to breathe life into it, was "the people with whom all power remains that has not been given up in the Constitution derived from them." He also raised one further consideration, that if the state legislatures were to approve the Constitution, then "succeeding Legislatures having equal authority could undo the acts of their predecessors."[28]

Jefferson, in his *Notes on the State of Virginia*, had expressed similar concerns about the Virginia Constitution of 1776. Since only the legislature had approved it, it was subject to legal challenge under the principle of *Quod leges posteriores priores contrarias abrogant*: in a conflict between two legislative acts of equal status, the more recent one prevails. "If a constitution was adopted under conditions that made it indistinguishable from a statute or ordinance," the historian Rakove writes, "it could not bind or constrain subsequent legislatures." Madison was well aware of, and shared Jefferson's concerns. He had proposed to Washington before the Convention opened that the people would need to ratify the new Constitution through some form of ratifying conventions. As the debate closed on July 23, Madison said that "He considered the difference between a system founded on the Legislatures only, and one founded on the people, to be the true difference between a *league* or *treaty*, and a *Constitution*." Madison's intent was to form one American nation through the adoption of the Constitution, and not another league of sovereign states.[29]

The exact wording that opened the draft version of the Constitution produced by the Committee on Details' was: "We the people of the States." It then went on to list the thirteen states. The final Constitution, as written by Gouverneur Morris and the Committee of Style, would remove the list of states, and change the wording to "We the people of the United States," a much stronger nationalist statement. As Beeman writes, the preamble in the Constitution "seemed to suggest that the people of the nation possessed…sovereign power," not the states. Morris would also expand the preamble to include the purposes of the new Constitution, which were to "form a more perfect Union, establish Justice, insure domestic Tranquility, provide for the common defence, promote the general Welfare, and secure the Blessings of Liberty to ourselves and our Posterity." The preamble listed those goals that the Articles of Confederation were unable to accomplish.[30]

During the debates of August 30 and 31, the Convention also determined that ratification by nine states would be sufficient for the Constitution to go into effect. The anti-nationalists, led by Luther Martin, had wanted all thirteen states to approve it before it could become effective, but his proposal was defeated. Ultimately, only Martin's home state of Maryland opposed the decision of ratification by nine states. The decision of those nine would not compel those who did not ratify to join the union. "No state could be bound by the new plan unless it chose that fate for itself," Amar writes, "instead, the text and act of constitution envisioned a possible dissolution of the old union, with nine or more states going one way while a minority of free and independent sovereign states veered off." Reed also argues that although states would enter the Constitution as sovereign entities, "they would not remain so after ratification." They would now be members of one new indivisible and indissoluble nation. Whether states could secede from the new union would be a source of contention for the next seventy-five plus years, until the Civil War settled the matter conclusively.[31]

The Convention also decided during the debates of August 30-31 that the approval of the existing Congress would not be required in order to advance the Constitution to the various ratifying conventions. The delegates apparently wanted to "spare it the embarrassment of taking an action inconsistent with the Articles of Confederation." Elbridge Gerry raised this issue once again on September 10. Hamilton supported Gerry on this issue, and proposed a process upon which the Confederation Congress would approve the document before referring it on to the states. Randolph also supported this position, and went one step further by proposing that the ratifying conventions be allowed to offer amendments to the document that would then be taken up by a "second general convention." Most of the delegates saw the danger in these proposals. First, it was difficult to imagine that the existing Congress would vote itself out of business. Second, allowing amendments that would go to a second convention was a way to ensure that the Constitution would never be ratified. "In the end, they reaffirmed the principle of ratification by nine state conventions, limiting the role of the Confederation Congress to that of receiving and transmitting the document to the states," Beeman writes. They agreed to present the Constitution as a take-it-or-leave-it proposition, although they left an opening for amendments to occur after ratification, a decision that would prove important during the battle for ratification.[32]

We the People – Who Gets to Vote and Hold Office?

Another major matter the committee dealt with was who should vote. The committee members left out any requirement that voters own property, contrary to the prior decision of the Convention. Gouverneur Morris attempted to add it back, arguing that property-less voters would "sell [their votes] to the rich who will be able to buy them." He equated those without property to children who are not allowed to vote, "because they have no will of their own." A number of other delegates, including Mason, Madison, and Franklin opposed his elitist views. In defending the vote of those who owned no property, Franklin said that the Constitution should not "depress the virtue & public spirit of our common people, of which they displayed a great deal during the war, and which contributed principally to the favorable issue of it." He did not think that the elected had any right in any case to narrow the privileges of the electors. Morris' proposal was defeated on a vote of seven to one, with one state divided.[33]

Charles Pinckney next tried to add a property qualification for holding federal office. Franklin once again responded, expressing "his dislike of everything that tended to debase the spirit of the common people" and indicating that the government should not be simply for the rich. This proposal, too, was defeated. For a group of men who feared that in the future an overbearing majority might strip them of their property, they ultimately ended up establishing a House of Representatives that indeed would be the people's house.

Enumerated Powers and the Necessary-and-Proper Clause

"The Federal Government is a government of limited and enumerated powers," Chief Justice John Roberts writes in his opinion on the Affordable Care Act in 2012. One of the major changes that the Committee on Detail made was to insert a list of eighteen enumerated powers for the broad grant of authority that had been in the Virginia Plan. Surprisingly, this change elicited little debate from the full Convention, especially in light of the recent tie vote on the issue. One historian argues that Madison was in fact supportive of granting a specific list of powers to the new government, and that the Virginia Plan's broad language was merely a placeholder. His view of the limited nature of federal power during the 1790s tends to support this position. Once they had settled the issue of representation, then the Convention could settle on the powers to be granted to the Congress. Two members of the committee, Rutledge and Randolph, both supported granting only specific powers, in part because they thought that would be required to gain the support of the public. They also feared that without such limitations the new government could "violate all the laws and constitutions of the states."[34]

The list of enumerated powers was designed to provide the federal government with the requisite authority to manage the problems the Confederation Congress could not. This list included the power of taxation, the ability to regulate both foreign and domestic commerce, the power to coin money and borrow funds, and to make war—later changed by the Convention to "declare" war. The committee also included one other key provision, which stated that the legislature had the power to "make all laws that shall be necessary and proper for carrying into execution the foregoing powers." James Wilson, who had preferred that the Congress be given a general grant of legislative powers, added this provision. The phrase, when combined with the addition of the words allowing the Congress to legislate for the "common defence and the general welfare," as added by the full Convention in September, would provide the nation with the flexibility needed for future generations to respond to problems that could not be contemplated at that time.[35]

The necessary-and-proper clause, as it came to be known, has been the subject of many disputes over the past 200-plus years. One of the first occurred in 1791, when Alexander Hamilton, in the role of Treasury Secretary, proposed creating the Bank of the United States. Madison, the strong nationalist, had argued in *Federalist* No. 44 that, "the whole Constitution would be a dead letter," without the necessary-and-proper clause. "No axiom is more clearly established in law, or in reason, than that wherever the end is required, the means are authorized; whenever a general power to do a thing is given, every particular power for doing it is included." But when the Bank bill came before the House, Madison reversed position and adopted a strict constructionist view, arguing that the idea of implied powers struck "at the very essence of the Government as composed of limited and enumerated powers." In fact, Madison's real concern was less that the Bank was unconstitutional and more that it was simply bad policy that would allow financial interests to have an undue influence over the federal government. "The stock jobbers will become the praetorian band of the Government, at once its tool and its tyrant," Madison told Jefferson.[36]

Washington, in a quandary over what to do with the Bank bill that passed Congress, asked both Jefferson and Hamilton to provide their opinions on the constitutionality of the legislation. Jefferson took the strict constructionist view, arguing that in order to be constitutional a bill had to be "more than just convenient in executing powers granted to the federal government: it had to be truly necessary—that is indispensable." While Jefferson took this position on the issue of the Bank, his strict constructionist views were not doctrinaire, as one of his biographers points out. He even closed his letter to Washington stating that if "pro and con hang" evenly, then the president should "decide the balance in favor of [Congress'] opinion." Jefferson's strict constructionist views would prove increasingly elastic once he became president and faced decisions on issues he cared about deeply. The Louisiana Purchase would fall into this category, which Jefferson originally thought would require an amendment to the Constitution to complete, a position he later rejected.[37]

Hamilton's response was highly detailed, a forty-page manifesto that has been called "the most brilliant argument for a broad interpretation of the Constitution in American political literature." Hamilton defended the concept of implied powers, arguing in the words of one of his biographers that "the government had the right to employ all means necessary to carry out powers mentioned in the Constitution." In the future, others would use Hamilton's views to justify the use of federal power to solve the problems of their day, including Supreme Court justice John Marshall, Abraham Lincoln, Theodore and Franklin Roosevelt, and Barack Obama. Ultimately, Washington signed the Bank bill, but not before requesting Madison to prepare a veto message, indicating his own divided mind on the subject.[38]

Wilson also inserted into the report by the Committee on Detail a number of restrictions on the states. Both he and Madison had supported a national veto over state laws, a proposal that the full Convention had defeated. The limits on state power were a way to regain at least some control over the states. The prohibitions included banning states from issuing paper money, from entering into treaties, from taxing imports, and from engaging in war. All of these limitations dealt with matters that had proved to be a problem during the 1780s under the Articles of Confederation.[39]

More Protections for Slavery

Before the Convention adjourned on July 23, Charles Cotesworth Pinckney had "reminded the Convention that if the Committee should fail to insert some security to the Southern States agst an emancipation of slaves, and taxes on exports, he shd. be bound by duty to his State to vote agst. their Report."[40] The committee took his warning seriously. With his fellow South Carolinian, John Rutledge, Pinckney managed to secure three additional limitations on the Congress as part of the committee's report. First, the Congress would not be allowed to levy taxes on exports. Since the southern states exported a large quantity of their crops (tobacco, rice, and indigo) overseas, they opposed taxes on exports that would raise their costs and reduce profits. Second, the legislature would be prohibited from passing any laws that would limit "the migration or importation of such persons as the several States shall think proper to admit." "Such persons" referred to slaves, and the purpose was to allow the slave trade to continue. This issue was of great importance to both South Carolina and Georgia, states that had a shortage of slaves. If the slave trade was ended, the cost of purchasing surplus slaves from Virginia and Maryland would rise. Third, the Congress would only be allowed to pass navigation acts with a two-thirds approval. Navigation acts referred to laws that regulated foreign trade, including the imposition of tariffs and quotas on imports. The southern states opposed such laws because they feared that the northern states would force them to ship their products only on domestic vessels, which could increase their shipping costs. On the other side of the issue stood the New England states, which supported tariffs and quotas as a way to protect their shipping industries.[41]

Interestingly, the committee had failed to clearly include the three-fifths clause for purposes of representation. That issue, along with the three new proposed limitations on the Congress, reopened the debate over slavery during the month of August, when the Convention added back in explicit language on the three-fifths clause. Rufus King of Massachusetts wanted to end the slave trade, and thought that counting slaves for purposes of representation "was a most grating circumstance." Gouverneur Morris launched into a fiery speech denouncing slavery, and proposed that they eliminate the three-fifths clause from the document. Morris was clearly the most vocal opponent of slavery at the Convention. Although his family had owned many slaves in New York, Morris had freed his only slave. He considered slavery "the curse of heaven on the States where it prevailed," which had caused "the misery and poverty [of] the barren wastes of Va. Maryd. and other States having slaves." His proposal quickly went down to defeat, since the other delegates were not interested in revisiting a decision they had already made. Despite his moral outrage, Morris was more concerned that the South would receive a primary benefit from counting slaves for purposes of representation, but not have those same slaves included for purposes of taxation. As he put it, the states of South Carolina and Georgia would "have more votes in a Govt. instituted for the protection of the rights of mankind, than the Citizens of Pa or N. Jersey," due to the nefarious practice of slavery.[42]

Beginning on August 21, the Convention debated further the issue of slavery, specifically the Committee of Details' proposals. A new compromise began to emerge, which one historian has referred to as the "dirty compromise." The New England states, which were highly dependent on shipping the staple products of the South, found their economic interests aligned with the slave states. In a series of votes that took place over the next eight days, one or more of the New England states would support the South in opposition to taxes on exports, and in return, the states of the Deep South would support the removal of the two-thirds requirement to pass navigation acts.[43]

Luther Martin of Maryland opened the debate on August 21 with a proposal to levy an import tax on slaves. As with Morris, Martin's support of an import tax had both a moral and a practical economic motive to it. Martin was rightly concerned that the three-fifths clause, in combination with the prohibition against ending the slave trade, would encourage a substantial increase in that trade. He believed that the slave trade was "inconsistent with the principles of the revolution and dishonorable to the American character to have such a feature in the Constitution." His economic motive arose because both Maryland and Virginia had a surplus of slaves. To the extent that the African slave trade continued, the value of their surplus slaves would diminish. John Rutledge opposed Martin's proposed tax, and threatened that the South would abandon the union if such a tax were implemented. He then made a pitch to his New England allies to consult their interests, since the increase in slaves "will increase the commodities of which they will become the carriers." Ellsworth of Connecticut took the bait, indicating that he did not want to debate the "morality or wisdom of slavery," and that "what enriches a part enriches the whole."[44]

Debate continued on August 22, including an impassioned speech by George Mason of Virginia, a slave owner, exclaiming the evils of the slave trade and of slavery itself. "Slavery discourages arts & manufactures...They prevent the immigration of Whites, who really enrich & strengthen the Country. They produce the most pernicious effect on manners. Every master of slaves is born a petty tyrant." Ellsworth challenged Mason, stating that if slavery "was to be considered in a moral light we ought to go farther and free those already in the Country." This may have been a ploy on his part in support of the Deep South position on the slave trade, since he knew that abolition was politically impossible. After much additional debate, Gouverneur Morris moved that the matter, "including the clauses relating to taxes on exports & to a navigation act," be sent to a new committee that "may form a bargain among the Northern & Southern States."[45]

The new committee proposed that the slave trade could not be prohibited prior to 1800, which was soon amended to 1808. The importation of slaves would be subject to taxation, and Congress could pass navigation acts by a simple majority of the Congress. The first two provisions passed on a vote of seven to four, with the New England states voting in support with all of the southern states except Virginia. Though Madison was supportive of providing the central government the power to regulate international commerce through a simple majority vote, and knew that a political bargain would need to be struck to do this, he was greatly concerned over the twenty-year extension of the slave trade. "Twenty years will produce all the mischief that can be apprehended from the liberty to import slaves."

When the motion on navigation acts came up for a vote, one of the southern delegates attempted to reinstate the two-thirds vote requirement. This was defeated when South Carolina joined all of the northern states in allowing navigation acts to pass with a simple majority vote of the Congress. Madison was unable to convince his fellow Virginians to support the motion, and Randolph was so unhappy with the result that he began to question whether he would support the new Constitution[46]

Evidence of a bargain between the New England states and those of the Deep South is contained in one of Madison's margin notes, where he indicates, "an understanding on the two subjects of *navigation and slavery* had taken place between those parts of the Union." Luther Martin, in a letter he sent to the Maryland ratifying convention, provided further evidence. Martin, who had served on the committee "found the *eastern* States, notwithstanding their *aversion to slavery*, were very willing to indulge the southern States, at least with temporary liberty to prosecute the *slave trade*, provided the southern States would in turn gratify them, by laying no *restriction* on *navigation acts*." In one final concession to the South, the North agreed to a provision that would require that fugitive slaves be returned to their master, despite "any regulations subsisting in the State to which they escape." Northern states that had abolished slavery were now required "to be actively complicit in keeping slaves in bondage."[47]

Could the Framers have done better? At one extreme, the abolition of slavery was too much to expect. The delegates had come to establish a strong union, and any proposals to eliminate slavery would have ended the Convention and any chance of creating a consolidated nation. None of the Framers even considered this as an option. From an economic perspective, the southern states were totally dependent on slavery, since their main crops were labor intensive. Any attempt to abolish slavery would have also required compensation to slave owners, since the protection of private property was one of the core values of the revolutionary generation, perhaps on par with liberty. The Convention had been called, in part, to protect the property rights of elites from the potential for redistributive policies that were being adopted in some states. Any attempt to free the slaves would mean compensating slave owners, a very costly proposal, estimated at over $140 million. For purposes of comparison, the total budget for the new federal government in 1790 was only $7 million. One must wonder if Gouverneur Morris was serious or simply engaging in rhetoric when he said "I would sooner submit myself to a tax for paying for all the Negroes in the United States than saddle posterity" with a Constitution that sanctions slavery. Another alternative would have been to borrow a portion of the cost and add this to the national debt, and tie such a proposal to gradual emancipation so that the cost would not all fall at once. Still another alternative, one that would be proposed in the 1790s, was to use the proceeds from the sale of western lands to compensate slave owners. Madison would also make such a proposal in 1819, but none of these would ever be implemented.[48]

Even if they had solved the economic issue, social factors remained that made the abolition of slavery impossible. American society was racist, believing blacks and other non-white races inferior. There existed substantial doubt that blacks could ever "function responsibly as equal citizens in a free republic," as historian Beeman writes. Still, we must refrain from too harsh a judgment on the founding generation. "No model of a genuinely biracial society existed anywhere in the world at that time," Ellis writes, "nor had any existed in recorded history." Even John Adams, who did not own slaves, clearly opposed the practice, and supported gradual emancipation, feared there would be significant social disruptions if slaves were liberated too quickly. Many at the time thought liberated slaves should be repatriated to Africa, including Jefferson and Madison, who later became the President of the American Colonization Society.[49]

For most of his life, Abraham Lincoln, who would emancipate the slaves, was not an abolitionist. In 1862, he told a delegation of black leaders that they could never "be placed on an equality with the white race...whether this is right or wrong I need not discuss." For much of his life, Lincoln supported the idea of colonization. In his eulogy for Senator Henry Clay of Kentucky in 1852, Lincoln came out in favor of "returning both free and emancipated blacks to their "long lost fatherland" in Africa. It was an idea he supported through much of the Civil War.[50]

While abolition was too much to expect, did the North need to give up so much during the debates on slavery? They not only approved the three-fifths rule for representation in the House, which also benefited the South in presidential elections, but they allowed the slave trade to continue for twenty years, and approved the fugitive slave law. Historian Paul Finkelman argues that had the northern states been willing to drive a harder bargain, they could have at least ended the slave trade. "Although some southerners talked of not joining the Union unless the slave trade were allowed, it seems unlikely they would have risked going it alone over a temporary right of importation." Madison was one Southerner who would have been willing to end the slave trade if that were the price for union, but he was also willing to concede that risking the union was not worth it, expressing concern that "great as the evil [of the slave trade] is, a dismemberment of the union would be worse." The extension of the slave trade would lead to a significant expansion in the number of slaves. Over the prior 170 years, two hundred thousand slaves had been imported into the county. Then between 1788 and 1808, an additional two hundred thousand slaves were imported. "Moreover, the dramatic increase in slave numbers, in conjunction with the operation of the Constitution's three-fifth provision, further strengthened the political power of the slave-owning South, making a political solution to the problem of slavery in the United States all the more difficult," Beeman points out.[51]

As we have seen, many of the founding generation knew that slavery was wrong and that they could never square it with their dedication to the twin values of liberty and equality. This is why the Constitution never mentions the word slavery. When Gouverneur Morris attempted to insert the word slave for "such persons" in the slave-trade provision, his motion was defeated. Only the delegates from the Deep South attempted to make any defense of the practice of slavery. During the August 21 debate on slavery, George Mason, in a moment of great foresight, said: "As nations cannot be rewarded or punished in the next world they must be in this. By an inevitable chain of causes & effects providence punishes national sins by national calamities." Slavery was indeed America's original sin, and the nation would pay a heavy price for it in the future, almost suffering the dissolution of the union to rid the nation of slavery.[52]

Completing the Constitution

The delegates were nearing the finish line. On September 8, the Convention "appointed by Ballot" their final committee, the aptly named Committee on Style, whose job was to finalize and rearrange the new Constitution. Not surprisingly, its members included Madison, whose ideas had so influenced the Convention, Gouverneur Morris, who by some accounts spoke more than any other person at the Convention, was also appointed. Alexander Hamilton, who had missed much of the summer session, and who had alienated many with his speech extolling the virtues of the British monarchy, was named to the committee as well. Perhaps this was due to the esteem he was held in by many of his colleagues, or perhaps the other delegates wanted to ensure his strong support as part of ratification in New York. The committee was rounded out by the chair, William Samuel Johnson of Connecticut, and Rufus King of Massachusetts.

Over four days, the committee reduced the twenty-three articles contained in the previous draft down to seven, with those seven further split into sections. It was what one historian has called "a master piece of draftsmanship." Morris was the main author, as he later indicated in an 1818 letter, saying the "instrument was written by the fingers which write this letter." Madison provided further corroboration in 1831, when he revealed that, "The finish given to style and arrangement of the

Constitution fairly belongs to the pen of Mr. Morris." Morris proved equal to the task, converting awkward phrases and stilted language into crisp and concise wording, as historian Carol Berkin writes.[53]

The document opened with the words "We the people of the United States," replacing the list of states the prior draft from Committee of Detail had included. The new preamble's opening indicated that the people of the new nation, and not the individual states, had sovereign power.[54] It then went on to provide a list of the reasons for the creation of the new Constitution, including "to form a more perfect Union, establish Justice, insure domestic Tranquility, provide for the common defence, promote the general Welfare, and secure the Blessings of Liberty to ourselves and our Posterity." This was a vision of a new national government that would support a new nation.

Article I placed the legislative branch in the most prominent and important place, at the beginning. This befitted the Framers, who believed that the legislature was the primary branch of government. What was also noteworthy for this elite group of men was that they required no property qualifications to vote or to hold office, a revolutionary concept for those who feared an excess of democracy. To be elected to the House, one need only have reached the age of twenty-five and have been a citizen for seven years. To become a senator, a candidate need only be at least thirty years old and have been a citizen for nine years prior to running for office. The Congress would have a list of enumerated powers, but also the broad power to provide for the general welfare and to make all laws necessary and proper to carry out its duties under the Constitution.

The second branch of the government was the executive, as contained in Article II. Unlike Article I, which specified the powers of the legislative branch, the document vested the president with the amorphous "executive Power." That power would be limited through a series of checks and balances, including:

- The president would serve as commander in chief of the armed forces, but Congress had the power to declare war;
- The president could make treaties, giving him significant influence over foreign affairs, but only with the advice and consent of two-thirds of the Senate;
- The president could veto bills, but the Congress could override his veto with a two-thirds vote of both houses;
- The Congress was given the power to remove the president and the vice president, and "all civil Officers of the United States" due to "Treason, Bribery, or other high Crimes and Misdemeanors."

Article III contained the judicial branch, as revised over the course of the summer. The Virginia Plan had proposed three branches of government, with the judiciary being the third branch. It stated that "a National Judiciary be established to consist of one or more supreme tribunals, and of inferior tribunals to be chosen by the National Legislature." In addition, select members of the judiciary, along with the executive, would be members of a council of revision with the power to veto both state and federal laws. Of all of the branches of government, the Convention spent the least amount of time on the judicial branch. "Few delegates felt as passionate about the character of the judicial branch of the government as they did about the need to protect their state interests in the contest for representation or about the prospects and perils of a strong chief executive," writes Beeman.[55]

The Committee of Detail's report from August had made the first revisions to the proposals contained in the Virginia Plan, much of which would end up in the Constitution. One area that elicited debate was who should appoint judges. The Convention went back and forth over this matter, with some favoring appointment by the Senate, and others wanting the president to make the appointment. They finally settled on a role for each, with the president appointing judges with the advice and consent of the Senate.

The Convention rejected the concept of a council of revision, due at least in part to concerns about having judges involved in such a council. On June 4, Elbridge Gerry had expressed doubts about having the judiciary be a part of the council, since "they will have a sufficient check agst encroachments on their own department by their exposition of the laws, which involved a power of deciding on their Constitutionality." Luther Martin too expected the courts to play a role in determining whether laws were constitutional. John Rutledge argued that judges should never be asked "to give their opinion on law till it comes before them." Overall, the Framers expressed a very real concern that judges should not take a part in the creation of laws that they would later be asked to determine the validity of.[56]

Still, the Constitution makes no mention of the power of judicial review of laws, even if the Framers had assumed the Supreme Court would have a role in deciding whether laws are constitutional. Legal scholar Akhil Reed Amar argues that the Framers wanted "a rather modest judicial role" for the courts. It was the last branch mentioned in the document, tracking "a more democratic logic in which the institutions mentioned earliest in the document rested on the broadest electoral base, with later mentioned entities layered atop broader tiers of the democratic pyramid." The Congress would approve laws, and the executive would then either sign them into law or veto them.

The courts would only then become involved, and were expected to largely defer to the other two branches, according to Amar. The early Supreme Court, even under John Marshall, who had introduced the concept of judicial review, tended to yield to the judgment of the political branches. Over time, and particularly in the twentieth century, the role of the Supreme Court would grow.[57]

Article IV of the Constitution governs relationships between the states and the federal government, and also contains the fugitive slave clause. It also allows for new states to be formed and to enter the union. The provision governing the entering of new states is very broadly outlined: "New States may be admitted by the Congress into this Union." The Northwest Ordinance, which the Confederation Congress had approved at almost the same time as the three-fifths compromise had been formulated by the Convention, provided a detailed process for the admission of new states. The Framers no doubt understood that future legislation adopted by Congress would cover such details.

Article V allows for the amendment of the document under a specific set of circumstances. The amendment procedures under the Articles, which required all states to approve major changes, had made it all but impossible to amend the document, and caused men like Madison to scrap the Articles altogether and replace them with a new Constitution. The Framers were attempting to strike a balance between the need to allow for amendments while at same time avoiding trivial changes to the document or allowing a future Congress to make amendments that were self-serving (like postponing future elections). Originally, the Committee on Detail had allowed for amendments when two-thirds of the states called a new convention into existence. But some of the Framers had concerns that the purposes of a general convention would be too open ended, allowing for numerous and unlimited changes. This was an ironic twist, as one historian writes, given how the Framers had themselves exceeded their authority. Madison's proposed solution was to allow for amendments when two-thirds of Congress or two-thirds of the states proposed specific amendments and when three-quarters of the states ratified such amendments, either by their legislatures or through ratifying conventions. Rutledge added a provision that no amendments could be made affecting the slave trade until 1808. The Committee of Style added a clause allowing for the calling of a general convention to consider amendments to the Constitution, which surprisingly passed with no debate, a provision that has never been used.[58]

Article VI allowed the new government to assume the debts of the Confederacy, and also declared that the Constitution was the supreme law of the land. This was included to placate those nationalists, like Madison and Wilson, who had held out for a congressional veto power over state laws. Article VII concluded the document in a simple manner by stating that the "Ratification of the Conventions of nine States, shall be sufficient for the Establishment of this Constitution between the States so ratifying the Same." The Committee of Style had removed the method for approving the Constitution, choosing instead to insert these provisions into two resolutions. Legal scholar Akhil Reed Amar has referred to the placement of "We the People" at the beginning of the document, along with ratification by people through conventions, as the "matching bookends" of the Constitution. "The Philadelphia architects preferred instead (of placing them together) to erect them at opposite ends of the grand edifice so that both the document's front portal and rear portico would project the message of popular sovereignty, American style."[59]

While the Committee of Style was preparing the document, the Convention continued in session, reaching numerous decisions. The most consequential of these concerned a bill of rights. On September 12, the same day that the committee submitted the new version of the Constitution to the delegates, George Mason proposed that a bill of rights be added to the document as a means to gain greater support from the people. He believed that "a bill might be prepared in few hours." Gerry supported Mason and made a motion to include a bill of rights in the Constitution. Roger Sherman opposed the motion, stating that since the Constitution did not alter the various state bill of rights, that there was no need for one in the federal charter. Mason responded that since the new Constitution was to be the supreme law of the land that a bill of rights was indeed necessary. The Convention voted to exclude a bill of rights, with all ten states present voting no. This major blunder would cause the Framers much criticism in the upcoming state ratifying conventions. The reason the Convention voted so overwhelmingly against the inclusion of a bill of rights was simply fatigue. The other delegates knew that, although Mason was correct in terms of the time it would take to prepare a bill of rights, debate over its contents could potentially consume several more weeks.[60]

Between September 12 and September 15, the Convention debated the Constitution submitted by the Committee of Style. Historian Clinton Rossiter writes that despite the delegates' desire to complete the job, they could not resist the urge to tinker with the document, and "a full two dozen changes were made, and another two dozen considered and then rejected." In addition to those already discussed, some of the most important included a provision that states could not, without their consent, be denied their equal vote in the Senate; the removal of a provision that would have allowed the Congress to appoint a Treasurer, a position that would instead fall under the president; and a reduction in the ratio of representatives from one in forty-thousand people to one in thirty-thousand people. This latter change was added at the urging of Washington, one of the only provisions that he directly lobbied for, since he was convinced that the legislative districts were too large. The document was now ready to be signed.[61]

But not before one more round of debate ensued, spearheaded by those who had expressed reservations over the Constitution during the past several weeks. Randolph, who had introduced the Virginia Plan, opened with a statement of concern about the "indefinite and dangerous power given by the Constitution to Congress." Given his prior support for an open-ended grant of power to Congress in the Virginia Plan, and his own role in in gaining a statement of enumerated powers as part of the Committee of Detail, it seemed a disingenuous position to take. Perhaps he only opened with this issue to pave the way for his real concern that "amendments to the plan might be offered by the State Conventions." Without this change, it would "be impossible for him to put his name to the instrument."[62]

George Mason followed Randolph, stating his view that the new government "would end either in monarchy, or in a tyrannical aristocracy." His views were in accord with those who held that any increase in power of a distant central government would lead to tyranny, a view rooted in the experience of the colonies when they broke from Great Britain in 1776. But Mason's primary objection was that there was "no Declaration of Rights, and the laws of the general government being paramount to the laws and constitution of the several States, the Declaration of Rights in the separate States are no security." He supported Randolph's position, and "with the expedient of another Convention as proposed, he could sign" the document.[63]

Charles Pinckney took up the burden of responding to the protests. "These declarations from members so respectable at the close of this important scene, give a peculiar solemnity to the present moment." But calling a second convention would lead to "nothing but confusion & contrariety could spring from the experiment." He went on to argue, "Conventions are serious things, and ought not to be repeated." While he had his own reservations, he would support the current plan due to his fear of "a general confusion, and an ultimate decision by the sword," if the Constitution were not approved.[64]

The final protest came from the great contrarian, Elbridge Gerry, a man Clinton Rossiter has referred to as a "grumbletonian" who objected "to everything he did not propose." He listed multiple reasons for his opposition, many of which were trivial in nature. (For example, he complained about the power of the House to conceal its journals.) He also complained that his home state did not get its fair share of representatives. He too supported the idea of a second convention.[65]

When the vote came, all states voted no to Randolph's proposal for a second convention, and all agreed to the Constitution as amended. The Convention then adjourned at "6 oclock" as noted in Washington's journal, thus ending the longest day of a long and arduous summer. Ultimately, as part of the ratification process, those opposed to the Constitution would take up the call for amendments to the document to be considered by a second convention. They too would fail.[66]

Pinckney and the dissenters were not alone in having reservations about the new Constitution. Probably each of the thirty-nine delegates that would ultimately sign the document had some level of disappointment. Madison certainly did. In a letter to Jefferson on September 6, 1787, he indicated that, "the plan should it be adopted will neither effectually answer its national object nor prevent the local mischiefs which everywhere excite disgusts agst the state governments." Madison was no doubt still upset over losing the issue of proportional representation in the Senate, and the lack of a veto power over state laws. "So powerfully committed had he been to his own proposals and to the intellectual discoveries on which they had rested that he could not yet fully bring himself to accept the higher wisdom that regards politics as the art of the possible," Rakove writes. Within a month, in another letter to Jefferson, it appears that he was beginning to see how important the work of the Convention was and just how difficult an undertaking they had pursued. Discussing the difficulties encountered in framing a new government and balancing the interests of the different states, he remarked that it "was a task more difficult than can be conceived by those who were not concerned in the execution of it. Adding to these considerations the natural diversity of human opinion on all new and complicated subjects, it is impossible to consider the degree of concord which ultimately prevailed as less than a miracle." Madison signed the Constitution, and became one of the most tireless workers in urging its ratification.[67]

Hamilton also had clear concerns over the proposed new government, as indicated from his marathon speech in June, when he had urged a stronger central government and a much-reduced role for the states. Hamilton, who was a member of the New York Manumission Society, was also concerned over the issue of slavery and specifically the three-fifths compromise, although he admitted "that no union could possibly have been formed" without it. Madison records Hamilton as telling the delegates in September that "he had been restrained from entering into the discussion from his dislike of the scheme in general, but as he meant to support the plan…as better than nothing," he too ultimately signed the document.[68]

Washington had his own reservations and understood that the document was not perfect, but one of his biographers argues that he believed the document would be amended and evolve over time. "Its very brevity and generality…meant it would be a constantly changing document, susceptible to shifting interpretations." He also wrote to

Lafayette that it was "little short of a miracle [that] delegates from so many different states...should unite in forming a system of national government so little liable to well-founded objections."[69]

It would ultimately fall to the oldest and wisest delegate, Benjamin Franklin, to urge his colleagues to act in a unanimous fashion. It was Franklin who had begun the business of trying to form one nation with the Albany Plan so long before; who had helped Jefferson refine that great statement of the American mind, the Declaration of Independence; who had worked to bring France into the Revolutionary War and who had negotiated the peace with England; who had proposed the core compromise over representation at the Convention; and who now attempted to get all those present to sign the Constitution. In a speech read for him by Wilson, he indicated that he did "not entirely approve of this Constitution at present; but sir, I am not sure I shall never approve it." Given his long life, he found that his opinions would change over time as he received more information, and he needed to "pay more respect to the opinions of others." While he knew that the document had its faults, the country needed a strong general government, and any convention of men with "their prejudices, their passions, their errors of opinion," could not be expected to put forth a "perfect production." He concluded by saying that "it therefore astonishes me, sir, to find this system approaching so near to perfection as it does... Thus I consent, sir, to this Constitution because I expect no better, and because I am not sure that it is not the best." He urged that "for the sake of our posterity, we shall heartily and unanimously" approve the document. While he was unable to convince Mason, Randolph, and Gerry to sign it, he was able to convince thirty-nine others present to affix their name to it. As the signing went on, he remarked about the sun carved on the back of Washington's chair that he was happy to "know that it is a rising and not a setting sun."[70]

Endnotes

1 Solberg, p. 224

2 Beeman, p. 228

3 In this section, I have generally followed the presentation by Rakove, *Original Meanings*, p. 259-260. This is the most precise discussion on the debates over the nine-day period from July 17 to July 26.

4 Solberg, p. 247; Berkin, p. 127 and 121 for the Mason quote; Rakove, *Original Meanings*, p. 260

5 The Morris quote is from Rakove, *Original Meanings*, p. 259

6 Solberg, p. 249

7 Read, p. 157-158

8 Beeman, p. 299-300; Rakove, *Original Meanings*, p. 264; Solberg, p. 306

9 Solberg, p. 304-306; Joint possession was Hamilton's phrase, as taken from Arthur M. Schlesinger, Jr., *The Imperial Presidency*, (New York, 1973), p. 19

10 Solberg, p. 310; Rakove, *Original Meanings*, p. 265; Berkin, p.143-144

11 Berkin, p. 146; Amar, p. 164; Beeman, p. 306

12 The quotes are from Best, p. 216 and 220

13 James Madison letter to George Hay, August 23, 1823, retrieved October 18, 2013 from http://press-pubs.uchicago.edu/founders/documents/a2_1_2-3s10html

14 The Jefferson quote is from his letter to Francis Hopkins on March 13, 1789, retrieved from www.let.rug.nl/usa/presidents/thomas-jefferson/letters-of-thomas-jefferson/jetfl75.php on 9/25/2013; the quote from Adams is from his letter to Jonathan Jackson on October 2, 1789 retrieved from www.notable-quotes.com; see also Richard Hofstadler, *The Idea of a Party System: The Rise of Legitimate Opposition in the United States, 1780-1840*, (Los Angeles, 1969), especially Chapter One

15 Hamilton, *The Federalist Papers*, p. 79; Hofstadler, *The Idea of a Party System*, p. 28

16 Hofstadler, *The Idea of a Party System*, p. viii

17 Robert A. Dahl, *James Madison: Republican or Democrat*, retrieved from htttp://faculty.rcc.edu/sellick/DahlEssay.pdf on 10/10/2013

18 Robert Dahl, *Pluralist Democracy In the United States: Conflict and Consent*," (Chicago, 1967), p. 86; Rakove, *Original Meanings*, p. 268

19 Beeman, p. 302

20 Dahl, *Pluralist Democracy in the United States*, p. 92; U.S. Electoral College: Who are the Electors? Retrieved from www.archives.gov/federal-register/electoral-college/electors.html on October 17, 2013

21 Dahl, *How Democratic is the American Constitution*, Kindle location 673; Fair Vote. Org, *How the Electoral College Became Winner Take All*, retrieved from www.fairvote.org/how-

the-electoral-college-became-winner-take-all.html on October 18, 2013

22 Dahl, *How Democratic is the American Constitution*, Kindle location 666

23 Dahl, *How Democratic is the American Constitution*, Kindle location 714

24 Madison letter to Hay; the Madison letter came to my attention from an interesting article by Rob Ritchie and Devin McCarthy, *Why James Madison Wanted to Change the Way we Vote For President*, published June 18, 2012 retrieved October 18, 2013 from http://www.fairvote.org/why-james-madison-wanted-to-change-the-way-we-vote-for-president/#.UmKbXhTn_cs; Reid Wilson, "The GOP's Electoral College Scheme," *National Journal*, December 17, 2012, retrieved October 18, 2013 from http://www.nationaljournal.com/columns/on-the-trail/the-gop-s-electoral-college-scheme-20121217 ; see *Proposed GOP Changes to Electoral College Election Laws*, January 28, 2013, retrieved October 18, 2013 from http://www.whiteoutpress.com/articles/q12013/proposed-gop-changes-to-electoral-college-election-laws/

25 Solberg, p. 246 and p. 247

26 Beeman, p. 270-271

27 Rakove, *Original Meanings*, p. 104; Solberg, p. 243

28 Solberg, p. 241

29 Rakove, *Original Meanings*, p. 99-101; Ketchum, p. 218

30 The historian quoted is Beeman, p. 348

31 Solberg, p. 297-299; Beeman, p. 293-295; Reed, p. 29 and p. 33

32 Rakove *Original Meanings*, p. 106; Beeman, p 340

33 Beeman, p. 279-280; Solberg, p. 271-272

34 Rakove, *Revolutionaries*, p.379; Clinton Rossiter, *1787: The Grand Convention*, (New York, 1966), p. 208-209; Stewart, p. 170-172

35 Solberg, p. 263; Stewart, p. 172

36 Madison, *The Federalist Papers*, p. 294-285; Ketchum, p.320-322

37 The quote is from Chernow, *Hamilton*, p. 352; On Jefferson's pragmatism as a strict constructionist, see Jon Meachman, *Thomas Jefferson: The Art of Power*, (New York, 2012), p. 250 and p. 389-390

38 Chernow, Hamilton, p. 352-353; Ketchum, p. 321

39 Beeman, p. 274; Solberg, p. 267 has the list of items the state were banned from doing.

40 Soldberg, p. 246

41 Beeman, p. 275

42 The Morris quotes are from Paul Finkelman, "Slavery and the Constitutional Convention: Making a Covenant with Death", p. 212, in Beeman, *Beyond Confederation;* Rakove, *Original Meanings*, p. 86-87; Beeman, p 317. All of these historians raise the issue that Morris' primary concern was the interest of his state and not the immorality of slavery.

43 Finkelman, p. 214

44 Finkelman, p. 214

45 Solberg, p. 281-282; Beeman, p. 334 points out the motivation for Ellsworth's challenge to Mason

46 Beeman, p. 328-329

47 Finkelman, p. 220; Beeman, p. 330

48 Beeman, p. 317; Ellis, *Founding Brothers*, p106-107 discusses the cost of emancipating the slaves and the possibility of issuing debt and utilizing the proceeds of western land sales to pay the compensation to slave owners.

49 Beeman, p. 334; Ellis, *Founding Brothers*, p107; Eric Foner, *The Fiery Trial: Abraham Lincoln and American Slavery*, (New York, 2010), p. 17-18

50 Foner, *The Fiery Trial*, p. 224; p. 61

51 Finkelman, p. 221; Beeman, p. 333-334

52 Stewart, p. 202; Solberg, p. 280

53 Rossiter, p. 228 and p. 225; Berkin, p. 150

54 Beeman makes this point on p. 348, although his statement is somewhat more equivocal.

55 Solberg, p. 78; Beeman, p. 236

56 Solberg, p. 97; Rakove, *Original Meanings*, p.236

57 Amar, p. 208-218

58 Beeman, p. 337-339

59 Amar, p. 29

60 Beeman, p. 342-344; Bowen, p. 243-246

61 Rossiter, p. 230

62 Solberg, p. 333; Beeman, p. 355

63 Beeman, p. 356 raises the point about Mason's fear of a strong central government; Solberg, p. 334; Mason also outlined an entire list of objections to the new Constitution on his copy of the September 12 draft, which was later printed in a pamphlet and used by the opponents of the document. See Solberg, p. 335-338.

64 Solberg, p. 334

65 Solberg, p. 334-335

66 Solberg, p. 335; Rossiter, p. 233

67 Rakove, *James Madison*, p. 78; Madison letter to Jefferson October 24,1787, retrieved November 13, 2013, from http://press-pubs.uchicago.edu/founders/documents/v1ch17s22.html

68 Chernow, *Alexander Hamilton*, p. 239

69 Chernow, *Washington*, p. 538-539

70 Isaacson, p. 457-459

Chapter 10

The Public Debate Over Ratification / Fall 1787 to Spring 1788

"It is a national government and no longer a Confederation."
– George Mason, 1787 –

"To all general purposes we have uniformly been one people; each individual citizen everywhere enjoying the same national rights, privileges, and protection."
– John Jay, Federalist No. 2 –

The Convention had met in secret, but in the fall of 1787, a great public debate began over the proposed new government contained in the Constitution. The debate occurred in the press, in pamphlets, on street corners, and most of all in thirteen separate ratifying conventions held in each state. While the supporters of the Constitution attempted to use the momentum of the Philadelphia Convention to push through a quick up or down vote, the opponents began to organize and urge either rejection, or at a minimum , the addition of amendments to the document. The outcome was uncertain as the great debate began. At the core of the debate was whether the United States would form one nation under a stronger central government, or remain as thirteen separate states linked together in a loose confederation.

Federalist versus Antifederalist

After the Convention, supporters of the Constitution began to call themselves Federalists. Historians have long been critical of the use of this term, arguing that the supporters of the Constitution were nationalists, men who supported the creation of a consolidated nation. The word Federalist, in this telling of events, should be reserved for those "who continued to support a league of friendship and cooperation among independent sovereign states," as the historian Carol Berkin writes. There is much truth to this view, since men like Madison, Hamilton, Washington, and Wilson all went to the Convention with the goal of creating a strong national government that would be superior to the states. Still, they did not prevail to the extent they had hoped. Hamilton would have all but eviscerated the states. Madison wanted sovereignty to reside in the national government, and in private was critical of the decisions reached at the Convention over proportional representation and elimination of the veto of state laws. The new government that emerged from the compromises reached at the Convention was in fact a hybrid, partly national and partly federal, with the ultimate question of where sovereignty resided left obscure. Both Madison and Hamilton used this to great effect in defending the Constitution, even though both were critical of the outcome.[1]

More troubling was the term applied to those who opposed the Constitution: the Antifederalist. This term cast them as a group opposed to all measures to strengthen the central government, which they were not. "The labels affixed to the two sides…defied logic," Ellis writes, "for both sides were federalists, meaning that they advocated a confederated republic, but disagreed over the relative power of the states and the central government in the confederation." The term Antifederalist was meant to be a term of reproach, as one supporter of the Constitution saw it when he said, "I do, and always did, treat the appellation with contempt."[2]

The Federalist strategy was to use the momentum they had built from the Convention to pursue ratification. Most major newspapers were on their side, with only twelve of over ninety publications printing Antifederalist essays. They also had the advantage of having the two most distinguished Americans as supporters: Washington and Franklin. One Boston newspaper complained that the influence of the two made "too strong an argument in the minds of many to examine, like freemen, for themselves." Both sides in the great struggle over ratification tended to distrust public opinion, some because they doubted the capacity of the people to make sound judgments about complicated matters, others because they "feared that cunning leaders would manipulate even well-meaning citizens." Madison shared both concerns. In a letter to Randolph in January 1788, he expressed a grave reservation that complicated constitutional issues are "subjects to which the capacities of the bulk of mankind are unequal and which they must and will be governed by those with whom they happen to have acquaintance and confidence." While Franklin and Washington were on his side, Madison fretted that men like Patrick Henry, whom he considered a demagogue, would mislead his fellow Virginians to reject the Constitution.[3]

Washington had decided to return to Mount Vernon and not take an active part in the ratification process, but he was far from a dispassionate observer. He followed the debates in newspapers, and both Madison and Hamilton kept him apprised of the status of the battle for ratification. Mount Vernon became "the electoral headquarters for plotting strategy and tracking the state-by-state results as they rolled in."[4]

The Federalists anticipated most of the major arguments that the opponents would raise, since they had heard them in the Convention. They also planned to pursue an up-or-down, take-it-or-leave-it strategy in which they would ask the state ratifying conventions to vote yes or no without amendments to the new plan of government. This strategy would evolve over time in order to win approval in the key states of Massachusetts and Virginia. But they drew the line on allowing the consideration of amendments in a second convention, instead contending that the Constitution be ratified first, with amendments to be considered by the new Congress. Given the difficulties of achieving compromise at the Convention, the Framers shuddered at the thought of a second convention. "Once begun, how could this cycle of deliberation and revision ever end?" was the great concern of the Framers, argues Rakove.[5]

The Antifederalists

The Antifederalists also had an elite group on their side, including Mason, Gerry, and Randolph, the three dissenters from the Convention. The two New York delegates who had left the Convention early, Lansing and Yates, were also opponents, as was Governor Clinton. John Hancock and Samuel Adams were undecided, and if they opposed the Constitution, the chances for victory in Massachusetts would be remote. Richard Henry Lee and Patrick Henry were opponents in Virginia. In all three of these large and crucial states, the Constitution's ultimate approval was very much in doubt.

Still, the Antifederalists faced an uphill battle, even though they may have had a majority of the public on their side. One of the major problems they faced was the lack of an agreed upon strategy for defeating the Constitution. Whereas the Federalists had worked out their plan over a four-month period of private meetings at the Convention, the opponents did not have this luxury. Also, the Antifederalists did not agree among themselves. At one extreme stood those who wanted to reject the new Constitution and continue with the government under the Articles. At the other extreme were those who saw the need for a stronger central government and would accept the Constitution, but wanted certain amendments added. In between the extremes, opinions also varied widely, leaving the Antifederalists with little by way of an effective alternative to the Constitution. Despite these disadvantages, they were a formidable group that would make ratification of the Constitution difficult for the Federalists in certain key states, and their influence would lead to the post ratification amendments known as the Bill of Rights.[6]

Despite disagreements among the Antifederalists over goals, there was broad concurrence on certain matters.[7] First, they almost all agreed that the Constitution created a consolidated national government with too much power, one that would act directly on the people, and that would strip the states of their sovereignty. The core concern was their fear of centralized power, and they laid claim to be the true inheritors of the revolutionary movement of 1776. "The Antifederalist argument was anchored in the revolutionary ideology that regarded any powerful central government as a domestic version of the very British government they had supposedly repudiated forever," according to Ellis. To the Antifederalist, a republic could only exist in a small and homogenous territory. A strong central government would result in "the loss of liberty, ending in aristocracy, monarchy, or some other form of despotism." They stood squarely against the creation of the type of national government proposed by the Constitution.[8]

The Antifederalists pointed to several provisions of the proposed Constitution to support their position that the new government would be national and no longer federal. The opening words: "We the people," clearly indicated this was no longer a Confederation. Samuel Adams observed that, "as I enter the Building I stumble at the Threshold." The Constitution conferred the power to levy direct taxes, which Mason claimed, "entirely change[d] the confederation of the states into one consolidated government." They also pointed to the sections of the Constitution that indicated it was the supreme law of the land, the inclusion of the necessary-and-proper clause, and the failure to explicitly reserve any powers to the states as indications that the Federalists intended to create a consolidated national government of unlimited means. Control over the army, when combined with the power of taxation, was another great fear of the Antifederalists, who opposed standing armies that could be used to oppress the people and deny them liberty, as the British had done.[9]

The Convention had gone beyond its mandate, which had been limited to proposing amendments to the Articles of Confederation, and the Antifederalists made sure this issue was aired. Many of the Antifederalists admitted there was a need to reform the present system, and they were willing to provide Congress with the power to control commerce, to generate revenue through an impost, and if needed to allow the central government to requisition additional funds. But only if those funds were not paid were the Antifederalists willing to allow the Congress to impose direct taxes. They also denied the claims of the Federalists that: 1) the country was facing a major emergency due to the inability of the government to meet its debts; 2) property rights were in danger; 3) the states were weak; 4) foreign governments endangered the United States; and, 5) only a stronger central government would make the country "prosperous, respected and safe."

Finally, the Antifederalists protested that the Constitution contained no bill of rights. The major mistake the Framers had made at the

Convention by not including a bill of rights was coming back to haunt them in the battle for ratification. The Antifederalists argued that since the new national government would have power directly over individuals, then a bill of rights was essential. This was perhaps the most important contribution the Antifederalists would make during the debate, an argument that resonated with many Federalists as well, and led to the first amendments to the document following ratification.

It would fall to the Federalists, and especially men like Wilson, Hamilton, and Madison, to defend their handiwork from the criticisms leveled by the Antifederalists. In many ways, it would be a battle between optimists and pessimists. "The hopeful men of 1787-1788 were the Federalists," historian Clinton Rossiter writes, "and that may be one reason why they got their charter ratified." In American politics, the optimists tend to win.[10]

Federalist Responses

James Wilson was the first to provide a response to the criticisms being raised by the opposition in Pennsylvania when he spoke before a large group at Independence Hall on October 6, 1787. Regarding the lack of a bill of rights, Wilson indicated that the new powers given to the federal government were enumerated and limited, therefore "it would have been superfluous and absurd to have stipulated with a federal body of our creation, that we should enjoy those privileges of which we are not divested." In other words, there was no need for a bill of rights, since the federal government had no power to interfere in such basic rights as freedom of speech, press, and religion. Wilson concluded by stating that not only was a bill of rights unnecessary, but "the very declaration might have been construed to imply that some degree of power was given" to the new government over certain rights, when none in fact existed.[11]

On the fear of standing armies during peace time, Wilson indicated he did not "know a nation in the world which has not found it necessary and useful to maintain the appearance of strength in a season of the most profound tranquility," and that a military force was necessary so long as it was "under the control and with the restrictions which the new constitution provides." He then disputed that the Constitution would eliminate the states. In fact, the continued existence of the states was needed for the new federal plan to be effective, as Wilson argued in this passage:

> *The President is to be chosen by electors, nominated in such manner as the legislature of each State may direct; so that if there is no legislature there can be no electors, and consequently the office of the President cannot be supplied. The Senate is to be composed of two Senators from each State, chosen by the Legislature; and, therefore, if there is no Legislature, there can be no Senate. The House of Representatives is to be composed of members chosen every second year by the people of the several States, and the electors in each State shall have the qualifications requisite for electors of the most numerous branch of the State Legislature; unless, therefore, there is a State Legislature, that qualification cannot be ascertained, and the popular branch of the Federal Constitution must be extinct.*

Wilson defended the power of taxation vested in the proposed federal government, since it would be responsible for "national safety, to support the dignity of the union, and to discharge the debts contracted upon the collected faith of the States for their common benefit." He closed with what would become a common refrain from the Federalists, that those who opposed the strengthening of the central government were pursuing their own selfish interests and not those that would serve the public good. "Every person, therefore, who enjoys or expects to enjoy a place of profit under the present establishment, will object to the proposed innovation," Wilson declaimed.

The speech received wide spread press coverage, with a summary of it first printed on October 9 in the *Pennsylvania Herald*, and then reprinted in just about every other state. It quickly elicited significant and numerous responses from a host of Antifederalists, writing under pseudonyms such as "Centinel," an "Old Whig," "Cincinnatus," and "Brutus." The most salient criticism came over Wilson's dismissal of a bill of rights. This would prove to be a losing argument in the end, not the least because the Antifederalists pointed out that the Constitution included a "partial bill of rights," including the protections for a writ of habeas corpus, the prohibition on bills of attainder, and the prohibition on *ex post facto* laws. "Wilson's speech thus emboldened the opposition as much as it heartened his supporters," Jack Rakove writes, and "far from crushing early objections to the Constitution...Wilson gave Anti-Federalists something of the intellectual focus they initially lacked."[12]

The Federalist Essays

Hamilton conceived of *The Federalist* while aboard a sloop sailing between Albany and New York City. He designed it to be a comprehensive analysis and defense of the Constitution, geared toward a New York audience as a means to sway the election of Federalists to the ratifying convention in that state. Hamilton first asked fellow New Yorker John Jay to assist him with the project. Jay, a successful lawyer who had played a central role in drafting New York's Constitution, was also a member of the negotiating team, along with Franklin and

Adams, which had negotiated the peace treaty with Great Britain that had ended the Revolutionary War. Finally, Jay had served as the Secretary of Foreign Affairs under the Confederation Congress, a job that gave him a unique insight into the weaknesses of the government to manage foreign policy under the Articles of Confederation. [13] Hamilton next reached out to Madison to join the team. Madison had rushed from Philadelphia to New York City in order to shepherd the Constitution through the Congress, and was thus available to assist with the writing of the essays. Each of the men would cover those areas of the Constitution for which they had the greatest expertise, writing under the shared name of Publius, who had been instrumental in the overthrow of the monarchy and had helped establish the Roman republic. Soon after beginning the project, Jay came down with a terrible bought of rheumatism, and was only able to contribute five of the eighty-five essays. Madison prepared twenty-nine, and Hamilton contributed the balance of fifty-one.[14]

The Federalist represented an upbeat and positive explication of how a republican form of government could exist on a continental scale without endangering but in fact promoting and protecting liberty. The Framers were willing to try such an experiment, even though the implementation of such a government, one that derives its power from the people, had never before been successfully attempted over such a large area. Madison chided his opponents on this point in *Federalist* No. 14, when he posed the question: "But why is the experiment of an extended republic to be rejected merely because it may comprise what is new?" He then goes on to list all of the innovations that Americans had endeavored to undertake over the previous twenty years, including a "revolution which has no parallel in the annals of human history." The Antifederalists feared an experiment in nationhood, and were unwilling to accept that a republican form of government could indeed exist over a large geographic area. Their political ideas emanated in part from Montesquieu, whose writings Antifederalists treated "as a source of incontrovertible rules that needed only to be quoted, not examined or assessed or interpreted," and that made up "a set of near universal or absolute statements capable of predicting the destiny of all political systems," according to Rakove. *The Federalist* writings, particularly those of Madison, challenged the precepts of Montesquieu that underlay the intellectual position of the Antifederalist.[15]

The essays that comprise *The Federalist* are remarkable, since they were composed by practical politicians, and not by philosophers or political theorists such as Locke, Montesquieu, or David Hume, who had influenced Madison. In addition, the authors composed the essays under incredible time constraints, giving them little opportunity to review their own work, never mind consulting with each other over their handiwork. Some have criticized *The Federalist* as a work of propaganda; but this overstates the case if one defines propaganda as spreading generally false or exaggerated ideas.[16] The work is certainly not an effort at dispassionate analysis, since the goal of the authors was to defend the Constitution from its critics and convince a wavering public to support its ratification. In this vein, neither Hamilton nor Madison reveals his own reservations about the Constitution. Still, it is quite amazing how much the essays reveal about the political views of the two primary authors, and how little concerned they were with the political correctness of some of their opinions of the general public, as we shall see from certain specific statements contained in the essays. Such open and honest writing would never survive the modern political world, where a politician's every utterance is subject to intense criticism and censoring by political consultants.

The political theory that underlay the *Federalist* writings, particularly those penned by Madison, was grounded in the authors' views of human nature. They were realists and considered man a self-interested creature that often acts based on passion and not reason.[17] But they balanced that view with a belief that man also had a "capacity for reason and justice," as historian Clinton Rossiter has framed it. The capacity to act with reason, wisdom, and judgment was thought to reside largely in those men "who possess the most attractive merit and the most diffusive and established characters," according to Madison in *Federalist* No. 10.[18] In other words, Madison and the other Framers wanted to rely on the elite of society, on the natural aristocracy that rose to prominence due to merit and achievement, to govern.

To Madison, society was segregated into numerous factions based on the different skills, abilities, and wealth that occurred naturally. The greatest source of faction was the uneven distribution of property. In framing a government grounded in majority rule, the great challenge is to ensure that the rights of the minority, which owns most of the property, are protected from a majority that may attempt to confiscate their possessions. "This distrust of man was first and foremost a distrust of the common man and democratic rule," as historian Richard Hofstadter writes. Rather than trying to rely solely on the virtue of the citizenry, the Framers believed the country needed a well-formed Constitution to regulate conduct between men.

While the Framers had concerns about placing too much power with the common man, they also feared giving too much power to the elite. Even Gouverneur Morris, clearly a voice of the natural aristocracy, had said, "Wealth tends to corrupt the mind and to nourish its love of power, and to stimulate it to oppression." Hamilton, no friend to the common man, said "Give all power to the many, they will oppress the few. Give all power to the few, they will oppress the many." [19]The key was to ensure that no single interest became too powerful. As Madison told the Convention, the problem remained "of so adjusting the claims of the Two Classes [those with property and those without] as to give security to each, and to promote the welfare of all."[20] This would be achieved by first providing for a system of checks and balances that could work best in an extended republic. Under such a system, an overbearing majority would need to seize not only the multiple branches of the federal government but all of the state governments. Second, rather than establishing a direct democracy, the Constitution would establish a republic in which the principle of representation would take place. As discussed above, Madison believed that those elected to the new federal government would come from men with "the most attractive merit," and that such men would act with greater independent judgment and integrity. "One reason the Framers believed in representation was that it would refine leadership, acting as a kind of a sieve that would separate and elevate the more virtuous elements," according to political scientist James MacGregor Burns. The third step to balancing the two classes was this: Ensuring that the government was kept in its place by establishing a separation of powers under the Constitution. This would keep the representatives from becoming tyrannical and attempting to deprive the public of their liberty. The Constitution would augment this separation of powers by having the two main branches of government, the legislative and the executive, elected directly or indirectly by the people at different times and by different majorities, and by having them serve different and staggered terms of office. Such a system would place a high premium on the ability of elected officials to work together, to bargain with one another, and to reach compromise.

One of the criticisms leveled by the Antifederalists was that no real economic crisis existed that would require a change in government. In response, the first nine essays largely focused on the weaknesses of the Confederacy in both foreign and domestic affairs. Hamilton opened *Federalist* No. 1 with a challenge to the people of the United States "whether societies of men are really capable or not of establishing good government from reflection and choice, or whether they are forever destined to depend for their political constitutions on accident and force."[21] Americans have the opportunity to choose a new government, Hamilton argued, and not have it forced upon them. Jay followed in *Federalist* No. 2 by directly taking on the charge that the Federalists intended to implement a consolidated government. Rather than hide the ambitions of the nationalists, he asks, "whether it would conduce more to the interest of the people of America that they should, to all general purposes, be one nation, under one federal government." Jay saw that America was in many ways one nation already, "a people descended from the same ancestors, speaking the same language, professing the same religion, attached to same principles of government, very similar in manners and customs," and that most of all, Americans had fought side by side to achieve independence. What they lacked was a government sufficient "to preserve and perpetuate" the nation.[22]

Madison joined the fray with *Federalist* No. 10, considered by many not only one of the most important of the essays but the classic statement of Madison's political theory. In it, he built upon the themes first developed in *Vices of the Political Systems of the United States*. Madison took on two of the lines of argument put forth by the opponents of the Constitution: 1) that a republic could only exist over a small and homogeneous geographic territory; and 2) that there were too few members of the legislature in the new system to adequately represent the people.

Factions are the great problem that face governments whose authority is grounded in the popular will. Madison argued that factions are a byproduct of human nature, with "the most common and durable source of factions" being the "unequal distribution of property," which splits society into different classes and interests. His focus was how to control the effects of an "interested and overbearing majority" faction. Madison's view on the tyranny of the majority included a self-interested element, a fear that the lower classes would control government and eliminate debts, redistribute property, and issue paper money, all actions that had occurred to one degree or another at the state level. But the protection of minority rights extended beyond just property rights and applied to freedom of speech, religion, and conscience. In dealing with factions, society could choose to destroy liberty, but such a cure was "worse than the disease. Liberty is to faction what air is to fire, an aliment without which it instantly expires." A better method exists, which is to control the effects of factions. In this regard, Madison argued that a republic has the advantage over a democracy (here Madison was referring to a direct democracy), since in a direct democracy there is no means to check factions. "A common passion or interest will, in almost every case, be felt by a majority of the whole...and there is nothing to check the inducements to sacrifice the weaker party..." But in a republic, where individuals are selected to represent others in the government, the public views are passed "through the medium of a chosen body of citizens, whose wisdom may best discern the true interest of their country." But even in a republic, "men of factious tempers" may "betray the interests of the people." This is where the importance of a larger republic comes into play in controlling factions. "Extend the sphere and you take in a greater variety of parties and interests; you make it less probable that a majority of the whole will have a common motive to invade the rights of other citizens."[23]

As an ancillary benefit, an extended republic would result in the election of men of independent judgment, a benefit of larger legislative districts. "In the next place, as each representative will be chosen by a greater number of citizens in the large than in the small republic, it will be more difficult for unworthy candidates to practise with success the viscous arts by which elections are too often carried; and the suffrages of the people being more free, will be more likely to center on men who possess the most attractive merit and the most diffusive and established characters." For Madison, being a legislator was similar to acting in a semi-judicial role, and he wanted to see elected officials act with independent judgment. "Madison thought that government should be essentially arbitrative, with neutral umpires weighing competing interests, to strike a just balance," historian Garry Wills writes. "This meant separating the officials, in some measure, from their local ties, freeing them to be impartial." Thus, the union to be established would not only protect liberty, but also result in the election of more able representatives. "The image here is akin to skimming a small amount of cream (the representatives) off the top of a bucket of milk (the polity)... In order to get the same absolute amount of cream, we need skim an even thinner (and thus richer) layer off the top" when dealing with an extended republic, as Amar writes.[24]

One of the core criticisms made by the opponents of the new Constitution was that it would eradicate the states. Madison, in *Federalist* No. 14, refuted this charge. "The general government...is limited to certain enumerated objects, which concern all of the members of the republic...The subordinate governments, which can extend their care to all those other objects which can be separately provided from, will retain their authority and activity." [25] Hamilton, in *Federalist* No. 15, builds a case for why the national government needs the authority to act directly on individuals. Because the government under the Articles of Confederation had no direct authority over the people, and no means to sanction the states, its actions "are mere recommendations which the States observe or disregard at their option." Hamilton admits that the states will lose some sovereignty under the Constitution, but that the

Antifederalists are trying to do the impossible by augmenting "federal authority without a diminution of State authority; [to have] sovereignty in the Union and complete independence in the members." Without the granting of additional powers to the federal government, the states will continue to "fly off from the common center," and act in their individual interests "without that knowledge of national circumstances and reasons of state," which are needed to make correct judgments. Hamilton builds his case further in *Federalist* No. 16 when he argues that under the current Confederation, the only means to compel the states to follow federal law is through the use of force, which will lead to civil war and ultimately the dissolution of the union. By granting the federal government power over individuals, these problems can be ameliorated.[26]

In a series of essays beginning with No. 23, Hamilton defends the powers of taxation and the military power given by the Constitution to the new government. This was in response to Antifederalist charges that the Constitution would result in the creation of large standing armies that would be led by a president who would act like a monarch, and that taxes would need to be high to support such a military establishment. Hamilton argues that the central government "ought to be invested with the full power to levy troops; to build and equip fleets; and to raise the revenues which will be required for the formation and support of an army and navy." He reminds the reader that even "though a wide ocean separates the United States from Europe," there are still dangers in the world that require a people to defend themselves. And the power over taxation is needed not only for national security purposes, but also "for the payment of national debts…and in general, for all of the matters which will call for disbursements out of the national treasury."[27]

Reading the essays, one gets the sense of frustration the authors must have felt toward some of the criticisms of the Antifederalists. Given the extensive debates and resulting compromises that the Framers engaged in at the Convention, the difficulties in balancing interests of different regions, the making of accommodations for large versus small states and slave versus free states, some of the attacks seemed unrealistic to both Hamilton and Madison. Some of these frustrations come through in *Federalist* No. 37, when Madison explains the difficulties that the delegates to the Convention faced, and then concludes by writing: "Would it be wonderful if, under the pressure of all of these difficulties, the convention should have been forced into some deviations from that artificial structure and regular symmetry which an abstract view of the subject might lead an ingenious theorist to bestow on a Constitution planned in his closet or in his imagination." He added that the "real wonder is that so many difficulties should have been surmounted" with such a degree of unanimity as to make one "perceive in it a finger of [the] Almighty."[28]

Another of the disturbing charges the Antifederalists leveled was that the Constitution would lead to government by an aristocratic few. The Antifederalists believed the transfer of power to a national government would also result in the "transfer of power from the people to the well born," since "power concentrated led to aristocracy" while "power diffused" led "to democracy."[29] This too must have been a somewhat galling charge to men such as Wilson and Madison, who had fought to ensure that the Constitution was built on the consent of the governed. Certainly, the Federalists wanted the most able men to serve as elected representatives in the new federal government, which opened them to the charge that they wanted a government run by the elite of society. But then by definition, representative government is one in which a small group of individuals make decisions based on the consent of the governed. And many of those who were counted among the ranks of the Antifederalists, including Mason, Gerry, Randolph, Richard Henry Lee, Patrick Henry, and George Clinton were themselves a part of the elite of revolutionary society.

Madison answers this charge in *Federalist* No. 39, along with the criticism that the Constitution would establish a consolidated national government. He begins with a definition of a republican government as one "which derives all of its power directly or indirectly from the great body of the people and is administered by persons holding their offices during pleasure and for a limited period, or during good behaviour." He goes on to show how that definition conforms not only to the state constitutions, which the Antifederalists defend, but also to the branches of the new government. "The House of Representatives… is elected immediately by the great body of the people. The Senate, like the present Congress…derives its appointment indirectly from the people. The president is indirectly derived from the choice of the people, according to the example in most of the States." Madison then addresses the issue of national versus federal governments, and how the Constitution has established a unique hybrid of both:

> *In its foundation it is federal, not national; in the sources from which the ordinary powers of the government are drawn, it is partly federal and partly national; in the operations of these powers, it is national, not federal; in the extent of them again, it is federal not national; and, finally in the authoritative mode of introducing amendments, it is neither wholly federal nor wholly national.*[30]

Some historians have criticized Madison for being disingenuous at best, or engaging in propaganda at worst, in part because he was defending the ambiguous character of relations between the central government and the states, which the Framers had settled on. Madison had clearly argued for a much stronger national government, with proportional representation in both branches of the legislature and a national veto over state laws. But as the debate over ratification unfolded, he used his greatest defeats at the Convention to the advantage of the Federalist cause.[31]

Madison was not quite so successful in defending the Convention from charges that the Framers exceeded their mandate by writing a completely new Constitution. In a tortured analysis contained in *Federalist* No. 40, Madison relies in part on the recommendations from the Annapolis Conference, a strained rationale at best, since he and Hamilton had used a loophole in the instructions given to the delegates from New Jersey to frame those recommendations in such a way as to justify the end they sought. At the conclusion of this essay, Madison grants for the moment that the Convention may not have been "authorized by their commission" to propose a new Constitution, but still he asks if this is reason enough to reject it? In fact, the states seemed to agree, since all of them except Rhode Island formed special ratifying conventions to consider the approval of the Constitution. And even Rhode Island held a statewide referendum on the Constitution, which "vindicated the theory of popular sovereignty the framers had invoked," according to Rakove.[32]

Another line of attack from the Antifederalists was that the Constitution did not adhere to a strict separation of powers. One Antifederalist, who wrote under the nom de plume Centinel, argued that the new government to be formed under the Constitution was not "founded on those balancing and restraining powers recommended by Mr. Adams and attempted in the British Constitution." Centinel was referring to Adams' recently published work called *Defence of the Constitutions of*

Government of the United States of America, in which Adams argued that "power is always abused when unlimited and unbalanced," a view widely shared by the other founders. Beginning with *Federalist* No. 47, Madison defends the Constitution from this charge by first stating that his opponents do not actually understand the concept of the separation of powers. They view the fact that each of the three branches of government is not totally separate from each other as a violation of the precept originally laid down by Montesquieu, but in fact "he did not mean that these departments ought to have no *partial agency* in, or no *control*, over the acts of each other. His meaning [was] that where the *whole* power of one department is exercised by the same hands which possess the *whole* power of another department, the fundamental principles of a free constitution are subverted." Madison points out that the British Constitution, along with the state governments, which the Antifederalists held up as their model, did not totally separate the legislative, executive, and judicial branches from each other.[33]

In *Federalist* No. 48, Madison explains that some blending between the three branches is needed to maintain the separation of powers. He disparages the use of what he calls "parchment barriers," impediments in the written document that prevent the abuse of power. Madison builds on this point in *Federalist* No. 51, another of the seminal essays, in which he outlines how to develop a true system of checks and balances. Each of the branches of government must be given the constitutional means to protect itself from encroachments from the other branches, and the officeholders need to have a personal stake in the protection of the power of their office. "Ambition must be made to counteract ambition. The interest of the man must be connected with the constitutional rights of the place." An example may help explain what Madison was attempting to achieve. In 1981, after the election of Ronald Reagan as president, his administration attempted to write specific language to implement their budget, which the House of Representatives had passed. In reply, Tip O'Neil, then the Speaker of the House, responded as follows: "Did you ever hear of the separation of powers? The Congress of the United States will be responsible for spending. You're not supposed to be writing legislation."[34]

Madison believed that a system of checks and balances was necessary because of the very nature of man, since people strive to obtain as much power as possible, as illustrated by the confrontation between President Reagan and Speaker O'Neill. Madison, in one of his most famous and perhaps politically incorrect statements, frames it this way:

> *If men were angels, no government would be necessary. If angels were to govern men, neither external nor internal controls on government would be necessary. In framing a government which is to be administered by men over men, the great difficulty lies in this: you must first enable the government to control the governed; and in the next place oblige it to control itself. A dependence on the people is, no doubt, the primary control on the government; but experience has taught mankind the necessity of auxiliary precautions.*[35]

What jumps out in this passage is that the government must first control the governed. But Madison was alluding to the most basic function of government, the need to provide order in a society by ensuring that laws are followed and that individuals are safe from harm. In order to avoid tyranny, government must also control itself, through a well-structured system of checks and balances.

Madison was ambivalent about the role of public opinion in governmental decision making, which comes through clearly in *Federalist*

No. 49. On the one hand, he knew that all power in a republic flows from the people, since "the people are the only legitimate fountain of power." But in deciding major constitutional questions, he feared that decisions "could never be expected to turn on the true merits of the question." Madison was writing specifically about an observation that Jefferson had made that whenever two branches of government encroach on a third, a new convention should be called to fix the breach. Madison had numerous concerns about Jefferson's proposal, despite their friendship and his complimentary remarks that Jefferson's writing, "marks a turn of thinking, original, comprehensive, and accurate." But his major concern with Jefferson's proposal was that complicated subjects would be decided based on "passions" and self-interest, and not on reason. "But it is the reason, alone, of the public, that ought to control and regulate the government. The passions ought to be controlled by the government." Madison's concerns went well beyond just the issue raised by Jefferson, but extended to the entire public debate that was taking place over the Constitution, one he was concerned would be decided on the basis of emotion or the demagoguery of the Antifederalists, and not on the merits of the case. In this, Hamilton shared his concern, and worried over the outcome of the public debate taking place over the Constitution. "It is almost arrogance in so complicated a subject, depending so entirely on the incalculable fluctuation of the human passions, to attempt to even conjecture about the event."[36]

The concerns of the duo reflect the tensions inherent in democratic politics. The consent of the governed is essential to implement any major public initiative, yet the public may lack the knowledge to weigh the full ramifications that will occur from policy choices they confront. Most people lead busy lives, and do not have the time or the inclination to become experts on the whole range of matters that face the government, from budget and fiscal policy, to military matters, to foreign relations. That is why the founders generally preferred a republican form of government, in which the people elect representatives who study complicated issues and act with independent judgment on behalf of the people, with adequate checks on those who are elected to ensure they don't become despotic or act only in their own self-interest.

The Antifederalists had a series of criticisms of the structure of the proposed federal government. They claimed that the House of Representatives was too small and would therefore represent the interests of the few and not the many. One Antifederalist leader, Melancton Smith of New York, charged that the House would represent the "natural aristocracy" rather than the "middling class." Because there would be too few members of the House, they would not be able to identify with the common people and would "be obliged to rule through corruption, force, and fear—with monopolies and standing armies—rather than mutual confidence," according to constitutional scholar Akhil Read Amar. Some of the Antifederalists criticized the proposed two-year terms for representatives, believing that annual elections were needed to ensure that the House would represent the people. They also criticized the long terms of office for the Senate, the lack of any provision for recalling its members, and for its treaty-making power. As with the House, the Antifederalists were concerned that the Senate would become an aristocratic body that the state legislatures could not control.[37]

Madison defended the House of Representatives from these charges in a series of essays in *Federalist* No. 52 through 58. First, he responded to the critique of his opponents on the need for annual elections. He agreed that frequent elections are important to ensure that the government has "an immediate dependence on, and intimate sympathy with, the people." But he questioned why the frequency must be annual, pointing to examples from Great Britain, Ireland, and the

American colonies where terms of office extended beyond one year, and concluded that, "the liberties of the people can be in no danger from *biennial* elections." In *Federalist* No. 53, Madison expands his defense of longer terms of office on the basis that the more complicated nature of federal legislation requires "sound judgment" that can only come from "a certain degree of knowledge," which results from serving for a longer term of office.[38]

On the issue of the small size of the House, it is interesting to note that in *Federalist* No. 55, Madison was defending one of those elements of the Constitution which he in fact disagreed with. At the Convention in July, he had proposed to double the initial size of the house to 130 members, and had supported Hamilton in a later motion to increase the size of the House. Both motions had been defeated, and it wasn't until Washington spoke at the very end of the Convention that the ratio of House members to population was decreased, thereby allowing for a larger House in the future. Madison was in fact trying to find the sweet spot, where the first branch would not be too big, yet not too small. In *Federalist* No 55, Madison defended the original sixty-five member House with the query as to whether there are "any circumstances" under which the people "will choose, and every second year repeat the choice of sixty-five...men who would be disposed to form and pursue a scheme of tyranny or treachery." In fact, once ratified, Madison would pursue an amendment to increase the size of the House, an amendment that failed to receive the required votes for ratification by the states.[39]

In his final series of essays, Madison defended the Senate in *Federalist* No. 62 and 63. He rested his case largely on the need to have a second chamber of the legislature that would act with greater wisdom and stability, since the House could too easily "yield to the impulse of sudden and violent passions, and to be seduced by factious leaders into intemperate and pernicious resolutions." For the Senate to have the ability to resist this impulse, it must have "great firmness, and consequently ought to hold its authority by a tenure of considerable duration." Madison concludes *Federalist* No. 63 by rebutting the charge that the Senate will be transformed "into a tyrannical aristocracy." His answer was found in a reliance on the system of checks and balances and separation of powers, which the Constitution contains. The Senate would first have to "corrupt itself; must next corrupt the State legislatures, must then corrupt the House of Representatives, and must finally corrupt the people at large." And should the Senate ever become "an independent and aristocratic body…the House of Representatives, with the people on their side, will at all times be able" to restrain them.[40]

John Jay returned to write his final essay in *Federalist* No. 64, where he defended the combined treaty-making power of the Senate and the presidency. He relied on the fact that both institutions would be composed "of the most enlightened and respectable citizens," with the greatest "abilities and virtue," and would therefore be able to act in the national interest. "With such men the power of making treaties may be safely lodged."[41]

Some historians find the Antifederalist charge that the Framers were elitists who wished to establish control by an aristocracy valid. Gordon Wood argues that, "the Constitution was intrinsically an aristocratic document designed to check the democratic tendencies of the period." By aristocratic, Wood is referring to the natural aristocracy that consists of those who had risen to the top of society based on education, experience, and accomplishments. It is true that Madison was greatly concerned over the types of people who controlled the state governments, and intended that the natural aristocracy would dominate at the national level of politics, as he wrote in *Federalist* No. 10.[42]

But does the fact that the government is run by an elite made up of the most knowledgeable and capable people really lead to a conflict "between aristocracy and democracy," to an "aristocratic tyranny" as one Antifederalist described it? While the opponents of the Constitution legitimately feared such an outcome, the future of the federal republic would disprove the charge. Madison and Jefferson, two members of the natural aristocracy, would establish the Republican Party in the 1790s as a means to organize common people in opposition to rule by the Federalist Party, which they believed pursued policies designed only to help the upper class. Abraham Lincoln, who started life as the most common of men, would join the natural aristocracy, but he never forgot his roots, and pursued policies such as the Homestead Act to provide free land for farmers. Later, Theodore and Franklin Roosevelt proposed and implemented policies designed to aid average Americans, despite the fact that they came from the elite of society. In our own time, George W. Bush pursued an agenda based on "compassionate conservatism," which was rooted in the idea that individuals have a responsibility to one another in a good society, that the rich owe something to those less fortunate. These leaders have proved that one need not come from the lower or middle class of society to represent those interests.[43]

Wood discusses, in the conclusion to his seminal book, *Creation of the American Republic,* how the Federalists, in order to counter the charge that they planned to establish an aristocratic tyranny, needed to show that the branches of government created by the Constitution did not represent different divisions in society but rather the entire people. In Great Britain, the various branches of government had represented the one (the monarchy), the few (the House of Lords), and the many (the House of Commons). But Federalist theory held that all of the branches of government were responsible to the people through the process of representation. Government in the United States would not just be republican in form, but a "Democratic Republic," as Nathaniel Chipman of Vermont would refer to it in 1793, or a "representative democracy," in the words of Hamilton. The separation of the government into the legislative, executive, and judicial branches was "functionally but not substantively different"; they were not designed to check different social elements of society, but rather to segregate power based on the functions to be undertaken and to serve as checks on each other. But all three of them derived their power from the people. "The executive and judicial powers are now drawn from the same source, are now animated by the same principles, and are now directed to the same ends, with the legislative authority; they who execute, and they who administer the laws, are so much the servants, and therefore as much the friends of the people, as those who make them," as James Wilson framed it.[44]

On March 4, 1788, Madison left New York for Virginia to stand for election to the ratifying convention in his home state. He had not intended to serve, but was convinced by his friends that his presence would be essential, especially in countering the opposition of Henry, Mason, and Lee.[45] It was left to Hamilton to complete *The Federalist* by countering the attacks being made upon the presidency. "The principle objection of most Antifederalists to the executive branch was that the President had been given too much power," including "his right to make appointments and treaties, his influence over the army, his right to pardon, and most of all his veto power," according to historian Jackson Turner Main. While most Antifederalists were willing to accept a stronger executive, they thought the Constitution went too far.[46]

Hamilton's answer would come in series of eleven essays that extend from *Federalist* No. 67 through 77. The most famous of these was *Federalist* No. 70, in which Hamilton argued that, "energy in the executive is a leading character in the definition of good government." A feeble executive would lead to a government that was "ill executed" and would result in "bad government." For Hamilton, the "ingredients which constitute energy in the executive are unity; duration; an adequate provision for support; and competent powers." In the next seven essays, Hamilton would develop each of the ingredients. One can see in these essays a foreshadowing of Hamilton's "ambitious use of executive power" that would occur in his role as secretary of the treasury under Washington. In a broader sense, Hamilton was laying the groundwork for the presidency as the central political actor on the American stage. As historian Arthur M. Schlesinger, Jr. writes, "A system based on the tripartite separation of powers has an inherent tendency toward inertia and stalemate." Among the Framers, Hamilton saw the presidency as the one institution that could overcome this tendency, and Lincoln felt the same, saying that the office needed to be and was "clothed with great power."[47]

While most of the critics of the Constitution acknowledged the need for a national court system, certain provisions of the federal judiciary came under scrutiny from the Antifederalists. Melancton Smith was concerned that the powers of the Supreme Court were too extensive and would make it "totally independent, uncontroulable and not amenable to any other power in any decisions they make." There were also concerns that the Supreme Court would have the power to decide the meaning of the Constitution, and that this would lead to ever greater consolidation of power under the national government.[48]

Hamilton responded to these charges in a series of six essays beginning with *Federalist* No. 78. While the Convention had spent little time on the judicial branch of the government, and had not explicitly included the power of judicial review in the Constitution, Hamilton defended the concept. As with Jefferson and Madison, Hamilton believed that the Constitution as a body of law was superior to acts passed by the legislature, what he called fundamental law, since the Constitution came from the people. "The Constitution ought to be preferred to the statute, the intention of the people to the intention of their agents" in the legislature. Since the legislature is in no position to judge whether the statutes they have passed are valid under the Constitution, "the interpretation of the laws is the proper and peculiar province of the courts." Given that the judiciary is the weakest branch of the government, since it has "neither Force nor Will, but merely judgment," the lifetime appointment of judges is needed to provide the courts with the "independent spirit" needed to serve as a "bulwark" against "legislative encroachments."[49]

For all of the high-minded political theory the *Federalist* essays represented, their "reasoned and erudite defence of the Constitution," their influence was largely restricted to New York and Virginia. The essays were long and complicated, leading one Antifederalist to complain that the authors had "endeavored to force conviction by a torrent of misplaced words." The *Federalist* essays were only published in about a dozen newspapers outside of New York. "The Federalist worked only a small influence upon the course of events during the struggle over ratification," according to Rossiter. "Promises, threats, bargains, and face-to-face debates," what Madison referred to as the "vicious arts," would carry the day in the ratifying conventions.[50]

Endnotes

1 For historians that have been critical of the use of the word federalist as applied to the supporters of the Constitution, see Main, p. viii-xii; Berkin, p. 175; Beeman, p. 375.

2 Ellis, *American Creation*, p. 114; Pauline Maier, *Ratification: The People Debate the Constitution, 1787-1788*, (New York, 2011), p. XV

3 Maier, *Ratification*, p. 74; Rakove, *Original Meanings*, p. 134 and 139

4 Chernow, *Washington*, p. 542-543; Ellis, *His Excellency*, p. 181

5 Rakove, *Original Meanings*, p. 112

6 On majority support for the Antifederalists, see Ellis, *American Creation*, p. 116 and Richard E. Ellis, "The Persistence of Antifederalism after 1789," p. 295, in Beeman, *Beyond Confederation;* see also Berkin, p. 174-175 for the disadvantages faced by the Antifederalists.

7 This section generally follows the analysis prepared by Main in Chapters VI-VIII.

8 Ellis, *American Creation*, p. 117; Main, p. 129

9 The Mason quote is from Main, p. 123

10 Rossiter, p. 285

11 The quotes in this section are from a summary of the *Speech of James Wilson*, retrieved December 1, 2013, from http://www.constitution .org/afp/jwilsono.html

12 Maier, p. 80-81; Rakove, *Original Meanings*, raises the issue of the partial bill of rights on p. 144-145 and the fact that Wilson's speech helped focus the arguments of the Antifederalists.

13 He is the fourth member of *The Quartet* that Ellis writes about.

14 Chernow, *Alexander Hamilton*, p. 247-248; Ketchum, p. 239

15 All quotes from the *Federalist* are from the edition edited by Rossiter and are footnoted based on the primary author and page number. The quote from Madison is from p. 104; Rakove, *Original Meanings*, p. 151

16 See the basic definition of propaganda contained in the online Merriam-Webster dictionary retrieved December 12, 2013 from http://www.merriam-webster.com/dictionary/propaganda; Beeman makes the case that *The Federalist* was propaganda on p. 407; Rakove, *Revolutionaries*, takes the opposite position on p. 388, arguing that *The Federalist* contains "careful reasoning and prudent distinctions" that would not be found in true works of propaganda.

17 This section was largely influenced by three particular writings. One was from James MacGregor Burns, *The Vineyard of Liberty*, (New York, 1983), p. 60-63; the second Richard Hofstadter, *The Founding Fathers: An Age of Realism*, retrieved December 31, 2013 from http://cf.linnbenton.edu/artcom/social_science/clarkd/upload/the%20founding%20fathers---hofstadter.pdf; and the third was from Wood, *Creation of the American Republic*, especially Chapter XV

18 The quote from Rossiter is taken from his introduction to *The Federalist Papers*, p. xiv; Madison, p. 83

19 Michael P. Federici, *The Political Philosophy of Alexander Hamilton*, (Baltimore, 2012), p.79

20 Quoted in Wood, *Creation of the American Republic*, p.504

21 Hamilton, p. 33

22 Jay, p. 37-38

23 Madison, p. 78-83

24 Madison, p. 82; Wills, p. 33; Akhil Reed Amar, *The Bill of Rights: Creation and Reconstruction*, (New Haven, 1998), p. 10

25 Madison, p. 102

26 Hamilton, p. 108 and p. 111

27 Hamilton, p. 154-155, p. 160 and p. 188

28 Madison, p. 230

29 Main, p. 130

30 Madison, p. 246

31 See Rakove, *Original Meanings*, p. 161 and Beeman, p. 407 for their criticisms of Madison's defense of the partly federal and partly national nature of the government.

32 Madison, p. 254; Rakove, *Original Meanings*, p. 112

33 The quote from the Centinel essay was taken from Antifederalist Paper No. 47, which reflects excerpts from the original letters of October 5 and 24, 1787, and were retrieved December 20, 2013 from http://www.rightsofthepeople.com/freedom_documents/anti_federalist_papers/anti_federalist_papers/ ; Madison, p. 302-303

34 The quote from Tip O'Neill is from Chris Matthews, *Tip and the Gipper: When Politics Worked*, (New York, 2013), p. 144

35 Madison, p. 322; for an excellent short summary of the meaning of this essay, see Federalist # 51 Explanation retrieved December 21, 2013 from http://www.webpages.uidaho.edu/pols101_online/lessons/Handouts/Fed.%2051%20Handout.pdf

36 Madison, p. 317; Rakove, *Original Meanings,* develops the theme of the concerns with the public debate on pages 140-142, where the Hamilton quote is taken from.

37 Amar, *The Bill of Rights*, p. 11; Main, p. 134-136

38 Madison, p. 327 and 332

39 Madison, p. 344; Amar, p. 12

40 Madison, p. 379, p. 387-390

41 Jay, p. 391

42 Wood, *Creation of the American Republic,* p. 513

43 Wood, *Creation of the American Republic,* p. 485 and p. 513; on Lincoln and Bush, see Dionne, p. 160-161 and p. 114-115

44 Wood, *Creation of the American Republic,* Chapter XV contains his full argument.

45 Rakove, *Revolutionaries*, p. 390

46 Main, p. 141-142

47 Hamilton, p. 423-424; Rakove, *Original Meanings*, p. 283; The Lincoln quote is from Doris Kearns Goodwin, *Team of Rivals: The Political Genius of Abraham Lincoln*, (New York, 2005), p. 687

48 Main, p. 156

49 Hamilton, p. 467-469

50 Ferling, p. 305; Chernow, *Hamilton*, p. 261; Rossiter's introduction to *The Federalist Papers*, p. xi

CHAPTER 11

The State Conventions / September 1787 to July 1789

"As the instrument came from [the Convention] it was nothing more than a draft of a plan, nothing but a dead letter, until life and validity had been breathed into it by the voice of the people, speaking through the several State Conventions."

– JAMES MADISON, APRIL 6, 1796 –

Historians have pretty well repudiated any attempt to explain the framing of, or the debate over, the Constitution on purely economic or class terms, as proposed by historian Charles Beard. Beard had seen the Federalists as an undemocratic and self-interested minority that owned much of the public debt and personally gained from the establishment of a new system of government with the capacity to repay them. In fact, many of the Antifederalists who attended the state ratifying conventions were wealthy men who owned public debt that rivaled the Federalist leaders. Perhaps a more accurate description of the split between the two sides was geographic. Support for the Constitution tended to be strong among those who lived in cities on the Atlantic seaboard and were dependent on trade and manufacturing, whether wealthy merchants, middle class artisans, or poor laborers. Those who lived further west, in the backcountry of "western New

England, Pennsylvania, New York, South Carolina, and Virginia" and who made their living from farming small plots of land, tended to oppose the creation of a strong central government. The divisions of the state ratifying conventions occurred along these same geographic lines.[1]

Action from the Confederation Congress

George Mason's opposition had an immediate impact on the debate over the Constitution. Mason had circulated his objections to some of his allies in Virginia, including Richard Henry Lee. Lee, born into one of the most prominent old-line Virginia families, had been involved early on in the American Revolution, opposing the various taxation schemes that the British had attempted to implement in the 1760s. A delegate to the Continental Congress, Lee had introduced the resolution declaring independence in 1776. He was an old line "Whig," a man whose experience with the British made him fear the power of a strong central government. Along with Patrick Henry, Lee had refused to serve at the Convention, believing it was wrong for members of Congress to "pass judgment at New York upon their opinion at Philadelphia." Although he and Mason were part of the Virginia aristocracy, they were both concerned that the Constitution would lead either to a monarchy "or a corrupt, tyrannical aristocracy," as Mason framed it.[2]

Lee used the debate that began on September 26 in the Confederation Conference as an opportunity to put forward his opposition to the Constitution. He argued for a bill of rights, a council of state to restrict the president, and a provision that would make the Senate elected based on proportional representation. "Perhaps this last proposition drew a brief smile from Madison, who certainly agreed with it in principle," according to Rakove. Lee also maintained that Congress had the power to amend the Constitution before sending it on to the states for ratification. Madison immediately saw the danger in the latter proposal. If the Congress amended the document, it would become an act of Congress and under the Articles of Confederation would require the unanimous consent of the states to become effective. Madison was also hoping for the support of the Congress, but he eventually accepted a compromise proposal under which the Congress unanimously agreed to send the Constitution on to the states for consideration through the ratifying conventions without expressing either support or opposition. "The reference to unanimity referred only to the willingness—grudging on the part of many—to transmit the [Constitution] to the states," as Beeman writes.[3]

Ratification in Pennsylvania

Even before Congress acted to refer the Constitution to the states, the Pennsylvania legislature attempted to form a ratifying convention. Members of the Pennsylvania Assembly, the sole legislative branch under the state's constitution, were meeting at the State House, where the Convention was also meeting. Immediately after adjournment of the Convention, Pennsylvania was the first state to receive a copy of the new Constitution. A group of supporters for a strong national government controlled the General Assembly, and they wanted to be the first state to ratify the document. They went to great lengths to attempt to achieve this result. By September 28, the Federalist majority had still not received word that the Confederation Congress had acted on the Constitution. The General Assembly was scheduled to adjourn the next day and the Federalist members were anxious to adopt resolutions outlining how delegates were to be elected to the ratifying convention. Late in the day, word finally reached them that the Congress had acted. By then, nineteen members of the opposing party in the Assembly refused to attend that day's session, which denied the majority party the minimum two-thirds quorum required under the state Constitution to take action. The next morning, the Federalists organized a group of men (variously described as a gang or a posse) to forcibly escort two of the missing men back to the state house so the vote could take place.[4]

The hardball tactics of the Federalists in Pennsylvania, which other states were watching, almost backfired. Sixteen of those who had boycotted the September 28 session sent an address to their constituents that was widely published, which called into question not only the motives of the supporters of the Constitution but of the document itself. Richard Henry Lee complained that the supporters of the Constitution in Pennsylvania were acting "[a]s if the subject of Government were a business of passion, instead of cool, sober, and intense consideration," words that must have made Madison blanch. Despite the rough start, the Federalists were able to dominate the election of delegates held on November 6, with their greatest strength in and around Philadelphia. When the state convention opened, the Federalists held a two-to-one advantage in delegates. With such a large majority, they could have called for an immediate vote for ratification. Instead, they allowed for "a free and ample discussion of the federal plan," but intended to limit the actual vote to an up-or-down decision on ratification. Thomas McKean, one of the supporters of the Constitution and a former chief justice of the Pennsylvania Supreme Court, framed the convention's role as being restricted to one question: "whether we will ratify and confirm, or, upon due consideration [,] reject, in the whole, the system of federal government that is submitted to us."[5]

The debate in Pennsylvania revealed the fault lines between the Federalists and the Antifederalists that I explored in the earlier chapter. For over two weeks, the two sides made their case. The Antifederalists believed the Constitution established a consolidated government, based on the theory that sovereignty could not be divided; that it was not possible to create a government within a government (*imperium in imperio*). "If sovereignty could not be divided, the establishment of a sovereign nation would necessarily end state sovereignty and establish a highly centralized...government," according to Maier. James Wilson's response at the convention was quite ingenious, and formed the theoretical justification for American federalism. He reasoned that, in fact, sovereignty was not in the state governments or the national government, but rather was vested in the people. As such, the people "can delegate it in such proportions, to such bodies, on such terms, and under such limitations, as they think proper." The people "may take from the subordinate governments powers with which they have hitherto trusted them, and place these powers in the general government." Since all power emanated from the people, sovereignty was not being transferred from the states to the federal government, since the states had no sovereignty to transfer. Wilson made the case that while the states were losing nothing, the country as a whole had much to gain: "By adopting this system, we become a NATION; at present we are not one." In a moment of great foresight during his speech to the convention on December 10, Wilson also saw that the government proposed under the Constitution would "probably lay a foundation for erecting temples of liberty in every part of the earth."[6]

The Antifederalists attacked the document's lack of a bill of rights. Wilson made his standard defense, that since the Constitution only granted the federal government certain enumerated powers, and these did not include interference in the people's basic rights, such as freedom of speech and the press, a bill of rights was not needed. Also, any attempt to enumerate those rights that were to be protected could well fall short of being comprehensive. "Everything that is not enumerated is presumed to be given," with the result that, "an imperfect enumeration would throw all implied powers into the scale of government,"

Wilson claimed. The Antifederalists responded by pointing out that the Constitution protected certain rights, such as habeas corpus and trial by jury in criminal cases. Using Wilson's logic, it could be inferred that all other rights were not protected.[7]

Essays began to appear in newspapers that supported the Antifederalist position on the bill of rights. Perhaps had they limited their proposed amendments to this one issue, the Antifederalists would have had more success and they would have been able to attract some votes from the more moderate Federalists. Instead, they overplayed their hand. As the convention neared its end on December 12, Robert Whitehill of Cumberland County proposed an extensive series of amendments that would have changed the Constitution completely, including "that the sovereignty, freedom, and independency of the several states shall be retained." Whitehill also proposed that the convention adjourn to an unspecified date so that the people of Pennsylvania could consider his amendments. The Federalists voted down his proposal, 46-23, and approved the Constitution on the same vote. In a final defeat for the Antifederalists, the Federalists also purged the proposed amendments from the minutes of the convention.[8]

Unfortunately, the hardball tactics used at the beginning of the process by the Federalists in Pennsylvania left a bad hangover with their opponents in the state. As Rossiter writes, "The manner in which the Federalists had won this important battle…raised serious doubts about their claims to wisdom and virtue." During a celebration rally in Carlisle on December 27, a crowd of Antifederalists attacked James Wilson, and may have killed him, had an old soldier not shielded him from their blows. The Antifederalists also began to circulate petitions signed by the voters, which requested that the legislature nullify the convention's decision to ratify the Constitution.[9]

While the debate raged in Pennsylvania, Delaware became the first state to ratify the Constitution when they voted unanimously for approval on December 4, thus denying Pennsylvania that distinction. New Jersey soon followed on December 18, followed by Georgia on December 30. Both states approved the Constitution on unanimous votes. As the year ended, four states had ratified. But the heavy lifting had just begun, and the outcome was very much in doubt in Massachusetts, Virginia, and New York. Without those key states, there would be no union.

The Battle for Massachusetts

As the year 1788 opened, Connecticut became the fifth state to ratify the Constitution. The vote was 128-40, with the Federalists holding several key advantages in the state. First, almost every newspaper supported the Constitution. Second, three delegates to the Constitutional Convention (Sherman, Ellsworth, and Johnson) put their significant influence behind the ratification effort. Finally, allowing the new federal government to regulate interstate commerce was in Connecticut's interest, as it received many of its imports through New York, which would no longer be able to levy an import tax on those goods.[10]

On January 9, Massachusetts kicked off a series of state ratifying conventions where the results would very much be in doubt. The state had elected 355 delegates to the convention to be held in Boston, by far the largest number of any state. With so many delegates, plus a large number of spectators, the convention had to move three times before finally settling in the Congregational Church, which had large balconies from which the public could observe the debates.[11]

The Federalists faced several challenges in Massachusetts. The impact of Shays Rebellion still hung over the state. Delegates from the three westernmost counties, (Berkshire, Hampshire, and Worcester), were strongly opposed to the Constitution. They believed the proposed government gave too much power to the wealthy. Unlike other states, class differences would play a major role in the Massachusetts ratification vote. Rufus King, who had been a delegate to the Convention, wrote a letter to Madison in which he bemoaned the fact that the opponents did not show concern about any specific aspect of the Constitution, but rather "that some injury is plotted against them, that the System is the production of the Rich" and will result in "the establishment of two Orders in Society, one comprehending the Opulent & Great, the other the poor and illiterate."[12]

Two of the leading politicians in the state, John Hancock and Sam Adams, were either noncommittal or hostile toward the Constitution. Hancock, who had recently been elected governor, had pardoned the remaining participants in Shays Rebellion and had helped heal the divisions in the state "by persuading the legislature to relieve the economic distress that lay behind the unrest," according to Maier.[13] He was also a delegate to the convention, which elected him its presiding officer. But a bad case of gout kept him from attending until later in its sessions. Hancock kept his views, and his options, open on the Constitution. Eventually, the Federalists would need to make a major strategic decision to accept potential amendments to the Constitution to secure the governor's support.

Sam Adams, who had been one of the major leaders of the independence movement in the 1770s, was suspicious of the concentration of power contemplated under the Constitution. Lee had sent Adams a copy of his proposed amendments to the document, and in reply, Adams mentioned that he had trouble from the opening wording of the Constitution and that: "I meet with a National Government, instead of a federal Union of Sovereign States." Six days before the convention opened, he came out in opposition to the Constitution. He was forced to change his mind due to lobbying by his primary supporters, Boston's tradesman and mechanics, who advocated the establishment of the new federal government. While personally opposed to the new Constitution, he remained largely silent for much of the convention in order to placate his core constituents.[14]

One man who was missing from the debate, and who could have been of great help to the Federalists, was John Adams, who was serving as American minister to Great Britain. Adams received a copy of the Constitution in the fall of 1787, and was greatly impressed. He sent a letter endorsing the proposed plan to John Jay that was widely quoted. "The public mind cannot be occupied by a nobler object than the proposed plan of government. It appears to be admirably calculated to cement all of America in affection and interest as one great nation." His only criticisms were that the president should have been even more powerful, and that there was no bill of rights included in the document. Since "provision is made for corrections and amendment as they may be found necessary, I confess I hope to hear of its adoption by all of the states," Adams wrote in the letter.[15]

Given the even divide between supporters and opponents, the Federalist strategy in Massachusetts was to move through the document slowly, with the intent of convincing those in the opposing camp open to persuasion to support the Constitution. The Federalist Theophilus Parsons explained that the focus was on "men of integrity and candor" who were "ready and desirous of being informed." The Federalists supported an open dialogue, but voting would only occur at the end of the convention once they were assured they had the votes to win. The leadership of the Federalists included King, Gorham, and Strong, all of whom had attended the Philadelphia Convention. It also included a number of other fine speakers, including Francis Dana, Fisher Ames, and Theodore Sedgwick. Interestingly, Elbridge Gerry was not elected as a delegate, but the Federalists allowed him to attend in order to answer questions. His role soon caused controversy, and he left the convention in a huff after only a few days, having made very little impact.[16]

The debate went on for three weeks, with the convention going paragraph by paragraph through the document. The Federalist speakers, made up of successful lawyers and experienced politicians, were also great orators. For each objection to the Constitution raised, the Federalists provided a ready answer. The opponents pointed out that the House was too small to be truly representative of the people, and two-year terms were considered too long, since in Massachusetts representatives were subject to annual election. Ames responded that the federal government was more complicated and would require "at least two years in office...to enable a man to judge of the trade and interests of states which he never saw." Dana pointed out that in terms of size the combined number of House and Senate members was the same as the current Congress under the Articles of Confederation. The Antifederalists also complained that the Congress had the power to levy direct taxes. "Old Revolutionary sensitivities over taxes were rekindled by recent experience, particularly in sections of Massachusetts where men had been driven to desperation by high direct taxes leveled by the state legislature," writes Maier. But the Federalists responded that during normal times, taxes on imports would be sufficient to meet the expenses of the federal government, and that direct taxes would only be needed in times of war.[17]

Despite the superior debating skills of the Federalists, by the end of January they knew they had not changed enough minds to ensure ratification. They decided to change tactics, and came out in support of certain amendments to the Constitution which would be recommended to the first Congress should the document ultimately be ratified. They also enlisted the support of John Hancock, dangling in front of him their backing for his re-election efforts and the possibility that if Virginia did not ratify that he, rather than Washington, would become president. Hancock, who up until then had not attended the convention, arrived on January 30, carried into the meeting by his servants. Many thought his illness was, in part, a handy excuse, which bought him time to see which way the political winds were blowing. Hancock wanted to "avoid alienating either his constituents in Boston, who were ardent Federalists, or those in rural parts of the state who were opposed to or had strong reservations about the Constitution," Maier writes.[18]

On January 31, Hancock rose to state his support for ratification of the Constitution...as long as certain amendments—that would be introduced in the new Congress by the Massachusetts delegates—accompanied the approval. Hancock proposed nine amendments, including two that would make their way into the bill of rights. One dealt with the use of grand juries in criminal cases, which would become incorporated into the Fifth Amendment, and the other required that the states would retain all powers not delegated to the federal government, and would become the Tenth Amendment. Surprisingly, the Antifederalists took the position that the convention lacked the authority to propose amendments. But Adams backed Hancock's motion, which settled the matter. On February 6, the convention approved the Constitution on a razor thin vote of 187-168. Half of the no votes came from the three most western counties, with many of the rest from other rural parts of the state.[19]

In Pennsylvania, the heavy-handed tactics of the Federalists led to continued opposition to the Constitution. But in Massachusetts, many of those who voted no pledged their support and agreed to work to convince their constituents to do the same. One Antifederalist, William Widgery, said they had lost to "a majority of wise and understanding men," and he would try to "sow the seeds of union and peace among the people he represented." Benjamin Swain indicated that "the Constitution has had a fair trial...that many doubts which lay on his mind had been removed," and that he would "support the Constitution as cheerfully and as heartily as though he had voted on the other side of the question." As Maier writes, the reason for the reaction in Massachusetts owed much to the way in which the Federalists were willing to listen to their opponents, and "addressed their concerns and answered their questions with seriousness...and treated them publicly with the respect their power demanded—even if they were uneducated, had no wealth to speak of, and had supported Shay's Rebellion."[20]

The Federalists in Massachusetts expected their support of the Constitution to carry over to New Hampshire, which opened its convention on February 13. This didn't happen, and after ten days of deliberations, the Federalists in New Hampshire moved to adjourn the convention without taking action. The Rhode Island legislature, in late February, asked their constituents to express their views through local town hall meetings. The meetings overwhelmingly opposed even the call for a convention, and Rhode Island would remain outside of the union until January of 1790, after the new government had already been formed. Undeterred by these setbacks, conventions in Maryland and South Carolina approved ratification of the Constitution in the late spring. All eyes now turned to Virginia, whose convention was set to open on June 2, 1788. Eight states had ratified at this point, but no one expected that the union could survive without Virginia.[21]

Virginia: Henry versus Madison

An all-star lineup faced off against each other in the Old Dominion state, although Virginia's meeting was almost as interesting for those that did not attend the convention as for those that did.

George Washington, despite his role as president of the Constitutional Convention and the first delegate to sign the document, did not attend. He intended to stay above the fray, and he knew his incredible influence could cause resentment among those who opposed the Constitution. A Boston newspaper complained of the influence of both Washington and Franklin, stating that their support for the Constitution had made "too strong an argument in the minds of many to suffer them to examine like freemen for themselves." When Washington became aware that Maryland might postpone its convention until after Virginia's, he wrote to Governor Thomas Johnson, an old friend, arguing that this was but a ploy by the opponents to undermine the effort for ratification in both states and other parts of the South. Coming on the heels of New Hampshire's adjournment, Washington greatly feared that the entire enterprise was facing failure. Although Maryland moved forward with their convention and went on to ratify, rumors circulated that Johnson was so greatly "displeased" by Washington's meddling that he urged the convention to recommend amendments to the Constitution.[22]

Washington was also concerned that some would see his lobbying for the Constitution as campaigning for president, which would have been unseemly during that era. But while Washington attempted to stay out of the way during the ratification process, he was far from a disinterested observer, as the Maryland incident shows. Upon his return from the Convention, he had sent copies of the Constitution to several key leaders in Virginia, including Patrick Henry and Thomas Jefferson. In his correspondence to Henry, he indicated there were flaws in the document, but that it was "the best that could be obtained at this time; and as a constitutional door is opened for amendment hereafter, the adoption of it under the present circumstances of Union is, in my opinion, desirable." Henry disagreed and went on to actively oppose the Constitution.[23]

Both Madison and Hamilton kept Washington in the loop in the battle for ratification. Madison had sent Washington the first installments of *The Federalist* in November of 1787. Washington sent a copy of them to a publisher in Richmond, hoping they would be widely printed and read in the Virginia newspapers. Washington was so impressed with the essays that he wrote to Hamilton that, "when the transient circumstances and fugitive performances which attend the crisis shall have disappeared that work will merit the notice of Posterity." He also encouraged Madison to run as a delegate to the convention in Virginia, knowing his leadership was needed if Virginia were to ratify.[24]

The other missing man was Jefferson, who was serving as foreign minister to France. Prior to the start of the Convention in Philadelphia, Madison had sent Jefferson a letter alluding to the problems that the country faced and some of his proposed solutions, including a separation of powers and a federal "negative *in all cases whatsoever* on the local legislatures." While Jefferson agreed with his good friend on the need for a separation of powers, the federal negative was a new idea that was "for the first time, suggested to my mind. *Prima facie*, I do not like it. It fails in an essential character; that the hole and the patch should be commensurate."[25]

After the Convention adjourned, Jefferson received a copy of the new Constitution from Washington. His initial inclination was to oppose the document, in large measure because of his fear of a strong central government. In a letter to John Adams in November 1787, he wrote, "there are things in it which stagger all my disposition to subscribe to." He was particularly concerned about the president, which he equated with "a bad edition of a Polish King," and was considerably troubled by the lack of term limits for the office. Overall, he thought that the "Convention had been too much impressed by the insurrection in Massachusetts," and should have simply added "three or four new articles" to the current system of government.[26]

Madison was influential in changing Jefferson's mind. In his letter of October 24, 1787, Madison explained in detail the problems the Convention had to address. He opened by stating that the Convention had come to the realization that "a voluntary observance of the federal law by" the states "could never be hoped for." Given this, the only alternative was to design "a Government which instead of operating, on the States, should operate without their intervention on individuals." Knowing Jefferson's suspicions of executive power, he spent time explaining the challenges that the Convention faced in designing a president that would have sufficient independence without fostering "heredity tenure." But Madison spent most of his letter explaining his concern with how best to balance the rights of individuals and minority groups with the need for majority rule. As previously discussed, Madison believed the key lay in the establishment of an extended republic. "What remedy can be found in a republican Government, where the majority must ultimately decide, but that of giving such an extent to its sphere, that no common interest or passion will be likely to unite a majority of the whole number in an unjust pursuit," he wrote to Jefferson. [27]

Jefferson was persuaded to support the Constitution, in part by Madison, and in part based on time, distance, and reflection on the matter. "Jefferson's being in Paris rather than Philadelphia proved a major advantage, by providing time to adjust to political ideas that ran counter to his own and that he would in all likelihood have opposed if present," Ellis writes.[28] In response to Madison's letter, Jefferson wrote:

> *I like the general idea of framing a government, which would go on of itself, peaceably without needing continual recurrence to the State legislature. I like the organization of the government into legislative, judiciary, and executive. I like the power given the legislature to levy taxes, and for that reason solely, I approve of the greater House being chosen by the people directly.*[29]

But he was also candid with his friend, pointing out what he considered to be flaws in the document. Most importantly was "the omission of a bill of rights," that provided for "freedom of religion, freedom of the press," and other core rights. Despite Madison's explanation, he still struggled with the lack of term limits for the president, and feared too powerful a government. "I own, I am not a friend to a very energetic government. It is always oppressive." And he had a much more optimistic view of the role of majority rule than Madison, telling him "peace is best preserved by giving...information to the people," rather than "energy to the government." Given his belief that the "will of the majority should prevail," he stated that he would support the proposed Constitution if the people approved it. Jefferson's thinking on the best approach for implementing the Constitution would continue to evolve during the spring of 1788. He first thought that once nine states had ratified the document, "that the others might, by holding off, produce the necessary amendments." But after he learned of Massachusetts' decision to pursue recommended amendments, he decided that was the preferred course. Jefferson's views were so mixed and evolving that both sides in the Virginia ratifying convention attempted to claim him, according to historian Lance Banning.[30]

Madison had initially resisted running as a delegate for the Virginia ratifying convention, since he thought it was wrong for those who had drafted the Constitution to sit in judgment of it. This decision seemed wise at first, as the document met with significant support in Virginia, to the point where Mason's opposition made it impossible for him to be selected as a delegate from his home County of Fairfax. But opposition soon jelled around the protests of Richard Henry Lee, Mason, and, most importantly, Patrick Henry. By November of 1787, Madison's family, friends, and supporters were urging him to return home and run for election as a delegate. Madison hated campaigning for office, which he considered part of "the vicious arts" of politics. He remembered all too well his first run for office, when his unwillingness to buy drinks for the electorate cost him the race.[31]

Both Washington and Edmund Randolph urged Madison to return home before the election for delegates to the convention, which was to be held in March 1788. Madison had been lobbying Randolph to support the Constitution, and it must have been heartening for him to be coaxed by Randolph "not to hazard [his election] by being absent at the time." In an exchange of letters with Randolph, Madison first mentioned that as a way to form "a coalition of the real Federalists," he would be willing to support "recommendatory alterations" along the same lines Massachusetts had followed, but he was still unalterably opposed to a second convention. Madison also expressed the same sentiment to an influential Baptist preacher, James Leland, who had expressed opposition to the Constitution because it did not protect freedom of religion. "In return for Leland's promise to withdraw his objections, Madison...would support a bill of rights...after its ratification," his biographer Ralph Ketchum writes. While Madison still personally considered a bill of rights unnecessary, he was also a practical politician willing to support amendments to the document, if such a position would win him the support of Randolph and the religious community in Virginia.[32]

On a cold and windy day at the end of March, Madison stood before a group of voters to ask for their support in selecting him to serve at the convention. For almost two hours, he "addressed himself in a speech to the people in defence of the new Constitution, and there appeared much satisfaction," according to one observer. Another said that Madison "convinced a majority that he had acted as he ought & that the Constitution ought to be adopted." He was easily elected, and must have felt great satisfaction that one of those he defeated was Charles Porter, the man who had beaten him for a seat in the Virginia legislature in 1777, by plying the voters with liquor.[33]

The Virginia convention opened on June 2. Madison did not arrive until that evening, having assumed that, just as with the Federal Convention, this one would start late. With 170 delegates, and a packed house of spectators, the convention had been forced to move from the State House in Richmond to the Quesnay Academy across the street. As the convention opened, eight other states had ratified, and before the convention ended, New Hampshire would make it nine. Even though the union would now be formed, if ratification failed in Virginia, New York would likely follow suit, and the experiment in nationhood would collapse.

As the convention began, the outcome was too close to call. As in other states, the rural areas tended to oppose the Constitution, while those sections of the state that had been settled the longest and where commercial interests resided tended to be Federalists. Many thought the result would hinge on the votes of the delegates from Kentucky, which was still a part of Virginia. Those delegates worried that the new national government might agree to close the Mississippi River, an issue Madison tried to assure them was untrue.[34]

No other state could claim the galaxy of stars that attended the Virginia convention, even with the absence of Washington and Jefferson. Edmund Pendleton, who served in the equivalent role of chief justice of the Supreme Court, was chosen to chair the meeting. Not only were Madison, Mason, Henry and Randolph elected as delegates, but so was the future fifth president of the United States, James Monroe, and John Marshall, the second chief justice of the Supreme Court. But this would largely be a battle between Henry and Madison, with Randolph backing Madison when he surprisingly announced his support for the Constitution on June 6, four days after the convention opened. Both Madison and Washington had urged Randolph to change his position, but the outcome in the other state conventions was what finally swayed him. Since eight other states had already ratified, Randolph no longer believed it would serve Virginia's interests to stay outside the union.

"I believe, that as sure as there is a God in Heaven, our safety, our political happiness and existence, depend on the Union of the States," Randolph told the convention.[35]

Madison and Henry made quite a contrasting pair. Ellis aptly frames their styles as follows:

> *Henry was animated, passionate, spoke without notes, and combined the appearance of an actor on the stage and an evangelical minister at the pulpit. Madison spoke calmly, in a voice so low that the stenographer complained he could not catch his every word. He held his hat in one hand, which contained notes that he consulted like a professor delivering an academic lecture. But as a result his arguments arrived without flourish or affectation, in a sense the more impressive because of their austerity.*[36]

On the second day of the convention, Mason proposed they go line by line through the Constitution, in order to avoid a vote until the opponents had enough support to ensure that amendments would be approved to the document. Madison agreed immediately, in part because he wanted to act in a conciliatory manner, and in part, because he felt this would work to his advantage. Henry almost immediately broke the agreement, and his speeches over the course of the next three weeks reflected a broad based attack on the Constitution, rather than a limited critique of specific provisions. Indeed, one of the problems the Antifederalists faced in Virginia was that Mason and Henry operated at cross-purposes with one another. Mason wanted to elicit support for amendments, while Henry preferred to reject the Constitution outright. Madison framed their differences in a letter to Washington when he wrote that the two "made a lame figure & appeared to take different and awkward ground."[37]

Henry's salvos were a litany of all of the charges that the Anti-federalists had leveled against the supporters of the Constitution, as explored in the previous chapter, including:[38]

- There was no crisis in the affairs of the Confederacy. The nation was at peace and prosperity was returning to Virginia.
- The Convention had exceeded its authority, and rather than proposing a whole new government, they should have proposed amendments to the Articles of Confederation.
- The Constitution would create a consolidated government that would act directly on the people, destroy the states, and endanger the liberty that the public enjoyed.

As he spoke, Henry assumed the mantle for all of those who believed that a strong central government would undo all that had been gained since the revolution, that such a government would violate the true spirit of 1776, in which liberty needed to be protected from a distant central government. "If we admit this consolidated government, it will be because we like a great, splendid one," he charged. Those who supported the Constitution were after a "mighty empire" with an "army, and a navy, and a number of things. When the American spirit was in its youth, the language of America was different; liberty, sir, was the primary object."[39]

Echoing the views of Montesquieu, Henry alleged that the government would be unresponsive to the people, since a republic could only survive in a small and homogenous community. "There never was a government over a very extensive country without destroying the liberties of the people," he claimed, "popular government can only exist in small territories." Although Henry and Mason were working at cross-purposes with each other, some of Mason's specific comments helped to build support for Henry's more general attacks. This included Mason's criticism of the power of direct taxation, which would ultimately make the central government supreme and destroy the division of power between the states and the federal government. "These two concurrent powers cannot exist long together; the one will destroy the other; the general government being paramount to, and in every respect more powerful than the state governments, the latter must give way," in Mason's view. He also believed that the House of Representatives was too small and could not adequately represent the people. "Sixty-five members cannot possibly know the situation and circumstances of all the inhabitants of this immense continent," Mason argued. Given the small size of the House, and the even smaller size of the Senate, the new central government would be a bastion for the "natural aristocracy." Washington, from his vantage point at Mount Vernon, observed that it was "a little strange that the men of large property in the South should be more afraid that the constitution should produce an aristocracy or a monarchy than the genuine democratical people of the east," in what Ron Chernow calls a veiled criticism of slavery in the South.[40]

The Federalists decided that Randolph would be the first one to respond to Henry. Randolph, who was seventeen years younger than Henry, reminded the delegates that he too was "a child of the revolution." He was claiming the mantle of the revolutionary era, not only for the younger generation that he and Madison represented, but also for the Constitution as a plan of government that would fulfill, rather than endanger, the promises of 1776. Both he and Madison disclaimed that the Federalists wanted to fashion an empire. "National splendor and glory are not our objects," Madison argued, but rather their goal was to provide for security and happiness at home, and to be viewed as "respectable abroad."[41]

Henry's claim that the Federalists were out to destroy liberty must have greatly irritated Madison, since he believed that a stronger central government would protect liberty. Madison challenged his opponents to provide specific examples to support their claims "that this Constitution ought to be rejected, because it endangered the public liberty… Let the dangers which this system is supposed to be replete with be clearly pointed out." If there were powers being given to the Congress that were "dangerous and unnecessary," then those should be "plainly demonstrated," but the convention should not be "satisfied with general assertions of dangers, without examination." To Madison, the real threat to liberty was a feeble federal government, which was the bane of confederacies throughout history. He framed his point to the delegates with this query: "Does not the history of confederacies coincide with the lessons drawn from our own experience?"[42]

Madison then went on to describe those experiences. Foreign governments would not enter into treaties with the United States because they considered its government feeble and untrustworthy. The country could not pay its debts, and the "government was totally destitute of the means to protect itself or its members." Hostility between the states, and the threats from foreign nations, would eventually lead to disunion and the formation of numerous smaller confederations, each of which would have its own army and interests to protect. Madison argued that, "the same causes which have rendered the old world the theatre of incessant wars and have banished liberty from the face of it, would soon produce the same effects here." The dangers of continual wars would crush liberty "between standing armies and perpetual taxes," if the union under the Constitution were to fail. Far from threatening liberty, the Constitution would create a government that would protect it and the nation's people.[43]

After having lost the battle to create an even stronger national government at the Philadelphia Convention, Madison next countered the charge that the Constitution created a consolidated government that would place all power in the hands of a distant federal government and destroy the states. This new and "unprecedented" form of government stood by itself. "In some respects it is a Government of a federal nature; in others it is of a consolidated nature," Madison pointed out. Ultimately, it derived its power from the people, but the people acting as "thirteen sovereignties." Echoing James Wilson, he indicated that the Senate would represent the states, and that electors selected by the states would chose the president. As part of the "mixed nature" of the government, the people would directly elect the members of the House of Representatives.[44] Although Madison intended the new federal government to be in a better position to control majority factions than the states had been, he knew that the bedrock of any democratic republic was the people.

> *But I go on this great republican principle: that the people will have virtue and intelligence to select men of virtue and wisdom. Is there no virtue among us? If there be not, we are in a wretched situation. No theoretical checks, no form of government, can render us secure. To suppose that any form of government will secure liberty or happiness without any virtue in the people is a chimerical idea.*[45]

As part of the debate on taxation, Mason had proposed an amendment to the Constitution under which the federal government would first requisition funds from the states, and only if they did not pay would the federal government be authorized to levy taxes directly on the people. Randolph ridiculed the proposal, stating that it would be no more successful than the current scheme laid out by the Articles of Confederation, which had left the central government bankrupt. He asked what the result would be if state officials took the same approach with local governments, concluding, "You would be laughed at for your folly." No one paid taxes voluntarily, Randolph argued. Supporters of the Constitution, using the same arguments as the Massachusetts Federalists, claimed that taxes on imports would normally be sufficient, and that it would only be during times of war or emergencies that direct taxes would be needed so that the government would have the "full scope and complete command over the resources of the nation," in order to "borrow with ease," since creditors would know they would be repaid. Left unsaid was had the central government had this power during the war with England, it may have avoided much of the inflationary pressures that had occurred, when the greenback had become worthless. The Federalists were of one mind that no government could be sovereign without the power to tax, that this was "essential to the very existence of the union."[46]

Surprisingly, Madison was not the one who presented a response to the charge that the United States was too large to be a republic. Perhaps this was because he fell ill during the convention with what he referred to as a "bilious attack," which caused him to miss several days. Ever since his youth, Madison had suffered from numerous illnesses. He preferred to work from behind the scenes, and at other times during his life, had been shielded from the limelight by men like Jefferson and Washington. But during the Virginia ratifying convention, he was front and center in the battle with Henry and the Antifederalists. Francis Corbin, John Marshall, and Randolph all took up the slack, making the arguments that Madison, had he been there, may well have made.

Corbin referred to the Antifederalists as putting forward an "old worn out idea." Marshall indicated that the concept that a republic could only exist over a small territory was based on a review of countries "where representation did not exist" and therefore did not apply to the United States. Corbin pointed out that under the Antifederalists' argument, only Delaware and Rhode Island would qualify as a republic, making it an absurd argument belied "by our own experience," since even Virginia would not qualify.[47]

Many of the delegates to the convention were concerned that the North would dominate the new central government and pass laws that were inimical to the interests of Virginia and the South. They pointed to the proposed Jay Treaty of 1786, which would block navigation of the Mississippi for a generation in return for an opening of trade with Spain, as an example of the types of policies that northern politicians would pursue to the detriment of the South. This was a particular sore point for the Kentucky delegates, which was not yet a state, who needed access to the Mississippi to trade for goods they needed. "Accordingly, though most Virginia politicians readily conceded the necessity for federal reform," Banning writes, "most also wanted constitutional amendments that would guarantee additional protection for their state, along with additional protection for the people's unsurrendered rights." These amendments included a bill of rights plus changes to the structure of, and additional limitations on the power of, the federal government to regulate trade and implement navigation acts.[48]

The only way Virginia would ratify was with amendments, and the only question would be whether the amendments would be in the form of recommendations to the new Congress, or whether they would be a mandatory requirement under which the state would stay outside of the union until the amendments were added to the Constitution. By June 24, Mason had finally convinced Henry to support his position, and together they proposed forty amendments that included a bill of rights and changes that would shift power back to the states. Henry thought it was lunacy to ratify the Constitution without the amendments, which would then need to go back for approval by the other states before Virginia would join the union. Both Madison and Randolph warned that such a process would in all likelihood lead to chaos. Each of the states, even those that had already ratified, would need to hold new conventions and approve all forty amendments before Virginia would ratify. Achieving consensus would be impossible and the other states would be placed in a position of having "to gratify Virginia" so that she would join the new nation. Randolph told the convention that such a move was "another name for rejection" of the Constitution, and Madison added that it risked "losing the union."[49]

The Federalist arguments swayed enough votes, with a majority having decided that the interests of Virginia were "inseparable from the perpetuation of the Union," according to Maier. Henry's proposal was defeated on an extremely close vote, 88-80. Virginia then ratified the Constitution, with its forty proposed amendments, 89-79. Madison found many of the amendments "highly objectionable," especially "an article prohibiting direct taxes where effectual laws shall be passed by the States for the purpose." He had tried to explain why such a law would be detrimental to the new federal government, but "it was impossible to prevent this error." At least the amendments were not mandatory. But, true to his word, Madison would later do everything in his power to see that a bill of rights was added to the Constitution, even though he still thought they were unnecessary. Henry, although he would resent Madison for his loss and later exact a political cost, would reject attempts by others to undermine the Constitution. In the future, he chose to work "to retrieve the loss of liberty and remove the defects of that system in a constitutional way."[50]

Madison, who had done more than any other single person to bring about the design and ratification of the Constitution, was exhausted. He had planned to return to New York immediately, but Washington convinced his young friend to take some time off and spend it at Mount Vernon as his guest. "Moderate exercise, and books occasionally with mind unbent, will be your best restoratives," he wrote to Madison, who took him up on his offer.[51]

New York: The Last Major Challenge

As the New York ratifying convention opened in Poughkeepsie on June 17, the Federalists were in trouble. Under the leadership of Governor George Clinton, opponents of the proposed Constitution outnumbered the supporters 46-19, although not all of the forty-six were firmly in the Antifederalists' camp. Clinton was a populist politician embraced by the small yeoman farmers of upstate New York, which was where the strength of the Antifederalist movement was located. He stood unalterably opposed to the leading patrician families in the state, including the Schuylers. Since Hamilton had married into the Schuyler clan, this placed him at odds with Clinton. Although the two had gotten along well during the Revolutionary War, Hamilton had gradually come to see Clinton as the type of politician he despised, a man who manipulated the masses for his own well-being. "George Clinton's friends considered him a man of the people; his enemies saw him as a demagogue," writes his biographer John Kaminski. Still, Clinton was a natural leader who drew men to him. Washington considered him a friend, despite their disagreement over the Constitution. Whereas Washington's relationship with Mason was never the same after they parted ways over ratification, Washington remained friends with Clinton.[52]

Hamilton knew that ratifying the Constitution in New York was tied to success in Virginia and New Hampshire. "Our only chance will be the previous ratification by nine states, which may shake the firmness of [Clinton's] followers," he wrote to Madison. To this end, he proposed that they debate the Constitution clause by clause. Not only would this buy time for Virginia and New Hampshire to act, but no person (other than perhaps Madison) was in a better position to debate the fine nuances of the document. The debate that occurred from June 17 until July 2 would feature Hamilton and his Antifederalist opponent Melancton Smith, who had written under the name of the "Federal Farmer." Both sides had other able speakers, including John Jay for the Federalists and John Lansing for the Antifederalists. Clinton was elected as the chairman, which somewhat limited his ability to engage in the debate.[53]

The criticisms leveled by the Antifederalists covered familiar ground. These included:[54]

- Whether the Articles of Confederation should have been amended to add powers to the central government, instead of writing a whole new form of government;
- That the House of Representatives was too small to truly represent the people, and that it and the Senate would be controlled by a natural aristocracy that would result in a "government of oppression";
- That the power to levy direct taxes should be limited only to those circumstances where a state does not first pay its requisitions.

One revealing moment occurred when Governor Clinton indicated that the United States was so large and diverse that no general free government can suit "all of the states." Hamilton's response echoed the sentiments which Jay had written in *Federalist* No. 2, that indeed America was one nation. "From New Hampshire to Georgia, the people of America are as uniform in their interests and manners as those of any established in Europe," Hamilton told the convention. What was lacking was a government capable of ruling this newly emerging nation.[55]

The debate went on until July 2, when word arrived that Virginia had ratified the Constitution. At that point, the Federalists abandoned the debate and allowed the other side to put forward a dizzying array of amendments, which amounted to a complete rewriting of the Constitution. But the Antifederalists were in a bind, since they lacked the votes to either reject the Constitution outright, as some of their members wanted, or to ratify with amendments. Melancton Smith was in the latter group. He concluded that since ten states had already ratified, the ground had "totally shifted." Smith realized that the only way to make changes to the Constitution was as a part of the new government that was to be formed. The lack of unity among the Antifederalists forced Smith and the other moderates to enter into negotiations with the Federalists over the terms and conditions under which amendments would be approved.[56]

John Lansing, who had attended the Convention in Philadelphia and left early due to his opposition to the direction the delegates were heading, organized the fifty-five amendments that the Antifederalists had generated into three distinct categories: "explanatory," "conditional," and "recommendatory." The Federalists were willing to accept the explanatory and the recommendatory amendments, since those largely dealt with a bill of rights, and most Federalists by now realized that these were likely going to be added to the Constitution. But they firmly rejected any conditional amendments. Jay pointed out that if New York did not ratify without conditions, it could have no input into proposing amendments as part of the new government. Robert Livingston followed this with an implied threat that the southern part of the state, including New York City, might secede from New York in order to join the union. The Antifederalists then attempted a different tactic, under which New York would withdraw from the union if a second convention were not organized within two years of ratification. But Hamilton was ready with a reply from Madison, whose opinion he had sought on this matter. Madison responded that "such a conditional ratification would not make New York a member of the Union. The Constitution requires an adoption *in toto* and forever."[57]

It would take another two weeks of debate between the two sides, but the basic bargain would trade unconditional ratification for a proposal that a second convention would be called under Article V of the Constitution. Smith was able to engineer a change in the wording of the ratification motion, eliminating the words "on the express condition," and replacing them with the wording "in confidence that" the Congress would assent to New York's interpretation of the document and that a second convention would be called. This minor wording change transformed the action of the convention from a mandatory to a discretionary one for the new Congress. By the razor thin margin of three votes, 30-27, New York ratified the Constitution. Both Jay and Hamilton signed a circular letter that was to be sent to the states requesting that a second convention be called.[58]

Madison was unhappy with the outcome in New York, and was unable to grasp that his ally Hamilton had supported the circular letter as the price they had to pay to get New York to ratify the Constitution. He went so far as to argue that it would have been better had the state rejected the Constitution, since such an outcome "would have necessarily been followed by a speedy reconsideration of the subject." Washington was much more understanding, writing to Jay that "considering the great majority that appeared to cling together in the Convention…I did not, I confess, see how it could be avoided." Madison's concerns would prove unfounded, as within the next year only New York and Virginia would pass resolutions for a second convention, although more states may have joined them had Madison not led the effort in the new Congress to pass the first ten amendments.[59]

It would take a second convention, but North Carolina would finally ratify the Constitution in November 1789. Rhode Island held out until May 1790, when it ratified it by two votes. By then, Washington had taken the oath of office as President. The thirteen original colonies that had fought and defeated the British had formed a new and stronger national union.

The Federalists had achieved a great victory, in part by designing a new, extra-legal approach for ratification that went around the rules established under the Articles of Confederation. As the process unfolded in the individual ratifying conventions, the Federalists' tactics also evolved, largely based on necessity. Pennsylvania had used a rushed approach that treated their opponents with disdain. In Massachusetts, Virginia, and New York, the Constitution was given a full and fair hearing, and the Antifederalists were treated with the respect they deserved as the loyal opposition. The Federalists, in part, were forced to change tactics due to the strength of the opposition in those states. As the late Robert A. Goldwin pointed out, "a change of just eighteen delegate votes" in those states would have either led to the defeat of the

Constitution, or at least have required amendments to the document as a condition of ratification. The process itself, and the compromises needed to achieve victory, would allow the Antifederalists to also leave a lasting mark on the Constitution. They had proposed a series of amendments, many of which would never be implemented because they would have reduced the power of the federal government over such vital issues as taxation and commerce. But the most frequently requested changes dealt with a bill of rights, and these amendments would ultimately strengthen and add legitimacy to the Constitution. The ratification process proved that no group of men, even the Framers, held a monopoly on wisdom or good ideas. Madison would come to realize this was the case, and that if the new Constitution were to long endure, they would need to add amendments.[60]

Endnotes

1 Wood, *Creation*, p. 484; Maier, *Ratification*, p. 72-73; Ferling, p. 295

2 Beeman, p. 372; Rakove, *Original Meanings*, p. 108

3 Rakove, *Original Meanings*, p. 109-110; Beeman, p. 372

4 Beeman, p. 376-377; Rakove, *Original Meanings*, p. 110; Maier *Ratification*, p. 57-64 provides the most detailed account of the incident.

5 Rakove, *Original Meanings*, p. 111; Beeman, p. 381; Maier *Ratification*, p. 105

6 Maier, *Ratification*, p. 109 and p. 114; Wood, *Creation*, p. 530

7 Maier, *Ratification*, p. 108

8 Maier, *Ratification*, p. 118-120

9 Rossiter, p. 286; Bowen, p. 277

10 Beeman, p. 384-385

11 Beeman, p. 386; Maier, p. 166

12 Beeman, p. 387

13 Maier *Ratification*, p. 159

14 Maier *Ratification*, p. 163-165

15 McCullough, p. 380-381

16 Maier, *Ratification*, p. 168-169

17 Maier, *Ratification*, p. 170-180

18 Maier, *Ratification*, p. 192

19 Beeman, p. 388-390; Rakove, *Original Meanings*, p. 120; Maier, *Ratification*, p. 207

20 Beeman, p. 390; Maier, *Ratification*, p. 209-210

21 Beeman, p. 391-395

22 Chernow, *Washington*, p. 542-543; Flexner, p. 139-150

23 Flexner, p. 139-140

24 Chernow, *Washington*, p. 544; Ellis, *His Excellency*, p. 180-181

25 Ellis, *American Sphinx*, p. 120; Madison letter of March 19, 1787 to Jefferson, retrieved February 5, 2014 from http://founders.archives.gov/documents/jefferson/01-02-0227 ; Jefferson letter to Madison of June 20, 1787 in Koch and Peden, p. 422-423

26 Meacham, *Thomas Jefferson*, p. 213; Jefferson letter to Adams of November 13, 1787 in Koch and Peden, p. 435-436

27 Madison letter of October 24, 1787 to Jefferson, retrieved February 5, 2014 from http://press-pubs.uchicago.edu/founders/documents/v1ch7s22.html

28 Ellis, *American Sphinx*, p. 121

29 Jefferson letter to Madison of December 20, 1787, p. 436-437

30 Jefferson letter to Madison of December 20, 1787, p. 440-441 ;and Jefferson letter to Carrington of May 27, 1788, p. 446; Lance Banning, *The Sacred Fire of Liberty: James Madison & the Founding of the Federal Republic*, (Ithaca, 1995), p. 234

31 Banning, p. 235; Ketchum, p. 250

32 Banning, p. 236; Ketchum, p. 251

33 Ketchum, p. 251; Richard Labunski, *James Madison and the Struggle for the Bill of Rights*, (New York, 2006), p. 47

34 Banning, p. 234-236; Beeman, p. 396

35 Labunski, p. 87

36 Ellis, *American Creation*, p. 120

37 Banning, p. 237; Ketchum, p. 254; Rakove, *Original Meanings*, p. 123

38 The best summaries of Henry's views are in Ellis, *American Creation*, p. 121-122 and Banning, p. 238-242

39 Banning, p. 239

40 Banning, p. 242-43; Chernow, *Washington*, p. 545

41 Maier, *Ratification*, p. 267-268

42 Labunski, p. 89-90; Ellis, *American Creation*, p. 122-123

43 Banning, p. 248-249

44 Ellis, *American Creation*, p. 123; Maier, *Ratification*, p. 269-270

45 Quoted from Banning, p. 247

46 Maier, *Ratification*, p. 272

47 Maier, *Ratification*, p. 270-271

48 Banning, p. 258

49 Rakove, *Original Meanings*, p. 124; Banning, p. 258-259

50 Maier, *Ratification*, p. 309; Banning, p. 264

51 Maier, *Ratification*, p. 318

52 Beeman, p. 401; Chernow, *Hamilton*, p. 220-221; Maier, *Ratification*, p. 321

53 Chernow, *Hamilton*, p. 262; Beeman, p. 401

54 Maier, *Ratification*, p. 351-369 has the complete discussion of the debate over the two week period and the response of the Federalists.

55 Chernow, *Hamilton*, p. 265

56 Maier, *Ratification*, p. 383; Rakove, *Original Meanings*, p. 125

57 Maier, *Ratification*, p. 380-381; Rakove, *Original Meanings*, p. 125-126; Robert A. Goldwin, *From Parchment to Power: How James Madison Used the Bill of Rights to Save the Constitution*, (Washington, 1997), p. 45

58 Rakove, *Original Meanings*, p. 126-127

59 Rakove, *Original Meanings*, p. 127; Goldwin, p. 47

60 Goldwin, p. 47-48

Chapter 12

The Bill of Rights / July 1789 to December 1791

"Congress shall make no law..."
– First Amendment –

National Public Radio personality Peter Sagal produced a PBS series on the Constitution in 2013. In the second installment, he said, "Ask anybody on the street about the meaning of the Constitution and they will give you a one word answer: freedom." But the Constitution does not mention the word freedom anywhere. The first ten amendments, known as the Bill of Rights, rectified this problem. For many Americans, the protections contained in the Bill of Rights, including freedom of speech, religion, and press; the right to bear arms; the provision for jury trials; and other protections of civil liberties, are the very heart of the American Constitution.

Madison Changes His Mind on a Bill of Rights

James Madison had gradually changed his mind. Originally opposed to adding an enumeration of rights to the Constitution, Madison remained silent when George Mason proposed one at the end of the Federal Convention. During the Virginia ratification process, he had acquiesced to the need for amendments, but only after the Constitution was approved. At that point, he was still personally opposed to such amendments, largely because he believed they would be ineffective in protecting rights. But in June of 1789, Madison proposed a series of amendments to the Constitution in the first Congress, most of which dealt with rights.

Madison's evolving views on the subject resulted from several factors. Jefferson's insistence on the need for a bill of rights played a part, as did practical politics. To get elected to the House of Representatives, Madison promised his constituents he would support a bill of rights. Another part of his support was based on his view of the dangers of a second Constitutional Convention, which he hoped to forestall by offering amendments to the Constitution. He knew the Antifederalists would use a second convention not just to add an enumeration of rights, but to weaken the federal government. Most importantly, Madison became a fervent supporter of adding a bill of rights because he saw it as a way to create national unity. The struggle for ratification had been divisive, and he knew that the union would not long endure if half of the people opposed it.

Just as Jefferson was convinced to support the Constitution by Madison, so Jefferson's view on the need for a bill of rights influenced Madison. In response to Madison's lengthy letter describing the Constitution, Jefferson had responded with his overall support for the new government in his December 1787 letter, but he remained disappointed in the lack of a bill of rights. "Let me add that a bill of rights is what the people are entitled to against every government on earth, general or particular, and what no just government should refuse, or rest on inference," Jefferson wrote to Madison. It wasn't that Madison was opposed to protecting individual rights, far from it. He had, from an early age, taken a great interest in protecting the rights of conscience, especially freedom of religion, and was "in favor of liberty both civil and religious," as he wrote in his autobiography. In 1776, he had strengthened the provisions related to freedom of religion in Virginia's Declaration of Rights, and had worked with Jefferson on adopting a Bill for Religious Rights and on eliminating Anglicanism as the official state religion in 1779. Almost every element of his thinking on constitutional changes prior to and during the Federal Convention had focused in one way or another on structuring government in such a way as to protect the rights of the minority from the whims of an overbearing majority. "His concern about the security of private rights was rooted in a palpable fear that economic legislation was jeopardizing fundamental rights of property" through paper money and debtor relief schemes, according to Rakove.[1] Madison explained his thinking on the subject in his October 17, 1788 letter to Jefferson. "My own opinion has always been in favor of a bill of rights; provided it be so framed as not to imply powers not meant to be included in the enumeration," a statement some historians have called disingenuous, given his history on the subject. Madison immediately qualified this remark, stating that he never "thought the omission a material defect" but that he was willing to support the inclusion of a bill of rights because it was "anxiously desired by others." His real concern was that "experience proves the inefficacy of a bill of rights" when it is most needed. "Repeated violations of these parchment barriers have been committed by overbearing majorities in every State." Madison drew a distinction for Jefferson on the difference between monarchical governments and a republic. In a monarchy, power is controlled by one person, and a bill of rights can act as a barrier to violations of individual rights. But in a republic, a majority of the people rule, and it is from this source that the violation of individual rights may arise. "Wherever the real power in a Government lies, there is the danger of oppression. In our Governments the real power lies in the majority of the Community, and the invasion of private rights is *chiefly* to be apprehended, not from the acts of Government contrary to the sense of its constituents, but from acts in which the Government is the mere instrument of the major number of the constituents." In other words, the government may deny an individual or a minority its rights, not because governmental representatives are scheming to increase their power, but because they are acting on behalf of a majority of their constituents. Given this, Madison thought a bill of rights would be nothing more than a "paper barrier" that would be "least effective when most needed."[2]

Yet, Madison was also beginning to see that a bill of rights could have value. In his letter to Jefferson, he indicated that, over time, citizens would come to value "the political truths" contained in such a statement. A bill of rights could "counteract the impulses of interest and passion" that motivated much of political activity. The idea that a bill of rights could cause people to put aside their own self-interest to support more enduring principles and come to value the protection of minority rights seems to contradict much of Madison's concerns with the way in which overbearing majorities may act. But it is also the key to his conversion on the need for a bill of rights. Madison's argument was that as people come to value the rights included in the Constitution, they will also defend them. Robert A. Goldwin, in his book on Madison and the bill of rights, describes how this works in our own time:

> *Ordinary citizens [will] say to themselves... "Even if that person's speech, book, or religious doctrine is obnoxious to me and to the majority of my fellow-citizens throughout the nation...the Constitution forbids us, even though we are an overwhelming majority, from silencing him. And I am for the Constitution, first and above all else."*[3]

Of course, there have been times when "parchment barriers" did not act to constrain a majority. Madison also admitted to Jefferson that in rare circumstances government itself, or "a succession of artful and ambitious rulers" could become oppressive, although he saw "no tendency in our governments on that side," a perspective that would prove false in the future.[4]

Madison's campaign for election to the House of Representatives in the winter of 1789 contributed to his conversion on the need for a bill of rights, especially the input he received from the public on their fears and concerns for the new and more powerful central government. Although he abhorred campaigning for political office, Madison realized his active participation was needed to "repel the multiplied falsehoods which circulated" about him. Patrick Henry, from his position in the legislature, made sure that Madison was not appointed to the Senate. Two other Antifederalists, Richard Henry Lee and William Grayson, were instead elected by the legislature, with Madison finishing a close third. Henry then got the legislature to draw the boundaries of the congressional district that Madison would need to run in, which included his home of Orange County, to include several counties that had been opposed to the Constitution. The legislature also added a provision requiring residency in the district for twelve months prior to the election, thus making it difficult for Madison to run in another district.[5]

The Antifederalists selected James Monroe, a formidable candidate, to run against Madison. Monroe was a war hero who crossed the Delaware with Washington during the battle of Trenton, where he was seriously wounded. "At slightly over six feet with broad shoulders and a large frame, Monroe looked the part of a Virginia statesmen," writes political scientist Richard Labunski. Monroe and Madison had been friends for a long time, and had invested together in western lands. Traveling together during a very cold and snowy winter in Virginia, Madison and Monroe debated the issues at joint appearances. One of those issues was whether the Constitution would be amended. Madison found he had to counteract Antifederalist charges that he "did not think that a single letter of [the Constitution] would admit of a change."[6]

In response, Madison issued a series of letters, many of which were published in newspapers in Virginia, in which he pledged his support for a bill of rights. "Amendments, if pursued with proper moderation and in a proper mode, will not only be safe, but may serve the double purpose of satisfying minds of well-meaning opponents and of providing additional guards in favor of liberty," he wrote. He was especially in favor of amendments that would protect "essential rights, particularly the rights of conscience in the fullest latitude, the freedom of the press, trials by jury, security against general warrants, etc." Madison had become aware, based on his travels around the district, that opposition to the Constitution was widespread among the public. "He had learned from countless face-to-face discussions in his counties that anxieties about the new regime were not confined to several dozen hopelessly recalcitrant opponents of the Constitution; they were widely shared among the body of the freemen," writes Lance Banning. The public's concerns were not focused on major structural changes to the government or the reduction of federal power, unlike the position taken by the Antifederalist leaders, but rather were centered on the need to protect individual rights. "The great mass of the people who opposed it, disliked it because it did not contain effectual provisions against encroachments on particular rights," observed Madison. The inclusion of a bill of rights would establish the "Constitution as the focus of national unity, to which the whole community, regardless of faction, could pledge its allegiance."[7]

Madison won the seat in the House by a margin of 336 votes out of 2,280 cast. In his home county of Orange, Madison received 216 votes to only nine for Monroe, which helped push him over the top. Monroe also had his strongholds, including his home in Spotsylvania and Amherst County, where he won by a combined 175 votes. Despite the close-fought election, Madison and Monroe maintained their friendship. Writing to Jefferson, Madison indicated he and Monroe were able to keep their political and personal views separate, which "saved our friendship from the smallest diminution."[8]

Some thought Madison's conversion on the bill or rights was simply political expediency. Robert Morris said Madison "got frightened in Virginia and wrote a Book," a reference to the letters he had written. While Madison had strong political reasons to change his mind, he also had undergone a true conversion on the need for a bill of rights. The best evidence for this was how doggedly he worked to see a bill of rights added to the Constitution, especially given the opposition he faced from both his friends on the Federalist side and his enemies among the Antifederalists.

Introducing the Bill of Rights

Implementing a new government was a daunting task. When the first session of Congress opened on April 1, 1789 the representatives first had to determine the rules under which they would operate. Some of the most pressing needs facing the new nation were the establishment of a revenue system so the government could pay its bills; the creation of the various offices needed to form a cabinet in the executive branch; and the creation of a federal judiciary, along with the fashioning of a set of federal laws. Given this workload, Madison waited until May 4 before he announced that he soon planned to introduce amendments to the Constitution. It was no coincidence that the next day, Theodoric Bland, an ally of Patrick Henry, introduced Virginia's petition for a second convention. On May 6, the representative from New York presented a similar petition. Madison was able to convince his fellow congressmen that they had no power to act on the petitions, since the Constitution required that two-thirds of the states needed to request a second convention, and then one would be held. "The best mode was to let it [the petition] lie upon the table till a sufficient number of applications appeared," Madison told the House.[9]

He was forced to wait another week beyond his intended date, but finally on June 8, he asked the House to go into a Committee of the Whole to consider amendments to the Constitution. His motion immediately caused controversy. The Antifederalists assumed that his proposed amendments would not create the changes they wanted in the new government, changes that would weaken the power of the federal government and return that power to the states. But Madison found resistance from the Federalists as well. William Smith of South Carolina, James Jackson of Georgia, and Benjamin Goodhue of Massachusetts all expressed reservations that a debate over a bill of rights would divert their attention from more pressing matters. They were also reticent to amend the Constitution before it was implemented. Smith said, "It must appear extremely impolitic to go into the consideration of amending the Government before it is organized, before it has begun to operate." He also expressed a concern that they needed to pass the revenue system before undertaking other business. Jackson argued that the Constitution should "have a fair trial; let it be examined by experience, discover by that test what the errors are, and then talk of amending." Banning writes that the source of the resistance of the Federalists was rooted in their sense that "Madison was asking them to sacrifice their own opinions to the views of the opponents of the Constitution." They considered the amendments unnecessary and improper, much as Madison had previously believed.[10]

Madison's speech was designed to convince the Federalists that the amendments he was proposing were the best way to forestall more radical changes that would strike at the most important powers that had been delegated to the new federal government, including the power to tax and to control the military forces of the nation, which the Antifederalists hoped to undo through a second convention. Jackson had thrown Madison a lifeline, suggesting that a special select committee take up his proposed amendments. Madison accepted his proposal, and then plunged headlong into the rest of his speech.

He opened by telling his fellow representatives why he was introducing the amendments. The most important reason was to ensure unity among the people and to prove that those who supported the Constitution "were as sincerely devoted to liberty and a Republican Government as those who charged them with wishing the adoption of this constitution in order to lay the foundation of an aristocracy or despotism." During his campaign for the House, Madison had come to realize that "there is a great number of our constituents who are dissatisfied with [the constitution]." They were people who were "respectable for their talents and patriotism" who might "join their support to the cause of Federalism" if they could be convinced that "the great rights of mankind [are] secured under this constitution." In addition, by adding a bill of rights, the two states that stood outside the union, North Carolina and Rhode Island, might be encouraged to join "as soon as possible." Madison also reassured the Federalists that "if we can make the Constitution better in the opinion of those who are opposed to it, without weakening its frame or abridging its usefulness in the judgment of those who are attached to it, we act the part of wise and liberal men."[11]

Madison then turned to the changes he sought in the Constitution. He opened with two proposals that would not survive the legislative process. The first was that the Constitution should contain an additional declaration at the beginning:

> *...that all power is originally vested in, and consequently derived from, the people. That government is instituted and ought to be exercised for the benefit of the people; which consists in the enjoyment of life and liberty, with the right of acquiring and using and generally pursuing and obtaining happiness and safety.*

He concluded this declaration by stating that the people have the right to change their government "whenever it be found adverse or inadequate to the purposes of its institution." As Banning writes: "Adoption of this language would have meant, of course, that it would never have been doubted that the fundamental principles of the Declaration of Independence are part of the Federal Constitution."[12]

In his second proposal, Madison suggested integrating the amendments directly into the body of the Constitution, believing that if they added amendments at the end, they would be ignored. Roger Sherman opposed this recommendation because it would change the original words that the Framers had crafted in Philadelphia and might call into question the legitimacy of the ratification of the document. Ultimately, to garner the votes needed for passage Madison had to concede this point "to a few who knew their concurrence to be necessary to the dispatch if not the success of the business." Had his proposal succeeded, the way in which we view the "Bill of Rights," as a stand-alone statement of enduring political rights, may well have been buried within the body of the Constitution. "Today, far from being regarded as a mere footnote or afterthought to the Constitution, the amendments that make up the Bill of Rights hold near sacred status in America—perhaps revered even more than the original Constitution itself," Professor Richard Labunkski writes.[13]

Working from a starting point of over two hundred proposed amendments submitted by the various state ratifying conventions, Madison pared the list down to nineteen changes to be made to the Constitution. Two had to do with congressional salaries and the size of congressional districts, neither of which would ultimately be ratified by a sufficient number of states to become part of the Constitution. Two concerned general principles of government, and the balance covered basic rights. Most of Madison's proposed rights would ultimately be found in the amendments approved by Congress, although the wording was changed. The table below shows a list of the proposed rights that Madison introduced on June 8, and their location and wording in the final Bill of Rights.[14]

Madison's June 8 Proposals	Location in the Constitution
The civil rights of none shall be abridged on account of religious belief or worship, nor shall any national religion be established, nor shall the full and equal rights of conscience be in any manner, or any pretext, infringed.	*First Amendment* Congress shall make no law respecting an establishment of religion, or prohibiting the free exercise thereof; or abridging the freedom of speech, or of the press; or the right of the people peaceably to assemble, and to petition the Government for a redress of grievances.
The people shall not be deprived or abridged of their right to speak, to write, or to publish their sentiments; and the freedom of the press, as one of the great bulwarks of liberty, shall be inviolable.	*First Amendment*
The people shall not be restrained from peaceably assembling and consulting for their common good; nor from applying to the legislature by petitions, or remonstrances for redress of their grievances.	*First Amendment*
The right of the people to keep and bear arms shall not be infringed; a well armed, and well regulated militia being the best security of a free country: but no person religiously scrupulous of bearing arms, shall be compelled to render military service in person.	*Second Amendment* A well regulated Militia, being necessary to the security of a free State, the right of the people to keep and bear Arms, shall not be infringed.
No soldier shall in time of peace be quartered in any house without the consent of the owner; nor at any time, but in a manner warranted by law.	*Third Amendment* No Soldier shall, in time of peace be quartered in any house, without the consent of the Owner, nor in time of war, but in a manner to be prescribed by law.
No person shall be subject, except in cases of impeachment, to more than one punishment, or one trial for the same offence; nor shall be compelled to be a witness against himself; nor be deprived of life, liberty, or property without due process of law; nor be obliged to relinquish his property, where it may be necessary for public use, without a just compensation.	*Fifth Amendment* No person shall be held to answer for a capital, or otherwise infamous crime, unless on a presentment or indictment of a Grand Jury, except in cases arising in the land or naval forces, or in the Militia, when in actual service in time of War or public danger; nor shall any person be subject for the same offence to be twice put in jeopardy of life or limb; nor shall be compelled in any criminal case to be a witness against himself, nor be deprived of life, liberty, or property, without due process of law; nor shall private property be taken for public use, without just compensation.

Excessive bail shall not be required, nor excessive fines imposed, nor cruel and unusual punishments inflicted.	*Eighth Amendment* Excessive bail shall not be required, nor excessive fines imposed, nor cruel and unusual punishments inflicted.
The rights of the people to be secured in their persons, their houses, their papers, and their other property from all unreasonable searches and seizures, shall not be violated by warrants issued without probable cause, supported by oath or affirmation, or not particularly describing the places to be searched, or the persons or things to be seized.	*Fourth Amendment* The right of the people to be secure in their persons, houses, papers, and effects, against unreasonable searches and seizures, shall not be violated, and no Warrants shall issue, but upon probable cause, supported by Oath or affirmation, and particularly describing the place to be searched, and the persons or things to be seized.
In all criminal prosecutions, the accused shall enjoy the right to a speedy and public trial, to be informed of the cause and nature of the accusation, to be confronted with his accusers, and the witnesses against him; to have a compulsory process for obtaining witnesses in his favor; and to have the assistance of counsel for his defence.	*Sixth Amendment* In all criminal prosecutions, the accused shall enjoy the right to a speedy and public trial, by an impartial jury of the State and district wherein the crime shall have been committed, which district shall have been previously ascertained by law, and to be informed of the nature and cause of the accusation; to be confronted with the witnesses against him; to have compulsory process for obtaining witnesses in his favor, and to have the Assistance of Counsel for his defence.
The trial of all crimes (except in cases of impeachments, and cases arising in the land or naval forces, or the militia when on actual service in time of war or public danger) shall be by an impartial jury of freeholders of the vicinage, with the requisite of unanimity for conviction, of the right of challenge, and other accustomed requisites; and in all crimes punishable with loss of life or member, presentment or indictment by a grand jury, shall be an essential preliminary, provided that in cases of crimes committed within any county which may be in possession of an enemy, or in which a general insurrection may prevail, the trial may by law be authorised in some other county of the same state, as near as may be to the seat of the offence.	*Sixth Amendment*
In cases of crimes committed not within any county, the trial may by law be in such county as the laws shall have prescribed. In suits at common law, between man and man, the trial by jury, as one of the best securities to the rights of the people, ought to remain inviolate.	*Seventh Amendment* In Suits at common law, where the value in controversy shall exceed twenty dollars, the right of trial by jury shall be preserved, and no fact tried by a jury, shall be otherwise re-examined in any Court of the United States, than according to the rules of the common law.

The rights which Madison put forward, and which formed the basis for the first eight amendments, reflected limitations on the power of the federal government, or as he phrased it "the great object in view is to limit and qualify the powers of government ... and in some cases, against the community itself; or in other words, against the majority in favor of the minority." Many of those he proposed would be diluted in certain ways. He also made a proposal to extend the Bill of Rights over the states in certain critical areas. "No state shall violate the equal rights of conscience, or the freedom of the press, or the trial by jury in criminal cases." Madison was still concerned that state governments were the most likely to violate individuals rights, but this proposal was ultimately defeated in the Senate. It would take the addition of the Fourteenth Amendment in the aftermath of the Civil War to finally extend the power of the federal government to ensure that the states did not violate rights.[15]

One of Madison's other proposals worth considering ultimately became the Ninth Amendment. "The exceptions here or elsewhere in the constitution, made in favor of particular rights, shall not be so construed as to diminish the just importance of other rights retained by the people; or as to enlarge the powers delegated by the constitution; but either as actual limitations of such powers, or as inserted merely for greater caution." This was his way of ensuring continued protection for those rights not enumerated. The Supreme Court largely ignored this amendment until 1965, when it was used in the case of *Oswald v Connecticut.* "In his concurring opinion, Justice Arthur Goldberg invoked the Ninth Amendment to support the claim that state prohibition on contraception even for married couples violated a fundamental right of privacy that did not need to be specifically identified to be deserving of constitutional protection," Rakove writes.[16]

Congressional Debate and Ratification

It would take the House until July 21 to finally decide whether a special select committee should consider the amendments or whether the House sitting as a Committee of the Whole should consider them. The House finally agreed to assign a special select committee, which included one representative from each state, with Madison representing Virginia. The committee completed its work in one week. They changed some wording in Madison's proposals, narrowed the provisions dealing with freedom of conscience, and all but eliminated the opening declaration. The full House finally began the debate over the amendments on August 13.[17]

The most interesting element of the congressional debate was the attempt by the Antifederalists to incorporate more sweeping amendments into the Constitution. Elbridge Gerry opened the subject when he proposed "that all the amendments by the respective states" should be considered. On August 18, Thomas Tudor Tucker of South Carolina put forward seventeen amendments that, had they been approved, would have limited the power of the federal government in a number of areas. "The intention was to alter radically the structure of government established under the Constitution, and the thrust of the proposed revisions was to transfer power from the several branches of the federal government back to the states," according to Goldwin. The proposed amendments included restricting the ability of the federal government to levy direct taxes only when a state had failed to meet its requisitions; removal of any power over Congress to control federal elections; limiting presidential terms to no "more than eight years in any term of twelve years"; and allowing the states to levy their own duties. The Federalists in the House did not even allow debate over the proposed amendments, and the congressional record simply indicates "it was determined in the negative" that the amendments should be given further consideration. The Antifederalists would bring back the amendments again several days later, but with no better results.[18]

On August 24, the House approved sending seventeen amendments to the Senate for their consideration. To secure the requisite two-thirds vote, Madison had to use all of his political skills to convince the Federalists, many of whom still felt they were conceding too much to the other side, to vote with him. The gathering of votes and the required compromises were a process he referred to as "the nauseous project" in his private correspondence to a friend. He gave up on his opening declaration and on the ability to interweave the amendments into the body of the Constitution, but he won on all the major issues of substance.[19]

Several members of the Senate, which the Federalists dominated, were hostile to the proposed Bill of Rights. Robert Morris thought Madison had only proposed the amendments because he had gotten "so Cursedly frightened" from his close election in Virginia. Morris considered the amendments nonsense. Fortunately, the majority of his colleagues did not agree, and the Senate moved rather expeditiously to approve the amendments. The senators took the seventeen amendments approved by the House and condensed them down to twelve, making numerous wording changes that generally strengthened the Bill of Rights. Especially noteworthy was the provision on religious freedom, which they joined with the rights of freedom of speech and the press to form the First Amendment. The Senate also rejected the amendment that Madison considered the most important, "that no State shall infringe the equal rights of conscience, nor freedom of speech, or of the press, nor the right of trial by jury in criminal cases." Given that senators were appointed by their state legislatures, it is little wonder they rejected this amendment. The only major issue the two houses disagreed on was the wording for the anti-establishment clause dealing with religion, but the Senate eventually accepted the House version, after they met in a joint conference committee. The Bill of Rights was sent to the states for ratification on September 25, 1789.[20]

Surprisingly, the public showed little interest in the state ratification process, including the legislative debates. Unlike the original ratification of the Constitution, the ratification of the Bill of Rights evoked little public involvement and very little newspaper coverage. Goldwin attributes this to the fact that Madison had succeeded in splitting the public from the Antifederalist leaders. "The great mass of the people had been won over to the Constitution," he argues, "the public's fears had subsided, and their attention had turned to more pressing matters." By the end of January 1790, five states (New Jersey, Maryland, South Carolina, New Hampshire, and Delaware) had approved all or most of the proposed amendments. North Carolina had by then ratified both the Constitution and the Bill of Rights. Only Madison's home state of Virginia proved problematic.[21]

During the spring elections of 1789, the Virginia House had turned over, with many more Federalists elected. Edward Carrington, who had served in the Continental Army with Washington, reported to Madison that his "information from the various parts of the Country is that the people are at ease on the subject of amendments." Henry had little support left in the lower House and departed the legislature part way through the session. With little opposition, the House was able to approve all twelve of the amendments. But the Senate remained in the hands of the Antifederalists, and they refused to approve what would become the First, Sixth, Ninth, and Tenth Amendments. When the House refused to concur with the Senate's changes, ratification in Virginia stalled until December 1791. Goldwin observed that "ironically, by taking so long, it fell to Virginia...to be the decisive eleventh state to ratify," and thus bring the Bill of Rights into effect. By then, over two years after Madison had first proposed the amendments to the House, even Rhode Island had ratified the Constitution and joined the union.[22]

As Madison had suspected, the Bill of Rights would sometimes be nothing more than a "parchment barrier" to the will of a determined majority. In 1798, the Congress would pass and President Adams would sign the Alien and Sedition Act, which made it illegal to criticize the federal government, despite the protections of the First Amendment. In the South in the aftermath of the Civil War, Jim Crow laws were enacted to deprive African-American's of their basic rights, even in the aftermath of the addition of the Fourteenth Amendment, which extended the bill of rights to the states. During World War II, the federal government incarcerated Japanese-Americans without due process of law, in violation of the protections contained in the Bill of Rights.

But Madison was also correct that over time the Bill of Rights would become "incorporated with the national sentiment." As Labunski notes: "A culture of tolerance for even controversial speech had to develop over time." In the aftermath of the First World War, the Supreme Court handed down the first decision protecting freedom of speech. The Court was aided in its decisions by the adoption of the Fourteenth Amendment in the aftermath of the Civil War, which applied due process of law to the states and made them subject to the Bill of Rights, as Madison had originally proposed. Many more Supreme Court decisions that protected rights followed in the twentieth century, and today the Bill of Rights is more than just a "parchment barrier" in the United States, but is an essential part of American national sentiment.[23]

Endnotes

1 Goldwin, p. 61; Rakove, p. 310 and p. 314

2 The historians mentioned are Banning, p. 281; Rakove, *Original Meanings*, p. 331; the quotes are from Madison letter of October 17, 1788 to Jefferson, retrieved March 14, 2014 from http://www.constitution.org/jm/17881017_tj.htm; the concluding quote is from Goldwin, p. 63

3 Goldwin, p. 99-100

4 Madison letter of October 17, 1788

5 Labunski, p. 136-140

6 Labunski, p. 152; Ketchum, p. 146; Jack N. Rakove, *James Madison and the Bill of Rights*, retrieved March 14, 2014 from http://www.apsanet.org/imgtest/jamesmadison.pdf

7 Banning, p. 272-274; Goldwin, p. 81 and 73-74

8 The election results are from Labunski, p. 175; the quote from Madison is from Ketchum, p. 277

9 Labunski, p. 185-191; Goldwin, p. 76

10 The quotes are from the *Congressional Record* of June 8, 1789 that were retrieved March 12, 2014 from http://memory.loc.gov/cgi-bin/ampage?collId=llac&fileName=001/llac001.db&recNum=223; Banning, p. 286

11 *Congressional Record*; Banning, p. 286

12 *Congressional Record*; Banning, p. 288

13 Labunski, p. 200; Banning, p. 288

14 Rakove, *Madison and the Bill of Rights*

15 Rakove, *Madison and the Bill of Rights*

16 Rakove, *Madison and the Bill of Rights*

17 Labunski, p. 207-217

18 Goldwin, p. 118-139

19 Goldwin, p. 156; Labunski, p. 235

20 Goldwin, p. 159-164; Labunski, p. 236-239

21 Goldwin, p. 168; Labunski, p. 245

22 Goldwin, p. 173

23 Goldwin, p. 183; Labunski has a good overview for why the Bill of Rights did not become effective until the twentieth century on p. 257-260

Epilogue

The Ongoing American Debate

"This land is your land
This land is my land...
This land was made for you and me."
— Woody Guthrie —

George Washington, who symbolized the unity of the entire American nation, was unanimously elected president of the United States by the electoral college on February 4, 1789. John Adams received the second most votes, and became vice president, thereby giving the office of the executive sectional balance between the North and the South.

During the ratification process, Washington had expressed some reticence about serving as president. Some of his hesitancy was dictated by the times. "In Washington's world no prominent statesman regarded the forthright expression of political ambition as legitimate," Ellis points out, since to do so was to confess that one was unworthy for election. But that was not the whole story. At age 57, he struggled with his health and had concerns that, like his father, he would die young. Financially, Washington was also struggling, and needed to borrow money both to keep Mount Vernon afloat and to cover the costs of his journey to New York to be sworn in as president. Washington wrote to

Hamilton that he longed to "live and die, in peace and retirement, on my own farm."[1]

Yet, Washington also knew that when called upon, he would serve. His friends lobbied him ceaselessly. Hamilton wrote to him that he could hardly walk away from the new government, given all he had done to bring it about, including his service as the President of the Federal Convention. "You will permit me to say that it is indispensable you should lend yourself to [the new government's] first operations. It is of little purpose to have *introduced* a system, if the weightiest influence is not given to its firm *establishment* in the outset," Hamilton insisted. The policies to be implemented in the first few years of the new republic would need to be moored on solid ground, since "all the great arrangements under the new system [will] fix its tone for a long time to come," Madison told Washington. Lafayette wrote to Washington from France, saying, "you alone can make the political machine operate successfully."[2]

On April 14, 1789, Charles Thomson, Secretary to the Congress, arrived at Mount Vernon to formally announce that Washington had been elected president of the United States. Washington was ready to accept the office, and they set off for New York two days later. All along the way, adoring crowds greeted him and he was honored at regal receptions fit for a king. Just after departure, Washington stopped in Alexandria where the leaders of the town held a dinner in his honor, with the standard thirteen toasts given. When he arrived in Philadelphia, twenty thousand people lined the streets to show their support and appreciation, as church bells rang. The Federal Gazette wrote "What a pleasing reflection to every patriotic mind, thus to see our citizens again united in their reliance on this great man who is, a second time, called upon to be the savior of his country." In Trenton, where he had routed the Hessians during the war, "the townsfolk had erected a magnificent floral arch in his honor with the words 'December 26, 1776' sewn from leaves and flowers," according to Chernow . Washington finally arrived in New York City to great fanfare, and took the oath of office on April 30, 1789.[3]

Although Washington avoided making any policy recommendations in his inaugural speech, he indicated that he planned to not succumb to "local prejudices or attachments...[nor] separate views nor party animosities." But it was not to be, for as President Kennedy told a group of state governors on July 4, 1962, "to govern is to choose." Over the coming years, despite his best intentions to create a sense of unity, Washington would choose a set of domestic and foreign policies that would ultimately lead to partisan differences. Of particular importance would be those policies proposed to deal with the finances of the new government.[4]

The first of these policies was Alexander Hamilton's program for establishing public credit and paying off the nation's debt, which stood at $77 million. The debt consisted of monies owed to foreigners ($11.7 million); the public ($40.4 million); and the debts of the states ($25 million). Hamilton proposed that the federal government assume repayment of the state debt, and that they refinance the debt through the issuance of new bonds. He assumed wealthy northern investors would purchase the bonds, which would then give them a stake in the success of the new federal government. The existing public debt would be redeemed at full face value to the current owner. The new debt would be fully secured through a stable system of taxation, primarily through the impost that Congress had recently approved. The proposal to pay the public debt at face value caused a rift with Madison, who saw that such a proposal would benefit speculators, who had begun to buy up much of the public debt from its original holders at pennies on the dollar and stood to make a windfall profit. Many of the original holders of the public debt were Revolutionary War veterans and the picture soon emerged of a grave injustice in which "battle-worn veterans of the war for independence [were] being cheated out of their just rewards by mere moneymen." Madison's preferred approach, which he called discrimination, would have ensured that the original owners would get a share of any windfall, an approach that Hamilton rightly thought unworkable. The plan to assume the state debts was even more controversial, since states such as Virginia had largely paid off their debt. Madison's opposition ensured that the assumption plan stayed bottled up in Congress for over six months.[5]

Ironically, it was Jefferson, recently returned from France to serve as Washington's Secretary of State, who broke the impasse. The two men had met outside Washington's office one day, with Jefferson reporting that Hamilton looked "dejected beyond description," over his inability to get his debt plan through Congress. He may have been especially dismayed that Madison, his recent collaborator, stood opposed to him. Hamilton knew that Madison had supported the assumption of state debts back in 1783, and would later remark he had expected his friend's "firm support…in the *general course* of my administration." There were also numerous other discussions going on in Congress for how to resolve the issue, but Jefferson helped to break the impasse when he hosted a dinner in late June for Madison and Hamilton. Madison agreed to withdraw his strenuous opposition in return for certain concessions to his home state. His fellow Virginians opposed the plan for assumption of state debts, since they saw no value in it for their state. Madison felt duty bound to support his constituents and so he personally vote against the plan. In return for Madison's agreement to allow the debt plan to move forward, the seat of government would be permanently relocated to what would become Washington D.C. The permanent location of the new capital was another controversial issue, with numerous states competing to become its home. As he later wrote to James Monroe, Jefferson had decided, despite his own personal opposition to the assumption plan, that "in the present instance I see the necessity of yielding for this time...for the sake of the union." In other words, without some accommodation between the two sides, the experiment with a more robust federal government might collapse and lead to disunion or civil war. Jefferson would later rue the deal that was struck.[6]

Washington was largely silent on the issue of assuming the debt, choosing to stay out of the middle of a debate between some of his most valued advisors. Although he sympathized with the plight of the veterans who were losing out to speculators, he had also warned his former soldiers back in 1783 not to sell their hard-earned securities "at a very great discount." When Hamilton made his next controversial proposal, to create a Bank of the United States, it sailed through Congress. This occurred despite vehement opposition from Madison, who objected to the establishment of the Bank on the grounds that the Constitution did not authorize it and would give Congress "unlimited power" over legislation. Washington was uncomfortable that two of his most trusted advisors, Madison and Hamilton, saw the issue so differently. He then asked both Hamilton and Jefferson to provide opinions as to whether the Constitution would permit the establishment of the Bank and whether he should sign or veto the bill. Jefferson, following on Madison's lead, "propounded a rigidly strict interpretation of the Constitution, which if adopted would have placed the national government in a straightjacket," according to historian Jacob E. Cooke. Hamilton, on the other hand, put forward an expansive view of the implied powers of the new federal government, arguing that a sovereign government has "the right to employ all of the means to attain the ends of such power" so long as the Constitution did not expressly forbid the use of such power. Hamilton must have taken particular pleasure in quoting from *Federalist* No. 44, written by Madison, which stated: "wherever a general power to do a thing is given, every particular power for doing it is included." Ultimately, at the end of February 1791, Washington signed the Bank bill. Perhaps he realized the establishment of a stable system of public credit for the nation would avoid a repeat of the problems he had faced as the general of an army that lacked adequate supplies and pay because the Confederation Congress could not borrow sufficient money to fund the war.[7]

Historians have provided alternative explanations for why Madison, the fervent nationalist of the 1780s, gradually became a champion for an alternative and more limited view of the Constitution. Had he changed his mind, or did he not envision the uses Hamilton intended to put the new government to? Exploring that question is beyond the scope of this Epilogue, but some of his opposition to Hamilton's program, especially on the plan to assume state debts, was grounded in the political realities of his home state. The assumption of state debts, as Hamilton originally proposed it, favored certain northern states that had large war debts. The original proposal was of no benefit to Virginia and could actually cost them, since the state would be required to pay taxes to the federal government that it would then use to retire the debts of other states. The compromise that Jefferson helped broker placed the new national capital in the South, and required that Virginia receive federal payments that would be equal to any losses they would sustain from the assumption plan, thereby allowing Madison to remove his active opposition to the legislation. The assumption plan did not ultimately involve great political principles, and each side could "calculate its specific gains and losses," according to Rakove, and find room for accommodation. Hamilton bank plan involved far larger issues, making it difficult to reach compromise, and ultimately two sides emerged from that debate with vastly different conceptions of the path the new nation should be on. Madison and Jefferson would lead one side, Hamilton the other, and out of this process would emerge America's two-party system. "The ideas and issues that divided these two Founders [Hamilton and Jefferson] have persisted from generation to generation in American politics," historian John Ferling writes. "Their opposing views are like the twin strands of DNA in the American body politic."[8]

Hamilton envisioned the development of a strong nation-state with an economy built on commerce and industry. Both he and Washington wanted to ensure that the United States, through its own means, could build a strong enough military to protect the country. Hamilton championed policies intended to create a stable public finance system, a funded debt, and a national bank that would control the money supply, all of which would help foster new industry. He believed the country needed an active federal government, especially a strong executive, to promote economic development. As part of this, "he converted the new Constitution into a flexible instrument for creating the legal framework necessary for economic growth," and specifically leaned on the "three still amorphous clauses—the necessary-and-proper clause, the general-welfare clause, and the commerce clause—making them the basis for government activism in economics," Chernow writes. [9]

Unlike today's conservatives, Hamilton's policies were not grounded in a laissez-faire approach. In his report on manufacturing that he delivered to Congress on December 5, 1791, his stated goal was to promote such measures that will "render the United States, independent on foreign nations, for military and other essential supplies." While he admitted in the report that agriculture has "intrinsically a strong claim to pre-eminence over every other kind of industry," it should not be the exclusive path to economic growth. As for the claim that the economy should be allowed to grow based on the invisible hand of the market, Hamilton spent much of the report demonstrating why this could not work for newly emerging economies. Those nations that had already "perfected a branch of industry" made it difficult for new nations to compete "without the extraordinary aid and protection of government." Such aid would include protective tariffs on selected industries, trade restrictions, and direct subsidies, which Hamilton called bounties. Such subsidies would be restricted to "new undertakings," since there are "natural and inherent impediments to success." Government also had a role in regulation and inspection of manufactured products as a way to "prevent frauds upon consumers at home," and to "improve the quality...[of] national manufacturers." Finally, as a means to promote economic growth, the government should invest in public works projects, including "good roads, canals and navigable rivers."[10]

Like Madison and many of the founding generation, Hamilton had concerns about majority rule. He defended many Tories (those who had supported England during the war) in the immediate aftermath of the revolution, and saw that popular passions had led to attempts to deny them their rights. In the turbulence of the mid-1780s, Hamilton "fell prey to lurid visions that the have-nots would rise up and dispossess the haves," according to Chernow. And during the Philadelphia Convention, he had extolled the British system of government and life tenure for the Senate and the president, which he referred to as an "elective monarch." His vision was of a political system in which authority would flow down, one designed to control popular passions, to place checks on democracy, and promote order.[11]

As with so many of the founders, Hamilton was complicated. A self-made man, he had worked his way to the top of society, and he identified with the interests of the commercial elite. Yet he was not a closet monarchist, as Jefferson thought, and he did not intend his economic policies to create greater wealth for the already affluent, as many of his critics at that time charged. Hamilton "believed that government ought to promote self-fulfillment, self-improvement and self-reliance," according to Ron Chernow. His policies were designed to promote entrepreneurship and the expansion of industry, an approach that would allow the most talented to succeed as he had. Gordon Wood writes that, "Hamilton's financial program, like all his measures, was designed not to make money for any particular group but to create a powerful nation-state." Still, Hamilton's Achilles heel was his inability to empathize with the common person and to show compassion for the struggles that the poor experienced. His policy proposals also had a sectional bias, favoring northern commercial interests over those of the agrarian parts of the country. In the newly emerging American nation, there was the need for an alternative political organization that would give expression to the concerns of agricultural interests and the average person, which Jefferson and Madison would provide.[12]

Both Jefferson and Madison believed the future of self- government and the preservation of liberty were dependent on the United States continuing as primarily an agricultural society. They each had grave concerns that the premature industrialization of America would lead to the creation of large cities teaming with the urban poor.

Jefferson thought that people who worked for others, as was the case in manufacturing, would become dependent "which begats subservience and venality, suffocates the germ of virtue, and prepares fit tools for the designs of ambition." The resulting growth of inequality would call into question the survival of republican government, which they believed required a more equal distribution of wealth, which could best be preserved through a rural society. [13]

Madison wrote that "health, virtue, intelligence and competency in the greatest number of citizens" could best be nourished through farming as a lifestyle. Jefferson, who had a somewhat mythical view of the ideal of farming, wrote that "those who labor in the earth are the chosen people of God, if ever he had a chosen people, whose breasts He has made His peculiar deposit for substantial and genuine virtue." It is understandable that these two men, raised on plantations in rural Virginia, would prefer agriculture to commerce and industry. The duo saw Hamilton's plan for an expanded industrial base for the United States as a threat. To both Jefferson and Madison, the policies that Hamilton was proposing would heavily favor the interests of the northern financial sector (they referred to such men as stockjobbers and speculators), create a cadre of the ultrarich, and ultimately provide them with too much power and sway over the federal government, leading to rule by an aristocratic elite. Jefferson wanted to pursue alternative policies that would promote a more inclusive democracy, protect the interests of yeoman farmers, and provide a role for the common man, a rather ironic position for a slave owner.[14]

It wasn't that Jefferson and Madison opposed all industry or commerce in America. Rather, they felt that the country should have the right types of manufacturing. "For the well-being of the nation's agriculture, a commerce functioning primarily as a carrier of surplus produce to worldwide markets was indispensable," historians Stanley

Elkins and Erick McKitrick write. Industry should support a primarily agricultural economy, and provide basic goods that could be supplied through home industries and artisan production, without the need for large-scale industrial production. Most of all, Jefferson opposed any type of governmental subsidies for industry, which would create favored businesses and link the wealthy to a government that they would then control. [15]

Jefferson and Hamilton had fundamentally different views on human nature. Hamilton was a pessimist who distrusted people and wanted to preserve the status of the elites of society. Jefferson was an optimist. Ferling summarizes Jefferson's view this way:

> *If man's environment could be changed so that education was widespread, social distinction eliminated, and wealth more equally distributed, the good in mankind would predominate. Jefferson championed governments that permitted change, advocated listening to the will of the people, and denounced the oppression of the many through what he called the tyranny of the few.*[16]

Hamilton did not support the establishment of a monarchy in America. In 1792, he wrote, "I am *affectionately* attached to the republican theory. I desire *above all things* to see the *equality* of political rights, exclusive of all *hereditary* distinction, firmly established by a practical demonstration of it being consistent with the order and happiness of society." Still, Jefferson thought he did support a monarchy, and was present when Hamilton told Adams that the British government "was the most perfect model of government that could be formed." After the dinner at which Hamilton made this remark, Jefferson claims that Hamilton told him "the greatest man that ever lived was Julius Caesar." Chernow doubts the veracity of this story, pointing out that

"Hamilton's collected papers are teeming with pejorative references to Julius Caesar." Given their differing views on policy, and his knowledge of Hamilton's speech at the Federal Convention, Jefferson told Washington that "the ultimate object of all this [Hamilton's policies] is to prepare the way for a change from the present republican form of government to that of a monarchy, of which the English Constitution is to be the model." One of Jefferson's biographers, Jon Meacham, points out that he did not trust the "old mother country" nor any American who had looked favorably upon "its trappings—aristocracy of birth, hereditary executives, lifetime legislatures, standing armies…and centralized financial systems." He viewed Britain and those who admired her as a threat to the republic they had established, and in Hamilton, he had found the perfect foil.[17]

Jefferson and Madison formed an alternative party, the Republicans, to battle Hamilton and his Federalist policies. In another example of the ironies of history, two anti-party individuals formed a political party. Madison, who had done so much to implement a constitutional order designed to counteract parties and the formation of majority factions, now became the leader of a party. (We should not confuse the Republican Party of Jefferson and Madison with the modern Republican Party. Instead, it would gradually evolve into the Democratic-Republicans, and ultimately into the Democratic Party under Andrew Jackson.) Madison justified the creation of the Republican Party as a means to counteract what he saw as the Federalists' approach to government by the few. He argued there was a need to organize those people who believed "that mankind are capable of governing themselves." Madison, with Jefferson's full support, began to place an emphasis on the need for "political equality among all" as a way to counteract the Federalists. Given their concerns over inequality, Madison proposed that laws be adopted that "reduce extreme wealth towards a state of mediocrity, and raise extreme indigence towards a state of comfort." By the early 1790s, Madison was concluding that parties could not be avoided, and that the alternative was to make "one party a check on the other," to have one party play off another. Such a view is consistent with Madison's earlier writings that in an extended republic, different interests and factions would compete with one another. What was different now was that he and Jefferson would attempt to establish a party that could form a majority that could ultimately take over the reins of government. That party would include an uneasy alliance between many of the former Antifederalists and those like Madison and Jefferson who had supported adoption of the Constitution. The coalition would include those in the rural backcountry of the northern states, along with southern plantation owners.[18]

Jefferson had a utopian side to him, and believed that by removing governmental control a mythic world could be created where all people lived together amicably. His view was moored to a belief that "America would be a happy land if it remained the habitation mostly of independent yeoman farmers" who would be "model citizens for America's experiment in republicanism," according to Ferling. Jefferson saw no need for an activist government to pursue the ends he sought, believing that the best government is one that governs least. In part, he thought that an active government would end up benefitting society's elite, as it had in Europe, especially given the recent growth in industrialization, urbanization, and the existence of monarchical rule in the old world. To Jefferson, Hamilton's policies were designed to recreate European society in America. "I think our governments will remain virtuous for many centuries as long as they are chiefly agriculture… when they get piled upon one another in large cities, as in Europe, they will become corrupt as in Europe," Jefferson wrote. He thought that limited government would allow people to compete on a natural basis, with opportunity open to all, and that "people's inherent sociability and moral instinct would create a natural ordering of society" without the need for governmental involvement. Ellis argues that Jefferson thought that once people were freed from the "last remnants of feudal oppression" they would "interact freely to create a natural harmony" in society without the need for extensive government involvement.[19]

The newly emerging Republican Party and the Federalists engaged in a no-holds-barred, brass-knuckled battle over the future of the nation. In 1791, Madison convinced his friend Philip Freneau to start a republican newspaper, the *National Gazette*, to counteract the influence of John Fenno's *Gazette of the United States*, a Federalist newspaper that served as a mouthpiece for Hamilton. Madison had begun to see the importance of relying on the public to counteract what he considered Hamilton's attempts to turn the government over to the wealthy. Meanwhile, Jefferson operated behind the scenes, supporting Freneau's efforts and hiring him to work part-time in the State Department. It was an odd position for Jefferson to occupy, essentially "playing the part of leader of the opposition," as Meacham writes, even though he was still a key member of Washington's cabinet.[20]

The war of words between the two sides raged during the 1790s, both in newspaper accounts and also within the government. Jefferson and Hamilton were "daily pitted in the Cabinet like two cocks," according to Jefferson. Hamilton, who felt hurt by what he saw as Madison's betrayal, now referred to him as a "clever man" who was "very little acquainted with the world," and who had fallen under Jefferson's spell. Writing under a pseudonym in Fenno's *Gazette*, Hamilton incorrectly charged that Jefferson had opposed the Constitution, that he was "a man of profound ambition and violent passions," and that his views would lead to "National disunion, National insignificance, Public disorder, and discredit." Madison responded with a series of essays in the *National Gazette* that charged that Hamilton was focused "less to the interest of the many than of a few" and that he wanted the government to be controlled by "fewer hands" until it "approximated... an hereditary form." Both Jefferson and Hamilton attempted to get Washington, who was caught in the middle, to fire the other. Washington attempted to mediate the conflict with little success, and told Jefferson that his fears of monarchy were overblown, since most Americans were "steadily for republicanism." But by and large, Washington supported the economic policies Hamilton put forward, and largely blamed Jefferson for the partisanship that had infected his administration. Washington took the attacks on Hamilton personally, seeing them as attacks that "filled me with painful sensations."[21]

Hamilton's view of the future, and the policies he espoused, helped lay the foundation for the future American economy, "the embryo of modern America," as Ferling writes. What he could not foresee, and what Jefferson seemed to grasp, was the problems that large-scale industrialization would eventually create. This included the concentration of wealth into ever fewer hands; the exploitation of factory workers and the need for unions to protect those workers; the creation of urban blight in cities, where people were forced to live in tenements; and the movement of political power into the hands of the few. Jefferson would triumph with his election to the Presidency in 1800, but he would also continue many of the Federalists' policies, including the stable financial system that Hamilton had designed and which had allowed the United States to prosper. The western frontier also provided a safety valve for a continued rural lifestyle in America, especially with Jefferson's acquisition of the Louisiana Purchase. [22]

Not until the aftermath of the Civil War did the industrial revolution hit the United States with full force, leading to the creation of large corporations that had substantial political power. In the twentieth century, first the progressives and later Franklin Roosevelt and his New Deal, would turn to the use of the federal government as a means to counteract corporate power and advance greater equality for the average person. As FDR observed, "It was the purpose of Jefferson to teach the country that the solidarity of Federalism was only a partial one, that it represented only a minority of people, that to build a Great Nation the interests of all groups in every part must be considered, and that only in …national unity could real security be found." Starting with FDR, liberals would use Hamiltonian means (activist government) to achieve Jeffersonian ends (greater equality). At the same time, conservatives would use Jeffersonian means (limited government) to promote Hamiltonian ends (capitalist growth). This battle continues to this day, a part of the ongoing American argument. [23]

While debate did not end in the aftermath of the Constitution, its terms had shifted in a clear and dramatic way. People no longer questioned whether America would be one nation, but rather they debated what that nation would become. Although Madison and Jefferson led a movement to overturn Federalist policies, they did so within the framework of the Constitution. Countries like France and Russia, in the aftermath of their revolutions, would resort to violence to settle their differences, which would ultimately lead to despotic rule by a dictatorship. Americans largely settled their disputes through debate. As Ellis writes: "The revolutionary generation found a way to contain the explosive energies of the debate in the form of an ongoing argument or dialogue that was eventually institutionalized and rendered safe by the creation of political parties." Part of that debate over the next sixty years would revolve around the issue of federalism: how much power should the central government exert, and how much power should be left to the states. Different leaders would view this question from varying perspectives over the coming half century, with important ramifications for the future of the American nation. Only with the outbreak of the Civil War would the constitutional arrangement completely collapse, due to the unresolved issues of slavery and federalism left over from the founding. The Civil War would determine, in Lincoln's words, whether "a nation conceived in liberty and dedicated to the proposition that all men are created equal," could "long endure." The scourge of slavery would finally be eliminated, although the battle for equal rights continues to this day.[24]

Despite their differences, both sides in the early republic venerated the Constitution, which provided the glue that held them together. Put another way, the Constitution provided a roof over the nation, and allowed the time needed to build the walls of shared experience that are central to nationhood. "The Constitution became a substitute for any deeper kind of national identity," writes historian John M. Murrin. "American nationalism is distinct because, for nearly its first century, it was narrowly and peculiarly constitutional. People knew that without the Constitution there would be no America."[25]

The Constitution provided a whole host of benefits in addition to allowing a sense of nationhood to gradually emerge over time. The new federal government was given the power to solve the problem of financial solvency; deal with common problems; resolve issues between the states on commerce; and speak with one voice with foreign nations. The document was also structured to allow for sufficient flexibility so that future generations would be able to deal with problems that the founding generation could not envision and a process for amendment in those instances where the Constitution clearly was lacking. Our constitutional arrangements have allowed the "ongoing argument" which began with the founders to continue through to our day. Although our founders had concerns about democracy, they provided for a remarkably democratic Constitution through elections to the House by the people, the lack of property qualifications to vote, and only very general requirements to run for office. The United States has become increasingly more democratic over time, with ever-greater numbers of people eligible to participate in the system.

The Constitution created a wholly new system of federalism in which the central government would deal with common problems, leaving to the states those matters best left at the local level. Unfortunately, the founders were unable to provide a solution to whether the states or the federal government would ultimately be sovereign. They blurred that issue, since "any effort to enforce an unambiguous answer to the question would probably have killed the infant American republic in the cradle," Ellis writes.[26]

The compromises that allowed the Constitutional Convention to succeed also came with a cost. The compromise between large and small states created a Senate in which people from some parts of the country have a much greater level of representation than those from other parts of the country. The Constitution created a process for electing the president that can, in certain instances, result in the person with fewer votes filling the office. Most egregious of all, the founding generation was unable to come up with any solution to the issue of slavery, a problem that not only violated the most basic human rights, which the revolutionary generation had fought for, but ultimately led to disunion.

We have inherited a great nation, one that, despite its ideological differences, conquered a continent; survived a Civil War; built a vast industrial empire; endured the Great Depression; and defeated both fascism and communism. We are also the heirs of the founding generation's great debates, and in many ways, their arguments still resonate today. What is the proper size and role of the federal government and that of the states? Where should the line be drawn between individual liberty and the public good? What do we mean by equality, and how do we ensure that all people are treated fairly? How do we organize a government of the people, by the people, and for the people but still ensure that the rights of the minority are protected from the tyranny of the majority? These questions do not lend themselves to simple answers. The founders struggled with them, and so do we. Former Supreme Court justice David Souter writes of the difficult task that faces the Court each time it reaches a decision on the meaning of the Constitution, since the document itself is rooted in a "pantheon of values," including liberty, order, fairness, and equality, values that can sometimes be in conflict with each other. "And the very opportunity for conflict between the good and the good reflects our confidence that a way may be found to resolve it when a conflict arises," Souter observed.[27]

Some in the United States today, particularly those on the far right wing of the Republican Party and its tea party adherents, have attempted to hijack the founders for their own purposes. The Tea Party Patriots, for example, describe themselves as "a community committed to standing together, shoulder to shoulder, to protect our country and the Constitution upon which we were founded!" Another tea party group has referred to itself as a "user driven group of like-minded people who desire our

God-given individual freedoms written out by the Founding Fathers." A part of what these groups have in common is a belief that the founders were universally anti-government and that the sole value of merit at the time of the founding was individual liberty. They completely downplay or ignore concerns the founders had that in a republic the people needed to act with virtue and promote a broad view of the public interest beyond just individual gain; the concerns expressed among the founders on the need for equality; and the pursuit of the Framers of the Constitution to create a stronger federal government.[28]

Michael Gerson, one of the more astute observers of the modern political scene, wrote an essay in the magazine *Nation Affairs,* accompanied by a summary in the opinion section of the *Washington Post* entitled: "Anti-government stance ignores founders focus on public good." Gerson, a conservative who was a speechwriter for President George W. Bush, argues that the founders put forward "a strong governing system," and he correctly points out that the Framers wanted to replace the weak government under the Articles of Confederation with a more energetic federal government. The founders "believed that good government was essential to promote…the public good." They did not believe that the government should be "frozen in amber," but instead "designed a constitutional system that could accommodate" future change. Gerson points out that "durable majorities have endorsed the existence of Social Security and Medicare," even though these governmental programs "were not envisioned by the founders." The founders may have argued among themselves over whether such programs were in the public interest, but would have left such decisions to the people through the democratic process. Gerson points out that it is dangerous when debates of this type are "short-circuited by simplistic and legalistic appeals to the Constitution as a purely limiting document." It simply leaves no room for the public to debate the merits of alternative public policies.[29]

While the right wing of the Republican Party has assumed extreme positions in today's America, there have been times when liberals also took extremist positions, denying the importance of private property rights or how strongly individualism is rooted in American history. In the aftermath of the ascendancy of the New Deal, some on the left thought conservatism was dead. "The habit of historians and social scientists in the period after World War II was to dismiss conservatism," E.J. Dionne writes. America needs both a strong conservative and a strong liberal side that engage in vigorous debate and compete for political power, just as Hamilton and Jefferson did. Among other things, the conservative side puts forward the importance of individual initiative, the limits to governmental power, and the importance of a strong private sector. Liberals remind us that we are all in this together, that equality is also a part of our founding heritage, and that government can assist in solving persistent societal problems.[30]

In the twenty-first century, Americans must find ways to break the political paralysis that has set in. Madison and the Framers designed a constitutional system that requires a great deal of bargaining among political actors and makes it difficult, but not impossible, for majorities to form in order to take action. The problem is not debate, which the founders extensively engaged in; the problem is in failing to find the principled compromises needed after differing opinions have been expressed, and one side or another wins an election. Whether from red state or blue; liberal, conservative, or moderate; Democrat, Republican, or Independent; we are the inheritors of the founding generation. If they could find ways to compromise and move the nation forward, we can also. Despite our differences, as Americans we are united in our love of country and our esteem for the Constitution. This is what continues to make us one nation.

Endnotes

1 Ellis, *His Excellency*, p. 182; Chernow, *Washington*, p. 548

2 Chernow, *Washington*, p. 548-549

3 Chernow, *Washington*, p. 561-564

4 Berkin, p. 202; The quote from President Kennedy was retrieved March 23, 2013 from http://www.pbs.org/capitolfourth/kennedy.html. A good summary of Washington's attempts to create unity is from Don Higginbotham, *George Washington: Uniting a Nation*, (Lanham, 2004). Although not dealt with in this Epilogue, many historians see foreign policy issues as even more important for the rise of party government in the 1790's. For example, see Jacob E. Cooke. Organizing the New National Government, in Leonard W. Levy and Dennis J. Mahoney (Ed.), *The Framing and Ratification of the Constitution*, (New York, 1987), p. 329

5 Ellis, *Founding Brothers*, p. 56-60 has a more detailed discussion of the issues involved; see also Cooke, p. 322

6 Ellis, *Founding Brothers*, p. 50-51; Chernow, *Washington*, p. 621; Rakove, *Madison*, p. 104-108 and p. 111

7 Cooke, p. 324; On the issue of the need for a strong public finance system and its relationship to supplying the military during times of war, and how this relates to Washington's experience during the Revolutionary War, see Rakove, *Revolutionaries*, p. 400-431

8 For the disagreements between the historians on Madison's conversion from a strong nationalist, some believe that Madison had changed his mind while others maintain that his thinking was consistent throughout and he never intended to support the type of program Hamilton put forward. For those who think he changed his mind, see Rakove, *Madison*, p. 110-111 and Ketchum, p.314-315. For the opposing view, Banning's book on Madison is dedicated almost entirely to this issue, especially Chapter Ten. Wood also deals with this issue in *Revolutionary Characters* in Chapter 5; John Ferling, *Jefferson and Hamilton: The Rivalry That Forged a Nation,* (New York, 2013), Kindle location 56

9 Chernow, *Hamilton*, p. 345

10 Alexander Hamilton, "Report on Manufacturers," retrieved April 8, 2014 from http://www.constitution.org/ah/rpt_manufactures.pdf

11 Ferling, *Jefferson and Hamilton*, Kindle location 3921; Chernow, *Hamilton*, p. 219

12 Wood, *Revolutionary Characters*, p. 129-130 also argues that Hamilton intended to "use monarchical like government influence…to tie leading commercial interests to the government" and create a dependency between the two. The quote from Wood in the text is found on p. 130. For a succinct criticism of the outcome of Hamilton's policies and the relationship between wealth and power, see Ferling, *Jefferson and Hamilton*, Kindle location 7902-7903. Ferling does not directly criticize Hamilton for wanting to create a

plutocracy, but argues that Jefferson was correct in fearing that Hamilton's policies would lead to such a result, which in many ways they have. For an alternative view of Hamilton see Chernow, whose views are more charitable toward him.

13 The best analysis on the relationship between Jefferson's views on politics and economics is Drew McCoy, *The Elusive Republic: Political Economy in Jeffersonian America*, (Chapel Hill, 1980). The Jefferson quote is from page 12 and is taken from his *Notes on the State of Virginia.*

14 Ketchum, p. 328; Jefferson, p. 280

15 Stanley Elkin & Eric McKitrick, *The Age of Federalism: The Early American Republic 1788-1800*, (New York, 1993), p. 20

16 Ferling, *Jefferson and Hamilton,* Kindle location 4206

17 Chernow, *Hamilton*, p. 398-401; Jon Meacham, *Thomas Jefferson: The Art of Power*, (New York, 2012), p. 259-263 and p. xxvii-xxviii

18 Hofstadter, p. 81-82; Richard E. Ellis, "The Persistence of Antifederalism after 1789," in Beeman (Ed.), p. 344-345

19 Ferling, *A Leap in the Dark*, p. 332; Chernow, *Hamilton*, p. 346; Wood, *Thomas Jefferson, Equality, and the Creation of a Civil Society*, p. 2146; Ellis, *American Sphinx*, p. 359-360

20 Meachum, *Thomas Jefferson*, p. 256

21 Meachum, *Thomas Jefferson*, p. 262; Ferling, *Jefferson and Hamilton,* Kindle location 5031-5111; Ferling, *A Leap in the Dark*, p. 351

22 Ferling, *A Leap in the Dark*, p. 347-348 and p. 350

23 Meachum, *Thomas Jefferson*, p. 502

24 Ellis, *Founding Brothers*, p. 15

25 John M. Murrin, *A Roof Without Walls: The Dilemma of American National Identity*, in Beeman (Ed.), p 346-347

26 Ellis, *American Creation*, p. 242-243

27 Dionne, p.1-33

28 Dionne, p. 31-32

29 Michael Gerson and Peter Wehner, *A Conservative Vision of Government*, National Affairs, retrieved January 3, 2014 from http://www.nationalaffairs.com/publications/detail/a-conservative-vision-of-government; Michael Gerson, "Anti-Government stance ignores founders focus on 'public good,'" *Sacramento Bee*, January 3, 2014

30 Dionne, p. 59

Index

A

CPSIA information can be obtained at www.ICGtesting.com
Printed in the USA
BVOW08s1335190216

437360BV00002B/12/P

9 780997 080506